"A writer of dazzling intelligence."   —Janette Turner Hospital

"Roberts's style is passionate, angry, and often very funny. [Here is] a writer in love with his subject."

—Oriana Fallaci

"Superbly composed scenes capturing the complexities of modern-day Egypt juxtaposed with the mysterious legacies of its ancient past...A compelling and brilliantly recorded quest."

—Los Angeles Times

"Roberts writes like an angel...brilliant, funny, moving, and often profound."
—Colin Wilson

Paul William Roberts graduated from and taught literature at Oxford University. After stints in India and Hollywood, he settled with his wife and their two children in Toronto, where he has been the recipient of numerous screenwriting, journalism, and fiction-writing awards. His travel writing has appeared in Condé Nast Traveler, Harper's, The Toronto Star, and many other publications. His books include a nonfiction work on Egypt titled The River in the Desert, a work of fiction, The Palace of Fears, and the recent Empire of the Soul, his book about India. Roberts is currently at work on a book about the apostle Thomas.

ALSO BY PAUL WILLIAM ROBERTS

Empire of the Soul: Some Journeys in India
River in the Desert: Modern Travels in Ancient Egypt
The Palace of Fears: a novel

IN SEARCH
OF THE
BIRTH OF JESUS

The Real Journey of the Magi

P AUL W ILLIAM R OBERTS

Riverhead Books
New York

Riverhead Books
Published by The Berkley Publishing Group
200 Madison Avenue
New York, New York 10016

Copyright © 1995 by Paul William Roberts
Book design by Debbie Glasserman

Riverhead hardcover edition: October 1995
First Riverhead trade paperback edition: November 1996
Riverhead trade paperback ISBN: 1-57322-567-3

The Putnam Berkley World Wide Web site address is
http://www.berkley.com/berkley

The Library of Congress has catalogued the Riverhead hardcover edition as follows:

Roberts, Paul William.
     In search of the birth of Jesus : the real journey of the Magi/
Paul William Roberts.
          p.   cm.
Includes Index.
     ISBN 1-57322-012-4 (alk. paper)
     1. Magi.   2. Jesus Christ—Nativity.   3. Roberts, Paul William—
Journeys—Middle East.   4. Middle East—Description and travel.
5. Bible, N.T. Gospels—Evidences, authority, etc.   I. Title.
BT315.2R59   1995
232.92′3—dc20   95-19689 CIP

Printed in the United States of America

10   9   8   7   6   5   4   3   2   1

Acknowledgments

I am greatly indebted to the generous assistance of the Canada Council during the year spent writing this book, and to the Writers' Development Trust for the months preceding that. Without the help of Chris Wendland and Lufthansa German Airlines, the preliminary research would have been entirely impossible; and without the help of both Lufthansa and Gholam Ali Khosroo of the Iranian Mission to the United Nations in New York, getting to Iran at all would have been entirely impossible. I extend my deepest thanks also to President Hashemi Rafsanjani and the government of Iran for their kindness and hospitality during my stay; I sincerely hope that our respective nations will soon heal their wounds so that more Westerners will be able to experience what is and has always been one of the most remarkable places on earth. I am also deeply grateful to Andy Morpurgo for his lightning translation and brilliantly concise verbal summation of Giuseppe Messina's *I Magi a Betlemme* (Romae, Apud Pont. Institutum Biblicum, 1933). For hours of painstaking and diligent work under bizarre conditions, I thank Tracy Bierstock; and for a refuge from the storm, I am indebted to her parents, Don and Pam Bierstock. My thanks to Jennifer Yoo, who had no idea what she was getting into, but got in anyway. And to John Anthony West, Graham Hancock, and Colin Wilson I owe much inspiration and a good deal of sheer fun. It was a year when I learned the difference between friends and acquaintances, too. For their friendship and from the bottom of my heart I thank Norman Snider, Simon and Kate Harling, Steven and Alison Alix, Daniel Lynch and Isobel Beveridge, Nagui Ghali, Michael Coren, Anne Collins, Alexander Epstein, Douglas Pepper, Lewis H. Lapham, "Rick" Macarthur, and Malcolm J. Kaswan. For those who believed in a crazy whim from square one, I'm amazed: Don Bastian, Angel Guerra, Sally Tindal, and all at Stoddart in Toronto. For Amy Hertz, who took the book with her from one publisher to a far, far better place, I thank her courage, admire her unerring sensibility, fear her censure, look forward to her laughing voice, and remain in awe of her ability to edit at 30,000 feet on a nettlesome computer. Jane Leibowitz became a welcome voice on the phone, and her general, my dear, dear agent (and greatest provocateur) Mildred Marmur became everyone and anything necessary to keep wolves at bay and obtain a manuscript on schedule. To Marc Gabel, a sage's sage and a friend's friend, I can only say: *I wouldn't have endured me,* but thank God you did. To Cathy Stilo, patron saint of tolerance, I would say the same — if I didn't know she whirled with Dervishes on the side. And, always last but never lost, to my partner and best friend, Tiziana Buttignol Roberts: "My love she speaks like silence, without ideals or violence, she knows there's no success like failure, and that failure's no success at all . . ."

For Nelson Doucet

There is a crack, a crack in everything,
That's how the light gets in . . .

—Leonard Cohen

Contents

Author's Note

In any dealings with ancient history one faces the usual problems of transliteration from archaic tongues and the ceaseless geographical metamorphoses that are booty from the game of grab we've come to view as progress and political-economic evolution. However, since the research for this book made me lose what little respect I'd retained for contemporary academia's monopoly on truth, I've taken a more ad hoc approach to these problems. Thus "Persia" is usually "Iran" except when the term refers to that specific region, or when another writer uses "Persia" to mean "Iran," for instance, and "Israel" is generally "Palestine" when it's not specifically the empire of King David or Solomon, or either the ancient kingdom of Israel or its southern counterpart, the kingdom of Judah. When the context urges it, I substitute the term "God" for names like "Ahura Mazda" and "Jehovah," only using "Yahweh" or "Ormazd" if the distinctions are crucial. I find the temporal designations "B.C." and "A.D." as biased and arbitrary as many people do, yet I retain them merely because their alternatives, "B.C.E." and "C.E." still sound so pointedly contrived and even offensive. Although the Church of Rome only existed officially from the eleventh century on—when it broke with the Eastern orthodoxy—I use the term to mean orthodox Pauline Christianity during and after the third century, because all the facts point to the Roman Empire's plans for an imperial faith from around this period on, and the journey from minor Jewish sect to Holy Roman Empire is a leap of such startling scope that it could only be the work of human beings, not God. The history of the world keeps changing to fit the current needs of the world, so I make no apology for presenting a history that fits my own needs. In using primary sources, on the whole one can be freed from tertiary expediency and see epochs or events in all their pristine purity. Whenever possible or advisable, I have tried to let the facts speak for themselves without interference from my subjective requirements. There are thus, at times, more questions than answers in these pages; but if the reader remembers that such a condition has always been the case for humankind, this apparent shortcoming will not seem as vexing as it sounds. Pedantry is the last refuge of the truly ignorant.

In Search of the Birth of Jesus

INTRODUCTION

⁂

WHO WERE THE MAGI?

In 1992, a nineteenth-century edition of Marco Polo's *Travels* appeared mysteriously beneath our tree on Christmas morning—a gift to me from Santa. The book was more consolation prize than gift, really, because a winter Caribbean vacation was what I'd actually requested in my November memo to the North Pole. After reading a mere sixty pages of the musty old tome, I began to view it more as a penance than any kind of prize. The immortal Venetian had been a merchant, not a poet, but no one had ever told me that he possessed such a radiantly mercantile mentality.

With the foot of slush in our driveway suddenly sculpted by a wind-chill factor 38 degrees below zero into a Hyperborean maquette of the

Moon, and with my bargain-store logs steaming wearily beneath two pounds of dying kindling, I needed a riveting, exotic adventure in virtual-traveling to curl up in my draughty roost with—not a self-help manual for thirteenth-century global sales reps. So the travelogue was not considered a literary form back then the way it is now . . . fine. But the inventory still isn't considered one, as far as I know.

Polo's world generally sounds more like a huge, chaotic bazaar, with whole nations reduced to crowded stalls whose wares are given a cursory and often disparaging glance in passing, their vendors "mean and vile" folk who are "remarkable only for being hard drinkers," or alternatively "simple people, speaking a very rude language" (usually Turkish), who are fond of bathing in hot springs, sell costly spices, eat fruit, and build large gardens.

Idly wondering, as I yawned and shivered, how the merchant of Venice would have employed his literary gifts to describe contemporary New York and Los Angeles in two paragraphs, I turned a page to find this:

Persia is a very extensive province, anciently very rich and flourishing, but now in a great degree wasted and destroyed by the Tartars. It contains a city called Sava, whence the three Magi came to adore Jesus Christ when born at Bethlehem. In that city are buried the three, in separate tombs, above which is a square house carefully preserved. Their hearts are still entire, with their hair and beards. One was named Balthazar, the other Gaspar, the third Melchior. Messer Marco inquired often in their city about these three Magi, but no one could tell him anything, except that they were ancient kings, who were there buried. They informed him, however, that three days' journey farther was a tower called the Castle of the Fire-worshippers, because the men there venerate fire, and for the following reason. They say that anciently three kings of that country went to adore a certain prophet, newly born, and carried three offerings, gold, incense, and myrrh, to know if he were a king, a god, or a sage; for they said that if he took gold, he was a king; if incense, he was a god; if myrrh, he was a sage. They went in one after another, and though they were of different ages and fashions, he appeared to each of them exactly like himself. When they came out and compared what they had seen, they wondered much, and then went in all together, and the child then appeared to them what he really was, a boy of thirteen days old. They presented to him the three offerings and he took them all, whence they concluded that he was at once god, king, and sage. He presented to them a closed box, desiring them not to open it till their return home. After having traveled a number of days, however, they were curious to see what was in the box, and opened it, when they found only a stone, which was meant to express that they should remain firm in the faith which they had received. They did not understand this meaning, and despising the gift, threw it into a well, when immediately a great fire came down from heaven and began to burn brightly. When they saw this wonder, they were quite astonished, and repented that they had thrown away the stone. They, however, took a portion of the fire, carried it to their country, and placed it in their church, where they kept it continually burning. They revere it as a god, and use it for burning all their sacrifices; and when at any time it goes out, they repair to that well where the fire is never extinguished, and from it bring a fresh supply. This is what all the people of that country tell, and Messer Marco was assured of it by those of the castle, and therefore it is truth. One of these kings was of Saba, the other of Ava, the other of the castle. Now let me tell you of Persia, its cities, and the actions and customs of its people.

—*Travels*, ed. Hugh Murray

Messer Marco goes on to achieve the ambitious goal stated in his last sentence in scarcely more space than he devotes to this unusual version of the Nativity, I might add. And, not letting Polo tell me any more on that portentous day, it struck me that his was most definitely an unusual version of the Nativity.

I scanned the footnotes to see what Polo's editor had to say about it. Hugh Murray, in the 1870 Harper & Bros. edition, tackles his task much like a Victorian schoolmaster sternly correcting the homework of an eager but dim-witted pupil. The Magi chapter, he comments, "is strongly stamped with the credulity of the age, from which it would be unreasonable to expect our traveler to be exempt. On his part it is mere hearsay . . ." I wondered what else but "mere hearsay" Murray imagined any Nativity story could be after 1,300 years. He goes on to observe that this section had been omitted from several earlier versions of the *Travels*, yet that other editors had confessed to "its genuineness, of which there can be no doubt." Murray justifies his own inclusion of the chapter on the grounds that "we are giving an edition, not a selection, of the traveler's effusions . . ." He does generously concede in the case of the tombs and bodies that there "is some appearance of the author's here speaking as an eye witness," but he still cautions his readers that Polo "only stands committed . . . to the extent of having seen three bodies partially embalmed." Apart from speculating somewhat wildly that the natural "burning wells or caverns that occur at Baku and other places in Persia" not only suggested the well in Polo's story but also produced "the adoration of fire in this region," Murray sees nothing else worth annotating here. His edition is not very highly thought of, I now realize. Santa really stiffed me.

I'd had 191 pages of the "traveler's effusions" by this stage and knew that Polo habitually made no discernible distinction between folklore and facts of history. However, I also knew that he was incapable of the kind of imaginative leap that creating this story would have entailed. Thus, like the dourly pedantic Hugh Murray, I too felt entirely certain that Messer Marco had seen the embalmed bodies he mentioned and had also been told an extremely strange, if not blatantly nonsensical, story concerning them—and been told this story by people who went out of their way to convince him it was true. Who were these people, though? I wondered. Muslims?

Like much else between Venice and Xanadu, the existence of the Zoroastrian religion in Persia completely escapes Polo's attention. Zoroastrianism is one of the oldest and most influential religions in the history of civilization. Although none of the few scholars who can be regarded as experts in the history of it—including details like when the prophet Zoroaster lived, where you encounter dates more than three millennia apart—there are some hard facts (a few of them literally carved in stone) proving the faith was widespread by the fifth century B.C. Polo, and any other Christian at the time, would have referred to them as fire-worshippers, though the reference is not accurate. Fire is a symbol of God in Zoroastrian temples—just as light is in many religions—and symbolic items like milk and Haoma flowers are offered to the flames of a central sacred fire during certain rituals. Some of those temple flames have been tended, their keepers claim, for two and even three thousand years. Magi, wrote Pseudo-Lucian fifty years before Jesus' birth, were "an order of seers who are dedicated to the service of the gods, and who are found among the Persians. . . . They have strong constitutions and live to a great age, for their profession as Magi makes it incumbent on them to observe strict rules of life." But Polo sees only Muslim "Tartars" on his trip, even when he is in the city of Yazd, the center of Iranian Zoroastrianism then and now. Yazd gets a brief paragraph—most of which is in fact devoted to the landscape beyond it—merely mentioning its silk-manufacturing industry and stating the bald fact that its citizens "all adore Mohammed." Nowhere in thirteenth-century Iran would such a statement have been less true. It's not even true today. But enough of Polo's shortcomings.

At this point, I set aside the *Travels* and excavated from the trolls' grave-yard in my three-year-old daughter's room a Bible she had been studiously illustrating with wax crayons. For those who have not done so recently or ever, I highly recommend reading this text upon which the world's largest religion and much of Western civilization itself is based. The content is often surprising. It certainly surprised me: what I read was nothing like the Holy Bible I had once listened to daily for fifteen years in icy churches and odorous school chapels. Many passages struck me as downright weird—alien, and almost risibly pagan in their preoccupations. Two years later, when my journey with the Magi was finally over, the nature of Christianity—not to mention Christmas—had been irreversibly transformed for me. But what they both perhaps lost on the swings of research, they gained on the roundabouts of my travels.

The original Nativity tale, which was what I first sought out, seemed even odder than most of the other oddities encountered on my trek through the Gospels. Only two of them—Matthew and Luke—even have a Nativity tale. And for authors who go on to give essentially the same accounts of Jesus' (surprisingly brief) ministry, death, and resurrection, Matthew's and Luke's versions of the same Nativity could hardly differ more drastically from each other in every detail.

Take Luke. He first devotes considerable space to the fairly miraculous birth of John the Baptist, Jesus' cousin; and then has Mary and Joseph traveling to Bethlehem from Nazareth to be taxed in accordance with the decree of Emperor Caesar Augustus and the census regulations of Quirinius, governor of Syria. Historically, this occurred around A.D. 6. Mary is "great with child" and gives birth while in Bethlehem, wrapping the child in "swaddling clothes" and placing him "in a manger; because there was no room for them in the inn." Already, the birth is six years later than we thought. Luke tells us that local shepherds, "keeping watch over their flock by night," were informed by an "angel of the Lord" that the Messiah had been born "this day in the city of David . . . Ye shall find the babe wrapped in swaddling clothes, lying in a manger." The shepherds seek out Mary and Joseph, see the divine child, and make "known abroad the saying which was told them concerning" him. When Mary's period of ritual purification is complete, she and Joseph take Jesus to be blessed in Jerusalem's Temple, where they sacrifice at the altar two doves or two pigeons "according to that which is said in the law of the Lord." Then Simeon, a "just and devout" man who had been assured "by the Holy Ghost that he should not see death before he had seen the Lord's Christ . . . came by the Spirit into the temple," where he finds Jesus and "took him up in his arms and blessed God." He blesses Mary and Joseph, too, telling Mary, "Behold, this child is set for the fall and rising again of many in Israel; and for a sign which shall be spoken against; (yea, a sword shall pierce through thy own soul also) that the thoughts of many hearts may be revealed." An aged renunciant named Anna, who apparently lived in the Temple and was renowned as a prophetess, similarly recognizes Jesus as the messiah, speaking "of him to all them that looked for redemption in Jerusalem." After this, the Holy Family returns to "their own city Nazareth" in Galilee, where Jesus spends most of the next three decades without, it would seem, doing anything worthy of note, let alone indicative of divinity. Nazareth, by the way, probably did not exist until nearly two hundred years after Christ's death.

Now take Matthew. His gospel makes no mention of John the Baptist's birth and has Mary and Joseph living at Bethlehem, where they apparently own the house in which Jesus is born during the reign of Herod the Great. Herod died in 4 B.C., which puts the Nativity ten years before Luke's version, and four years before that of conventional wisdom. Matthew mentions no shepherds, but he has "wise men from the east" arriving in Jerusalem and asking, "Where is he that is born King of the Jews? for we have seen his star in the east, and are come to worship him." When Herod "heard these things, he was troubled."

He had good cause to be troubled, too: besides being governor of Jerusalem he'd recently been promoted by his Roman masters to king of the Jews, and he now had big plans for a royal dynasty. Not being Jewish was a slight handicap for these plans, and Matthew deftly underlines the king's shameful ignorance of his subjects' religion here: Herod has to summon "the chief priests and scribes" to find out where the promised messiah (who is clearly also considered to be "King of the Jews") will be born, according to prophecy. Bethlehem, King David's home town— as any Jew of the day would have known—is the Old Testament answer. Herod next summons the wise men to a private meeting. He is clearly anxious about adding to their credibility in the eyes of the public by being seen to take them seriously himself. But at first glance Herod's covert encounter with the mysterious Magi seems somewhat ludicrous. He merely asks them one precise astronomical question: "what time [their] star appeared." Then, employing his newly acquired Judaic lore, he directs the "wise men" to Bethlehem, instructing them to send word when they have found the child "that I may come and worship him also." Herod was keener to meet the messiah than any man alive in those days. The wise men set out, "and, lo, the star, which they saw in the east, went before them, till it came and stood over where the young child was." Stars cannot perform such maneuvers as far as we know. The wise men arrive at Mary's house, fall down and worship her child, "and when they had opened their treasures, they presented unto him gifts; gold, and frankincense, and myrrh." We are never told how many wise men there are, and although there are three gifts here it would appear that these items are a communal offering. Matthew's wise men are also never referred to as "kings," let alone never ascribed separate kingdoms, as myth would have it. Indeed, they apparently come from the same place, since after "being warned of God in a dream that they should not return to Herod, they departed into their own country another way." Matthew then tells us that Joseph, too, is warned by an angel in a dream that Herod "will seek the young child to destroy him," and the family should "flee into Egypt . . . until I bring thee word." Mary, Joseph, and Jesus immediately leave for Egypt, where they remain until Herod's death. Furious at being double-crossed by the wise men, Herod orders the slaughter of all male children under two years of age "in Bethlehem, and in all the coasts thereof." Only when the family returns and Joseph is warned in another dream that Herod's son, the new ruler of Judaea, might not be any more kindly disposed to Jesus than his father was, do they all settle in Nazareth, Galilee, "that it might be fulfilled which was spoken by the prophets, He shall be called a Nazarene." Matthew then omits the next quarter of a century or so, picking up the narrative where the Gospels of Mark and John open—at Jesus' baptism.

Only one of the two Nativities can be historically accurate—unless Mary or Joseph or Jesus, or all three of them, forgot where Jesus was born, forgot even which decade he was born in, forgot whether it was local shepherds or Oriental wise men who showed up to celebrate the birth, and—still less likely—forgot that they had spent the years before Herod's death in Egypt, not in a non-existent town in Galilee.

Comparing Matthew and Luke further, I noticed that they are at least in agreement on one point: the virgin birth. They both also share a conviction that gospels need to include genealogies showing Jesus to be directly descended, via his father Joseph, from King David. But it struck me that there is a slight contradiction here: doesn't the virgin birth make Joseph (and his ancestors) somewhat irrelevant to Jesus? Luke's genealogy differs from Matthew's quite seriously at certain points, charting the bloodline to David via a more obscure son, Nathan, rather than the royal heir, wise King Solomon. Initially this seemed trifling—until I realized that it effectively denies Jesus descent from the royal messianic line, making him ineligible to be "King of the Jews." My school chaplain never mentioned this anomaly; probably because even people who read the Bible seem to feel justified in skipping its notorious genealogies. Luke names Jesus' grandfather Heli instead of Jacob, too.

I wondered if these alternative genealogies in Matthew and Luke, like the wildly different Nativity stories themselves, implied something more than just a variation in traditions. And why did they clumsily undermine the authority for a virgin birth by implying that Jesus carried Joseph's blood? Indeed, nowhere is this miraculous birth ever mentioned in the rest of the New Testament. St. Paul, prime advocate of Christ's divinity though he was, even states quite unambiguously that Jesus was "of the seed of David" (Romans 1:3). Elsewhere in the New Testament, I discovered Jesus had several brothers and sisters—a fact the Church apparently likes to ignore. Clearly, the Virgin Mary didn't remain a virgin all her life—unless Joseph had a previous or subsequent wife. But Joseph—as big a theological nuisance for the Church as Jesus' siblings—vanishes without trace after Luke's Passover story, never mentioned or even alluded to during Jesus' ministry, when the only father discussed is The Father. The gospel authors, I now find, have a more shamelessly functional approach to character than do the scribes of *Melrose Place*.

Looking at a Nativity tableau the next day, it was obvious that scriptural authenticity is not a big concern with the various creators and purveyors of Christmas imagery. Three kings dressed for some state jamboree or coronation, a stable bulging with domesticated beasts, the flock of sheep with its minders, awe-struck villagers, hovering angels, cherubim perched on the thatched roof, a plump and almost naked baby Jesus looking serenely cozy on his prickly mattress of uncovered straw: none of this has any sanction from Matthew or Luke, whose Nativity versions are invariably conflated in the various contemporary retellings that most people I've encountered assume to be the gospel truth. No one, however, seems to use Matthew's account of Mary's giving birth in the house in Bethlehem, which Matthew implies she and Joseph own. Luke's no-room-at-the-inn-and-manger makes for better myth—although Luke does not in fact mention any stable. This was added by someone who presumed the manger—an animal feed trough—was just doubling as crib, cows nibbling away at the baby's mattress while he slept upon it. The same sort of logic was at work when someone else decided three gifts clearly indicated three wise men—which by Marco Polo's time at least had established itself as indisputable.

These scriptural inconsistencies don't seem to have bothered most of history's great religious painters, though, or the lyricists responsible for some of our most popular Christmas carols—upon which many of us seem to rely entirely for hard facts regarding the Nativity. This is much the same as using the Beatles' "Back in the USSR" as an authoritative history of the Soviet Union. Whoever penned "The First Nowell," for example, appears convinced that Bethlehem is northwest of Jerusalem. The town has always been located to the south.

The New Testament's two conflicting Nativities ultimately shed little light on Marco Polo's Persian tale, however. In fact, they left me no more convinced of the events they described than the merchant of Venice's account did. Back in my roost before another batch of sighing fireproof logs, I wondered how tales of local lore 1,200 years and as many miles apart could be so similar in some details and yet so preposterously opposite in others.

But the nexus of all these differences and similarities, I began to conclude, was, in fact, the wise men of Matthew's gospel. The Magi. Their metamorphosis from the gospel's "some wise men" into three kings with names, respective ages, and kingdoms seemed to be one of history's great unsolved puzzles.

This was when my journey with them really began. If I could find evidence of the tomb Marco Polo insists he was shown eight hundred years ago, logic announced, and the remains of some nearby structure corresponding to a "castle of the Fire-worshippers," then I could be reasonably certain that Polo had not fabricated his bizarre yarn. Why and how I determined that it was utterly essential for cracking the enigma of the Magi that I re-create their theoretical journey from central Iran to Bethlehem—overland—is a mystery even now to me. Yet I did determine just that.

Exactly a month after opening Santa's gift, on a day when the temperature had soared to a balmy minus fourteen, I was hunched over an atlas with ruler, pencil, and a pair of dividers, muttering to myself. Iran to Iraq, up the Euphrates past Babylon; northwest to the Syrian border, then southwest through the desert to Palmyra; on to Damascus; into Jordan, crossing the Allenby Bridge to Israel, with a brief stopover in Jericho before heading for Jerusalem and finally Bethlehem. The prince of all peace accords, among Syria, Israel, and Jordan, would probably be signed the very day I entered the Church of the Nativity, I fantasized, admitting reluctantly that this was about as close as I'd get to the Magi's newborn messiah in our drab, pragmatic age.

Consulting no less an authority than Lawrence of Arabia, I conservatively estimated that the whole trip could be achieved by camel in under a month. Iran, Iraq, Syria, Jordan, Israel! By camel! In retrospect, I'm only surprised my plan didn't involve being disguised as an

Hassidic rabbi and dancing all the way from Iran yodelling "Hava Nagila" while waving a huge stars and stripes flag.

Waiting for an Iranian tourist visa that some clerkly mullah was apparently bringing on foot from Teheran to deliver personally, I ordered up books in the University of Toronto's Robarts Library; books that, in many cases, had last been requested in 1928, or still contained uncut pages over a hundred years after their publication.

The visa arrived eleven months later, during which time I'd acquired the acquaintance of acquaintances of a friend of a friend's cousin's brother in Teheran. Close ties in a strange country can be comforting and useful. I fantasized over the new best friends I was about to make in Iran, relationships that would pioneer the much-needed bridge-mending between our respective nations, as well as usher in regular vacations on the shores of the Caspian Sea, and FedEx couriers arriving on my doorstep bearing gifts of the finest caviar in gallon tubs, or eighteenth-century silk palace rugs from Shiraz. What harm is there in dreaming?

By now I'd also accumulated enough information about the Nativity Magi and Magi in general to make my wife warn visitors they'd sorely regret bringing up the subject in her presence. But no one had to bring it up: it was my sole topic of conversation, and I began to develop a missionary fervor for the task of preaching the Gospel of the Magi.

My desk groaned beneath the weight of Magi Christmas cards, Magi effigies, Magi documentary videos (all of them hopelessly inaccurate), and naturally thousands of photocopied pages from Magi books, Magi journal articles, Magi sheet music, Magi poems, and Magi carols. I even possessed Magi merchandising. Eventually, I managed to unravel the development of their myth.

It took several hundred years for Matthew's "wise men" to become the three kings, Balthazar, Gaspar—or Caspar—and Melchior. Early accounts—some of them by saints and Fathers of the early Church—give the number of "kings" present at the Nativity as high as fourteen and as low as two. Their names range from Hormazd to Karsudas and Melkon, ruling kingdoms like Arabia, Persia, Ethiopia, and in one case simply "the East." But by the early sixth century, when what was once a persecuted Jewish sect had become the official faith of the Roman Empire, the whole world suddenly reached unanimity on the number and identity of Jesus' first visitors. Emperor Justinian, ruling from Byzantium, had mosaics installed at Ravenna and Bethlehem that not only revealed the names and ages of the three kings, but also for the first time clearly showed them wearing traditional Persian clothes. Justinian was at war with Persia at the time, it's true, but there was more than just propaganda value in depicting Persians paying homage to the new god of the Romans. Ironically, the sight of their countrymen in a Christian mosaic prevented the Persian armies sweeping through Byzantine-held Palestine from destroying the Bethlehem church.

I found it to be commonly held that "Magi" was plural for the Latin "magus." Whenever I told people that Matthew's "wise men" were in fact Persian Zoroastrian priests, there was always the same glazed look of total disbelief. Thank God for the *Oxford English Dictionary*, my sole ally in the matter of Magi: "A member of the ancient Persian priestly caste, said by ancient historians to have been originally a Median tribe. Hence, in a wider sense, one skilled in Oriental magic and astrology, an ancient magician or "sorcerer." There is even a cautious reference to the term's specific use: "The [three] MAGI: the three 'wise men' who came from the East, bearing offerings to the infant Christ." The august dictionary clearly cannot quite bring itself to exorcise the haunting conviction that there were three Magi any more easily than most of its readers can, but at least it acknowledges the truth—that we don't know how many there were.

Marco Polo also knew a form of accepted truth about the Magi, I learned, and it's curious that he never refers to it while recounting his Nativity tale. In Germany's Cologne Cathedral is a calendar of saints which contains this dubious obituary:

> Having undergone many trials and fatigues for the gospel, the three wise men met in Sewa in A.D. 54 to celebrate the feast of Christmas. Thereupon, after the celebration of Mass, they died: St. Melchior on 1 January, aged 116; St. Balthasar on 6 January, aged 112; and St. Gaspar on 11 January, aged 109.

The "feast of Christmas," I should point out, was not established as a festival by the Church until somewhere near A.D. 336. But the reason for this obituary is that most of the mortal remains of the three Magi or kings are allegedly housed in a jewel-encrusted gold shrine behind the main altar of Cologne Cathedral. They've been there since 1164, over a century before Polo saw his embalmed bodies (although they, too, were reportedly discovered in Persia, but during the fourth century). Marco Polo would have known about this, since prior to 1164 the same jewel-encrusted gold shrine had been one of Milan's major spiritual tourist attractions. It was looted by the German monarch Frederick I Barbarossa, who at one point crowned himself Holy Roman Emperor and then established a rival papacy when the existing one expressed its disapproval.

Like many holy relics, the Cologne Magi are almost certainly bogus, a combination of political power play and moneymaking scam that was something of a Vatican trademark during the days when Roman Catholicism's hierarchy resembled Genghis Khan on Wall Street. Not a shred of evidence suggests that the jeweled shrine in Germany houses what's left of three fools, let alone wise men. But in the thirteenth century, holy relics were a booming business for the increasingly avaricious Church. Combined with the sale of indulgences (coupons for getting into heaven), the relics packed both congregations and coffers. No ruler of Christendom was about to let his pope spoil the lucrative fruits of this labor of centuries now.

Since the only resemblance Rome at this stage often had to anything mentioned in the Bible was Sodom and Gomorrah, it's hardly surprising to find many voices suggesting that incumbents of St. Peter's throne might occasionally behave more like men of God and less like robber barons. A visiting Martian would have been forgiven for thinking the Bishop of Rome fronted a prosperous merchant bank rather than a religion. Indeed, as many a budding martyr confessed, it was difficult to see how the teachings of Jesus ended up as a real estate empire and priceless art collection. Weren't they about charity, renunciation, compassion, and the search for a kingdom of heaven within?

The Albigensian heretics—or Cathars—certainly thought so, and said so. After some consideration, the Church responded to their criticisms by dispatching a mob of brutal mercenaries to kill every man, woman, and child. This genocidal action was deemed a roaring success—Catharism definitely lost its appeal, and the deterrent effect on wanna-be heretics pleased Rome greatly. So greatly in fact that a special unit called the Holy Inquisition was established to organize preemptive strikes against inchoate heresy and potential heretics. The unit still exists, except it's now called the Congregation for the Doctrine of the Faith. Between 1542 and 1965 it was known as the Holy Office. But today, as it was in the twelfth century, the unit's function is still to combat heresy. It's worth remembering that the term "heresy" comes from a Greek root meaning basically "to think for one's self."

Until 1991, the Holy Inquisition controlled almost all scholarship and translation of the Dead Sea Scrolls (especially the Ecole Biblique in Jerusalem, where work on the scrolls first commenced under Fr. Roland de Vaux) through one of its divisions called the Pontifical Biblical Commission. As the first truly accurate translations of the Scrolls appear, it's easy to see why the Church was so concerned with obviating independent study of the Essene texts for so long. They're poking holes in orthodox dogma everywhere. The Dead Sea Scrolls loom large in my journey with the Magi. In some cases, I have used material yet to be published from scrolls still only partially translated; and it's also only fair to warn readers that devout Catholics may find some of this material deeply disturbing. When the Qumran Scrolls are finally published in their entirety, I believe, the church of Rome will crumble into conflicted, autonomous factions much like the independent states of the former Soviet Union.

A profound secret about the origins of Christianity has been kept for nearly two thousand years, and Marco Polo's Nativity story is intimately connected to that secret. Polo and his various editors may well have sensed this, which is possibly why the chapter was omitted from many editions of the *Travels*. It is also perhaps the reason that Polo remained silent over the issue of the Cologne Magi.

And so what was supposed to be a straightforward little book about an ancient journey and the identity of those mysterious visitors at the Nativity nearly burgeoned into an alternative history of Western civilization. Santa's miserable little gift turned out to be an Aladdin's cave crammed with both earthly and spiritual treasures. I have endeavored to make the inventory of these treasures and curiosities as coherent as possible, but the sheer quantity of historical material involved has of necessity obliged me to truncate severely events that would be books in themselves, or to simply refer to other works dealing with the area, and, presumptuously I'm sure, to assume a basic level of familiarity with certain times and places that may well affront the reader's indulgence. Thus references to King Solomon, Darius the Great, or Zoroaster, for example, may seem at first confusingly irrelevant. But they are not— trust me. Everything relates to one subject: Who were the Magi? what was their connection to Jesus Christ? and why were they present at the Nativity? Like the sculptor who, when asked how he carved such an exquisite equestrian statue from a lump of rock, replied that he simply cut away everything that wasn't the horse, I have tried to cut away everything that isn't the Magi. But Matthew's "wise men" aren't horses, and it has been difficult to determine at times what was an extraneous protrusion and what was, say, a leg.

For this is not, by any stretch of the imagination, an academic historical text. It's the account of a contemporary journey in search of travelers who were themselves on a journey whose purpose was implicit in making that journey. Were it not for Marco Polo's chance encounter in Sava—or Saveh—while passing through Iran eight centuries ago, the Magi might have been left to rest in peace. Although other pioneers of the travelogue—such as Friar Odoric of Pordenone and the antic Sir John Mandeville (both writing in the fourteenth century)—have mentioned Iran as the Magis' country of origin (although both cite Kashan, not Saveh, as the city where the three met to start their journey), only Marco Polo recounts a "Zoroastrian Nativity" tale. No one I read, though, had been able to find the tomb Polo mentions, or his "castle of the fire-worshippers."

Besides myself, only William Dalrymple seems even to have found Polo's tale extraordinary enough to merit closer attention. Had I read Dalrymple's superb *In Xanadu* before leaving for Iran, I might never have gone. Following Polo's footsteps in 1989, Dalrymple noted the Nativity tale while in Saveh, and briefly endeavored to find the Magi's tomb—but to no avail. You have to admire someone who could tolerate Polo's company all the way to China, though.

By the eve of my departure I'd come to distrust the Venetian's memory and judgment so profoundly that I assumed Odoric and Mandeville were probably right and that Polo had confused Saveh with Kashan the way he sometimes confused north with south and days with weeks.

Yet, after a year in the library, I was pathetically eager to see what I'd been reading about, and woefully ill-equipped to wander 1,200 miles across virtually the only nations on earth still radiantly unimpressed by the glorious achievements of American foreign policy. About as close to the twentieth century as I'd ventured for some time was 1272 A.D., when Polo was where I would soon be. Things have certainly changed in eight hundred years, I kept saying to myself—until I started saying, Nothing's changed here in three thousand years. But when my journey with the Magi was finally over, I understood the nature of change for the first time, as well as a little more about the nature of life and death. That's what this book is really about.

—P.W.R.
Toronto, May 1995

Chapter One

THE JOURNEY

*Persia is a very extensive province, anciently
very rich and flourishing, but now in a great
degree wasted and destroyed by the Tartars. It
contains a city called Sava, whence the three
Magi came to adore Jesus Christ when born at
Bethlehem.*

—Marco Polo, *Travels*

ARRIVALS

The people who boarded Lufthansa's flight from Frankfurt to Teheran
were not the same people who stepped out onto Iranian tarmac. A stat-
uesque woman with dense, golden hair, pencil heels, and a leather
miniskirt, left the airplane as a pious nun, shrouded in black, her
scrubbed face older, humbler, more innocent. She also no longer appeared to know the playboy-businessman in a two-thousand-dollar
Hugo Boss suit she'd been chatting with in Germany, propped against
the departure lounge bar. He was then chain-smoking Dunhills while
daintily holding a tumbler of Chivas Regal between thumb and fore-
finger—displaying to full advantage the pinkie ring holding a rock

larger than anything in his drink, and the jewel-encrusted Rolex wristwatch embedded in an actual nugget of gold. Four hours later, the same man had become a weary merchant. The ring had gone and the Yukon-goldrush Rolex was a battered Timex. Even his shimmering suit seemed old and crumpled in Teheran, now owing its opulent sheen more to a decade of wear and ironing than to any costly exotic fabric. And his last inflight cocktail, judging by the fragrant wake in which I trailed as we left the plane, must have been Eau Sauvage with Listerine, not scotch and soda.

I passed the vast and lonely miles talking with a Norwegian executive from Britain whose company manufactured pharmaceutical items under some sort of partnership arrangement in Iran. His card read "Claus Fredman," but he explained that his name was really "Friedman."

"In Iran, though, I'm 'Fredman.'"

He was not even Jewish, he hastily added.

An anxiety-laden gloom appeared to be seeping into the airplane. It kept the mobile minibar busier than usual. The more Claus and I drank, however, the less drunk we seemed to be, and our attempts at humor constantly backfired, jokes plopping like eggs on concrete, or revealing hideous ambiguities that had never been suspected of them before.

A steward retrieved our platoons of empty miniatures. "I hope you have breath mints or mouthwash," said the flight bar attendant, somewhat sternly. "If they smell your breath, you go to jail. And we get punished, too, for serving you."

Claus smugly waved several rolls of Certs at her.

"It's not a joking matter," she stated. "It's very serious."

It sounded *very* serious. In fact, the *less* serious something was everywhere else, the *more* serious it seemed to be in Iran. Claus dumped a roll of Certs in my lap, along with a miniature bottle of industrial-strength Scope.

"In accordance with the laws of the Islamic Republic of Iran," announced a voice from the cockpit, "all women are required to cover their head and shoulders upon leaving the plane. Thank you for your cooperation. On behalf of Lufthansa, we hope you had a pleasant flight."

We had had a pleasant flight. In fact, I now hoped it would never end.

The reality of finally arriving in Iran hit, along with those images of the country all Westerners who have never been there inevitably have: something between a permanent storming of the Bastille and a ceaseless Nuremberg rally in medieval drag. I pictured a lengthy interrogation by Islamic police, my illegal luggage spread across the floor, tag-teams of brutal bearded inquisitors firing nonstop questions until I cracked.

Though relatively small, the airport terminal was immaculately clean and subtly opulent with white marble. Upon one wall hung a large portrait of the late Imam Khomeini flanked by the Islamic Revolution's current leader, Ayatollah Sayyed Ali Khamenei, and the nation's president, Hojjatoleslam Akbar Hashemi Rafsanjani. In their black and brown clerical gowns they reminded me more of benignly stern headmasters than they did tyrannical priest-kings. "Ayatollah" means "sign of God"; and the slightly lower title "Hojjatoleslam" translates something like "proof of Islam." The signs of God and proofs of Islam had been running Iran now for fifteen years; fifteen years which, according to Western media, were signal proof that both God and Islam should keep out of politics.

I retrieved my suitcase and joined the ragged lineup before a glass-fronted booth in which a uniformed man was laconically examining passports. The waiting allowed a fizzing dread to flood through me like toxic Alka-Seltzer. When a plainclothes official standing near the booth eventually caught my eye and beckoned me over, I thought a geyser of panic would blow through the roof of my skull. He snatched my passport, waved it at the man in the booth, who skimmed through it upside down, then stamped it, smiling insincerely. It was handed back and I was waved on.

On an upper level, behind vast sheets of plate glass, hundreds of eager faces peered down, waving or shouting joyfully. I wondered if Mostafa or Reza, those acquaintances of friends of friends' cousins, were there to meet me. Before the stairs leading to this upper level another bottleneck had gathered by a kind of small platform. Here a woman who looked and dressed like the Wicked Witch of the East was performing a third check of papers and bags. Blithely assuming, after my previous encounters, that such official obstacles did not concern me, I started to walk away. The witch made it very clear that my suitcase should immediately be placed upon her platform. She tugged its zipper open about three inches and peered down into the crack like a watchmaker. Then she closed the bag and dismissed me with a grunt.

This is it? I recall thinking, dragging myself and my luggage up the stairs. I've had more aggravation flying from Toronto to New York.

Rising from the bobbing field of faces was a crumpled sign reading DR ROBETS. It was held by a nervous-looking young fellow whose pencil-thin moustache gave him the appearance of a forgotten thirties matinee idol.

This was how I first met Reza, the maddening shadow who would dog my every step during this first stretch of my search for the Magi.

He thrust a bunch of flowers wrapped in aluminum foil at me, hoping I'd had a pleasant journey. Then, glancing around edgily—which I later learned he always did—seized both bags and strode forcefully through the crowd while I tottered in his slipstream.

TEN DAYS OF DAWN

Outside, I found neither hell nor the storming of the Bastille but rather Toytown. The dislocating glare of airport neon was replaced by a friendly glow from ten thousand colored fairy lamps reflecting off adjoining lakes formed by parked ranks of gleaming cars. These lamps hung from trees, telephone poles, statuary, fences, window ledges, even public benches. A major exponent of exterior novelty lighting had clearly been let loose here. And not just in the airport grounds.

As Reza lit up another Zagros Slim and plunged a powerful Japanese accelerator to the floor, oscillating his car like a weaver's shuttle through the ragged threads of more sedate traffic, I realized that the whole of Teheran was lit up like a forest of Christmas trees. There were even makeshift latticed arches festooned with evergreen branches and colored lightbulbs spanning many major thoroughfares. Banners and pennants fluttered in the breeze, and in places entire buildings were dazzlingly illuminated by irregular scaffoldings of green, red, and white fluorescent bars—as if some mad giant had been doodling with a wand of light. It was the merriest city I've ever encountered. If Santa himself had swooped past us on an incandescent sleigh I would not have been at all surprised. Against all odds, Teheran suddenly seemed like the perfect spot to begin a journey to the Nativity.

"What a jolly place," I remarked, inanely.

Reclining behind his small, leather-sheathed wheel like a Formula One pro, Reza merely grinned a somewhat loony assent, double-declutching as we maneuvered through three ninety-degree turns and burned rubber out onto an imposing square featuring a fifty-foot sculpture of white marble that was also sparkling with abstract constellations of multicolored electric stars.

"Looks like Paris. In a fairground," I added. "What's the name of this place?"

"Revolution Square," said Reza. "Used to be Square of the Shah. They name everything after themselves. Pahlavi this, Pahlavi fucken that. My mother even name me Muhammad Reza—same as bastard Shah name . . ."

The vanity of human wishes. Now everything was called "Liberation Avenue," "Unity Square," "Victory Place." But Muhammad Reza was just called "Reza."

"The alleys are named for the martyrs," Reza added, virtually with his head in my lap as we hung an impossible right and hit Mach Two up another avenue the width of a freeway.

The "alleys" were what I would term small streets.

REZA BURN

Reza had slid to a quivering halt in front of the Imam Khomeini Drugstore. I'd complained of a headache and he intended to buy me some pills whether I wanted them or not. He was like that, I discovered: your problems became his problems and were dealt with his way. His problems, however, were also assumed to be your problems. Thus everything was dealt with his way. To Reza, the world contained only one inhabitant. This soon became my biggest problem.

We two-wheeled onto yet another boulevard so enmeshed in speck-led webs of glowing color that it might as well have featured merry-go-rounds, big dippers, haunted houses, and hoopla stalls. Except there was not a person in sight, adding that dimension of eeriness you feel in big office buildings when everyone has gone home but the lights are still on. Hundred-foot banners flapped down like sails from high rise blocks, emblazoned with images of Khomeini solo, Khomeini and Khamenei, Khamenei and Rafsanjani, the entire revolutionary trinity together, each of them alone, and every other permutation, all sur-rounded by florid slogans in flowing Persian script extolling God, Imam Khomeini, the glorious revolution, the noble Iranian people, the glory of Islam and its Prophet—and its Prophet's "companion," Ali. The sails sagged and billowed in a friendly wind above the giant ship, but its crew had mysteriously vanished, sucked into the shadows be-hind those fairground lights.

Not wanting to labor the point, but feeling certain there must be an explanation, I said, "No one thinks of Teheran looking like . . . this . . ."

"Ten-day dawn," Reza apparently replied.

After a little more coaxing, he finally revealed that the decorations were not a permanent feature of the city but part of a nationwide an-nual celebration of the 1979 revolution. This was the fifteenth anniver-sary, thus cause for more elaborate festivities than usual. The whole event was known as "The Ten-Day Dawn," commemorating those eventful ten days that saw Imam Khomeini return from exile in France after the Shah's undignified departure, then narrowly avoid a civil war to proclaim the first Islamic republic, the advent of the rule of Allah on earth: the only theocratic government to exist since the Dalai Lama left Tibet. A slow dawn, to be sure, but certainly another ten days that shook the world.

"It must have been an extraordinary time," I suggested.

Reza agreed that it must have been, but not from personal experi-ence: he'd been a student in Boston during the revolution and the start of Khomeini's theocracy. He'd been a student in Boston and Los Ange-les during the capture of the American Embassy and the hostage crisis following it, too.

Moments later we came to a shuddering halt by a small building with glass doors and a fairy lit awning that proclaimed CHINESE RESTAURANT.

"This hotel," Reza announced. "I fucken hope it is not too expensive for you."

It was eight dollars a night.

"It looks more like a Chinese Restaurant."

"It is a fucken Chinese Restaurant. And also a hotel."

His command of the American language after those student years was impressive.

A pocked and pitted stick that probably belonged to a large dog was thrust through the door handles on the inside of the lobby, which was scarcely larger than a small trailer home. Reza smashed his car keys against the glass, soon producing a bleary-eyed man with a moustache like a fur stole and the sort of blue uniform that French postmen wear.

Beneath a sign reading RECEPTION and a framed photograph of headmaster Khomeini, this man produced a tattered ledger and several ball-point pens that did not function. About to pull out my own, I found Reza pushing me aside and scribbling in the ledger himself, occasionally asking questions about dates and numbers. The desk clerk mumbled something wearily.

"Give him your fucken passport," Reza told me.

I said I hated parting with passports but had made a photocopy of the entire document, which the man could have with pleasure. Reza sighed, conveying this information to the desk clerk and initiating an exchange that lasted a good five minutes, during which I began to feel the effects of traveling for over twenty-four hours halfway around the world.

"He needs the fucken passport," Reza eventually announced.

"Why won't the photocopy do?"

"The azzhole police don't like fucken photocopies."

I looked up at Khomeini, who seemed to be expressing disapproval, then reluctantly handed over my passport. In exchange I received a tiny old key attached to a slab of plexiglass as big as a book.

"You must have the fucken passport with you when you go out," Reza stated.

"Why?"

"In case you need it, azzhole."

I was trying his patience, I thought, not realizing that the world did this to him all day long without my help.

"Are there police checks?"

"No. Don't fucken take it, then," he said. "I thought you needed it with you?"

I think he was trying to convey that my passport would be safe with the desk clerk, and I could have it whenever I wanted to have it. No one was going to confiscate it. Meeting foreigners who had never visited the Islamic Republic before was something Reza did often, I learned later. Their petty, preconceived fears tried his patience.

The elevator was that European variety designed to hold a thin man with a pet mouse and a postcard. My nose was in Reza's eye. I wondered if my breath smelled as bad as his did.

Reza surveyed my room approvingly, rubbing his big violent hands and saying, "Very nice. Very nice. Is it nice?"

"Very nice."

All I first noticed was the stale, suffocating heat.

"It's a fucken nice room, no?"

"Very nice. Thank you, Reza."

"Are you sure it's nice?"

"Completely."

"I want you to be happy here."

"Thank you."

"I want you to have happy memories of Iran."

"I'm sure I will."

"I want this fucken room to be nice."

"It is, Reza. It's a very, very, *very* nice room."

"It's not as fucken nice as an American room, is it?"

"Oh yes," I protested. "Easily. It's nicer than many American rooms, in fact. *Much* nicer."

"Look," Reza urged, gesturing at a brown metal arrow that was attached to the wall diagonally, pointing toward a corner of the ceiling. A few white letters in Persian had been painted on it by a shaky hand.

I looked, wondering what important feature the arrow indicated for the benefit of guests.

"Kiblah," Reza explained in a reverent tone. "Direction of Mecca for your praying."

"Good."

Did he think I was a Muslim?

Reza announced his departure as if I might not expect it, adding that he presumed I'd want to sleep later than usual the following morning.

As it was already 4:30 A.M. in Teheran—and what felt like next year back in Toronto—I said I probably would want to do just that.

"We will come for you at eleven, then. Okay?"

"We?"

He meant Mostafa, who badly wanted to buy me lunch—or so it sounded. With this Reza backed out of the room in a courtly fashion, noting with a professional eye on the way any features that he may have missed.

"It's very, very nice," I reassured him. "And I really appreciate you coming to the airport . . . and the flowers . . ."

Reza gave me and the room the satisfied smirk of a crafty but top-notch butler, tugging the door shut with a thud as he vanished. Seconds later, there was a lesser thud from somewhere at the other end of the room. It took me a while to work out that the direction of Mecca had detached itself from the wall and landed deftly in a waste bin. It was the only convenience the room had afforded, which seemed unnecessarily luxurious. But for eight bucks a night I could hardly complain. In Toronto I can't even park my car long enough to watch a movie for eight bucks.

Parting the coagulation of webbed dust covering my window, I found a door leading out to a small balcony. Turning its key in both directions, however, I failed to open this door and gain access to the cool fresh air that it had kept out of my cell for what felt like decades.

I was in that cell for what felt like decades, too. Mostafa—who treated Reza alternately like a personal valet and an old dear friend—insisted that Reza would accompany me on my journey in the Magi's footsteps. This was something I didn't want but also didn't feel I could refuse. But no one was going anywhere until the Revolution celebrations were over, so I busied myself with meeting Iranian scholars, touring museums, attending concerts or plays in honor of the Revolution, and watching Reza eat. It was frustrating.

Reza became my shadow, refusing to countenance the idea of me going anywhere alone, and sulking with a mixture of hurt and fury when I did. He changed my dollars on the black market—which, strangely, is legal in Iran—but insisted on keeping the bricks of rials each hundred dollar bill commanded himself, doling out a little spare change for newspapers, if I pleaded for it, and paying all our restaurant checks and cab fares. He was keeping accounts, he claimed, and we'd settle up when my trip was over. Mostafa ran the Iranian affiliate of a Texas-based computer company, and Reza—despite their curious relationship—presented himself as Mostafa's school chum and partner. So I trusted him.

But I noticed that he began to treat me the way Mostafa treated him, and called me "azzhole" so often I began to wonder if he thought it was a term of endearment. Occasionally, however, he would spout something truly abusive, then pretend he was just joking. He enjoyed jokes, although I felt the countless ones he regaled me with concealed some kind of message and grievance. I knew much about him after a week, largely because he wanted me to know much about him. He never asked me anything about myself, though, and he soon made it very clear that he found my research and Marco Polo's Nativity story the very zenith of boredom.

He was married, of course, but had no children—which in a macho land is a problem. Macho men spend no time with wives or children, naturally, but they must have wives and children—sons, ideally—to not spend time with. The reason Reza had no offspring to not spend time with was his zero sperm count, for which he made me swear to send him some alleged miracle drug when I returned to Canada. There is no such drug, I learned later. He compensated for his low rung on the macho ladder by an obsession with sex that went far beyond the bounds of sanity and caused me to suffer many embarrassing moments and countless graphic accounts of his past conquests and prodigious copulations.

He also confessed a desire to sodomize me on several occasions, always quickly dismissing the confession as a joke, and he often remarked on my hair, eyes, and lips in terms that reminded me of Rodney Dangerfield seducing a Vegas bimbo. On one occasion I lost my temper and shouted at him to shut up, instantly vowing never to do it again because I realized he liked it.

His other most vexing medical situation was hypoglycemia. This manifested itself as a reasonable facsimile of raving lunacy that seized hold of him tenaciously the moment he felt hungry. Admittedly it distracted him from sex for a while. Yet it also became something of a problem for me to construct my days around Reza's capricious blood sugar levels. And this problem blossomed into howling nightmare when the Ramadan fast began.

Because the Muslim calendar is lunar and has intercalated months that retrogress through each season every few decades, Ramadan always begins whenever I visit an Islamic country and creates difficulties of varying degrees, depending on the official level of strictness in observance a particular country operates. But no country is more Islamic than the Islamic Republic of Iran, and, predictably enough, Ramadan began the very day Revolution festivities ended and my journey in search of the Magi began in earnest.

SAVEH

[Persia] contains a city called Sava, whence the three Magi came to adore Jesus Christ when born at Bethlehem. In that city are buried the three, in separate tombs, above which is a square house carefully preserved. Their hearts are still entire, with their hair and beards ... Messer Marco inquired often in that city about these three Magi, but no one could tell him any thing, except that they were ancient kings, who were there buried.

—Marco Polo, *Travels*

Heading south from Teheran, the lushness of earth watered by the melting Alborz snows quickly turned first to flat scrubland over which were scattered low mudbrick dwellings, then to a barren, grayish hilly desert. This landscape had not changed since Marco Polo traveled through it seven hundred years earlier. The evidence that such a dull two-lane stretch of relentlessly straight hardtop had once been the

Great Silk Road was now only crumbling square, fortlike structures that I noticed at rare intervals abandoned by the roadside: caravanserai. These were inns, guardposts, and overnight camps positioned a day's journey from each other for the trading caravans that passed, heading to India or China with gold and silver, or returning to Baghdad, Damascus, Constantinople, or even Venice, laden with silks and spices. Protection from bandits and weather, these caravanserai were also trading posts in their own right. Many a weary, saddle-sore merchant probably considered it worth his while to save himself a year or more of aggravation, danger, and illness by purchasing at an inflated price what he was traveling east for himself from those who had already been there and returned alive. China seemed a very long way from Teheran. So did India.

Saveh also began to seem a long way from Teheran after half an hour in Ghossam's car. A plump, good-natured man in his forties with a moustache that made him look like the genial sheriff from a cowboy movie in which no one gets shot, Ghossam was one of Reza's innumerable acquaintances. His vehicle was not licensed to drive through downtown Teheran—and, ideally, should not have been licensed to drive anywhere at all—so Reza and I had to take three cabs to a barren stretch of highway on the city's perimeter, then sit with our bags on the grassy shoulder until Ghossam and his four-wheeled hazard showed up.

An Iranian-built Paykan, this car suffered from a good many debilitating mechanical ailments whose symptoms varied from sudden explosions in its lower east side to a sustained and desperate metallic whine emerging from around the upper west side. The only things that worked faultlessly were its tape deck and four thumping speakers. Ghossam, however, only possessed two cassettes of music, both grimy with engine grease, both homemade dubs of forbidden Iran-Pop from Teherangeles—as Iranians referred to L.A., on account of its huge population of their fellow countrymen. One cassette was by someone called "Andy," who I thought was a girl but turned out not to be; the other was by a nameless band and contained Reza's favorite song, an irritating synthesized disco ditty featuring a shrill double-speed chorus that sounded like "Chickadee, chickadee, chickadee . . ." Reza played it constantly, swaying in his seat and producing a very loud castanetlike noise by pressing his palms together above his head and snapping the middle fingers against each other. He tried to teach me the technique but was extremely pleased to observe that I found it quite impossible. He must have practiced for months to master it himself.

In the middle of an especially bleak stretch of road a man stood by a clothes rack with wheels that held several dresses on plastic hangers. I asked what the man was doing.

"He sells women's clothes," replied Reza.

"Out here?"

"Why not?"

"Who buys them?"

"Anyone. You want to buy one? Gift for some Zoroastrian babe, eh?" He rasped out a laugh.

Lurching up to the crest of a hill after three hours in the groaning Paykan, I finally saw Saveh in the far distance, amid a flat plain ringed by foothills of the Zagros mountains. A huge, rickety sign in peeling paint proclaimed SAVEH WHITE CEMENT CO. Marco Polo had probably not seen that.

At first an uninspiring sprawl of low, dusty brown buildings, Saveh grew more interesting as we approached its center. Ancient mudbrick ruins were everywhere, built over or incorporated into new structures—an aspect of mudbrick that has turned many important archaeological sites into layer cakes of history, impossible to excavate without relocating entire communities. Archaeology was low on the list of the Islamic Revolution's priorities, too.

The office of the Saveh Antiquities Organization reflected this disinterest. Several men sat around drinking tea, listening with barely concealed boredom as I announced my purpose in visiting Saveh. Yes, they had heard of Marco Polo's story (yawn)—indeed, as Polo recounts, everyone here knew it—but it hardly (yawn) fired their imaginations.

But I persisted. Was there an old building—square with a dome—anything like the one Polo described, and ancient enough to have been standing in the thirteenth century? Expecting little more than disinterested shrugs, I was astonished to hear that there was indeed such a building. A guide would take us there. Soon.

While waiting, I examined various framed photo-enlarged engravings of ancient Saveh that hung on the office walls. It was quite clear that the city had once enjoyed much better days. Some pictures showed a high surrounding wall, beyond it elegant arches over cobbled streets where prosperous men rode camels. Others revealed a skyline of domes and minarets rising from enclosed courtyards thick with shady trees and fountains, the word "Saba" floating in the clouds. A common variant of Saveh or Sava, "Saba"—associated by scholars with Sheba—was also the realm where one of the three kings in Polo's tale is said to rule.

Hussein, the promised guide, a grizzled, portly barrel of a man, squeezed himself into Ghossam's car beside Reza, and the four of us set off toward the southern end of town. Saveh had gradually moved north since Polo's time, successive generations preferring that area because the mountains provided some respite from the biting winter winds of the southern plain, as well as from its choking summer dust storms.

South Saveh was very ancient indeed, with homes built on and with ruins, which themselves had been constructed upon the ruins of ruins. Turning a dusty corner, we came to a halt beside a large and very dilapidated mosque. Only one of its minarets, and this a stunted tower outside the northeastern corner of the walls, still stood. The minaret's brick courses had been heavily restored and it was unadorned apart from very early Islamic stone reliefs of deceptively simple geometric forms and stark Persian calligraphy. Only the magnificent pointed Mihrab dome, partially restored, retained any traces of former grandeur, its gilding patchy and faded, but the white and azure ceramic work still lending a simple design of interlinked octagonals subtle power and an elegance that often eluded more complex geometric decoration. The mosque's interior was entirely hidden behind a high square wall of crumbling stone and ancient mudbrick, some of it in reasonable condition, some not, and the rest only dissuaded from utter collapse by concrete buttresses placed against its interior at irregular intervals.

Beyond lay the open plain. Once outside the car, I could see what had impelled Saveh's citizens to move north: the wind was savage, mean-spirited, bullying clothes and hair, biting at ears, spitting dust and grit into eyes and mouths. Hussein led us to a huge pair of medieval doors studded with thick iron knobs. He produced a dungeon keeper's key ring and began trying its many massive keys in a padlock the size of a tombstone. None appeared to work, and I wandered around the exterior as he fussed and fiddled, urged on by Reza and Ghossam to try this key and that key again.

Long disused, this structure most certainly predated the twelfth century and seemed to have been constructed over an earlier building or compound, elements of which extended beyond its current walls across the dirt road and into someone's vegetable garden. I later learned that the owner of this garden—an influential man in town—had denied all requests to excavate his neat furrows of gourds and eggplants. Being "influential" obviously meant that he was rich enough to get away with such behavior toward local officials without fear of repercussions. The mosque was now at the very edge of Saveh, nothing beyond it but ruins of what must have been old city walls. The area itself was probably one of those portrayed in engravings back at the antiquities office.

A chorus of delight signaled that Hussein had finally won his struggle with the lock. Beyond that mighty door lay an inner courtyard whose dried-up ablutions fountain was about the only area not showing all the signs of an archaeological dig that had been begun decades before. The work was not so much abandoned as permanently interrupted, with ragged awnings still flapping over trenches whose sides were shored up by rotting wooden planks, and scaffolding made from desiccated tree branches surrounding precarious-looking walls and even parts of the central porch and its Mihrab dome.

I asked Hussein if there were ancient tombs anywhere. He nodded, suddenly more enthusiastic about his job now that a foreigner was showing interest, it seemed. He led me to the edge of a deep pit. At its base, some twenty feet below, stood two stone sarcophagi, badly scarred by sheer age as well as by more recent clumsy excavation techniques. In another pit, some thirty yards off, sat one more sarcophagus similar to the others. All three were reminiscent of very early monolithic Egyptian sarcophagi but utterly lacked ornamentation or inscriptions of any kind. Had there once been bodies in them?

Hussein shook his head. By the time French archaeologists had initiated work here in the 1930s, the vast stone coffins were empty. Excavation had apparently continued in a desultory fashion—supervised by various French or German or British missions—until just before the revolution. He motioned me further, down makeshift stairs of wood and rusty iron tubing, until we reached the lower levels.

At the lowest level of all, amazingly, was a ten-foot-square plinth of worn granite, with a saucerlike indented circle at its center: a Zoroastrian fire altar? Yet all around this area, too, were chambers built of polished limestone brick. Carved repeatedly into these, with a wallpaper effect, was a pattern that involved a kind of X over a P. This is one of the very earliest Christian emblems, the one that Emperor Constantine saw in his "vision" and carried into battle as a standard. Originally a combination of Hebrew letters with numerological significance used as a distinguishing mark by certain Essene sects like the one from which Jesus came—who also employed an alphabetical cipher—it was later used by gnostic Christians and other mystical sects. In Greek, conveniently, X and P—Chi-Rho—are the first letters in "Christ": the sign still appears on some Church paraphernalia. However, I've always believed—and it would not have been lost on Romans—that the P also stands for St. Paul, whose ideas were superimposed over the X or cross of Jesus (known as St. Andrew's cross). The essential conflict within the reasons for the Magis' journey—through time as well as space—involves the competing theologies of Pauline Roman Christianity and what can be termed Essene Jewish Christianity. Paul's emphasis on faith rather than the gnostic search for direct inner experience of God, which was the essential teaching of Jesus, divided early Christianity into a Roman state religion, on the one hand, and a spiritual underground of mystical movements on the other. It also provides an alternative history of Europe right up to the seventeenth century at least; the familiar events from classroom texts open to an entirely different interpretation if viewed from the perspective of a subjective spiritual truth with pure intentions versus an objective temporal lie whose motivations were political power and self-interest.

Elsewhere on the walls of these lower levels were patterns made by combining the first and last letters of the Greek alphabet, alpha and omega. In the Book of Revelation—the Apocalypse of St. John of Patmos—Jesus uses them to describe himself and God as the beginning and the end of all things. Revelation is the most obscure, sinister, and suspect of all New Testament texts, and has frequently been employed by men of ill will as a scare tactic to extract obedience from the masses. The real message of Jesus, like any great teacher, is one of liberation, compassion, and joy. Of this there is no doubt.

PALIMPSEST

This old mosque, then, had originally been a place of Zoroastrian worship, yet it had also later been built over and used by some kind of early Christian sect, too. And clearly the earliest Muslim builders had not minded the gnostic-style pattern, while the Mongols had plastered over it with their own designs. Then another generation of Iranian Shi'ites had plastered over the Mongol work, removing the indignity of conquest. Now, though, everyone's work was falling into untidy piles on the flagstones. Only the fire altar looked capable of surviving indefinitely. Which, as I was to learn, could hardly be more appropriate.

Deeper through superb brick arcades and into barrel-vaulted subterranean chambers we went, passing more evidence of ancient Zoroastrian presence, and eventually coming across a large windowless room hung with huge lengths of green and red cloth, the floor strewn with cheap rugs and cushions. Blackened oil lamps sat in carved niches, and a teeny wood-burning stove in one corner sprouted thirty feet of aluminum piping.

"Local womens, they still come here for the prayer," Hussein informed me.

It was at once an enormous relief to find evidence supporting the Saveh Nativity story, and yet at the same time it felt drearily anticlimactic. Were the uninspiring slabs of stone standing in muddy pits littered with rubble and garbage all that now remained of the tombs Polo had seen?

Perhaps not.

After managing to locate the key that unlocked it, Hussein ushered us into a large underground storeroom filled with objects unearthed many years before and left behind by the various archaeologists working at the site. Most items were certainly Islamic: storage jars—one with far too many handles—pots, oil lamps, ceramic tiles, sections of masonry carved with superb geometric designs. But some were quite clearly earlier. Sections of worn white marble sarcophagus lids and wall or floor plaques were decorated with Zoroastrian devices, especially the symbolic rendition of a hand holding the sacred Haoma flower. This flower is still, though reduced to a near-abstract circular emblem, the image retained on flags and letterhead as the Iranian crest to this very day. Ayatollah Khomeini was going to remove it, but—so I was told—Iran's most eminent Zoroastrian begged the imam to leave his nation's emblem what it had been for most of recorded history. To his credit, Khomeini acquiesced to this impassioned plea, and thus, bizarrely, the world's only theocratic state still flies a flag containing the symbol of another religion entirely.

The profusion of decorations on ceramic tiles that included images of humans and animals also surprised me. While the proscription against depicting such forms, so strongly adhered to by Sunni Muslims, did not apply in Iran, in my experience you still rarely saw these forms employed on anything but secular art. The lavishly tiled domes and minarets of Isfahan or Mashad, wild as they look from a distance, bear only, in supreme examples of elaborate Persian calligraphy, the ninety-nine names or attributes of God. Yet here in Saveh's ancient mosque were depictions of figures that appeared to have little that was traditionally Islamic about them at all.

Two tiles depicting kingly figures particularly puzzled me. One was beardless with a crown reminiscent of those worn when Zoroastrianism reigned supreme in Iran. He sat on a thronelike chair facing a curtain that seemed to be parting, and behind his right shoulder sprouted a green bush or small tree. The other figure wore a beard and turban, held what could have been a rosary in one hand and a ceremonial goblet in the other, but also faced something overtly symbolic—in this case a kind of suspended picture frame like a window without a building around it and containing only an expanse of green. A murky mirror perhaps? Or a window onto a mysterious world of green, the color sacred to Sufism (mystical Islam) and, for less mystical reasons, to Muslims in general. He, too, had the same tree as the other man beyond a wall behind him, although this image also had two smaller but identical trees on the other side. Both figures were on square tiles framed within identically designed eight-pointed stars on a ground of blue patterned with white Haoma flowers. The stars, the flowers, the most un-Islamically clean-shaven king, the curious symbols—it all intrigued me. In this palimpsest of Western religion, I was seeing through the Moslem layer, to the Christian, to the ancient Persian from which it all sprang.

A SQUARE HOUSE

Reza was getting hungry again. But this time he would not be eating so quickly. It was Ramadan, and although travelers were exempted from fasting—but should make it up later—it was still considered unseemly to eat around those who were fasting. So unseemly in fact that the only restaurants generally open for travelers were truckstops on the highway.

Ushered back outside, I assumed the tour was over. But, relocking the groaning portal, Hussein beckoned me to follow him toward a smaller door in the mudbrick wall, beyond the actual limits of the mosque although extending from its walls. This door led into an enclosure on the mosque's western side that might as well have been a garbage dump. Scraps of paper joined dust and grit to spin in a mad, rambunctious wind. I walked south, as Hussein indicated I should, looking into deep trenches that revealed foundations of what was presumably the original Mazdean temple.

Hussein's words were tossed like a juggler's balls by the turbulent air—I caught the odd one or two, but the rest, along with their meaning, were lost.

Only when I turned to squint south into the wind's abrasive, ghostly punches did I realize what he was trying to tell me. There, standing alone some twenty yards from the mosque's southern Qiblah wall and about the same distance from the crumbling remains of Saveh's old city walls, was a square, domed structure no more than twenty feet wide. It more closely resembled early Zoroastrian fire shrines than it did an Islamic tomb, except the walls were totally closed on two sides. A small arch, now barred, was built into the north wall, and another into the eastern wall. This latter now contained a door but had quite clearly once been entirely bricked up, an odd column of uncleared bricks still blocking about a third of the right hand side from the arch down. And this arch, too, was bricked off but from behind the other brickwork, making the actual entrance with its flimsy wooden door no more than four feet high. Here again was something curious and seemingly symbolic in intent.

"Tomb," Hussein shouted.

It was, too. And it exactly resembled the building Polo described — although, typically, he gave no indication of its size. I ran over, seeing that the structure was also of considerable antiquity, as I tripped and stumbled past ruts and rocks. The upper courses of brickwork had enjoyed some heavy restoration, but the rest was original, including the broad flat dome. The work also resembled that found in the deepest levels of the mosque, the old Zoroastrian and Christian levels. Inside this structure, however, were only two sealed rectangular sarcophagi, built into the stone-tiled floor, one smaller and lower than the other, both facing east-west, like the mihrab niche. The mihrab is supposed to face Mecca, which here lay to the southwest, suggesting that this was not the niche's original purpose. Like the niches in some later Mazdean temples it could have once contained the statue of a Hellenized Zoroastrian deity.

WE TWO KINGS . . .

I asked whose tomb this was, hoping Hussein would recount the same legend that Polo had heard not far from where we now stood. All he knew, though, was that the building had long been called "The Tomb of the Master and the Disciple." A great spiritual teacher and his favorite student were interred therein — or so went the local legend. Their names and any other details had long been lost in time. Certainly no one had visited the tomb in centuries, let alone venerated it. Rubbish and stray bricks and tiles were as close to floral tributes as these occupants had come for a very long time.

I searched inside for evidence of a third sarcophagus, but found none — although the two standing there were asymmetrically placed in terms of the available space. They would have been distinctly more balanced by the addition of a third, which is a valid observation in the context of an architectural tradition based upon geometrical harmony. The floor was also and undeniably far more recent than the walls, made of concrete's precursor, a paste of powdered limestone, water and who-knows-what-else, overlaid with rough stone tiles. Had the embalmed bodies that Polo claims he saw been removed when the tomb was later co-opted for Islamic cadavers? There was no way of knowing. I was not about to request disinterment.

But two kept cropping up. Had there been just two Magi, two kings? Did Polo add a third out of fear of the Inquisition? Several early accounts and fresco depictions in the catacombs of Rome did, after all, show just two Magi. I kept thinking about those two portrait tiles of the Persian "king" figures back in the old mosque.

Exposed out on this blasted wasteland, the tomb also seemed somewhat starkly humble for a resting place of holy priest kings. Yet, judging by the pattern of collapsed walls and half-exposed foundations extending across the entire area, the structure could have once been in its own enclosure—like Shi'ite shrines for saints and imams—surrounded by far more majestic elements.

No matter how inconclusive the evidence, I felt that the nexus of items that did support Polo's account was far too densely persuasive now to dismiss as coincidence. In fact, everything I'd seen backed him up in substance if not form: a major Mazdean temple, once a Christian church, containing sarcophagi, with an early mosque built over it, and a small tomb that matched the Venetian's description exactly, also containing sarcophagi for the bodies of venerated holy men. It was all where Polo had described it being but not quite *as* he had described it eight hundred years earlier. But then, not much Polo describes is remarkable for its accuracy.

CASTLES IN THE SKY

In some manuscripts of his account, Polo says he was told the story of the Magi not just "by those of the castle" but at the "Castle of the Fire-worshippers" itself—although one manuscript version ["Z"] says it was his father Nicolo who heard the story. Where exactly was this "Castle," or "Cala Ataperistan," as Polo himself termed it?

Hussein had no clue, had never heard of such a place.

The term "Cala Ataperistan" comes from the Persian *Qal'ah-i Atas-parastan,* literally "Castle of the Fire-worshippers." No one is sure why Polo, who did know Persian, dropped the š of *ataš,* but then again there are nine different versions of the term spread among the various manuscripts. In his definitive *Notes on Marco Polo,* Paul Pelliot gives the following frighteningly exhaustive account of scholarship on this subject:

> The "village" of "Cala Ataperistan" was, according to Polo, three days distant from Savah. Yule [the most eminent English translator and editor of *The Travels*], supposing the information was acquired on the homeward journey, sought for the place "between Savah and Abher"; but that was because Yule believed that, on the outward journey, Polo had gone to Ormuz via Baghdad. I agree with the view that, on the contrary, Polo never visited Baghdad ... and probably passed through Savah on both journeys. In such a case, the normal trend of the narrative is that Polo reached "Cala Ataperistan" on the outward journey three days after leaving Savah. This points in the direction of Kashan, where W. Jackson has proposed to place "Cala Ataperistan." But this also seems most improbable, now that we have a Kashan in Polo himself, in such circumstances that make it unlikely that Polo should have used both names for one and the same place. "Cala Ataperistan" was probably a fortified village in the vicinity of Kashan, but distinct from that city.

I had assumed that, along with Friar Odoric and Sir John Mandeville, Pelliot and his Polophiles were probably right about this, but then none of us had ever asked Dr. Morteza Zokaii where he thought "Cala Ataperistan" was located.

"There is dog-tor," Hussein suddenly announced, peeling a quarter page of newspaper from where the wind had just slapped it on his cheek, "who know much about this Markipollo story. You should be meeting with these man. He will tell you many ting."

The news that we were not yet through with Saveh hardly thrilled Reza. He complained about dying from hunger. He had not eaten since a truckstop lunch over two hours earlier. He hated my Magi. He hated the wind. He hated being away from Teheran. He hated Ramadan.

Hussein directed Ghossam to the home of Dr. Morteza Zokaii, all the same. I think he hated Reza for complaining about food during Ramadan—if for nothing else. The doctor's house was supposed to be off Ferdossi Street, but since most Iranian addresses look like three or four addresses muddled together, we seemed far from Ferdossi Street by the time Hussein told Ghossam to pull over. I wondered what made him so sure that the doctor would be home at 2:30 P.M. Hussein told us to wait, while he vanished through the door of a high white wall. Reza played "Chickadee, chickadee, chickadee" three times at migraine volume, presumably because he'd gathered by now how much I loathed the song and he badly needed to punish me.

No one had actually said that Dr. Zokaii would be an octogenarian professor of ancient history with a huge white beard, it was true, but no one had said he would be a twenty-four-year-old dentist, either. At first I imagined Hussein had misheard what I'd said about "Cala Ataperistan" as something like "Can I see an expert on pyorrhea?" But it soon became clear that Dr. Morteza Zokaii the dentist was also Dr. Morteza Zokaii the keen amateur local historian. Indeed, he had written a booklet entitled *Sava-Nama (The History of Saveh)*, which he proudly presented me with and signed, engraving a lavish encomium with a fountain pen. Printed in Persian, the booklet had, for no doubt scholarly reasons, occasional footnotes in English scattered throughout its forty-odd pages. One of these footnotes, I quickly noticed, referred to Yule's version of Marco Polo's *Travels*. The dentist did indeed know all about the story of the Magi, agreeing that the old mosque was definitely where Polo had seen their tombs. What about the "Castle of the Fire-worshippers," though?

He knew where that was, too.

"Kashan?" I asked nonchalantly—a man who knew his Polo—presuming this was the standard answer.

"I will show you."

It was apparently not far southwest of Saveh. Kashan lay very far to the southeast. I quizzed Dr. Zokaii to make sure we were talking about the same place. He asked me to call him "Mort."

"No question," Mort repeated several times. "Same place as Polo mention. I have seen through my eye."

With Reza now in a Wagnerian hypoglycemic rage—which fortunately also rendered him speechless—we dropped Hussein at a street corner and followed Mort's expert directions.

Before long we were in suburbs that increasingly resembled small villages until they were small villages, motoring along a road that increasingly resembled a country lane until it was a muddy, pot-holed goat track. Ghossam scarcely ventured out of first gear, negotiating hillocks, pits, boulders, herds of mountain sheep, until we reached a point where the track forked in three directions. For someone who had been to where we were going before, Mort seemed rather confused by the lay of the land. Suggesting we take the right-hand fork, the dentist soon changed his mind when we found ourselves in a deserted farmyard. He got out as if to seek directions from the farmer but disappeared behind a hedge for a meditative pee instead. We backed up when he returned, taking the central track. This took us out into a bleak, windswept plain crisscrossed by the meandering loops of a broad but shallow river rippling over gleaming rocks.

At one point there was the ruined arch of what had once been a stone bridge constructed with considerable engineering skill. Grids of ancient foundations were also visible amid green sprouting grasses like reeds. Long ago, it seemed obvious, this area had been a fairly extensive and sophisticated settlement of some sort. I realized after consulting a map that we could not now be very far from a place named Ava—a name mentioned by Polo as the kingdom of another one of his Magi—although evidently now we were heading due west, just like the burning gold disk in the sky. Ava was a few miles due south, although it was still the nearest place listed on the map. Blundering into another tiny village built over stone and mudbrick remains, we found ourselves menaced by an army of the most wicked-looking chickens I've ever encountered. As Ghossam blasted his horn, instead of scattering in clucking frenzy, some of these feathered demons leaped upon the hood and actually pecked at our windshield.

"Cheeken kebab," announced Reza abruptly.

In his state, all the world was food.

Mort laughed. "Not here," he said. "Here cheeken eat man kebab."

I certainly wouldn't have ventured out of the car unarmed.

Ghossam reversed, the Paykan screaming and farting beneath us, emitting dense clouds of charcoal-colored smoke, much of which we must have been breathing. An elaborate system of narrow canals surrounded this village, extending off across the plain toward where I now made out a line of steep mountains—the beginning of the Zagros range that basically continued from here over two hundred miles to the Iraqi border.

The plain grew wilder and bleaker, streams flashing like shattered mirrors in sunlight that, miraculously, never seemed to be interrupted by the huge, black warring clouds cruising through sapphire air to ram each other or fuse into monstrous shapes. Blurred sea monsters and steaming dragons reared and plunged on all sides, bouncing off mountain peaks to sink their vaporous teeth into each other. Macbeth's witches and King Lear would have been at home out here, but clearly no one else was. It seemed unlikely that this snaking ribbon of rutted mud we drove along even existed, let alone went anywhere.

"You sure you've been here before?" I asked Mort.

"Yes," he replied, uncertainly. "But I am only eight year old."

I think everyone wanted to hit him, but then he suddenly started pointing wildly, calling out, "There! Izz there!"

I could see nothing but a deep cleft running into the foothills, where the mountains had already cut off the day's sunlight, casting a cold and sinister shadow.

"Where, Mort?"

Then, as Ghossam turned into the cleft, directly ahead was a haphazard collection of huts and fenced enclosures strewn over low rocky hills.

"That?" I couldn't believe he had led us for nearly two hours that must have reduced the Paykan's brief life expectancy by twenty percent just to show us "A farm!"

"It is shepherd place," Mort protested. "This shepherd I am remember."

No one cared if the shepherd was Mort's long lost father. The dentist would have a long walk home the way things were going. Ghossam suddenly made a strange but optimistic-sounding noise with his teeth and tongue. And then I saw it.

Perched on the peak of a low mountain, overshadowed by the higher summits to the west behind, was a gigantic castlelike structure of dark reddish-gray stone. A hundred yards farther back it must have been all but invisible, melting into the rock around it. Now, a mere quarter of a mile off, it was there.

Dividing the sheer walls of its soaring central keep on either side of a broad arch were six narrower arches: Ahura Mazda and the Six Immortal Spirits, a trademark of Mazdean architecture. Yet this was no mere shrine or temple. It was a fortress, too, a "castle"—as Polo said it was. And, given the rough terrain—along with the Venetian's sporadic amnesia—this place could have easily taken his caravan three days to reach.

I hugged Mort, who seemed as excited by reaching the place as me. Possibly he had been wondering, as his companions certainly had, if his memory after sixteen years was merely a child's fantasy, that there was no castle to be found.

STARTING POINT

As far as I know, I am the first Westerner since Polo to find and identify "Cala Ataperistan," the "Castle of the Fire-worshippers," the place where, according to Messer Marco, the curious Persian legend of the Magi, that I'd read one Christmas morning and which had brought me here, had its origins so long ago.

Was this imposing edifice, hidden by the embrace of forbidding mountains at the edge of an even more forbidding plain riven with looping streams, once the base of St. Matthew's Magi? Or even just any magi? Had the watchtowers of its soaring walls been where they scanned the heavens two thousand years ago for signs of a long-awaited Savior?

The air around me became an electric shroud. It was a rare moment.

These are brief, of course.

"You must be mad," sneered Reza. "We came for this?"

Ghossam coaxed his car up a near-vertical incline of gravel leading past a series of thatched mudbrick huts in various sorry states of decay and several chicken-wire enclosures, through which dozens of sinewy, bad-tempered fowls passed back and forth quite freely, cackling disapproval at our intrusion. Two little girls in ragged headscarves peered out shyly from a darkened doorway. There was no other sign of human life. Only a profound distaste for any physical exertion not absolutely essential could have prompted Ghossam to force his ailing vehicle as far up this mountain track as he did. In fact, it was merely when a platoon of vast boulders started to indicate the end of any semblance of road at all that the driver finally came to a grudging halt, violently drawing up his hand brake as if intending to embed it in the roof.

Mauled by freezing gusts, I stood gazing up at the extraordinary structure now towering over this blasted yet breathtakingly dramatic landscape. The plain behind and its swirling pattern of sparkling gold waters was already far below and it stretched away for miles out to a muted blue horizon. Here and there thin streamers of smoke marked the invisible homesteads suspended from them.

"So, let's go," I said, indicating the craggy walls of dull ruddy rock brushed with grayish streaks of mud and rock slide.

"Please," Reza replied with a courtly gesture. "You're the insane one. You go. You not come after thirty minute, we leave you here with shepherd girls. Or maybe you prefer the sheeps?"

He slammed the door grumpily and stretched out in his seat, offering Ghossam a cigarette. The pair of them looked like British holidaymakers.

"Come," urged Mort, looking up in awe. "Whaat!" he repeated several times, shaking his head at the sight. "Whaat!"

The expression managed to convey both the lack of any adequate words to describe what he felt and the seemingly impossible task that those who had constructed this castle must have faced.

We started climbing toward the southeastern corner of the central keep along a route that Mort again appeared to know. But what looked at first like a track worn by countless previous feet heading up soon disintegrated into slithering gravel and small rocks. Before long I was clinging to bunches of grass that felt like porcupines' quills to prevent myself joining the steady stream of debris now pouring down a hundred feet beneath me. By now, too, I realized that what I had at first taken for rock face beneath the castle was in fact part of the entire structure, a series of walls and towers sloping down to the north that were ingeniously built upon natural rock and indeed looked as if they had metamorphosed out of the mountain itself. The camouflage effect was brilliant. You didn't even see them until you were less than fifty yards away. The sheer size of the building also became impressively apparent. It encompassed and incorporated the entire top half of the whole mountain, in three stages that were curiously interlinked in a spiral fashion reminiscent of ziggurats or illustrations of Babel's tower.

Before us now lay a sheer wall of natural and man-made rock structures some hundred and fifty feet high. Way above were lonely shadowed arches and oblongs of gaping windows, but no indication of any entrance. Below, the crumbling stones and scrub dropped away steeply to the south. Very steeply. Gasping in the thin cold air, I looked along the entire eastern face to the north for signs of an ancient path that once must have led to the entrance of this fortress. I cannot recall visiting any ruined castle where the traditional entrance route was not still fairly obvious. Yet here I saw nothing. The southern face and certainly anything farther west would have required considerable mountaineering talent, blending as it did back into the vertical crags of even higher mountains.

Easy to defend, the place must have been sheer folly to attack. There was not even any surface gentler than seventy degrees near the base of the outer walls upon which to mount a reasonable attempt at scaling them. Whoever lived here definitely *had* enemies—although they probably never got to see these enemies face to face. The place looked more abandoned than conquered.

"How old?" I wheezed to Mort.

"Twenty . . . four," he replied hesitantly.

"Not *you!* This thing. How old, do you think?"

Mort nodded, catching his breath, then gasping, "Twenty-four . . . hundred." He shrugged helplessly.

"Two thousand four hundred years old?"

"I sink . . ." He scratched his head, pondering, then nodded conclusively. "Yes, yes. It right. I sink . . ."

He beckoned me to follow him along the foundations of the eastern wall where what resembled a foot-wide track led down to the north. It was hard to tell where these foundations began and the actual mountain ended, so skillfully were the stones fitted together. Mort slithered and stumbled, clutching at flaking shards and clumps of weed for support as the ground beneath him turned into granulated liquid. I prodded with the toe of my boot at this dubious surface, initiating a virtual landslide in places. Beneath what had cascaded away near a bend where the track suddenly corkscrewed up drastically I saw what looked like a coin. Months later Dr. Robert Schoch of Boston University identified it positively for me: Hellenistic, second century B.C. Not much farther on, lodged between rocks that had been buried by the debris I kicked away, was an ancient ceramic tile, turquoise glazed, in the shape of an eight-pointed star. I confess I looted that, too.

Mort kept exclaiming "Whaat!" as I showed him pieces of the museum buried beneath our feet, yet he showed no interest in any treasure hunting himself—probably for the same reason Parisians never ascend the Eiffel Tower. Far from excavated, this extraordinary site, I later discovered, has never even been surveyed.

Soon Mort was creeping crab fashion down a suicidal stretch of track. The light was fading fast and it suddenly struck me how very foolhardy our attempted bid for the castle's summit had become. I gallantly let Mort forge ahead, seeing all too clearly that the track simply vanished into rock not far beyond where he clung. He next slid uncontrollably for twenty feet and only prevented a terminal plunge down into the northern gorge by forking his legs out forty-five degrees to slam both feet against a handy pair of boulders. By now, though, I could see the northeast corner of the castle's lower wall quite adequately. It sloped down to a point where what looked like a ruined stone tunnel had once bridged the chasm over to gnarled slopes of an equally sheer adjacent peak.

Mort was a mess, his loafers scratched and caked with mud and dust, his windbreaker and natty mohair trousers torn and soiled. Yet he seemed overjoyed by it all, as if a dream had finally come true. "What glory place!" he announced. "So much the wonder, yes?"

"Oh yes."

I persuaded him to abandon his futile course and follow me down to this tunnel. Wild winds lashed up from the plain, which had turned into a burnished copper sheet mottled by shadows of scudding clouds the color of bloodstained gold in a sky now more like a quivering mosaic made of fireflies, cobalt, lapis lazuli, and burning lava.

"Hey, azzholes!" cried Reza's voice far, far away.

The car itself was now just an ant on a thread somewhere below on the other side of the mountain. The unnerving echo of "azzholes" ricocheted off into the gloomy western chasms and crags. We ignored it.

Sliding down toward the north wall's base, we were soon out of sight, which had Reza's voice first shrieking faintly on reverb more imprecations, then becoming a muffled yell of anguish before getting drowned among a hundred million tons of rock.

It was pleasantly still at the point where that curious tunnel opened out above a steep gorge at whose base flowed a tiny mountain stream. We were suddenly sheltered from the wind, aware only of that chord of calm and steady silence you hear in your heart when surrounded by any mass of ancient stone: the music of nature's own unique reality, still and vast, but very far from sad.

Yet that chasm below reminded me of Zoroaster's description of the entrance to the next world: a bridge narrowing to the width of a razor as your soul is found wanting, then the fetid embrace of vile old arms as the hag from hell plunges with you down to an eternity of woe and bad food.

Seeing the stream, I realized that whoever had built this fortress knew a thing or two. It had its own fresh water supply and thus could probably withstand several years of siege without much hardship. The tunnel turned out to be a tubelike arch of stone bricks spanning a steep groove in the mountain into which steps had been cut. The steps ended at a place some six feet from the adjoining mountain slope. There had clearly once been some sort of drawbridge that could be lowered to allow entry. I had seen no visible path up to the castle because that path was in fact on the next mountain slope, a narrow track leading to where the theorized bridge had once reached out. Looking along the northern face, which veered away up above the gorge toward the peaks behind, it was plain that the fortress had no other possible entrance. And this one, a forty-five-degree flight of steps barely wide enough for two men abreast, would have been laughably easy to seal or defend. Around it the mountain and castle walls soared up sheer and unscalable. Looking across, it seemed possible to reach that point where the bridge would perhaps have once been, but also decidedly unwise to attempt leaping the six feet across a chasm whose bottom was now sickeningly invisible down there amid chortling waters and gathering shadows.

"Come," Mort trilled, brimming with enthusiasm. "We go there, then . . . pffftttt!" He made a flying gesture with one hand.

I made a falling gesture with mine, clapping the plunging five-limbed maquette of myself against the unyielding rock of my other palm.

"Splattt! Uh-uh, Mort. There are cavities to fill, abscesses to lance. Who will tend the teeth of Saveh if Dr. Mort ends up down there?"

I think he caught my drift, sighing and gazing up at the imposing corpse of stone towering over us. He returned to a baffled sequence of Whaats, shrugging his shoulders at me and shaking his head. I shared the feeling. How many castle builders had taken that swift route down to the base of the gorge which Mort still seemed so eager to try for himself?

Farther off than ever, the castle's enigmatic central keep—perhaps its temple and sanctum sanctorum—loomed over everything, silhouetted now in air that was like a shimmering mist of white gold.

"Whaat!" I said. "Whaat!"

Mort and I just stared at each other like children who've seen an angel.

IT BEGINS

Observatory, temple, fortress, Marco Polo's "Castle of the Fire-worshippers," "Cala Ataperistan," base of the Magi: I could now picture them up there on those battlements so vividly, their robes billowing in a soft night breeze, astrolabes and sextants gleaming red in flickering torch light, scanning the heavens, sighting along Orion's belt to Sirius, seeking out Polaris beyond the tail of Ursa Major, and then watching in awe as the conjunction of Jupiter and Saturn rose, an unfamiliar jewel in the constellation of Pisces exactly two thousand and one years ago. Then summoning aides and servants, ordering that preparations be made, provisions crated, gifts commissioned, and, finally, camels saddled for a long uncertain trip west to Bethlehem.

It *was* tempting to dream. But all I had really proved beyond any reasonable doubt was that Polo's account held up. Was there any way of proving that the story he was told also held up? The chances seemed slim. Very slim.

At the foot of the mountain, where its little torrent burgeoned into a tiny stream, I found evidence of a broader path skirting yet another ancient wall that was now merely a line of stones in the mud and grass. The path led round then over to the other mountain north of the castle where that one tiny, impenetrable entrance gaped. It also led back to the road where Reza and Ghossam sat in their yobs' car obscured by wreaths of tobacco smoke under a portentous sky, a sky half crazed with flaming serpents and ragged smoldering dragons now, inhabitants of the Middle Air in a frenzy of wind-blown activity, a last chance at whatever tasks they were obliged to perform before the night came falling.

"You find the babes up there?" Reza croaked.

"Yep. A whole harem."

The Paykan violently objected to ignition, grunting and shuddering around us, then exploding in a dreadful series of cracks and shrieks. Resigned finally, and after one more terrifying inner blast, it moved off almost with aplomb.

As we entered the shepherd's compound, six wild-looking men of varying ages emerged as one from a hut barely large enough to have contained three of them.

"Trouble," Reza stated.

"Shepherd peoples," announced Mort joyfully.

Ghossam pulled over and we all got out: this was what protocol demanded here. Wild-looking these men may have seemed at a distance, but close up they were as shy as their sheep, shifting nervously from foot to foot and grinning uneasily. Realizing that I was a stranger among strangers, they began staring at every odd inch of me, from tangled mop of hair to Ultralite hiking boots, whispering amused comments among themselves. The eldest—their father presumably—took a few tentative steps forward, extending a cracked and grimy hand with fingers like corona cigar butts. He bore an uncanny resemblance to

Norman Mailer. I took the proffered hand, which felt like tree bark, and asked Reza to convey greetings.

"He is a shepherd," Reza informed me, after the shepherd had spoken a few words that sounded like someone crumbling cellophane.

"Really? I thought he designed computer software out here."

"Shall I ask him if you can bang his daughters?"

"No, Reza. Why don't you ask him if he's ever been up into the castle?"

He had, as it turned out, but when asked what it was like could only say that there existed a water reservoir. This endorsed the castle's function as temple, however: baptism and ritual ablutions reached the West via Zoroastrianism. Did he know who had built it?

"A girl."

"When?"

"It was a long time ago. We were not here then and do not know."

It was a charming answer, so typical of replies to my stupid questions that I have received over the years from simple people in far-flung places. It has its own truth and wisdom, too. Who but fools would inquire of a past so distant that no man alive could possibly really know anything about it?

Hardly any one ever came this far out, I learned, and, yes, I was the only foreigner the shepherd had ever seen here—and he was eighty-seven years old. He would invite us for tea, we learned, but it was Ramadan and everyone would have to fast until the sun had set. In many Muslim countries the fact that the sun had long since disappeared below the gloomy western mountain ridges behind us would have sufficed, but in Iran things were stricter. The fast ended at a specific time, a time ordained in Qom, or so the shepherd believed. In fact, it was ordained in Cairo. I doubted very much if these isolated peasants were so pedantically strict in their religious observances. Strangers scared them. Any of us could be capable of imposing all manner of terrible punishments if we caught shepherds blasphemously sipping tea before the sun had officially set.

MARY'S TOMB

Navigating back across that tempest-tossed darkling plain proved even more hazardous than the outward journey. A dozen times Ghossam braked hard and then leapt out anxiously to find the car inches from a river bank or ditch.

"What's that about a girl building the castle?" I asked Mort.

The place was apparently known now as "Gheez Cala," or "the girl's castle." Mort did not know quite why, beyond reciting a legend that I was later to hear again in Yazd. It concerned one of the daughters of Yazdegard III, the last Zoroastrian monarch of Persia who lost both his life and his kingdom to the Arabs in 651. Indian Parsees, who use the Persian calendar, still number their years from Yazdegard's accession in 631. In reality he barely ruled at all. The Arabs already controlled most of Persia during his reign. Perhaps the castle had become a symbol of Zoroastrian resistance? The daughter in question acquired semi-divine status, too, fleeing with her faith from the Muslim invaders and eventually, so the story went, finding refuge when Ormazd, the Zoroastrian divinity himself, opened up a mountain to hide her.

"Shrine of Lady Maryam near here, too," Mort announced casually.

"Mary? Mother of Jesus: *that* Mary?"

He nodded proudly.

"Really? Where?"

It wasn't far, a fact that had Reza literally howling and gnashing his fangs in protest. Only hearing that there were just some ruined stones to see saved him. That and the night. The shrine of Mary would have to wait until another trip; but, real or legendary, it was still more evidence of a profound, mysterious, and ancient connection between this area and Christianity. What was this connection based upon, though? The more answers I found, the more questions seemed to arise. But such is life, and research.

A mile or so outside Saveh we pulled into a truck stop. Mort had been dropped off back at the office and was possibly filling molars again by now for patients who had been very patient indeed all afternoon. He'd implored me to write, to invite him to North American conferences on Saveh if there were any coming up in the near future, to send books, to request of him anything that I might need. He was a dear man. Eight months later he sent me a copy of the local newspaper. It contained an article illustrated by a picture of the castle in which the only words not in Farsi were "Dr. Rpberts."

The truck stop was dominated by a gigantic diesel furnace that almost glowed red hot. Kebabs were ordered from a waiter who was a dead ringer for George Harrison, then Reza and Ghossam asked where the prayer room was. Upstairs, they learned, heading off to check in with Allah. I tried to picture American truck stops with chapels full of mumbling, rosary-counting truckers as I stepped outside for a pee.

The washroom was allegedly at the rear, but it was so blindingly dark out there after the strip-lit restaurant-cum-wayside-mosque that I just stumbled behind the building and stood in refrigerated open air. As my eyes adjusted, however, I noticed that the truck stop was completely isolated. On all sides stretched out darkened countryside spotted with tiny fires. To the west I could just make out the serrated edge of those deep Prussian blue mountains where the castle lay. Above, the new crescent moon, the Ramadan moon, was stuck like a silver dagger into night's shimmering black flesh. Black silk flesh studded with tiny jewels, too, countless thousands of them. This was perfect air for stargazing still, and so I gazed. The constellations were familiar but repositioned. There was Orion in the south but leaning at a rakish angle almost on the horns of Taurus. Given precession, the Hunter would have been much lower two thousand years ago, almost at eye level with those Magi out there on their castle towers. And, almost incidentally, I realized that my journey in the Magis' footsteps was finally underway. It would have been a more sobering than thrilling thought had I also realized then where it would lead and how much longer it would detain me than it had probably detained those who preceded me two millennia ago. Despite the bone-gnawing chill, this sight, this night was breathtakingly beautiful.

Allah, however, had clearly not detained Reza long. My keeper sat hunched over the table, staring around the restaurant in a fury.

"Where's the fucken food?" he asked me.

"Being cooked probably."

"The cook's being fucked. Probably. Got some shepherd babe in there. I want to fucken *eat*. Sheet!"

He struck up a deafening tattoo with his knife and fork on the oak-patterned Formica, both legs leaping in an uncontrollable amphibian frenzy beneath him. Hypoglycemia cannot be much fun.

Chapter Two

THE BIRTH

Now when Jesus was born in Bethlehem of Judaea
in the days of Herod the King, behold, there
came wise men from the east to Jerusalem, saying,
Where is he that is born King of the Jews? for
we have seen his star in the east, and are come
to worship him.

—The Gospel of Matthew 2:1–2

And it came to pass, when the Lord Jesus was born
at Bethlehem of Judaea, in the time of King Herod,
behold, Magi came from the east to Jerusalem, as
Zeraduscht had predicted; and there were with them
gifts, gold, frankincense, and myrrh. And they
adored him, and presented him their gifts. Then the
Lady Mary took one of the swaddling-bands, and, on
account of the smallness of her means, gave it to
them; and they received it from her with the
greatest marks of honor. And in the same hour there
appeared to them an angel in the form of a star
which had before guided them on their journey; and
they went away, following the guidance of its light,
until they arrived in their own country.

—from The Arabic Gospel of the Infancy of Jesus

To set off after the Magi physically we need to become mental travelers as well. Indeed, most of my actual luggage consisted of notebooks and photocopied texts, because in the context of that ancient journey lay the real clues to its content. On finding the Syriac infancy gospel I knew that I had at last discovered not just a link between Matthew and Polo's story, but also conclusive evidence of a link between the Magi and Zoroastrianism—and thus with Iran. These Magi "came from the east, as Zeraduscht had predicted." Zeraduscht is, of course, Zoroaster.

To answer the question of why Persian priests would have been interested in the birth of a Jewish messiah, and why the author of this infancy gospel would have confidently asserted that Zoroaster himself had even predicted their Nativity visit, it is necessary to know that a profound connection existed between the Persians and the Jews. This connection began when Cyrus the Great, architect of Persia's brief but vast empire, conquered Babylon, freed the Jews from their Captivity, and decreed the rebuilding of Jerusalem as well as the construction of the Second Temple. For this, Cyrus had himself been termed "messiah" by the unknown prophet now called Second Isaiah. The connection ended some six hundred years later, in A.D. 135, when Roman forces finally crushed the Zealot leader Simeon Bar Khochba and razed Jerusalem at the end of the second and last Jewish Revolt against imperial occupation. Simeon's main ally in this conflict had been the Persian army, which was only prevented from coming to his aid at a final stand—where he was outnumbered against Roman legions ten to one—by marauding hill tribes from the north, who were themselves probably indebted to or in the pay of Rome.

ESSENES AND OTHER JEWS

The Judaism out of which Christianity emerged had long become hopelessly fragmented and increasingly secular in its concerns, producing various contending factions which claimed temporal authority over the people. These factions were ostensibly polarized between an aristocratic Sadducee elite who, with the more bureaucratic Pharisees, controlled the Jerusalem Temple and sought mainly material prosperity through cooperation with the Roman imperialists, and the more austerely pious Essene monastic orders, who not only refused to recognize the authority of the Temple's Roman-puppet high priest but also, holed up in remote but hugely elaborate monastery-fortresses—like Qumran near the Dead Sea—established a rival hierarchy to the one in Jerusalem. Essenes espoused a more mystical version of Judaism that also involved rigorous devotion to the true spirit of Mosaic Law; but, most vexing of all to the collaborationist orthodoxy, they were deeply involved with an increasingly ferocious Zealot resistance movement, too. This was far more potent and highly organized than is commonly believed, and in the early second century very nearly succeeded in driving the Roman legions from Palestine permanently. Nowhere in the empire had Rome's highly disciplined fighting machine encountered anything like the dedicated fearlessness, passion, and talent for extreme violence of the Zealot guerrilla warriors. At least two of Jesus' disciples were or had been Zealots, and the Essenes' Qumran fortress-monastery was even adapted as a major Zealot base throughout the Second Jewish Revolt in A.D. 135. Unlike the first one, this second campaign of terror was brilliantly planned and led by Simeon, who was himself hailed as the promised messiah by no less an authority than the great Rabbi Akiba. He adopted the sobriquet "Bar Khochba"—"Son of a Star"—to evoke the same Old Testament passage that Matthew alluded to in his Nativity account, and which associates the Magi's star with a Davidic messiah. Simeon, according to new research by Scrolls scholar Dr. Robert Eisenman, was probably also related by blood to the family of Jesus, proving that the connection with a royal Davidic blood line was not necessarily just a fabrication of the evangelists. This family would thus have been *expected* to produce the next messiah when he came.

The Jewish tradition—as is made quite clear in the Dead Sea Scrolls—refers to not just one promised Messiah but two: a spiritual master descended from the Aaronic line of David's high priest, Zadok; and also a great warrior prince descended from David himself, who will destroy Israel's enemies and bring about her own theocratic global empire. By this definition, from a Jewish perspective, Jesus hardly succeeded in his task.

A Messiah, as originally conceived, though, was not the unique manifestation it became in Pauline Christianity. King Solomon had been "anointed" as Davidic Messiah, for instance. And the Persian emperor Cyrus was hailed as a messiah by the great Unknown Prophet—called Second Isaiah by convention—for vowing to rebuild Jerusalem after he had freed the Jews from their captivity in Babylon. Second Isaiah, whose poetry ranks among the greatest literary achievements in the Bible, even has Yahweh himself make this pronouncement about Cyrus (Isaiah 42:1,4). Living in the fifth century B.C., during the period of Babylonian Exile, this Unknown Prophet is also the first Jewish writer to celebrate Yahweh—just after announcing the Persian emperor as messiah, too—unambiguously as the Creator, in exactly the way Ahura Mazda (God, for the Persians) had been celebrated by Zoroaster: "I, Yahweh, who created all things . . . I made the earth, and created man on it . . . Let the skies rain down justice . . . I, Yahweh, have created it" (Isaiah 44:24; 45:8,12). Parallels with Zoroastrian texts are so striking here that these verses probably represent the first imprint of the Mazdean faith whose profound influence was to transform Judaism from the sixth century B.C. onwards.

Essenes were most definitely not the passive, reclusive celibates they've been portrayed as by most contemporary scholars. The inhabitants of Qumran were members of an elite priestly caste, whose function in society was solely religious and deliberately shrouded in professional secrecy—just like India's Brahmans and the Persian Magi. Marriage for Essenes was mandatory—although it was governed by strict rules that included set periods of celibacy and an emphasis on communal rather than family life. Other rules included obligatory periods of manual labor, which would account for the anomaly of Joseph being termed a carpenter while also identified as a direct descendant of Israel's greatest king. Essenes, in sum, were expected to be very much in the world but not at all of it, the quotidian normality of work and marriage mixed in with monastic bouts of renunciation, isolation, meditation, and rigorous fasts. The extreme discipline achieved by these communities deeply impressed strangers who witnessed it—including Roman chroniclers, like Pliny and Josephus.

THE SCROLLS

Essene scribes were, of course, responsible for copying or composing most of the Dead Sea Scrolls. In subject matter these extraordinary documents are basically divided up almost equally between versions of Old Testament books on one hand, and then various "sectarian texts" on the other. Although the biblical scrolls are a thousand years older than any previously known versions of Old Testament books, they are surprisingly consistent with the texts we have come to regard as sacrosanct—a revelation that caused sighs of relief around the Judaeo-Christian world when it was finally established. The sectarian documents, however, contain the material that worried Roman orthodoxy sufficiently for it to have obstructed access to these scrolls, and actively blocked independent translation and publication of most of them for close to forty years. It was just during the last two years or so that what had been concealed for so long from all but a few sanctioned and mainly Catholic academics began to become available to any scholars who requested access to it when the Huntington Library announced that it possessed plate photographs of all the scrolls. Most had still not been translated even in 1991.

These documents are not scripture in any accepted sense but rather the product of mystics writing in the Jewish prophetic tradition or in the later apocalyptic tradition, which is not notable for its accessibility—as readers of the Book of Revelation may have observed. Some of these texts are notable for their startling similarity with Zoroastrian writings, though, and frequently expound a rarefied philosophy that is not merely reminiscent of Magian thought, employing both the ideas and the terminology unique to Zoroaster's unique vision of the secret architecture of the cosmos. The "Sectarian" scrolls are the real treasure unearthed at Qumran.

What is seen for the first time in these documents is not simply Essene Judaism as it was practiced two millennia ago; it is also quite clearly Christianity as it was practiced by Jesus and his followers—replete with baptism, bread and wine communions, and a God of justice and love. But what is also visible in the scrolls is the unfamiliar face of an entirely different philosophy from anything we think of as Jewish or Christian, one barely concerned with outer forms at all, one not really recognizable as an institution of any kind, and primarily one almost exclusively concerned with an inner life where spiritual truth is a living reality to be experienced directly, not a matter of faith and conjecture. At first glance these ideas have far more to do with Buddhism or Sufism than they do with anything remotely like contemporary orthodox Christianity or rabbinical Judaism. But what these Essene beliefs really are, I discovered during my journey with the Magi, is the fusion of Zoroastrianism with Judaism, which is why they seem both familiar and utterly alien at the same time. The Magi themselves, however, after this discovery, suddenly seemed to be less like occult strangers impelled to investigate an astrological portent, and more like visiting colleagues come to participate in a shared venture.

The best-known (and thus usually more abstract) scrolls translated to date speak of a coming war between "the sons of light" and "the sons of darkness," a war apparently viewed as both literal and metaphorical, ushering in an apocalypse both spiritual and temporal that will signify the dawn of a new age. Given the events in Israel that followed the writing and concealment of the scrolls in the caves of Qumran, these prophetic pronouncements were impressively accurate.

There can also finally be little doubt now, in the light of information about Essene Judaism found in the scrolls, that Jesus, his mother, father, sisters and brothers, as well as his cousin John the Baptist, were all members of an Essene hierarchy. Given Jesus' alleged royal Davidic blood line, they must have been very senior and revered members of that hierarchy, too, if not its leaders at some point. But this is not a success story, because something also appears to have gone disastrously and tragically wrong around the year A.D. 30, when Jesus was supposedly executed, and again later just before the Romans destroyed Jerusalem in A.D. 70.

A number of scrolls are concerned with a controversy of enormous importance to the community, and, now that we know that they were written during the first century A.D. rather than B.C., a controversy that plainly involves figures who easily correspond to Jesus, his brother James, the Roman puppet Jerusalem high priest, and Paul. This crisis threatens to divide the entire community and is recounted in terminology that makes it simultaneously a temporal event and also a cosmic parable. This loaded style is typical of Zoroastrian writings, quite common in the scrolls, and even evident in the New Testament gospels, where Jesus hardly ever utters a sentence that isn't ambiguous and teaches entirely through parables open to several layers of meaning. Thus every event contains the very nature of the universe because there is no division between the universal and the particular. Nothing can be dismissed as insignificant without the risk of overlooking something vital. This is why the Bible's verses seem so potent even when not carrying much apparent surface meaning. It is also why Matthew's brief twelve verses about the Magi can feel as if they contain an entire book's worth of information.

The Church understandably did not want to believe the scrolls concerned events surrounding the life of Jesus because the Jesus of Qumran is nothing like the divine incarnation of canonical scripture. Even the canonical gospels are not able to obliterate entirely the real Jesus, a man of flesh and blood and doubt and certainty and pain and joy. Far from meek and mild, this three-dimensional Jesus is as often angry and violent as he is wisely compassionate, as often sick and tired of human beings as he is endlessly patient, and blazingly irrational just as frequently as he is coolly philosophic. By making him a deity the Church in fact detracted from his real greatness as a mortal, besides making it nearly impossible for us to ever understand who, why, and what he actually was.

THE END TIME

The Magi were aware of something immensely important that was suddenly put at risk after the birth of Jesus, something that was at the very core of Zoroaster's doctrines: a war between forces of Truth and forces of the Lie. The anodes between which all creation lives are not as black and white in Zoroastrianism as they are in the good and evil of later Judaeo-Christianity: which is itself in fact part of the tragedy that could not, ultimately, be averted. Just as darkness is not the opposite of light but rather the absence of light, so the Lie is not Truth's opposite number as much as its simulation: a Truth that is seductive but not true, and thus prevents those who believe in it from realizing their mistake. A term used in the scrolls for those who mistake the arduous path to truth for a cakewalk is "the seekers after smooth things." Jesus warned materialists that they would find it easier to thread a camel through the eye of a needle than find any truth with their worldly philosophies. In the Zoroastrian schema, creation had entered its darkest era, when the forces of the Lie were massing for a final assault on Truth. The Magi and their Essene colleagues both realized that the point in Truth's defenses where the Lie's legions would attempt to break through first was religion itself. If that fell, humanity would be cut adrift, unable to ever find the road home again.

KING OF THE JEWS

The story that is told by the scrolls is in two parts. The first deals with a three-way conflict between people who, though never named, can be identified as John the Baptist, Jesus, and the high priest of Jerusalem's Temple; and it also mirrors events that occurred five hundred years earlier during the construction of the Second Temple, involving ancestors of Jesus and John as well as the Persian emperor Darius the Great, who ordered and financed the building in Jerusalem. Needless to say, Darius did not go through such expense and trouble because he wanted to impress Persia's tiny Jewish colony with his philanthropy. But we shall return to the Second Temple's construction again later, when the Magi reach the city of Susa, Darius' old imperial capital.

By the time the scrolls were written, Herod the Great had already finished building Jerusalem's Third Temple and the Romans were about to recycle it back to rubble along with the entire city. Rome's colonizing forces had not enjoyed their time in Palestine, thanks to the Zealots, and they wished to drive this point home. Herod had probably only been promoted to king of the Jews because no Roman wanted the job, which resembled a permanent blazing argument with the entire population over something no one any longer recalled but still felt strongly about all the same. The stress of it quickly reduced Herod to a sack of diseases featuring symptoms—like gangrene of the genitals—that were so graphically diabolical no contemporary chronicler could resist itemizing them in exhaustive detail. By the time hypertensive cerebral attacks had added a reasonable facsimile of raving insanity to the suppurating feet, ulcerated bowels, swamp breath, groin stench, and uncontrollable farting, Herod's highly successful suicide seems like a happy ending. Except the man never seems to die, since several of his sons all appear to be named Herod and keep cropping up even decades later, installed in positions of ever-decreasing importance until history loses all interest in their fate.

Herod Antipas—the Herod Jesus has to deal with as an adult—had been demoted to tetrarch of Galilee and Peraea. He also decided to build himself a new capital rather than live in fractious Jerusalem. But the move to Tiberias—named somewhat obsequiously after the emperor Tiberius—did little for "the Herod Syndrome": a compulsion to make bad situations truly terrible whenever possible. Consequently, this Herod decided to marry his niece Herodias, who was also married to his brother, who was also called Herod. Surprisingly, it was not the Herods who had a problem with their confounding domestic situation, but rather John the Baptist. Noisily deploring the marriage, John pointed out that Mosaic law quite clearly stated—as if there had previously been some question about the matter—that you shouldn't ever marry your brother's wife. This was later amended to *You shouldn't ever marry your brother's wife unless your brother is dead.* Herod's brother Herod did in fact die a couple of years after his wife became his sister-in-law. Their step-brother had murdered three thousand people for no apparent reason whatsoever before the emperor fired him, so Herod (the tetrarch) felt little need to agonize over whether or not criticizing his marriage could be considered bad enough a breach of subject-ruler etiquette to warrant the death penalty for one man. John the Baptist was jailed and beheaded before the tetrarch realized that a trial, ideally, should have perhaps preceded these events.

Problems were mounting up as fast as relatives by the time Herod, according to the Gospels, decided that Jesus was in fact the resurrection of John and, this being the case, was owed an explanation for his untimely death. Jesus himself apparently felt he'd be better off leaving Galilee than hearing Herod's views on crime and punishment. This time the Pharisees rather than the Magi warned Jesus that another Herod also wanted to kill him. The Gospel of Luke, always inventive, then comes up with a story about Pilate finding that Jesus is from Galilee during his trial and deftly avoiding a moral dilemma by sending him off for Herod, the Galilean tetrarch, to deal with instead. The other three gospels missed this somewhat too ironic twist of fate that made us believe, for two millennia, that the Jews had been responsible for a death ordained and carried out by the Romans.

The scrolls, however—untampered with since their composition— tell a story that is almost exclusively a private matter of inter-Jewish spiritual politics on its temporal level. The first Herod had once harbored dreams of creating his own Jewish empire to rival that of Rome. Since he was only a recent convert to Judaism—something half the Jewish orthodoxy regarded as impossible anyway—Herod's Jewish empire was a standing joke with his subjects.

The Jews regarded Herod as a bizarre form of Roman punishment. He was even obliged to import priests from Babylon to service his new temple, since he couldn't trust the local ones—a distrust evident in Matthew's Magi story, where news that a Jewish princely messiah has been born is the last thing Herod wanted to hear. The Essenes, however, showed a brief flicker of interest when the new Temple was being constructed, but largely because the event tied in with one of their prophetic calculations. Herod, however, took their interest as a sign of the approval he so badly craved. The Essene wealth was legendary—if the Copper Scroll can be taken literally, it amounted to billions of dollars in gold and silver. Their detachment from the Jerusalem orthodoxy and disdain for its corruption was something Herod found both frightening and intriguing, and also felt he might be able to take advantage of one day. The Essenes positioned themselves as the real guardians of the faith, their wealth popularly associated with the treasures reputedly once contained in Solomon's Temple—although such treasures are usually meant in the spiritual sense—and their Qumran headquarters now the only true Jerusalem.

This desert fortress, spread across an entire mountain like Herod's Masada palace, was laid out to contain in microcosm the entire land of Israel, with areas actually referred to as Galilee or Bethlehem, and the whole place as often termed Jerusalem or New Jerusalem as it was Qumran. This little quirk has resulted in much of the confusion caused by New Testament place names, and it explains such conundra as why Jesus, crossing a lake by boat, can arrive at his destination long after the crowd of followers who have walked there around the entire lake shore. It explains, too, why Paul at one point apparently travels

from Jerusalem to Jerusalem, a blooper traditionally written off as
scribal fatigue in third-century Rome.

THE TRAGEDY

The essence of what is portrayed as a dire brace of crises in the scrolls
first concerns Jesus' actions after the death of John the Baptist. John
had anointed Jesus as the Davidic Messiah, which thus made John
himself the priestly or Zadokite messiah. The two roles traditionally
worked in tandem, but the Zadokite's spiritual authority made him the
first among equals. John's brief but memorable career embodies Essene attitudes toward the worldly Jerusalem Sadducees and Pharisees:
he dressed like a crazed hermit and roamed the wilderness preaching
against urban corruption and the dangers of materialism, both of
which plagues afflicting struggling humanity, it was understood by all
concerned, could be blamed somehow on the Jerusalem Temple.

As we shall see, a temple according to Essene philosophy was supposed to be a spiritual structure, not a physical one. The only house
God needed was the individual soul, and the only sacrifice he required
to be made there was a selfless and compassionate life. The Jerusalem
Temple, of course, was virtually little more than a combination bank-
and-abattoir by this stage. Jesus himself made his feelings about the institution famously clear. But Luke's gospel even has Mary and Joseph
slaughtering doves and pigeons in it after their son's birth, an event that
certainly could not have occurred. The Essenes deplored animal sacrifice and were also, we're told, strict vegetarians.

When John the Baptist was executed, Jesus evidently tried to assume
both messianic roles and suddenly began to preach, something he
never did while John lived. Unlike his cousin's inspired and somewhat
fiery sermons, Jesus' public announcements were more reasoned and
traditional, full of quotations from Jewish scriptures to offset his more
idiosyncratic, multivalent Essene parables. At first, the Jewish orthodoxy seem to have regarded him benignly as something of another Hillel—the great teacher who died when Jesus was a child. Asked to
summarize the Torah as briefly as possible, Hillel once replied, "Do
not do to others that which is hateful to you—this is the whole of the

Torah." Jesus' famous maxim about treating others the way you'd like them to treat you is no radical innovation.

Where Jesus' conflict with the Essene hierarchs appears to have begun, however, is in the conciliatory tone of some of his remarks about Romans. The Jerusalem Jews were debased enough in Essene eyes, but the Romans were quite beyond the pale of redemption. Essenes, for all intents and purposes, were both cause and effect of the Zealots' resistance to Roman rule. When Jesus, asked about paying Roman taxes, replies that Caesar should get what belongs to him, he is directly flouting Essene policy. The scrolls indicate that this sudden compulsion to make peace with the invaders caused a rift within the Essene community between those who felt cooperation with Rome was possible and those hard-core Zealots who preferred to die than even contemplate negotiating a working relationship with the Evil One.

This schism, I believe, was what has created such a confusion over the various groups named in both the scrolls and the gospels. In reality, terms like Ebionites, Essenes, Zealots, and Nazareans (or Nazirites) merely refer to internal factions within the body of the Essene community as a whole. Jesus is not called a Nazarean because he was from Nazareth, which doesn't seem to have been Nazareth proper until the third century anyway, but because he belonged to the Nazirite or Nazarean wing of pious Essenes. The terms may have been purely symbolic or may relate either to ritual functions or even differing schools of thought.

The potentially disastrous rift is apparently healed, however, for the scrolls indicate that the schismatics finally returned to the fold. The events covered here, though, are somewhat mystifying since they include the period of Jesus' arrest and crucifixion. The betrayal by Judas Iscariot precipitates this in the gospels. "Iscariot" derives from the term "Sicarii," which basically means "someone handy with a knife" and was yet another name applied to Zealot warriors. No Zealot would betray anyone to Roman authorities, unless perhaps the person in question posed a threat to Zealots. Again, names are a problem. Judas was one of the most common names of the time and just means "Jewish man." Therefore Judas Iscariot would mean "Jewish man and Zealot warrior." One can never be certain whether or not some names are being used on a purely symbolic level, just as one can never be certain whether or not events are to be taken entirely literally.

Much is documented by the Romans about this period of history, but, as many have observed, no chronicler ever mentions any Jesus or any Jewish messiah being executed under Pontius Pilate's governorship. The gospels are equally baffling about the incident, if their stories are looked at carefully, and do not have the ring of authenticity they usually possess when recounting other events. They also pointedly have women as the only first-hand witnesses to both the death (crucifixion) and resurrection who are followers of Jesus.

Under Jewish law of the day—which pioneered patriarchy—a woman's testimony was not admissible in court—not valid, in other words. This, along with other incidents involving Jesus and women, has been interpreted in a revisionist light as an example of Christianity's pioneering feminism. It's a nice thought, but imposing contemporary values on the past is invariably a big mistake. It is far more likely, given the Essene fondness for coded and encrypted writings, that the episodes with women at the crucifixion and resurrection were designed to send a message to "initiates," readers who were watching for the indication that a passage had a "pesher," or other levels of meaning. This is not a paranoid conspiracy theory but a simple fact of Essene life. They regarded themselves as a chosen elite with heavy responsibilities, and they reserved the right to communicate only with each other, especially in matters concerning the community. Zealot activities were similarly, of necessity, placed under a rule of secrecy, and every warrior used a code name like Simeon's "Bar Khochba" to preserve the safety of his family as much as himself.

The other perplexing aspect of the gospels' crucifixion story is the behavior of the people of Jerusalem toward Jesus. When he enters as the Davidic Messiah they greet him with joy, paving the road with palm fronds. A few days later, we're expected to believe, they would rather save the life of a thief than even spare Jesus crucifixion. I therefore suggest that the whole incident relates to events in the other Jerusalem, Qumran, and represents the cathartic moment of what had been a major Essene crisis, but which, characteristically, was viewed as something universal in consequence. Jesus does not die, but, whatever really happened, he was still forced to leave the main community. As we shall see later, what probably did happen concerned the failed attempt by Jesus' followers to install him as both the Zadokite high priest and the kingly, Davidic messiah.

The gospel versions give the impression that the Romans overreacted to what was in essence merely a Jewish internal matter and no threat to imperial rule. When Jesus is arrested, for example, we're told a "band" of soldiers arrived for him. The original Greek, however, says a cohort of soldiers came. Cohort cannot be translated as "band"—it is a specific term meaning one tenth of a Roman legion. A legion contained 6,000 men; why, therefore, would 600 soldiers have been dispatched to arrest one man and a handful of followers? Either the events around Passover amounted to a full-scale insurrection that was brutally put down, the leaders executed, and the matter hushed up— or this story has another purpose altogether.

THE MAN OF A LIE

The second crisis the scrolls recount is a sequel to the first but involves, I believe, Paul and Jesus' brother James. Another schism had opened up, apparently, with Paul now arguing for reconciliation with Rome and James upholding the traditional Essene policy. Paul, however, is viewed as an outsider whose authority is not at all sanctioned by the Essenes. Paul's doctrine of faith directly contradicts the pure teachings of Jesus and causes its adherents to do what Jesus warned against: put off until tomorrow what should be done today. If faith alone got you to heaven, there was little point in good works or spiritual improvement. There are somewhat sinister undertones here, too: of the individual giving up power to the state. Unlike the first crisis, though, this one is never resolved, the account of it appearing to break off unfinished, but with the situation far more threatening than its predecessor. And this was essentially the crisis that the Magi had come from Persia to avert at the birth of Jesus.

Paul was far more involved directly with the Romans than Jesus had ever been, and his power base was exclusively among those Diaspora Jews Herod had to recruit for his dreams of empire because the locals would have nothing to do with him. Paul clearly fears James and keeps far away from Jerusalem, where, as he eventually finds out for himself, his life is in danger and only the Romans will protect him—his so-called arrest reads far more like a rescue and even puts him as a house guest in a Roman villa rather than in jail. Faced with a trial at the hands of Jerusalem Jews, Paul is quick to invoke his rights as a Roman citizen to be tried in Rome.

In his letters, Paul sounds bitter about the way James is treating him, constantly protesting that he is not a liar. But whatever the Essenes and the Magi feared might happen apparently did happen, because the Dead Sea Scrolls were buried soon after and the Zealots were fighting for their lives. Paul, along with some of Jesus' old followers—possibly, but not certainly, including Peter—end up in Rome as martyrs. Paul's death is unconvincingly documented, besides being highly unlikely given his cozy relationship with Roman authorities, and he seems to vanish when whatever he has been doing is deemed complete. According to the scrolls, what he has been doing is catastrophic in the eyes of those who appear to approve of Jesus.

THE NEW JEWS

During the three centuries that elapsed after Rome crushed the Jewish Revolt and razed Jerusalem, the burgeoning Christian world had become anything but unified under the watchful eye of an increasingly Roman Church. The cement of Hellenism had eroded and the great empire was now cracking apart along fault lines of religion and ethnicity. And beyond imperial fences, from Armenia through Egypt to Ireland, there were other churches with bishops who had never been formally ordained and often differed with orthodoxy on even the most fundamental issues of ritual, dogma, and spiritual practice. Many of these churches also continued to use scriptures like the Gospel of Thomas that, for one reason or another, had now been excluded from the orthodox canon; and most espoused a life of austerity, communal work, and meditation that still more closely resembled Essene Judaism than it did Pauline Christianity.

There were also mysteriously close ties between the autonomous monasteries that formed the heart of this other Christianity, ties that spoke of a dangerously threatening unity within the apparent diversity of spiritual freedom. The many heresies that Rome's bishops fulminated against were really just facets of the same big heretical gem, which sparkled brightly with an ancient light no power of earth could blot out. Egyptian monks regularly visited the great Celtic monasteries of Ireland, for example, bringing with them manuscripts of texts they knew that the Holy Synod condemned as Satan's work, but which the mystic soul of ancient Egypt deep within their new faith recognized as a part of the perennial truth that may change its name but never its nature. Wisdom could never be heresy no matter how many Roman theologians declared it such or had its champions burned alive along with the words they cherished.

Flames writhed above the public squares of Rome for days on end now, as the anti-heresy brigades piled on bales of anything that contradicted the tenets of that vast dark tool of state tyranny the Church had made from a teaching of individual liberty. For the mission of mercy that called the Magi to Bethlehem, back when storm clouds were just glimpsed far on the horizon, had ultimately failed. Three centuries later Truth itself was being threatened with extinction and appeared to have only its books for a refuge and fortress to protect it from the lie that proclaimed to all the world there was no truth but faith—yet faith was of course really no truth at all. So terrifying was this prospect of an end to truth as a reality humankind could experience—and thus not doubt—that books costing the equivalent of tens of thousands of dollars each to have copied by hand were sealed up in jars and buried, bricked up in the walls of tombs, stashed in remote caves whose mouths were silenced by tons of rock, or shipped off to the safety of distant monasteries where they could be slowly reproduced in the hope that one might live to see better days return. The Dead Sea Scrolls and the gnostic texts of Nag Hammadi had to wait nearly two thousand years to see the light of that new day. Countless works have been lost forever, though, and countless others probably still await some happy accident to free them from their graves.

In some cases, thanks to the busy traffic between Egypt and Ireland, the Gaelic translations of texts proscribed by Rome survived. And many of the so-called heresies are known now, ironically, solely through those works commissioned by Rome to denounce and ridicule them. Yet in among the fatuities of orthodoxy's hired apologists and vindictive hacks one can still see clearly enough the tableau image of a problem that the Church found so impossibly vexing in its stubborn refusal to disappear: the real teachings of Jesus. Furthermore, looking carefully at the components of this odd and alien tableau, one finds those enigmatic Magi staring back up through the dizzy centuries, as if waiting patiently for someone to ask their opinion of the world so far and what they're still doing in it. The irony of being forced to seek out the truth from those hired to brand it heresy is not lost on these Persian wise men either, but then they can no longer control their destiny.

It was at this point that the mental journey began to feel like a very complicated three-dimensional board game I was playing with a crew of talented cheats and liars.

HERETICS

Writing around A.D. 150, Justin Martyr—who taught his faith above a Roman bathhouse—mentions those "Christians" who regard Jesus as both Messiah and yet still a man. They adhere to many aspects of Judaic law and are despised by gentile or Pauline Christians.

Irenaeus, Bishop of Lyons, compiled a destructively influential list of prevailing heresies in the early second century, *Adversus haereses,* and in it he rages against a sect whom he calls "the Ebionites"—a term which can be translated as "the poor" and was also frequently used by the Essene authors of the Qumran scrolls to describe themselves— *ebionim,* in Hebrew—much as Knights Templar were the Poor Knights of Christ. Jesus was a man, not God, and Mary had not been a virgin, the Ebionites maintained, according to Irenaeus. They also insisted that Jesus only became the messiah after his baptism, an event viewed more like an anointing or coronation. The only gospel they used was that of Matthew, and—like Jesus himself—they preached and taught primarily from the Old Testament prophetic books. They followed Judaic law fastidiously, and, most telling of all, "they reject the apostle Paul, calling him an apostate from the Law."

Around the early fifth century, an unusually boring and self-righteous Church pedant called Epiphanius writes about those he calls both "Ebionite" and "Nazarean," the terms clearly interchangeable. They find no shame, Epiphanius is most upset to report, in denouncing Paul as *pseudapostolorum*—a "false apostle."

A collection of Arabic manuscripts, found in Turkey some thirty years ago by the medievalist scholar Schlomo Pines, proved to date from the tenth century, but also contained long verbatim quotes ascribed to a Nazarean text from around the sixth century, which, Pines theorized convincingly, might have been written originally in Syriac and have come from a Christian monastery in Khuzistan, southwest Iran. This older text reflected an unbroken tradition stretching back to the Nazarean or Essene hierarchy which—according to Dead Sea Scrolls scholar Dr. Robert Eisenman's latest findings—probably fled Jerusalem after James's execution in A.D. 63 immediately prior to the first Jewish revolt. Again, the beliefs entailed in this Nazarean-Essene document are very familiar: Jesus as man, not God; the overriding importance of Judaic law; and the usual tirade against Paul, whose followers are described as having "abandoned the religion of Christ and turned toward the religious doctrines of the Romans." Even the gospels are dismissed as all but useless secondhand accounts which merely contain "something—but little—of the sayings, the precepts of Christ, and information concerning him." For Professor Pines, however, the most startling news was finding the tenth-century Arab writer claimed that the Nazarean sect responsible for the earlier text still existed and, furthermore, was regarded as an elite by other Christians.

Pines would have been still more startled to learn that the Nazareans—or Mandaeans, as they're also called—still exist a millennium later. I met some of them in Khuzistan, near the Iraqi border in southwest Iran.

Mandaeans, of which the priests are termed Nazareans, view John the Baptist as the true spiritual Messiah but, contrary to what scholars have claimed, they regard Jesus as a "failed," not "false," princely or Davidic Messiah.

PAGAN MAGI

Taking the cue from Paul's Romano-hellenization of Christianity, far from recognized for its enormous contribution, Zoroastrianism was soon being branded pagan superstition by a new Holy Roman Empire. The Magi—instead of remaining as colleagues in the advisory capacity in which they probably came to Bethlehem to serve—now suddenly found themselves depicted by Church in-house artists apparently paying their traditional homage as much to Mary as to her child. Artists had been strictly decreed since the Council of Nicea in A.D. 325 to paint only in accordance with Church doctrine, not their own miserable imaginative inspiration, which explains their sudden common vision more easily than a mass-revelation engineered by angelic art critics.

Retaking Ravenna from the Goths for the second time in the sixth century A.D., Justinian commissioned the stunningly magnificent Nativity mosaics in its basilica of S. Apollinare Nuovo. This basilica had been constructed originally by the Arian Ostrogothic emperor Theodoric, whose own equally exquisite mosaic decorations depicting the life of Christ show the Savior oddly beardless and also omit any crucifixion scene. The teachings of the heretic Arius, like the Koran and even some early apocryphal Judaeo-Christian texts, maintain that Jesus was mortal, not divine; hence, logically enough, there could have been no resurrection. With no resurrection, a crucifixion is superfluous at best.

The two oldest extant versions of what is now widely agreed to be the earliest gospel written, that of Mark, are in New Testament collections known as the codices Sinaiticus and Vaticanus. Both of these versions of Mark omit the last twelve verses in the Authorized Version, which also just happen to be the ones containing any account of Jesus' resurrection from the dead. This would have concerned more people than it has so far if the gospel of Matthew—since it was placed first in the canon—had not been assumed to be the oldest for most of the last 1,700 years.

Yet it was the Nativity, with its virgin birth—and thus goddess Mary cult—that Justinian was more anxious to add to the visual theology deplorably lacking in Theodoric's Basilica. The pagan vacuum for a

mother goddess was still a more immediate problem than Gothic heresies were, so Nativity mosaics it was. And these new mosaics also included the earliest known representations of the Magi in Persian dress.
Justinian commissioned very similar mosaics—and probably from the
same politically correct artist—for his reconstruction of the emperor
Constantine's Basilica of the Nativity in Bethlehem itself, something
that must have been decreed during the same bout of imperial inspiration that had the decorators in Ravenna's Basilica while stray Goths,
dazed by looted wine, were still getting hacked to pieces in the alleys
outside. Oddly enough, the mosaics and reconstruction job in Bethlehem coincided with the final acceptance of December twenty-fifth as
the feast of Christmas by the Church in Jerusalem after six hundred
years of vacillation.

BIRTHDAYS

For the first three hundred years of Christian history—from which the
Magi are curiously absent—there had been yet another blazing difference of opinion between the Eastern and Western churches over the
celebration of Christmas and that of Epiphany, held on January 6.
Until A.D. 386 most of the Eastern churches considered Epiphany to
be both Nativity and the feast commemorating Jesus' baptism, his
"birth" as the Christ (and the beginning of his biography as far as one
half of the New Testament gospels are concerned). In a Pentecost sermon to the Christians of Antioch that year, St. John Chrysostom
(whose tooth is apparently in a church which also boasts a toe belonging to one of the Magi) quite clearly identifies Epiphany with Nativity.
But by December twentieth John had apparently changed his mind,
stating cheerfully in another sermon that he is looking forward to
Christmas as the festival of the birth, "the festival from which all other
festivals arise." This must have severely baffled the saint's congregation, for in his Epiphany sermon just over two weeks later, on January
6, 387, John goes out of his way to emphasize the sudden difference
between Christmas as Nativity and Epiphany as the "Manifestation of
Christ to the Gentiles." These particular "Gentiles" are also identified,
and apparently for the first time in history, as the Magi. John must have

been pleased with his brainstorm. Before this the term "gentiles" had been applied to the whole world, or as much of it as could have stood on the banks of the Jordan river when Jesus was baptized—or anointed Davidic Messiah by his cousin John, the Zadokite Messiah, as the Nazareans would put it.

The Magi's presence at the Nativity was soon to be rapidly promoted, too, becoming not only the much-needed explanation for a tricky riddle which the Church was increasingly requested to solve—how a Jewish rabbi came to be the Christian god—but also an emblem of the entire pagan world, with all its awe-inspiring mysteries and magical powers, relinquishing, like Prospero when the storm had passed, personal daemons, wands, arcane incantations, occult practices, and spell books at the feet of the infant Jesus: the invincible new super-god. There are strong parallels with the story of Moses humbling Pharaoh's court magicians with demonstrations of his own new god's superior powers. It was, in fact—not that anyone ever knows these things at the time—an image of the ancient world slipping imperceptibly into modernity.

December twenty-fifth was an inevitable Roman Christian choice for the Nativity because it had been decreed by the emperor Aurelian in 274 as *natalis solis invicti*, the birthday of his unconquered Syrian sun god. For solar cults, a noticeable increase in daylight time after the winter solstice (which occurs near the end of December) was always an understandably big deal. It also capped off the major Roman festival, Saturnalia: a celebration of astrological origins that concerned the victory of eternity over time.

For Roman Christians, Jesus therefore not only had to be born by miraculous means on the day when time was symbolically dislodged by eternity, but he also had to have been sacrificed himself in order to be resurrected as an acceptable god. In striving to find ways to make Christianity acceptable to pagan Rome—and change the diet of its lions—the early Church Fathers had gone a little too far in making the faith resemble paganism. Apart from sharing the solar deity's birthday and nimbus, he now also virtually shared the biography of Hercules. The son of Zeus, Hercules had been born of a virgin, who was with him along with his followers when he died after a heroic effort to combat evil hand to hand and, through his own suffering, win immortality for others—including his twin brother. The sky darkened, turning day into night as a sign after his death.

The Romans presumably had not considered, while they were busier than Frankenstein stitching various other body parts together around the brain of Christianity, how much evidence might exist out there about the brain's original owner. It was bad enough that a god had influential brothers or indeed any mortal brothers at all, but two entire rival churches—the Egyptian and Celtic—if not others, actually taught not only that James, the leader of Jerusalem's Christians, was a brother of Jesus, but also that the disciple Thomas was Jesus' twin brother (an idea durable enough to be embodied by Leonardo Da Vinci in his "Last Supper" painting). It was a variant of the Gemini myth that also had its roots in Zoroastrian mysticism.

There was no point now in cursing emperor Constantine's disastrous choice in state religions. He was at war with a pagan rival at the time and had to come up with some sort of spiritual gimmick of his own, but one that wouldn't alienate his people or troops. By now Christianity had made itself so presentable to Romans that there was even a lavish church among the temples to Zeus, the emperor cults, pagan Madonnas, all manner of Near Eastern deities, and a Jewish synagogue that sprang up at Dura-Europos, the urban-fortress experiment in inter-cult harmony established deep in Asia Minor—deep enough for safety if it failed. Thus, what with visions of the cross auguring military victory and Constantine's death-bed baptism, the Empire was now too far into Christianity for any turning back. It had to devise its own version of "Truth" and "the Lie"—which ended up as the canonical New Testament.

Thus efforts to bring all of Christendom into line with Roman doctrines really had little to do with theology and much more to do with power politics. Christian leaders were so happy to come in out of the cold that they no longer worried about what had become of their religion.

Most of the eastern churches deferred to Rome's pronouncement of December twenty-fifth for Christmas-Nativity, although Jerusalem held on to Epiphany's January sixth for nearly three more centuries. Pockets of the Egyptian and Celtic churches held out longer, however. Various bishops in Ireland and elsewhere also still remained so close to their faith's Jewish roots that they were even celebrating the sabbath on Saturday as late as the fifth century, and others refused to accept ordination from Rome for almost as long.

To this day, the Armenian church—still the major form of Christianity in Iran—observes Nativity on January sixth and does not observe Christmas at all.

The Armenian Bishop of Teheran told me this over tea. He also gave me a tin crucifix and urged me to visit Qom, the holiest city in Iran, where Imam Khomeini lectured for most of his life before embarking on a career in revolution when he was sixty-three. He returned there in triumph to briefly rule a country he had liberated from three centuries of monarchs whose idea of social policy appeared to be competing to see which of them could abuse his subjects and loot his own land more outrageously than his predecessors.

I had no desire to visit Qom, which was not on the route I had given the Magi, and which triggered sad memories of those days when Americans languished as hostages in their old embassy, and Iranians created for themselves an ugly image that was really far from their truth then and now, but which was far easier to scrawl across the world's TV monitors than it will be to erase.

"No-no-no," said the bishop. "You go to Qom for the spee-ritt truth. For the wheeze-dom."

I'm all for "wheeze-dom," of course, and the bishop seemed concerned enough about my Magi quest for me to risk taking his advice. Besides, it was easier to reach Kashan—the city where I'd been convinced I'd find Polo's Magi until I found them just where Polo had— via Qom than it was via the next stretch of Silk Route.

Chapter Three

THE HOLY CITY

This Kom is a place that, excepting on the subject
of religion, and settling who are worthy of salvation
and who to be damned, no one opens his lips. Every
man you meet is either a descendant of the Prophet
or a man of the law . . . Perhaps, friend Hajji, you
do not know that this is the residence of the
celebrated Mirza Abdul Cossim, the first mushtehed
(divine) of Persia; a man who, if he were to give
himself sufficient stir, would make the people
believe any doctrine that he might choose to
promulgate. Such is his influence, that many believe
he could even subvert the authority of the Shah
himself, and make his subjects look upon his firmans
as worthless, as so much waste paper.

—James Morier, *The Adventures of Hajji Baba of Ispahan* (1824)

THE LEADER SPEAKS

I'd often wondered what the Magi, and Marco Polo for that matter, did
during the long hours of riding through uneventful landscapes. The
one thing they didn't have to do, fortunately, was listen to local radio.
Ghossam's mobile sound system appeared to receive just one radio station, unless of course there was only one station to receive along the
Saveh-Qom highway. Our sole choice of entertainment on this lone
station was the mellifluous voice of Ayatollah Seyed Ali Khamenei,
Leader of the Islamic Revolution, the man handpicked by Imam
Khomeini to succeed to the nation's highest position—which itself

confused the rest of the world, where no precise parallels any longer exist for Khamenei's job. I wondered whether the similarity between the two men's names had been deliberate, whether the late imam had relished the thought of the inevitable confusion his successor's name would cause in the West. Or had it been mere vanity? No one, in Iran or abroad, can hear the name Khamenei without instantly thinking of Khomeini. Was it a spurious immortality the imam had guaranteed himself?

This, Reza informed me, was the first sermon that the Leader had delivered at Teheran University since a bomb hidden in a tape recorder had nearly blown his head off. These university sermons had become major events since Imam Khomeini had initiated them, their site soaked in revolutionary symbolism. Even the word "students" had taken on a numinous significance in Iran, rather than the euphemism for "not-yet-employed" it's become in the West.

"What's he talking about?" I inquired.

The Paykan crashed through an obstacle course of potholes. Reza burped contentedly.

"Satanic plots," he replied, turning to grin back at me like Tony Perkins in *Psycho*.

"What about them?"

"They should stop."

The ayatollah appeared to have a good deal more to say than this, so I decided to tax Reza's patience to its narrow limits by constantly demanding translations. He was more docile when well fed, however. Although the bomb had ripped open Khamenei's throat, the Leader's famous voice betrayed only a slight, sexy huskiness now to show for this injury.

"What other nation could get over one million people to attend rally for spiritual and political purposes of their free will?"

"Eh?"

"That is what Khamenei is saying," Reza explained. "He mean Ten-Day Dawn celebration."

In the East, "a million" usually means "a lot." I'd attended the celebrations in Teheran, and there were a lot of people milling around the gigantic space-age triumphal state-of-the-arch in Revolution Square that the late shah presumably imagined was an improvement on traditional Persian architecture. One hundred thousand people are still a lot of people, though.

"India."

"Huh?" He spun round again.

"India could."

"Could what?"

"Get over a million people to rally for church and state willingly."

"I think you lose some brain through your ear up that mountain," he informed me.

"He *asked*," I yelled back, "what other nation? And I just *answered* the question: *India* could. Five million people attended the Kumbha Mela."

I'd read that in the *Times of India*.

"Five million scum."

He cackled but he was not joking. So I insisted that he carry on translating.

The "Global Arrogance" ought to realize by now that it could never undermine the great Islamic Revolution, Khamenei wanted us to know, its plots were childish and had no effect. The leaders of Iran were happy to die, only too pleased to join all the other martyrs whose places in Paradise were assured. Allah Himself protected Iran, after all, and who could hope to defeat Allah? The people should, however, be ever-vigilant to protect what they had fought so hard for, just as they should protect their own faith by upholding moral standards no other nation on earth could boast of having in the first place. The People were great; the Prophet was great; his companion Ali was great; and, of course, God was great, was indeed the greatest. Et cetera. Khamenei's sermon was punctuated by stirring revolutionary cheers from the vast crowd of attentive students—"a million" of them.

The Leader of the Islamic Revolution sure could talk, though. Two hours later he was still talking. Reza had long since refused to translate, but no one switched Ayatollah Khamenei off. His voice was soothing, almost hypnotic, and if you did not know better you would have assumed that the thrust of his speech was a sort of inspirational self-help invocation liberally peppered with large chunks of mellow poetry and hip scriptural quotations. He sounded a bit like Baba Ram Dass. But anything was better than "Chickadee, chickadee, chickadee."

When I noticed that Ghossam's eyes were closed and he was actually beginning to snore, I snapped out of my own trance, beating the driver around the shoulders and elbowing Reza in the neck.

"Khoda!" yelped Ghossam, jerking forward to wrestle with the steering wheel as the car began to weave in drastic loops from one side of the road to the other.

"You azz . . ." began Reza, noticing our plight and abandoning the inchoate curse. "Holy sheet!"

We side-swiped an old van heading toward us, then went up an embankment and along a kind of sidewalk, where two makeshift stalls for dispensing fresh fruit juice suddenly appeared just ahead. Ghossam put a bear hug on the wheel, and we collided into the side of the first stall. It shattered into fragments of matchwood, straw, and fruit peel, which cascaded over the hood and windshield. Fortunately it was unoccupied; its owner or staff had probably gone home hours before. I looked out the rear window as we crashed back down on the hard top. The stall had vanished, a pile of garbage heaped where it had been, part of which was now tumbling down the grassy slope onto the road, just like us.

Reza screamed something in Farsi, throwing the "Andy" tape cassette at Ghossam.

"Khoda!" Ghossam repeated, mopping his brow on a sleeve.

No one came to complain or even to see what had happened. We were on the outskirts of a large town, but its inhabitants were nowhere to be seen—had all been abducted, perhaps, or fallen prey to Satanic plots.

"Go," wheezed Reza.

"You can't leave the scene," I reminded him piously.

"Here you can, long as no one ever realized you was in the scene to begin with."

"Come on! It's not right—they don't have insurance. Everyone's probably hiding from us."

"Yes, they think Mujahideen attack . . ."

"No, they think morons-in-a-car attack . . ."

Both Reza and Ghossam laughed heartily, untroubled by any nagging social conscience. They were like naughty schoolboys, though, energized by their crimes, as soon as they were sure they'd gotten clean away, that is.

ALI'S TOWN

"You are Martik Bargarian, Armenian sausage merchant," Reza announced, dangling a hotel key at me.

"What?"

The room apparently was four dollars, but would be fifty if the hotel manager suspected I was a foreigner.

"So you just talk sausage. Okay?"

Muttering in a stilted guttural drawl about sausages, I was virtually carried through the lobby between Reza and Ghossam. We had one room with six single cots in it. The bathroom was truly terrifying, a bat cave with faucets.

After listening to the duet for tuba and whoopee cushion that emerged from my companions' noses and mouths all night, I felt sure I had not slept even half a wink by the time an iridescent gray sheen appeared beyond the begrimed glass veil of our curtainless windows.

With the fertile Alborz foothills to the west, cooled and irrigated by the Qomrud River carrying melting snows and mountain streams, the holy city of Qom also stands on the very edge of the great salt desert of Dasht-e-Kavir, an inhospitable and totally unpopulated plain of salt, sand, and brackish streams that is an empty space on even the most detailed maps, stretching some two hundred miles east to Khorasan province, whose own eastern border is Afghanistan. Considering what Qom represents, politically and spiritually, this location seemed almost excessively replete with symbolism.

Bastion of Shi'ite Islam, the tidy, tree-lined little city spirals out from its focus, a golden-domed mosque housing the shrine of Fatima, sister of the eighth imam, Ali al-Rida. Yet its green, shady streets and often near-rural suburbs also contain the tombs of at least ten kings and some four hundred other saints. In 1666, for example—the year London burned to the ground, and the year Mogul emperor Shah Jehan, builder of the Taj Mahal, died bankrupt in an Indian prison—Iran's Shah Abbas II, revered by the clergy for his piety, was interred at Qom in an exquisite mausoleum adorned by fourteen silk rugs that rank among the finest ever woven in Persia. Some shrines there even date back to the fourteenth century and earlier.

Yet the first sights that greet the visitor today are watchtowers and

high barbed-wire fences guarding a military base near the turnpike
ending Iran's new Teheran–Qom Expressway. Although also guarding
what became Imam Khomeini's political base for a while after the Revolution, and what had been the clergy's theological base for centuries,
the watchtowers initially give an impression that the whole of Qom is a
fortified city. This impression is swiftly dispelled, however, not far beyond the turnpike, by a small fairground of swings, slides, and a miniature Ferris wheel featuring images of Yogi Bear, Donald Duck, Tom &
Jerry, Minnie Mouse, and other great Americans, emblazoned ten feet
high on its surrounding wall. Beyond this point, central Qom lies irreg-
ularly spread out around the valley below, its most prominent feature,
initially, a titanic image of Khomeini's face painted on one entire side
of the tallest building in sight. Though still some two miles away, its
stern and vigilant expression is clearly visible—a giant tutelary genie
watching over the nation's spiritual core.

At dawn Qom was extraordinary. There were mullahs everywhere, in
brown or black abayas, with white or black turbans, riding motorcycles
or crammed in cars, standing in huddles talking or striding down the
sidewalks with their robes billowing behind them. Everywhere too,
usually in gaggles of five or more, were black chador-shrouded
women, their sparkling almond eyes peering out of the shadows cast by
flaps of material usually held between their teeth, and through which
they had learned from habit to talk effortlessly.

Everyone appeared to be heading toward the great gold onion dome
and the candy-striped lighthouse minarets of Fatima's shrine. But there
were many distractions on the way. Barrow boys hawked pyramids of
dried fruit; sidewalk vendors shouted out the virtues of their oranges,
bananas, melons; a shabby old man leaned against a cart of partially
dried pomegranates looking as unenthusiastic as his squashed soggy
wares looked unappetizing. Tiny stalls sold religious knickknacks:
agates set into chrome-plated rings; green prayer beads; the Ka'aba
printed on red velvet with gold tassels; Khomeini wall clocks; framed
paint-by-numbers-style images of the martyr Husain ready to fight at
Karbala; pennants of green and red felt with "God Is Great" emblazoned in gold and green glitter over them, both in Persian script and
English. For Qom was also a spiritual resort town—and resorts will be
resorts.

Much interest was shown by these early-risers in everything on display, as if the like of such treasures had never been seen before. I started noticing the panoramic variety of faces here, too: Indonesian, Pakistani, African, Balkan. The city housed possibly the most prestigious Shi'ite theological school in the world, after all. To study here would mean much back in Jakarta or Khartoum, I realized, watching how proudly these young faces wore their new robes and spotless turbans, how importantly they walked, how intensely they talked.

Turning into a broad, flag-bedecked, palm-lined boulevard leading to the great shrine, I felt as if I were in medieval Oxford or Cambridge—which were both, ostensibly, theological institutions themselves eight hundred years ago. A Congo rubine sun had set fire to the great gold dome now and was splattering the geometric ceramic zigzags and spirals swirling around soaring minarets with exploding micro-galaxies of red hot stars.

Through the high ogee arch of the mosque's entrance there was an enormous courtyard surrounded by shady arcades. The giant marble ablutions pool had several layers of green, blue, orange, and red light-bulbs strung to a central pole. Behind it, recessed beyond a three-arched portico supported by high, thin, delicately carved columns in red, white, and blue, was a fifty-foot-high stalactite vault of pointed arches in antique mercury-backed mirror work. Catching flushed impressions of a new raw sun from the rippling pool, this huge crystal cave flashed and quivered like the entrance to some higher world, some paradise of light. Above it the swelling mihrab dome burned in the high blue air amid a forest of ceramic-sheathed minarets in turquoise, emerald, ivory, and cadmium yellow. Green banners with elegant white calligraphy extolling Allah, His prophet, and Iran's Revolution appeared suddenly to breathe like giants' torsos, pulsing to and fro in the cool morning wind. Standing in groups of three or four around the courtyard—but as if positioned by some fastidious art director for harmony's sake, were russet or black-clad mullahs engaged in animated discussions.

Feeling overwhelmed, as well as overtired, I performed ablutions in synch with a gnomish old peasant, letting water run from the elbow down in the Shi'ite manner, then washing my feet and carrying my boots to where a turbulent river of people was pouring into one absurdly small entrance. Behind a flap stood the footwear counter—get token, give shoes—and to the right, behind heavy, worn green velvet drapes lay the cavernous prayer hall. Some two hundred mullahs and civilians sat in circles or prayed alone on dozens of magnificent old carpets. I followed the steady troop of people heading through an arch to the left, however, soon finding myself facing the shrine of Fatima itself.

Beneath a stalactite mirror work dome in which glinted a thousand constellations of candle light stars, the resting place of the eighth imam's sister was a solid silver vault canopied in gold and green ceramic, patterned with the names of God formed from vibrant white script. Gold rosettes with floral ceramic hearts a foot in diameter stood side by side around the eaves of this majestic roof. A scrum of bodies heaved and struggled to approach the intricately worked silver walls. Hands were laid upon burnished metal misted by anxious breath and sweat, then prayers or pleas mumbled passionately, and folded rials posted through a slot which deposited them within, at the base of a sarcophagus entirely shrouded by ancient baize and gold-braided cloth. The glittering honeycomb of geometric alcoves above and all around made me feel like a worker bee in some celestial hive.

With certain places of worship a sense of proximity to the Eternal is tangible. It most definitely was here. I suddenly felt an aching need to pray, to be still for a while where the future meets the past. Not once did I ever sense any hostility toward my infidel presence. The universality and absolute egalitarianism of true Islam was very evident in every eye that met mine. We all had larger concerns within this sublime monument to faith, more important business. I could feel why so many of Iran's great men of God preferred this particular mosque above all others. A living, intelligent energy informed the place, permeated it, drove it like some vast arcane machine designed to focus minds on an absolute reality.

Wandering back to the prayer hall I found the tombs of numerous ayatollahs—some very recent, some mere plaques in the flagstones worn smooth by the centuries of passing feet. Over the resting place of Ayatollah Motaheri a man sobbed silently. Imam Khomeini had been very close to the revered Motaheri. When he was killed by opponents of the revolution, Khomeini is reported to have said "Now my back is broken." Then he did something he had never done before, or ever did again: he bent down and wept for an hour. Many observed that some kind of spark was permanently missing from Khomeini's eyes after the loss of Motaheri.

A TALE OF TWO MULLAHS

I sat near a donnish-looking mullah who wore the supercilious expression of a professional pedant. Cross-legged, he faced a burly argumentative student. The mullah held a tome that had what was presumably a commentary printed in curious, obelisk-shaped columns in its margins. He would recite a passage in his precise, nit-picking voice, and then the student, using pugilist's hands for emphasis, would grunt and grumble a retort, constantly seizing the book and prodding at its paragraphs of exotic calligraphy with belligerent objections to his tutor's discourse.

I begged the couple's pardon and asked if they spoke English and if so what exactly they were doing.

"There are two aspects to religion," the mullah replied in perfect English, politely but very smugly. "There is Faith and there are Principles. For example, Faith is observing the prohibition against drinking alcohol, observing it unquestioningly. But the mind is gift of God and it will have questions, no? So Principles is examining why alcohol is bad. Yes?"

It seemed straightforward enough.

I asked about the obelisklike columns, learning that they indeed contained commentaries by subsequent scholars, and even commentaries on those commentaries.

Apologizing for my churlish ignorance, I then inquired what the Wise One knew about Fatima, the eighth imam's sister who was interred not thirty feet from where we sat.

"But perhaps I'm interrupting you?" I added hastily.

"No, no! It is my pleasure, friend."

The apprentice nodded to confirm this, possibly relieved to terminate his lesson for the day.

"It has been told," began the mullah, "that when al-Ma'mun, the son of Caliph Haroun al-Rashid, wished to make al-Rida his successor, he gathered together the great-great-grandchildren of the Prophet (Peace Be Upon Him) and said to them, 'In truth, I wish al-Rida to succeed me.'

"The Prophet's descendants envied al-Rida and said, 'You appoint an ignorant man who does not have the essential intuitive skills to direct the caliphate. Send for him now. He'll come here and you will see how his shameful ignorance makes it impossible to consider him for such a noble position.' So he sent for him and he came. The Prophet's descendants told him to ascend the pulpit and give some sort of sign to make them worship God's majesty."

The mullah looked at me knowingly, no doubt assuming that I was also the kind of person who needed signs to force him to worship, and could therefore relate to the people in his tale. The truth was, however, that I didn't have a clue what he was talking about and presumed he had misheard my question.

I had even less of a clue thirty-five minutes later when the brackish stream of his discourse suddenly dried up.

I thanked him and his student for their time, moving several yards back to sit. Soon I felt my body begin to hum and tingle with energy surging from ancient stones, a beneficent genius of place just rocking me gently back and forth, a reed in the wind like countless reeds before me had been and like countless others yet to come would be. Merely alive, breathing in and breathing out, being breathed back and forth through the eye of the needle separating being from non-being, keeping time from eternity.

JESUS OF THE KORAN

"Tell when He was not, and then I will tell you when He was," whispered a dry old voice. "Surely He is Seeing, but not like the sight of His creatures?"

I looked up to find an ancient mullah with bright eyes sparkling beneath his black turban and a beard like bleached horse hair.

"I heard Hojjat-ul-Islam Gilani reciting Imam al-Rida," he said.

"Then I saw you sitting with his words. I wished to help your meditations with a few simple thoughts. I am sorry if I disturb you . . . "

"No, not at all."

He was Ayatollah Khazzari, I learned, and soon I was telling him why I was in Iran, asking if he knew anything that might shed light on Polo's story and the Magi. I'd almost forgotten about them myself during that long moment of peace. One difference that I had always found striking between the Polo version and Matthew's was the absence of any astrological signs leading Polo's Magi to Bethlehem. I'd suspected that this might be connected to Islamic disapproval of pagan mysticism. So I asked Khazzari if the Koran touched on the subject of astrology at all. Without hesitation he began to quote:

> It is We Who have set out
> The Zodiacal Signs in the heavens,
>   And made them fair-seeming
> To all beholders;
>
> And moreover We have guarded them
> From every evil spirit accursed:
>
> But any that gains a hearing
> By stealth, is pursued
> By a flaming fire, bright to see.

I asked if this was perhaps somewhat disapproving, but the answer appeared to depend on the intentions of those interpreting heavenly signs. The "flaming fire" reminded me of the torrent of flame that gushed from the well when Polo's Magi threw away the stone that baby Jesus had given them. There was a pronounced Zoroastrian ring to that last verse, too: fire is the symbol for God, for truth—the force that would pursue those practicing occult arts with impure motives all the way to hell. Maybe. In answer to questions about the birth of Jesus, Khazzari quoted that most beautiful of verses in the Koran where Mary retires to a remote place after giving birth miraculously.

> And the pains of childbirth
> Drove her to the trunk
> Of a palm-tree:
> She cried in her anguish:

"Ah! Would that I had
Died before this thing! would that
I had been a thing
Forgotten and out of sight!"

But a voice cried to her
From beneath the palm-tree:
"Grieve not! for thy Lord
Hath provided a rivulet
Beneath thee;

"And shake towards thyself
The trunk of the palm-tree:
It will let fall
Fresh ripe dates upon thee.

"So eat and drink
And cool thine eye.
And if thou dost see
Any man, say, 'I have
Vowed a fast to God
Most Gracious, and this day
Will I enter into no talk
With any human being.' "

It was the wrong time of year for dates to be ripe according to the Koran, I learned—and you can't eat unripe dates—thus the fruit is also a miracle. There were also, I recalled, ripe dates on the trees behind the Persian Magi in Justinian's mosaics. The child Jesus talks from birth in the Koranic version, too, like the child in Polo's story. There is, however, no mention of Magi, or even shepherds. There's no crucifixion or resurrection either, for that matter. Yet the palm tree and the spring of fresh water, I was later to learn, were potent symbols in the esoteric version of Zoroastrianism that fueled Essene Judaism and thus lay at the heart of the Magi's journey.

"But Shia Islam gain much from Zoroastrian religion," Khazzari added, much to my surprise.

"Really?"

"Zardhusht [Zoroaster] was a very great philosopher. Very great. His religion and the great old knowledge of Egypt give to Judaism its basis; and to Christianity; and also to Islam."

I told him this sounded like a very radical statement, the kind that generates fatwahs. He chuckled.

"That is politics. This is truth. We have made a great error turning our faith into our politics. It has twisted the truth in it, making the inner outer, the particular general. Are not all religions one?"

"I've always wanted to believe so."

One what? was what I felt like saying, though.

For a moment it crossed my mind that he was a Komiteh plant, wired for sound, goading me on to say something derogatory about Islam, something worth twenty lashes and thirty years. But you can't fake goodness and sincerity. Usually.

I told him what Dr. Mort had said about Mary's shrine back in Saveh, asking why so many legends connected this area to Christian myth.

"Not myth," he corrected emphatically. "It is historical fact. The wise king Solomon was here also. Jesus was not crucified—Koran says so—and after his escape he came here with some followers, including his mother. She was old and sick, much troubled by Jesus' arrest and trial, and she died near Saveh. Jesus and his followers were heading to east—some say to India—but they buried Maryam and built a shrine before continuing on this journey."

"Do you believe Jesus died in Kashmir, then?"

"Some say he died in Rome. But it was wrong. He returned to the place where he had been educated as a youth—Kashmir and Himalaya hills—and he continue to teach a special few. His main mission is over, you see? but he still has some close companions. This, I believe, is the truth of what happen. Zardhusht also study in India. Christian religion now is far from original teaching of Jesus. Same thing in Islam. The Prophet is weep tears if he see what we have done with his glorious message."

"Where does Zoroastrianism fit in, then?"

My mind was reeling.

"It was . . . er . . . catty-list for all three faith that come out of Egypt. In Babylon the Zardhushtis bring together wisdom of ancient world, before history; this wisdom only remain in Egypt and India. Without Babylon exile the Jews would not have same religion at all. After exile they had absorbed the falsafa—philosophy—and also theosophy of

Zardhushtis and they are made it basis, with the Egypt wisdom, for new religion. Before this it is for masses very primiteeve: only the animals sacrificing and the fear. Your story of the Jesus his birth show how close bound these two faith were being at that point."

He added that Cabala was the true Judaism and that this was based totally on Mazdean (Zoroastrian) esoteric philosophy. Christianity was originally an offshoot and reformed version of esoteric, or mystical, Judaism. Zoroastrianism was to monotheism, it seemed, what the "missing link" was to evolution theory.

"You are having the Christian Cabala too," he told me. "The warrior priests who are ruling Jerusalem at time of Crusade learn this from the Jews and also from the Soof Muslim. You know the Soof?"

"Yes. Sufis?"

He nodded, adding, "Soof is the Islam of Prophet. Much love . . ." His eyes began to water and he gazed upwards. "Religion without the love is not true religion. Only with the love can we know God."

"Are you a Sufi?"

"There was a great man from your Britain who came here," he answered, "and I help him study the ancient Persian. He made translations. Poeticals, you see? Very beautiful translation he is making, this Professor Arberry—"

"Translator of Rumi?"

"Yes, yes. You know the Jalal a-Din Rumi?"

I certainly did know the poetry of one of the greatest Sufi mystics who ever lived. I knew Arberry's translations of his poetry, too. It was so transcendently beautiful that when I was a student I wrote Arberry a fan letter. Months later his daughter replied, saying that she was sure her father would have appreciated my kind words but, unfortunately, he was unable to thank me himself since he'd died three years earlier.

"You worked with him?" I asked Khazzari.

"I gave him some small little assistances. It was big honor."

"Can ayatollahs be Sufis?"

"All animals, they swim the ocean, yes? But only the fishes they live there . . ."

I took that as a yes. In my experience, asking Sufis direct questions and expecting direct answers was like wondering why dolphins don't learn how to write if they're so keen on communicating with humans. I asked Khazzari if he would have tea with me later. He had no trouble getting out of that one: it was Ramadan and he would fast until sundown.

"I must pray, then meet students," he said. "And you must continue your journey. The journey is very important for you."

"It is?"

He adopted an expression suggesting I had questioned the value of breathing.

"Of course. You will find what you are seek—is not that what you want?"

"Yup. What makes you think I will find it?"

"*Who* makes me think, not *what.* Those who wish to find what they are seek will find it. I think you wish to find, no?"

"Right . . ."

Had anyone ever said no?

He took both my hands in his and squeezed them tightly, staring into my eyes with sudden intensity. I felt a jolt of something surge up my spine.

"Khoda Afez," he muttered, shuffling off.

"Khoda Afez," I repeated. God be with you.

I sat for some minutes, reviewing every astounding thing that the old ayatollah had said. Thoughts raced in circles until they spun off their tracks, leaving me just breathing in the damp, perfumed air and bathing in the enormous peace of Fatima's otherworldly shrine.

REZA GETS HUNGRY

A hand smashed down on my left shoulder.

"Salaamat!" roared Reza. "We look everywhere for you. I think maybe some mullahs cut your British balls off and fuck your azz."

"You must be very disappointed."

He sniffed and shrugged, looking around edgily. Mosques are not like churches: there's no service; you come and do your thing and go as you please. They're more like community halls. Or pubs that only serve the kind of wine Omar Khayyam was addicted to. In a church someone would have told Reza to keep the noise down; here no one even noticed his voice above the echoing hubbub from scores of other animated conversations.

"Come," Reza hissed. "It's lunchtime soon. You have your breakfast?"

"No."

I don't think this answer would compute for him.

"Come!"

"Have you ever fasted during Ramadan, Reza? Being as devout as you are, I mean."

"Sure. Lots of time."

In Arab countries I have often encountered Muslims who usually stay up all night during the month of Ramadan, recovering from a thirty-course supper just in time to eat a power breakfast before sunrise, then snooze until evening. Doing this in Iran would be hazardous, though. Reza probably had another way around the problem.

"I bet you always suddenly have to take a trip somewhere during Ramadan?"

He threw me an almost plaintive glare.

"In Boston the Christian swine had their Lint—"

"*Lent* . . ."

"Lent? Stolen more like. And this Lent meant terrible sacrifices. One woman, she gave up putting salt on her food for the whole month . . ."

"Yeah. I once gave up having sugar in my tea. God was very pleased. By the way, there won't be any restaurants open for lunch, Reza. This is Qom, remember? You can't even chew your fingernails between sunrise and sunset . . ."

"Ghossam knows somewhere," he replied, a note of triumph blaring in his voice. "First we pray, though."

That would throw God off the scent.

"Why is this shrine for Fatima?"

"She is sister of Imam al-Rida," Reza said knowledgeably.

"Was she a saint, though?"

"Naturally."

"Why? What did she do?"

"She is sister of the eight imam," he replied, exasperated.

"And that's all? That makes her holy?"

"Of course it fucken does, azzhole!"

He went over to a trough of prayer-dust cakes and then to the nearest available space, embarking on his ritual of monotone recitation and postures of submission that looked more like pleas for leniency.

FAKE!

Ghossam had given the Paykan an oil change himself earlier on, and even rotated its tires—left front to right rear, right front to left rear—in order to even out tread wear. Unfortunately, he had neglected to replace the bottom screw cap where he'd drained out the mixture of molasses and Guinness that had been lubricating the machine until today. As a result, the new oil he'd poured into the top of the engine had drained out, too. This was not immediately obvious, but, by the time we were circling a mosque with a dome made of polished aluminum or steel like the lid of a giant wok, a noise of mice being tortured behind the dashboard quickly turned into a dreadful gnashing sound that was accompanied by violent jolts. The Paykan began to buck and whinny the way cars do in cartoons before they turn into wild horses. Ghossam needed reins, not a steering wheel, and all of us would have needed a good chiropractor had the vehicle not stopped suddenly in midjolt, sinking to its rubber knees silently as if struck dead.

"Khoda!" wheezed the driver, mopping his brow.

"Would you pay sixteen thousand dollars for this piece of sheet?" Reza asked me.

"No."

Cars were the only items in Iran that cost more than they did anywhere else.

We left Ghossam lying beneath the Paykan amid five lanes of traffic, a fifth of which hurtled by inches from his toes.

Reza loped into a joint that resembled the kitchen of a Depression-era factory cafeteria, with giant stoves whose burners could have been carved out of charcoal, and massive refrigerators secured by bolts and padlocks like jail cells. The rippled linoleum floor was awash with grease so thick it had gathered into furrowlike ridges in some places and in others was streaked with skid marks where many a patron had put up a valiant fight to remain vertical.

The proprietor was around four feet tall, with a Beatle haircut, a nose like a blighted strawberry, and a beard so dense and shiny it could have been a black vinyl surgeon's mask. Customers were clearly a novelty he was not used to dealing with—especially during Ramadan, in Qom—and he greeted us nervously, unable to decide which of the thirty empty tables we should be offered. Reza flopped down on a buckled folding chair by the nearest table, from which the proprietor snatched an ashtray brimming with butts and detritus, emptying its contents onto the floor and wiping what was left inside on the edge of his mottled apron.

Reza ordered two cups of tea. The proprietor bowed obsequiously, then skated back across the grease rink to his sarcophagus of a sink, where he commenced turning a faucet that was more like part of the valve system in an oil pipeline. Just when he appeared to be on the verge of employing a wrench to budge this piece of equipment, a torrent of steaming water gushed from the fire hose-sized pipe and thundered into the huge sink with such force that the entire building shook.

"Sheet!" croaked Reza. "Earthquake!"

"Why would he have a faucet like that for a kitchen sink?"

"These people steal equipment from American companies after Revolution—you know, oil companies?"

Maybe the restaurant had part of the trans-Iranian oil pipeline system connected to Qom's water mains?

The proprietor placed a rusty urn on his stove, struck a match, and ignited a burner that could have sent the space shuttle into orbit. Louder than a hundred welder's torches, the roaring inferno looked white hot, too, and within seconds steam gushed from the urn. Moments later the little man carried over two glasses of tea and a plate of cookies on a tray like the hubcap from an old ten-wheeler.

The cookies tasted the way petrified butter with pistachios riveted into it would taste. One mouthful made me feel I'd eaten a three-course meal. Reza fired off a burst of language at the restaurateur, whose pitted bulb nose seemed brighter and redder than it had when I first encountered it. He replied in a heliated voice, occasionally nodding at me.

"You wanna buy antique Armenians' picture?"

"What?"

"This man wants to know if—"

"What is it?"

He said something that required much shrugging and eyeball rolling and eventually sent the man skating off to a rear door.

"Thousand years old, the picture. Big thief, this man," Reza added, shoving a cookie into his mouth and sucking up his tea noisily. "You like these cookies? Special to Qom these. Imam Khomeini had them sheeped to France when he live there."

Learning this, I was surprised Khomeini had not weighed twice as much and lived half as long. But perhaps the sins of the father were visited on his son, who died while I was editing this book from a stroke: aged forty-three.

The proprietor returned with something wrapped in a potato sack. Inside was something wrapped in a ten-year-old newspaper. It turned out to be something else wrapped in a Marlboro duty-free bag. This proved to be a slab of worm-eaten wood the size of a large book. On one side of it was painted a Madonna who bore a striking resemblance to the late Richard Nixon, holding a fat child in a diaper. Clumsy stars like plus signs speckled the gloom behind them as if in the sky of an accountant's dream. I looked closely at this monstrosity. A brown film of age muted its colors. Judging by the craterlike indentations in various places, it had also been painted over something else. Judging by the dent my thumbnail was able to leave where the paintwork seemed thicker, the artist had employed acrylic colors—unusual in works of tenth-century art.

"It's a fake," I told Reza.

"Fake what?"

"It was painted last week."

He stared in utter amazement, saying, "I thought you supposed to be intelligent man, huh? Look how fucken old this piece of sheet is! Look at the fucken dirt on it!"

"That's brown varnish heated in an oven. The wood's old, though."

Reza sighed and shook his head in despair, then relayed my opinion to the little man. The thing did look like an old icon, I decided, and possibly had the remains of an old painting underneath the mug shots plastered on a few months earlier—possibly by the same artist responsible for forging Mickey Mouse uptown.

"He says you're a fucken moron," Reza informed me, after the proprietor had squeaked urgently for two minutes. "The thing was stolen from a church in Tabreez. It's been there for a thousand years."

"Maybe. But not with this painted on it. And whatever's beneath it is too damaged to bother with restoring."

"Give heem a hundred dollars."

"No. You buy it if you like it so much."

He sighed again, adding, "Back in States you sell it for half a million. More."

"Fine. Buy it and I'll send you the profit."

"All right," Reza growled, after another exchange with the icon's owner, "twenny dollars."

"Forget it."

"Okay, *ten*. Last offer."

"Sorry."

"Five?"

Finally the man carefully replaced the thousand-year-old icon in its customized containers, bearing the bundle back to where it had come from, disappointment emanating from the very bones in his little body.

"Really reep-off?" Reza inquired, genuinely wanting to know.

I presume he realized that I must have been fairly certain to turn down the chance of making half a million from five bucks.

"Yes."

"Beeg fucken bastard thief! We don't leave no tip, right?"

The proprietor returned with another, smaller bundle of filthy rags.

"Not again," I protested.

Reza barked something that sounded highly offensive at the man, who hopped about squeaking and waving his arms in protest. His nose was luminous by now.

"He has some old clock belong to fucken bastard shah family," Reza informed me, his tone, however, now suggesting we might be onto something.

"Nah." I pictured a rummage-sale alarm clock spray-painted gold with big rhinestones glued all over its casing and the legend "Property of Shah Pahlavi" daubed on the face. "Tell him to take a night-school course in art history or something, will you?"

"Less look," Reza pleaded.

"You look." I got up to leave.

Reza followed reluctantly, tossing about two cents onto the table.

"Could have been million-dollar clock," he complained.

"Sure, Reza. Could have been Cyrus the Great's own digital clock-radio."

"Yeah," he mused. "Cyprus the Greek . . ."

QOM'S SPEAKEASY

Ghossam drove up looking as if he'd been scuba diving in a tar pit. The Paykan, on the other hand, now had the cocky self-assurance of someone emerging from a post-workout shower. It fairly bristled with vigor and enthusiasm, purring contentedly, oxygenated oil running once more through its sclerotic old arteries.

Ghossam's illicit restaurant operated more furtively than a speakeasy and looked like an abandoned factory. A three-inch-thick door was unlocked only after someone had appeared from the side of the building, recognized our driver, and then signaled the okay to an unseen accomplice. The interior, however, was surprisingly opulent: marble floors, fake potted palms, a ten-by-eight-foot aerial photograph of Isfahan that gave you the illusion of being in a rooftop restaurant of a skyscraper—since there were no real windows at all—and waiters clad like royal footmen. All the place lacked was any other customers.

I wondered aloud how good the food could be if business was this slow.

"Place too much full when noon prayer finish," Ghossam assured me.

It was 11:55.

Freshly baked flatbread and salad arrived with a bowl of homemade garlic yogurt that was unbelievably tasty. Reza appeared to have sprouted four extra arms, tearing, shovelling, spooning, spreading, and ferrying wedges or blobs into his busy mouth so swiftly that he was blurred at the edges. Chicken and orange kebabs soon made an appearance, followed by pickles, braised leg of lamb in bean sauce, beef and onion kebabs, half a chicken baked between a sandwich of saffron rice with raisins until it was caramel crisp on the surface, a bushel of raw spring onions with radishes and mild peppers, and finally a cauldron full of fresh fruit.

"Did we order all this?" I inquired.

"House spezzal," Reza replied through a mouthful of it.

The food was exceptionally good, though, and would have been exceptionally good for five other people, too.

He drained his usual cup of boiling tea in one gulp and, without consulting Ghossam or me, jumped to his feet and announced that we were off. The bill was not twenty-five cents, but it was still only five dollars—including tip. By now the restaurant's clock proclaimed 12:20 and Ghossam's prediction turned out to be correct: the illegal eatery had mysteriously filled up with people fresh from their noon prayers, which had presumably included a plea for Allah's indulgence in this small matter of their stomachs. Missing lunch is only a big deal, it seems, when you are forbidden to eat lunch. Then food is all you think about.

SNOW IN SHUR AB

Leaving the holy city behind, we were once more back in the footsteps of the Magi on their first leg of the thousand-mile journey to herald the dawn of another age. The road southeast out of Qom skirted the edge of Dasht-e-Kavir's wilderness of salt. Everything about the area, the day, the journey and the mood, suddenly grew ominous. A clear blue sky was replaced by dense cloud more like an ectoplasmic winding-sheet in a confusing hue that was bone-white, milky gray, shimmering pastel violet, and pale rose all at the same time. Unnaturally low and solidified, it appeared to scrape the summits of a small mountain range on the eastern horizon, and was so massed where the twisting black ribbon of highway vanished far ahead that I felt sure the Paykan would grind to a halt inside it, leaving us groping blindly through a vaporous universe until we coughed ourselves to death.

Qom gradually deteriorated into a spectacularly ugly sprawl of industrial slums, culminating with a vast Dickensian prison so dark and forbidding that the mere sight of it was alone probably responsible for lowering by a further fifty percent Iran's already unusually low crime rate. What went on inside those walls, however, did not bear thinking about. The Islamic Republic espoused fundamentalist penology as well as religion.

A sign proclaimed the appropriately sinister name of the borough or town near Qom hosting this Gothic monument to the wages of sin: MORDADABAD. Just beyond it, on the crest of a low hill where the road bent out of sight, was a large tree that seemed to have huge black curly foliage. Behind it a series of wooden shacks leaned in different directions, the sole structures now visible in a flat wasteland of scrub and jagged stones. As we drew nearer I realized that the tree's odd foliage was in fact about sixty old car and truck tires dangling from its bare branches like bracelets.

"That's odd," I remarked. "Why would someone bother to do that?"

Reza turned, wearing his exasperated face.

"*Tires!*"

"I can see they're *tires*, Reza. Do you have them dangling from your trees?"

"I'd like to dangle *you* from my trees," he cackled. "It's a fucken tire repair place, azzhole!"

It was, of course, but I still felt the owner had gone maniacally overboard with his visual trade announcement. Most of all, though, the image of bleached skeletal branches, like a fleshless hand clutching at the sky and festooned with black rings, added to the sense of dread that I felt building. Seconds later another omen arrived: a tractor trailer transporting gasoline lay on its side in a shallow ditch just off the road. It looked as if it were taking a nap, the driver's cabin twisted slightly like a sleeper's head.

"Khoda!" gasped Ghossam, sucking air between his teeth and reducing the Paykan's cruising speed by twenty m.p.h.

"Truck drivers all mad men," announced Reza. "They try hard to die."

He played "Chickadee" to dispel intimations of mortality, and he lit cigarettes for all three of us to attract gratitude's good karma.

I had been seeing a white sheen for some time now far away on the horizon side of Dasht-e-Kavir's endless brown plain of foot-high scrub bushes and rubble, assuming it was just the salt in a salt desert. But it grew rapidly as we started heading due south beyond a mournful little place called Shur Ab, and, almost imperceptibly, it had covered the entire landscape twenty miles later, on the outskirts of Ab Shirim. Only the black macadam mysteriously remained untouched, a gleaming causeway heading off into what became merely a mottled white void. Everything else looked like it had suffered the consequences of a dog-fight between squadrons of rival cropdusting bi-planes. The odd clumps of scrub revealed patches of pale brown, but the rest were frosted with white, protruding from a shaggy white carpet that covered all the visible world.

"What the hell is that?" I asked.

Reza peered back over his seat affecting an expression of abject pity and said, "You sure you leeve in Canada?"

"Certain."

"And you not recognize snow?"

"Snow!"

It hadn't even occurred to me that the stuff might be snow. After all, it had not been snowing. I mentioned this.

"Then how it get here?" Reza said smugly. "Out of fucken ground?"

Clearly it had snowed south of Shur Ab, and snowed quite recently, too. The road remained unscathed because the snow was too wet to endure heavy traffic. By now, I also realized, the wreaths of ectoplas-mic cloud were invisible because we were *inside* them.

Coming up was yet more evidence of consummate Iranian driving skills: a ten-wheel Mercedes truck—belonging to a tire company ironi-cally—lay crumpled on its back in the snow, wheels akimbo, an in-verted turtle left by cruel children to await a slow, agonizing death.

"Khoda!" intoned Ghossam, slowing down yet again out of profes-sional courtesy.

Reza remained uncharacteristically silent. Entering this formless realm of white had affected all of us. For me it had been like driving out of Arizona and heading into Alaska half an hour later. Even Iran's geography had a Manichaean dualism about it.

MESSER MARCO SLEPT HERE

We were soon back on the Silk Route, and the path the Magi would have also taken: there was no other road between the mountains and the great salt desert.

Kashan was a two-hour drive from Qom—unless you stopped in Moshkan for six hours while your drive shaft was welded back together. Just before the Paykan's latest crisis, I had noticed the snow-capped ruins of a caravanserai, the one old enough for both Magi *and* Marco Polo to have taken shelter in it for a night of their three-day journey across this inhospitably barren and tedious zone. You could see all the way to the horizon in every direction. It was like sailing on an ocean of dust, which must have been unimaginably boring for cameleers. Only a constant threat of bandits could have made the monotony remotely attractive. At least I knew why Polo had nothing to say about this particular leg of his trip. And now I too had a brief layover in Moshkan, although the place barely existed even today—and the entire area could have only boasted that one crumbling caravanserai in the thirteenth century, let alone two thousand years ago. I doubt if anyone has ever yearned to revisit the place.

After an hour in a freezing shed, whose proprietor served tea made of boiling water and sugar into which perhaps one tea leaf had been briefly introduced, I certainly never wanted to see Moshkan again. Four hours later, convulsing with the kind of damp chill that feels as if your bone marrow has been replaced by crushed ice, I was ready to jog all the way to Kashan on my own. When you smoke cigarettes just for their heat you know that you're very cold indeed . . .

Ghossam was even colder, having spent much of the six hours lying beneath his Paykan's chassis outside. When we finally set off he had to get Reza to bend his frozen goose-necked fingers around the steering wheel. Another novel feature of his car was its lack of any heating system. The system had not broken, it just was not one of the "extras" Ghossam had seen any need to purchase. Fortunately, the engine always overheated after ten minutes and all we had to do was keep the windows rolled up, tolerating a 50/50 blend of carbon monoxide and air for the sake of general warmth.

NO IN AT THE ROOM

An unusually dark night poured down to coat the sky's crystal walls like tar. By the time we hit the prosperous perimeter of Kashan, the magnesium flares of high street lamps, flanking a broad boulevard with a forest planted down its central island, rendered all of us virtually blind. This and a heavy weariness that was probably the early stages of exposure sickness caused a unanimous decision to stop at the first hotel.

The first hotel looked like a colonial-era country club, approached by a long curving drive that led to a machicolated porch like something salvaged by crazed architects from a ruined castle. Reza ordered us to wait while he bounced through plate glass doors into an incandescent lobby where liveried staff thronged in a profusion that betrayed dire guest shortage. Soon he reemerged, asking us to come and sign the guest book. Although the shah himself would not have objected to staying in this place, a room was only five dollars. Or it was until I had carefully copied out my passport number in the register. Then inflation struck and the room price soared within three minutes to seventy dollars.

Reza ranted and raved at the desk clerk, banging the counter and sweeping registration forms and keys to the floor, insisting that I was Armenian and only carried a British passport because my mother had been shipwrecked near Dover when she was nine months pregnant. Besides, I was a close personal friend of President Rafsanjani, who would have the desk clerk fried in pig fat and the hotel razed to the ground if he ever learned of this insufferable insult. Et cetera. The tirade lasted at least ten minutes, with the desk clerk listening patiently, as if to a gripping yarn. When Reza fell silent, panting and wild-eyed from his exertions, the desk clerk said the room would still be seventy dollars. Take it or leave it.

"We'll leave it, azzhole!" yelled Reza. "You got three hundred empty room and you can afford to turn away guest?" Then he screamed at the top of his lungs, "I hope you motherfucking bastard sheet pieces watch Arabs fuck your sisters up the azz and piss on your fathers' eyes and your grandfathers' graves . . ." He wanted to say more but obviously ran out of abominations Arabs could commit.

The desk clerk thanked us all for our interest in his hotel, and other minions opened doors, directed traffic, waved farewell with inhuman courtesy.

Reza swore and sulked and growled all the way to what looked like Main Street, where a neon sign proclaimed SHAHIAH HOTEL over a modest little glass door.

"You be fucken Martik Bargarian from Armenia and you talk fucken sausage, sausage, sausage, or I'm gonna see how much luggage I can ram up your azzhole," Reza informed me as we approached the reception desk.

He also decided that I was deaf and dumb when discussing his companions with the manager—not that I knew this at the time. It was when I demanded a room to myself no matter what the cost, and the manager seemed excessively startled, and Reza dealt me a savage kick to the shin, that I realized something was amiss. I started mumbling gibberish about sausages and backed away very slowly out of sight.

The manager, however, didn't care where I was from or whether I could hear and speak, or what kind of business I was in. The room would cost six dollars whether I was from Neptune or Natanz.

I was so glad to be alone—or rather away from Reza—that even the bronchitic snore from a heating duct ten feet square and spanning one entire wall did not trouble me in the least. I sat on sheets so dry from lying in this tide of heat that they felt like baked newspaper, and I tried to get back to that place I had visited in Fatima's shrine when this interminable day was still young.

Although Kashan could no longer contain what I once imagined it might concerning the Magi, I was still convinced that there must be a good reason why so many for so long had associated this city with the meeting place of Matthew's wise men.

Chapter Four

※

KASHAN

*Then one travels for many days through many
countries, and comes to a city called Cassach
[Kashan], a good rich city, with plenty of corn
and other victuals. Some men say that it was at
that city the Three Kings met, who went to make
offerings to Christ in Bethlehem; it is fifty-
three days' journey from Bethlehem.*

— The Travels of Sir John Mandeville

If Sir John Mandeville ever traveled anywhere at all—if indeed he
even existed—he would have been in Kashan a few decades after
Marco Polo, in the early fourteenth century. But, as one critic gruffly
remarked, it is possible that "his longest journey [was] . . . to the nearest library." Mandeville's eccentric peregrinations, real or imagined,
took him to other places on my itinerary, too. No matter what his de-
tractors say, his *Travels* cannot be so easily dismissed. After all, he quite
clearly states at one point that the earth is round, so it comes as no surprise to find, nearly two hundred years later, that Christopher Colum-
bus perused him while preparing to sail west to China; Frobisher also
had a copy of Mandeville with him as he lay off Baffin Bay in 1576;

and it was the only travel book listed in the inventory made of Leonardo da Vinci's very extensive library when he moved from Milan in 1499.

THE CITY OF CUPOLAS AND WINDWARDS

The only travel book in the library of the Shahiah Hotel was a slim volume entitled *A Trip to the City of Cupolas and Windwards,* written by one Hossien Farrokhyar and published "By Cooperation of The Kashan Cultural Heritage Office." I found it lying in an otherwise empty bookshelf that stood in a lounge adjacent to the lobby and just outside the restaurant, which was closed. It was just after dawn and no one was about. At first I thought the desk clerk was praying over his desk, but a steady gurgling noise from somewhere deep in his throat made me realize he was asleep. Even the heating ducts were still snoring. I sat with the lone booklet, eager to learn something about the "City of Cupolas and Windwards." What were windwards, for instance? To me the word was only a term of direction, like "leewards." The flimsy cover featured a photograph showing stacked terraces of rectangular, clay-colored houses with large windows and flat roofs nestling halfway up the side of the first in a range of increasingly larger jagged mountains. There were no cupolas in sight. From my hotel room I had looked out over a hive of small brown buildings with egg-like domes, packed so closely together that even rats would have to diet in order to move around freely. The structures sprawled away over flat ground to where a square tower and several smokestacks indicated an industrial zone. No cupolas there, either, nor windwards—unless they were a species of chimney or window.

Kashan's "Historical Background" seemed intriguing, though; at least it did on the page.

> Generally, before "Aryan" Civilization penetrated into a land lated called Iran, there had been a civilization called "Sialk" which existed from 7000 B.C. up to the late 400 B.C. The hills with the same name in three kilometers of southwest of Kashan are the only remaining of that civilization. In 1932, this hill was registered as historical place of the country, under number 231.

I made a mental note to visit historical place number 231. The remains of a civilization that lasted 6,600 years without the rest of the world being aware of it were surely worth seeing. Kashan had certainly been around when the Magi came through town, and I still hoped to discover something of their presence there.

The most recent writer I came across to mention the city in connection with the Magi was a physician, Cyril Elgood. In his inordinately fascinating *A Medical History of Persia* (1951), the whole business is discussed, naturally enough, in terms of its effect on the progress of medicine. "With the death of Alexander," Elgood writes,

> another stage of Persian history came to an end and Persia entered into what may well be called the stagnation period. In the midst of this period, this lull, as it were, at least from the point of view of a medical historian, there was born at Bethlehem a baby at whose birth three Persian priest-physicians assisted. Christian and Zoroastrian tradition alike make the Three Wise Men to have come from Persia. The Bible gives them the official Zoroastrian title of Magus. The majority of the Fathers of the early Church agree in regarding Persia as their native country. Odoric says that Kashan was the city of the Three Kings. According to Marco Polo two of the "kings" came from villages situated in the neighbourhood of modern Teheran; the third came from a village about three days' journey away. Today at Urumiah a church is still known where one, if not two, of the Wise Men are buried. The prominence given to this Persian influence in the Gospel story suggests that the Persians had already begun to play their role as the scientific teachers of the world and that the Jews had already begun to modify their medical views in the light of Persian teaching.

It is not clear which version of Polo's account Elgood had read — if indeed he read one at all. "The majority of the Fathers of the early Church" don't seem to agree on anything at all, let alone the nationality of Matthew's Magi. Urumiah is known as Orumiyeh today, but not known for any church "where one, if not two, of the Wise Men are buried." Still, this could be another explanation for why there were only two tombs at Saveh. Elgood's theory that the Magi served as obstetricians or midwives at Jesus' birth is also unique. One assumes that Mary had a stand-in on hand, since the Persian priest-physicians, according to Matthew and Marco Polo, missed the actual birth by some days. Oddly enough, there is in fact some suggestion in one source that Mary did have a midwife present.

Among the pile of texts that could have been in the New Testament canon but aren't—because Church councils didn't want us to read them—are many fascinating items that survived Rome's organized literary extinction. A text called the Protoevangelium of James, for example—from whose internal evidence we learn that James was Joseph's son by a previous marriage (an attempt to make him unrelated by blood to Jesus and keep Mary's virginity intact?)—tells essentially the same story as Matthew does about the Magi, but it dates the Nativity as Luke does, during the reign of Caesar Augustus, and has Joseph traveling from Galilee to Judaea to be taxed. Jesus is born in a cave a few miles outside Bethlehem, however, where Mary has a midwife named Salome who experiences a vision that "salvation is born to Israel" just before the actual birth. As in Matthew, Herod's brutes seek to kill the child, but we cut back to Luke again for Mary to hide Jesus from the soldiers in a manger. This makes more sense of the manger: who would put their baby in an animals' feed trough unless they had very good reasons? The variant versions of events in the canonical gospels are problematical enough, but when you include in the mélange all the noncanonical versions it's clear that some form of consensus had to be imposed on the life of Jesus—historical reality or not. And so it was.

The Venerable Bede knew this consensus opinion well before the year 800. Bede was Anglo-Saxon Britain's leading historian—although, Venerable or not, he would have as much trouble obtaining a mail-order history degree from a P.O. box university these days as Marco Polo would in passing a high-school geography test. Bede, however, wrote the first account of the Magi in English, and with the same supreme confidence that characterized most of his early Christian peers:

> The Magi were the ones who gave gifts to the Lord. The first is said to have been Melchior, an old man with white hair and a long beard . . . who offered gold to the Lord as to a king. The second, Gaspar by name, young and beardless and ruddy complexioned . . . honored him as God by his gift of incense, an oblation worthy of divinity. The third, black-skinned and heavily bearded, named Balthasar . . . by his gift of myrrh testified to the Son of Man who was to die.

Bede's account is essentially the one depicted in Justinian's mosaics—where the Magi's names are embedded in the soil—and also, in basic details, the one Marco Polo heard. His Magi "were of different ages and fashions," too, and their gifts serve a similarly symbolic purpose—with the exception of myrrh.

But Polo's Magi bring their offerings for an entirely different reason. They appear to be some form of test, not unlike the one still used by Tibetan Buddhists to determine whether or not a newborn child is the reincarnation of a great Lama. The baby is offered a mixture of new shiny toys and old possessions of spiritual significance owned by the late lama whose reincarnation he may be. His interest in the old objects rather than the toys is viewed as one sign that he may be the one whom the priests are seeking. The process in Polo's account is very similar: "If he took gold, he was a king; if incense, he was a god; if myrrh, he was a sage . . ." I'd always assumed the three offerings were part of Jewish tradition, but although gold and incense are frequently paired in the Old Testament, they are never associated with myrrh. Christian tradition has come to link gold with divinity, incense with prayer (as in Hinduism and Buddhism), and myrrh with the suffering of Christ. But myrrh is an oddly flexible, all-purpose stuff—which is why few people can even tell you what it is at all.

Myrrh is in fact an aromatic gum resin from the tree of that name, and was widely used in the ancient world to make incense, perfume, and medicines. In Hebrew, the word—*mar* or *mor*—means "bitter," like the bitter herbs used in the ritual meal of Passover. In the Old Testament it is mentioned solely as a perfume, however (Psalm 45:8), or, mixed with olive oil, cinnamon, and other ingredients, recommended as "a holy ointment" for ritual anointing (Exodus 30:23). But the New Testament only refers to its medical uses, one of which is as a narcotic often administered out of compassion to victims of crucifixion. In Mark, Jesus himself reportedly refuses the potion: "And they gave Him to drink wine mingled with myrrh: but he received it not" (15:23). Polo witnessed "Tartars" in Iran heating wine with some other substance, believing they were getting around the Muslim prohibition against alcohol by concocting something that wasn't strictly wine. But, given his obliviousness to Zoroastrians, he may have been witnessing the preparation of haoma—identical to the Indian Vedic Soma—a sacred plant with narcotic properties that was often boiled in wine to mask its bitter taste, and used during exceptionally important rituals whose significance is still a matter of debate among scholars. The haoma flower appears on the Iranian flag to this day, and there are many portraits of Zoroastrian monarchs—and even Zoroaster himself—holding the flower between pressed palms: the traditional gesture of prayer. Like Soma, haoma, or Hom, is imbued with divine force through ritual incantations, then either pounded to extract the narcotic juice, or sacrificed to the temple's sacred fire. All Zoroastrian sacrifices are symbolic and do not involve any living creatures.

I have a hunch that myrrh and hoama are, in this case, if not one and the same thing, at least willfully confused in Polo's narrative, perhaps by whoever wished to highlight the bond between Jesus and the Zoroastrian faith.

Cyril Elgood's fanciful depiction of the Magi as traveling obstetricians is not, in fact, so far from the truth. The Zoroastrian priesthood, like the Indian Brahmans, performed spiritual functions and medical ones in tandem, and one of Zoroaster's many earthly personae was the Divine Physician. Jesus, too, was once also frequently termed Christus Medicus himself by the Eastern Church, in contrast to the western Christus Rex. The myrrh in Polo's story is thus a symbol for magical medicine, offered to determine if that will be the child's calling.

A REZA-FREE STROLL

Armed with *A Trip to the City of Cupolas and Windwards*, I stepped outside to explore Kashan, "Gate of world civilization," and "Bride of Iranian cities," as the booklet claimed the place was often termed. It was no longer in the depths of winter, which it had been when we'd arrived the night before. A few wispy clouds smeared the turquoise sky, but a brilliant early morning sun floodlit the world and seemed to be announcing to all that spring had unquestionably arrived. Despite a distinct chill in the air, virtually every tree in sight boasted its full allotment of blazing emerald leaves. In terms of where I currently live, the day felt like late April but looked like mid-July. "The Bride of Iranian cities" was obviously in her street clothes, though, for the line of uneven, square concrete boxes, and the profusion of overhead cables strung from a variety of poles made from functional materials that faced me did not exactly suggest an Oriental Venice or Paris.

As I walked along a sidewalk of tiny rectangular stones, however, I did notice that, like Saveh, this city was also very old indeed. The concrete kennels were often fashioned around undulating walls of hand-hewn stone blocks, many of them still set with massive wooden doors fortified by metal studs, pulled open or shut by plate-sized iron rings dangling over crude locks whose keyholes were large enough to receive mail.

In fact, locks seemed to enjoy an unusual popularity in Kashan. Within fifty yards I had passed five little stores with crowded windows displaying hundreds of different padlocks, some the size of Victorian novels, others small enough to secure a bee's sea chest. Many were apparently manufactured in China, and some of those not requiring keys even had Chinese numerals on their combination tumblers, which must have created a few problems for Iranian purchasers over the years.

Almost as popular as locks were clocks. Four stores I passed were piled high with everything from cartoonlike monster alarm jobs, boasting four big shiny bells that probably woke half the province, to little digital wristwatches, the kind that now come free in boxes of cornflakes and whose numerals often turn into Martian runes after a month. But, as seems to be the case everywhere east of Athens, the big seller in watches here resembled a gleaming manhole cover attached to sections of chrome-plated tank tread, its face covered in enough luminous paint to enrage a Geiger counter five miles away.

The citizens of Kashan looked different to me: smaller, slightly more Oriental and weatherbeaten than Iranians farther north. Everyone was still bundled up in wool hats, scarves, moth-eaten sweaters, nineteenth-century overcoats, and hiker's socks. The men, that is. They obviously didn't believe the world was anywhere near spring yet. The women could have been in bikinis beneath their billowing chadors, though. You never knew what Iranian women were wearing in there.

I watched a cheery little man in an elf's hat decapitate a chicken and hand the twitching corpse unwrapped to a woman who casually deposited it on top of about thirty big cabbages in a knitted rope bag, which she then hoisted onto her shoulder as if it weighed no more than an evening purse. Seeing me take such interest in his wares, the butcher-elf beckoned, directing my gaze to a wicker cage that held what may have been the outcome of some attempt to cross-breed ostriches with bats. It was huge, dark, and appeared to have teeth inside its trowel of a beak. I nodded appreciatively, indicating with my hands that this creature was certainly the biggest, blackest chicken I'd ever seen. This pleased its owner, who made a gesture I took to mean: *Shall I wrap it up, pal?* I backed away, shaking my head while still trying to look deeply impressed by the selection of poultry available.

Farther on at a perfumed fruit stand I bought several mandarin oranges for about three cents, then walked on peeling one and eating what tasted like little sheaths of vellum filled with cool orange juice. I'd devoured three of them when I started noticing that every other person passing me appeared to affect an expression of thorough disgust. One even spat forcefully and pointedly to emphasize his feelings. Was it something I'd said?

Once more, I remembered it was Ramadan, and hastily shoved the oranges into my pocket, wondering if I would live through this particular holy month. What would Italy be like if the Pope persuaded one of Rome's fleeting parliaments to pass a bill enforcing Lent?

THE MERCHANT OF KASHAN

When I returned to the lobby of the Shahiah Hotel, Reza was engaged in a belligerent argument with a new desk clerk. Seeing me walk in he screamed,

"Sausage! Sausage! Talk fucken sausage, you azzhole, or I tell this piece of sheet that you are a fucken Zionist spy motherfucker."

Muttering yet again, in what to me sounded like a west-central Asian dialect, about sausages, I crept by this conflict and headed upstairs to the safety of my room. The temperature in it by now felt like 130 degrees, so I attempted to open a window, succeeding only in detaching its handle. Then I saw Ghossam emerge from my bathroom wearing preposterously opulent pajamas. He bade me good morning and vanished out into the corridor.

By eleven-thirty we were in the hotel's restaurant eating chicken with rice and a salad with dressing that tasted like pine-scented disinfectant. Unlike Qom, Kashan didn't mind feeding travelers overtly.

"It's lemon, azzhole," replied Reza when I asked him what exactly was on the salad. "So what you wanna do here? Go to the fucken Antiquities Organization again, I suppose?" he speculated wearily.

Then he belched.

The Paykan had perhaps not enjoyed its night in the Shahiah's parking lot. It was having a bad battery day and only responded to the jump start offered by a second vehicle, which had to jump-start the first one as well, since that battery was now also drained of energy from the futile attempt to recharge ours. Ghossam spent a long time with his head under the hood, possibly reassuring the engine that he would never submit it to such indignities again, then feeding it from a can of special oil he kept in the trunk for such crises. I still have some of it on my knapsack.

Before too long, though, we were cruising into a dusty little street called Amir Ahmad Alley. It had a small mosque at the end, toward which batches of chadors were scuttling like baggy penguins. Reza lured me through a small doorway in the side of a nondescript mud-brick wall. Beyond was a cobbled entrance hall of old faded stucco festooned with classical Persian designs of vegetation and improbable animals. Another doorway led into a dank, zigzagging corridor that suddenly opened out into a majestic courtyard landscaped with a long rectangular pool and geometrical flower beds. All around it French doors opened a full yard above ground level—as they're supposed to do. The building in which they stood extended from a central structure consisting of an enormous basket handle arch flanked by two equally tall but narrow semicircular arches, above which rose a Baroque facade shaped like a fat trefoil covered with designs carved in deep stone relief and ranging from Greek urns to Chinese dragons. Behind the pediment of this facade, on the roof, there was a bizarre dome made of what looked like whitewashed mudbrick with around twenty funnel-shaped arched openings protruding from it. Upon this somewhat crowded dome there was another, slimmer dome that resembled a huge hard boiled egg sitting in an eggcup made from semicircular white marble purdah screens. The roof had no architectural links at all to what supported it.

Every inch of stone around the courtyard's polychrome tiles, marble pool, and mathematician's garden had been chiseled into some variety of shape, from the dentil-like band that outlined the facade and continued along flat edges of the other buildings' shared rooftop, to the small stalactite-vaulted alcoves every corner housed, and the Mogul-style mango cornices drooping from any available spot. The effect was overwhelming. It looked as if a master mason had decided to demonstrate his facility with every known architectural device on earth to show potential customers the range of choices his repertoire gave them. What the hell was this place?

"Antiquities Organization Office," replied Reza, staring gloomily into the murky waters of the pond.

"Really?"

"No, it's a fucken shopping mall—what you think it is?"

"A palace."

"Pah!" he spat in the pond. "We got fucken palaces everywhere here. Fucken bastard shahs shoulda built some apartment blocks instead."

If the triumphal arch back in Teheran was anything to go by, Reza was wrong about this.

He shouted at a gardener, who seemed to be discussing business with his hoe. The man pointed to the corner of an arcade on our left.

"Lezz go, eh?" Reza announced, bouncing off.

It wasn't the Antiquities Organization Office after all. It was the Kashan Cultural Heritage Office, whose cooperation had apparently made A *Trip to the City of Cupolas and Windwards* possible. Indeed, copies of the masterpiece were piled on shelves and tables everywhere inside a cavernous little room occupied by nine men in crumpled double-breasted suits that had probably cost them plenty back in 1952. A sulfurous miniature stove heated this den, where not much besides the perusal of carbon-copied forms seemed to be going on. There was no Antiquities Organization in Kashan, I learned, but its Cultural Heritage Organization was indistinguishable in function—although of course much, much more important. Nine pairs of ears listened to my business intently, then their owners discussed the matter among themselves for ten minutes before deciding that I really should be shown into the Director's office.

This proved to be a grim cell decorated with a ragged yellow poster celebrating the "25th Anniversary of the Glorious Reign of H.I.M. Mo- hammad-Reza Shah Pahlavi, on the occasion of the 2500th Anniversary of Establishment of Iranian Empire by Cyrus, the Great." Perhaps it was holding up the wall? Behind a schoolboy's desk sat a man who could have easily passed for a nineteenth-century British general. Be- hind him hung a dusty portrait of Khomeini standing on a very windy hill at sunrise holding an enormous flag, one arm and index finger urg- ing invisible hordes of triumphant Islamic revolutionaries on to victory. Like Lenin. Whoever painted it had probably never worked again.

"Yes," said the general, learning what my presence in his office in- volved. "Yes. True. Yes, yes, yes. Tea?"

"Yes."

I assumed he too had forgotten it was Ramadan. But when tea came he drank it, saying,

"Law says no tea during Ramadan. Yes. No tea. It is true. But a man must have tea in his intestine on cold morning. Yes, yes, yes. Yes?"

"Oh yes," I agreed.

"Yes, he must. It is true. Yes. The bowel does not function otherwise. Yes. Contagion will spread if the bowel does not function. Yes?"

"Yes."

"Contagion spreads there is sickness. Yes. Sickness. And a man, he cannot pray to God with sickness. Yes. This is true. Yes?"

"Yes."

"Yes. This cannot be denied. Yes, yes, yes. And so we drink tea. Yes. We drink and are not feared of Divine Punishment because now bowel will function. Yes. It is true. We are not feared. Yes?"

"Oh yes. I'm fine. Are you fine, Reza?"

Reza scowled, the expression melting into a fawning smile of obse- quious gratitude as he turned toward the general, whom I fully ex- pected to make an urgent dash for the can any minute now.

"You have this, yes?" The general slapped a copy of *A Trip to the City of Cupolas and Windwards* on his desk top.

"Yes, I do. Thanks."

"Yes, yes, yes. Take it, go on. Yes. Take it with you. Yes. We have pro- duced this wonderful book for famous tourists such as yourself, Doctor Poll. Yes. Have it." He leaned across to place it on my lap.

"What are windwards?" I asked.

"Yes," the general replied. "Yes. This is a city of cupolas and wind-wards—as this book shows. Yes. They are plentiful here. Too many windwards and cupolas we have. Yes."

"But what are they?"

"Yes. Windwards?"

"What are they?"

With terrifying alacrity the general bounded to his feet and flung aside shutters I had not even noticed were there. An avalanche of sun-light crashed into the murky cell, slowly dimming down until it was an incandescent, six-foot wedge of dust in colloidal suspension.

"Yes!" exclaimed the general, his arm outstretched like Khomeini's portrait, pointing forty-five degrees up at something beyond the blurred windows. "Yes, yes, yes. Too many windwards there are here."

I followed his finger up toward the egg-on-snowball domes behind the main building's facade. Was this kind of dome a windward?

"Yes, yes, yes. Not dome itself but dome windows."

The arched funnels were windwards, I soon learned. So called be-cause they caught the wind from every direction, forcing it down through the house below.

"Yes. Like the air condition, is it not? You know air condition, of course? It is true, yes?"

"Air conditioning?"

"Yes. Yes, yes. Condition of air is more cool," he elaborated. "Too much cupolas and windwards therefore the pleasant of cool. Yes?"

"Yes. I see. Thank you very much."

Windwards were unique to this area of Iran, apparently.

I asked about Polo's Magi, the tomb, and so on. He said yes a few hundred more times, then drummed his fingers on the desk and stared up at an adventure playground that generations of spiders had con-structed for themselves all over his office ceiling.

"Have some parnian," he finally stated. "Yes?"

"What?"

It took a few minutes, but I eventually gleaned that he had been re-ferring to a man called Hassan Parnian, not offering me what sounded like one of the sixty thousand varieties of sweet Iranian pastry. Hassan Parnian would show me around Kashan and environs, which according to the general had enjoyed civilization for "millions" of years. I remarked what a fine building his office was in, how appropriate it was for a Cultural Heritage Organization to actually occupy part of the cultural heritage it organized, and how inspiring it must be to work in such a place.

"Yes, yes, yes. Much of inspearing. This is true. Yes."

Then he informed me in so many words that his job was a little more difficult than I possibly imagined it was. He had six hundred monuments to maintain on an annual budget of $2,500. I can't maintain myself on $2,500 a *month*. I assumed that he'd got this amount wrong, but he had not. It amounted to less than $4.20 per monument.

When I saw the monuments themselves I felt like weeping and gnashing my teeth. Any one of them would be showered with restoration funds, pampered with yearly face-lifts, spotlit, fenced off, and photographed by millions of awestruck tourists a year in any North American city—or any village for that matter. What would a land that displays sixty-year-old Coca Cola bottles and Elton John's shoes in its museums do with a polychrome Mongol mosque or a palace built two thousand years before the Book of Genesis was written?

The general dispatched one of the nine men moving paper in their outer office to find Hassan Parnian, leaving Reza and me with the other eight. One of them handed me yet another copy of A *Trip to the City of Cupolas and Windwards*, which I thanked him for. I was mightily relieved when Hassan Parnian arrived to take me away from a sentence beginning "After porck and servant house as well as the river . . ."

Nearly five feet tall, Parnian wore two sweaters and a pair of striped pajamas beneath his mangled blue suit. He was a gentle, sweet-natured man with thick black wavy hair, a neatly trimmed beard, and spectacles like television screens. He smiled constantly and was tirelessly enthusiastic about everything he showed us. We stood marveling at the garden's delicate perfections while Parnian explained that the Cultural Heritage Organization's headquarters had once been the house of a seventeenth-century merchant named Haj Seyed Jafar Natanzi. One hundred and fifty artists and craftsmen had spent twenty years building it. It was one of those sagas of excess typical of the history of commerce—a subject I find devoid of interest. Only Hassan Parnian's winning personality lured me through the countless chambers of this particular merchant's monument to himself and Mammon. Compared to the historical riches surrounding Kashan, the place was really little more than a pauper's hovel.

THE SIALK ROUTE

What profit hath a man of all his labor which he taketh under the sun? One generation passeth away, and another generation cometh; but the earth abideth forever.

—Ecclesiastes 1: 3–4

Generations had been passing away and other generations taking their place under the burning sun in this part of Iran for longer than generations had been doing almost anywhere else on earth—or so we're told. To the southwest, some seven thousand years earlier, had been Elam, kingdom of the Elamites, whose civilization was well into decline even by the time Old Testament authors mentioned it. The word "Elam" means "high ground" in Hebrew, thus Susa, the Elamite capital, unsurprisingly, was located securely on a plateau protected by the Mesopotamian marshes to the west and the southern Iranian mountain ranges to the east. National security was literally a matter of life or death for nations back then—as governments would have us believe it is now.

The Elamites had developed their own semipictographic script independently of Sumer, it appears, and also at around the same time— according to current dating techniques—as the first examples of Sumerian script appeared. They spoke a language entirely unrelated to any other we yet know of and which had vanished long before the time Polo's Magi passed through the area, replaced by various tongues that in turn were themselves replaced by Aramaic. But four thousand years earlier even the mighty kings of Akkad and Ur had humbly built temples to and worshipped the gods of Susa. Around this heady period the Elamites may also have invaded Kashan and forcibly occupied the place, possibly to use as a trading post. It was not called Kashan then, of course, and it is not officially called Kashan now, either, but rather "historical place number 231," and located at the southwestern edge of town, where scattered cuboid suburbs cede to fields and hills.

To say that not much is known about the civilization of Sialk—as "historical place number 231" is usually termed outside Iranian bureaucracy—is an exaggeration of the kind contemporary archaeologists are prone to make frequently. In fact, nothing whatsoever is known for certain about this civilization, and even the assumption that Sialk was once invaded by the Elamites—about whom at least something concrete is known—is merely based on the discovery of some clay tablets in the hills southwest of Kashan inscribed in proto-Elamite script and tentatively dated to around 3,000 B.C.

HPN-231

Three long and tedious days after leaving Saveh, the Magi would have reached the first town of any size—the place that had once been Sialk. And, after three long and tedious hours exploring detours Hassan needed me to see, we finally reached "historical place number 231" along with Reza and Ghossam.

"Why the fuck we come here, azzhole?" was Reza's assessment of what remained of a civilization that had vanished long before any Christian, let alone any Shi'ite Muslim, got to see it.

"Cultural heritage," I replied.

"Pah! Good thing the Islam come for them. Sheet!"

We were at the edge of a windy plain, its yellow fields mottled gold beneath the shadows of scudding clouds that sped through sunlit air. Some hundred yards off, a low, uneven hill of pale, sand-colored rock and mud sprawled in a crescent. From where we stood it seemed a natural formation. But it was not.

"Sialk!" exclaimed Parnian, his innocent smile broad and triumphant.

At the edge of the hill there were still signs of an old and somewhat crude archaeological dig, probably the one that uncovered the proto-Elamite clay tablet. Pottery shards were everywhere, a sign that whoever directed the excavation work had little interest in recording the site properly. They were hunting for treasure.

"It is Frenchman," Parnian told me.

The work had been done sixty years earlier. Devotees of the English teaspoon-and-paintbrush school of archaeology constantly criticize French digs for their sloppiness and inadequate records. Just kicking around dust I found quite sizable fragments of ancient pottery, some with designs and even handles on them. If the French had been more careful with their work, some archaeology student could have spent a year gluing together enough pieces to make half an urn or oil lamp by now. I took a few pieces to an expert in New York, who'll be grateful for the anonymity. One he confidently identified as Ptolemaic, another "Neolithic, probably northern Europe," and a third "Pre-Columbian, southeast Mexico." I didn't tell him where I'd found them. On the other hand, if he was right, Sialk would be one of the most extraordinary civilizations known, attracting touring cavemen from Sweden, Alexandrian scholars, and Mayan or Aztec traders.

Except no one traveled with their clay vessels two millennia ago, and certainly never traded them. They were more like today's Chinese food cartons or yogurt containers: you used them until they broke and then tossed them out the window. Earthenware was also not usually fired to the hardness of ceramic ware: it was meant to be disposable. Will the students of A.D. 3199 be carefully laser-welding together Styrofoam McDonald's boxes and plastic Flintstones pop beakers? I wonder.

The hill was a mudbrick platform incorporating natural rock upon which a large building—presumably a temple or palace—had originally stood. Once you realized that what faced you was man-made, you began to notice how ingeniously men had made it with nature's cooperation. This platform design was strikingly similar to the architectural principle employed a few thousand years later for the palaces of Archaemenid kings. Although clearly far more elaborate, the fifth-century B.C. capital of Darius I at Susa is very reminiscent of the Sialk mound now, and not much more remains of it, either.

French excavators had tunnelled into the mound in places, revealing sophisticated mudbrick passageways. The architect of Sialk had cleverly employed his rock base to ensure that what were possibly storage chambers for food remained protected from winter rains. Even in the extreme dryness of Upper Egypt very little ancient mudbrick survived six thousand years, and now, thanks to the Aswan Dam's disastrous effect on the climate, the Nubians who still use mudbrick are obliged to cover it with plaster or concrete to keep increasingly more frequent spells of heavy rain from washing village walls away. Kiln-baked mudbrick structures were generally coated with mud, which was then dried by the sun and regularly patched up or replaced. But at Sialk the chambers within the rock platform have never been exposed to rainfall, or suffered through capillation the rising damp of subsurface water. Thus the skill of its bricklayers remains more or less unscathed and is impressive. They understood the principles of the arch, angling bricks toward a central supporting wedge; and they knew the techniques for maximizing a wall's strength by varying brick size and placement.

Below the northern side was a large cave, scarred with abandoned attempts by the French archaeologists to tunnel farther but containing a broad ledge carved out long before. The question was: had it been carved out long before the rock had been turned into the platform for a more ambitious structure?

It was strongly reminiscent of Ptolemaic cave tombs in Egypt's southwestern oases, which themselves had probably been adapted from caves used by people who cultivated grain in the region some 20,000 years ago. These oases contain some of the earliest evidence yet found of prehistoric agriculture. The area southwest of Kashan also contains such evidence.

So-called cavemen probably did not live in the caves associated with them, recent evidence indicates, using them rather for ritual purposes that would have included funerals as well as the unknown rite connected with those famous paintings of what appear to be hunting expeditions.

There were traces of petroglyphic animal forms in the Sialk cave, like those found in France. Weather patterns were vastly different here than in southwest Egypt, though, and had taken their toll on the messages left by our distant ancestors. Yet the shapes here were unmistakably the same ones found in France and in Egypt's Wadi Guedid. This means that Sialk had been important to human beings for even longer

than the author of A *Trip to the City of Cupolas and Windwards* realized, probably continuously inhabited for well over 20,000 years.

Although Susa was on one of the major ancient trade routes, Kashan
does not even feature on those of the Persian empire, only gaining importance when the Silk Route to India and China became in effect a
Europe-Asia expressway. There was thus no reason for the Elamites to
have invaded and occupied the place as a trading post. If maps drawn
during the reign of Darius do not show Sialk or Kashan as a significant
place, what made it so important to the Elamites? If it was important to
them, that is: because someone could have easily brought that clay
tablet back to Sialk after a trip to Susa. Archaeology is not a precise science.

Beyond this first hill there was a second one, almost a mile away to
the northeast. It looked virtually identical and was also known to contain ruins of an ancient structure, although no one has ever excavated
it. The positioning of the two platforms suggested that the area between them had once contained more humble structures from the
same early period. A stroll through the fields verified this: there were
remnants of walls made from crude rocks everywhere. And Parnian
told me larger carved boulders had been removed by farmers along
with much other stone, all of it used to build modern Kashan.

There had also, I discovered, once been a salt lake here that long
ago was connected to the vast salt lake north of Qom and formed part
of the great Dashst-e-Kavir salt desert.

"Lake dry up very long ago," Parnian had said. "But people here still
using the salt to eat."

Salt had once been a valuable commodity for people in hot climates
far away from a lake, the sea, or a salt desert. It was traded like spices
and even used as currency. The salt in salt lakes is not just sodium
chloride, either. In the Dead Sea, for example, there are numerous
other salts in the water that are essential to the body's cell development
and other functions. The salts can be ingested, but they can also be absorbed through the skin. Places like Vichy, in France, were popular ancient spas even in Roman times, and reveal evidence of continuous
habitation for thousands of years before. The so-called "cure" in Vichy
to this day consists of drinking various kinds of natural waters, some of
them revoltingly sulfurous or almost unpalatably saturated with salts,

as well as undergoing various forms of hydrotherapy—the most ancient medical treatment known. Given the undeniably close association that the Magian priests had with medicine, one would naturally expect to find evidence of them near any ancient spa in Iran. The connection between the Magi and Kashan suddenly seemed less of a mystery.

From the earliest times on record, tremendous importance was attached to water in general—and not just for obvious reasons. The Archaemenid kings always drank water from the river that flowed past Susa, and would drink no other water even when traveling. This water was boiled to insure its purity and stored in silver flagons conveyed along on four-wheeled carts drawn by mules. Many injunctions related to frequent washing of the body and the importance of keeping water clean. Indeed, Magian priests publicly castigated a king who allowed unclean bath water to drain into a freshwater stream. And to this day Zoroastrians attach a spiritual significance to running water, as have many ancient cultures. Numerous early medical texts devote much space to defining forms of water contamination and ways of purifying contaminated water. Baptism, of course—ritual immersion—was a practice of potent significance to the Essenes and early Christians, but its origins can be traced back further, through Zoroastrianism all the way to Vedic India. Stories of gods being born from it, prophets being fished from it, civilization being both saved and destroyed by it pervade these cultures. Water as symbol, metaphor, and reality: literally the fountain of life.

Although there was no reason why the Magi should *not* be associated with Kashan, its ancient medicinal waters flowed back unexpectedly far, further pulling me in another direction entirely, all the way to King Solomon, who, it seems, also had a fountain in Kashan. As is the way with hidden journeys, it was Solomon who finally returned me this time to where I'd left off following in the Magi's footsteps.

Chapter Five

STRANGE WOMEN,
STRANGE GODS

I am come into my garden, my sister, my bride;
I have gathered my myrrh with my spice;
I have eaten my honeycomb with my honey;
I have drunk my wine with my milk.

—The Song of Songs 5:1

Gentle and pleasant though Hassan Parnian most certainly was, I did not feel we could spare the time to visit his house for tea. Reza did not share this opinion. He tried various arguments, from claiming my wristwatch was ninety minutes fast to pleading that Ghossam needed some rest after such a strenuous morning.

Then he added, "Big insult to this Parnian if you don't go. People here can get fucken angry. Very dangerous people, Kashan people. Sleet your azzhole throat like this." He traced a line from earlobe to earlobe, emitting a squelching noise.

TEA AND URINE

Parnian opened a rusty iron door leading from the unpaved alley in which we had parked into a wide courtyard, where a woman bent sweeping with a broom made from thin twigs while a small girl wearing pigtails and a scarlet sweater watched her appreciatively. Parnian barked angrily, waving his little arms and gesturing at the three guests behind him. The woman snatched up the child in horror and ran for her life down a flight of concrete steps off to the left.

"Wife," Parnian explained, smiling apologetically.

It was as if we'd caught her nude sunbathing. I wondered if the sight of a woman sweeping perhaps had some taboo attached to it. Clearly Parnian was not such a gentle, pleasant figure in his own home. But who is?

He ushered us into the courtyard, down the same flight of steps his wife had taken, and into a large subbasement room where the temperature must have been just above freezing. This explained why Parnian and the other five members of his family all wore several layers of clothing. A large sheet curtained off part of the room, where several mattresses and a turmoil of blankets were spread across the flood. The main area was clean and tidy, dominated by a hand-loom twenty feet long and ten feet high positioned just beneath small windows set at ground level, presumably to catch what light they allowed in. About four inches of a large carpet formed a margin at the base of the loom's warp. Dangling from this woof were a pair of ancient spectacles whose lenses could have been chiseled from rock crystal, their buckled frames swathed in rubber bands and string. Blindness is an occupational hazard for weavers.

Apart from a battered dresser, the only furniture consisted of three large tapestry cushions set against the wall opposite the loom. Parnian apologized for his home, his wife, the mess, his poverty, life in general, and asked us to sit on the cushions while he went to restore order in his domestic world, vanishing behind a smaller curtain at the far end of the room to shout at its occupants.

"Much better than fucken old holes in the ground," Reza stated, his breath forming a slab of strato-cirrus cloud between us. "Why did we have to go to that fucken piece of sheet? Plenty of better places in Iran. Plenty . . ." He didn't sound that certain of this, though.

A small boy of eight or so in a crimson sweater and blue track pants emerged from what I presumed was the kitchen area, placing a large platter of pomegranates, cucumbers, and oranges at our feet, then sitting cross-legged watching Reza ram them into his mouth.

"This Amir Hussein," Parnian announced, indicating the boy who sat watching Reza. "Oldest son. He is very against the smoking, is this not, Amir? He says it is 'burning money,' this he says, is it true, Amir?"

Amir nodded righteously, adding, in remarkably good English, "Money can be spent on necessary item like the foods."

Parnian sat beside Amir on a garishly-hued carpet that bore an image of what looked like the Lion King, watching his guests dive at tea and cookies, but not partaking himself. He was fasting, or at least wanted us to believe he was: Reza obviously looked like a Komiteh agent to him as well. The three other children sat at a safe distance, and their mother virtually hid beneath the dresser, while Amir, apple of Dad's eye, emboldened by the popular reception his first attempt at conversation in English had received, continued a dissertation on the evils of smoking.

"It is same as burning the money . . ."

Teeth poised over the last cucumber, Reza asked me if I wanted it, mashing half between his molars before I had time to say yes.

"Too late, azzhole." He laughed, reaching to give Amir's cheek a savage pinch as the boy recited statistics on death by lung cancer. "Bet you're top of the class, eh, Amir?" Reza said, lighting up.

Parnian nodded proudly, ordering his wife to fetch an ashtray. Reza offered Ghossam and me a shot at his pack of Zagros Slims, but we both politely declined.

"Cigg-rett like pin in coffin . . ."

More tea, cookies, fruit, and cucumbers were ferried in.

"See!" Reza informed me, belching with satisfaction. "Poor people but great hospitality. That's what it's like here. Not like your fucken America where no one ever invites you home unless you fucken marry them."

I asked Parnian who did the carpet weaving.

"Wife, she is doing. But very lazy." He waved toward the loom. "This is all work for many week now."

The year-old rug rat flopping about at her side probably accounted for her "laziness."

"The Prophet (peeze be on heem), he not smoking . . ."

"How long does it take her to make a carpet that size?"

"If she work . . . maybe one year three month."

She then sold the carpet to a local dealer, I learned, for about $1,000. It was a contractual arrangement: she was self-employed but could only sell to one dealer. Victorian business practices still had a big future in rural Iran. Taking a closer look at the few inches she had completed, I realized that a carpet of such size and quality would cost $15–20,000 in New York.

"Does she have any smaller ones for sale?" I asked.

She did not. Considering how long they took to make, she sold them the moment they were cut from the loom. The family's own carpets were all cheap machine-made items with tacky patterns in synthetic fabric. The one on the loom, judging just from the part of its border visible, was going to be a traditional Persian carpet in the geometric floral design typical of Kashan, whose carpets are considered among the finest woven in Iran. I could smell the tang of *gomez*—bull's urine—still emanating from the wool.

A natural disinfectant mentioned in ancient Zoroastrian medical texts, bull's urine was long considered the most satisfactory method of purification in pre-Islamic Iran. The lips of a dying man were washed with it, and after death his whole body bathed in it by an assistant priest wearing sheepskin gloves. A woman who suffered miscarriage was given *gomez* both internally and as a douche to purify "the grave of the unborn." To this day, Parsees use it for a ritual purification ceremony once a year.

"In the Hell there smoking, not in the Paradise . . ."

Wool for carpet weaving has been soaked in bull's urine by the Muslims on Iran's central plateau since the earliest times on record, according to carpet historians. In India, too, various kinds of urine are also still applied to the skin or consumed as a treatment for numerous ailments. When I covered wars as a journalist, I was often told by doctors that a serious wound can be disinfected with urine if nothing else is available.

GARDEN OF UNEARTHLY DELIGHTS

Parnian chattered away about Kashan's inordinately long history, confirming at one point that it was a problem maintaining the monuments
this history had left for posterity on the $2,500 posterity could currently
afford for their maintenance. If fifteen months' skilled labor earned his
wife $1,000, I hated to think what he earned from whatever it was he
did for the Cultural Heritage Organization.

"For poor mans the smoking cigg-rett like burning family . . ."

In spite of Reza's noisy objections, I went through Polo's Magi tale
again, asking Parnian if he could shed any light on the matter. He
bowed his head, deep in thought, although I took the gesture as an ad-
mission of defeat. I threw in my thoughts about medicinal salts and
water cures, hoping this might ring a bell. It did.

"King the Sullyman, he had palace here with big fountain," Parnian
announced brightly.

"King Solomon?" I assumed he meant some other king.

"*Balay*, hah! Yes. Jewish king from the Ishrael."

"I don't think so."

"Yes!" he protested. "Holy Koran speak of this fountain. I will show
it for you. And place of Sullyman altar that the Zardhushti help him to
build with the magic."

I stood up, almost involuntarily.

> A garden shut up is my sister, my bride;
>   a spring shut up, a fountain sealed.
> Thy shoots are an orchard of pomegranates,
>   with precious fruits;
>   henna with spikenard plants,
>   spikenard and saffron,
>   calamus and cinnamon,
>   with all trees of frankincense;
>   myrrh and aloes, with all the chief spices.
> Thou art a fountain of gardens,
>   a well of living waters,
> and flowing streams from Lebanon.
>
> THE BRIDE: Awake, O north wind;
>   and come, thou south!

Blow upon my garden;
　　that its fragrance be wafted abroad.
Let my beloved come into his garden,
　　and eat his precious fruits.

—The Song of Songs 4:12–16

Whoever the author of "The Song of Songs" or "Song of Solomon" was, their style reveals a distinct Persian influence. A glance at the famous Fin Garden of Kashan was also enough to make anyone believe that the incomparably beautiful "Song" had been written right there, in the silence preserved by thick walls, among cool shady trees and perfumed flowerbeds planted beside sparkling pools dotted with small gurgling fountains. St. Bernard of Clairvaux, spiritual preceptor of the Knights Templar—warrior monks who ruled Jerusalem for over a century—called Solomon's "Song" the "heart of the mystical life." The only problem was that the poem was over two thousand years older than these gardens, which were themselves six hundred years younger than St. Bernard, being largely constructed during the reign of Safavid and Qajar monarchs, a mere few hundred years ago.

"There Feen Garden," said Parnian proudly, as we stepped through the high semicircular arch of a white-washed gatehouse inlaid with turquoise and jasmine tiles.

It was a magnificent sight. Avenues of sycamore trees with yard-wide canals running through them. Each canal was set every six feet or so with narrow blue ceramic domes that spouted arcs of flashing water at exactly the same height—although the level of the cobbled sidewalks sloped considerably. The Persian mathematician Jamshid Kashani had apparently designed the fountains, adjusting the width of spouts to even out exactly the distance their spurting waters could reach. With the geometrically laid-out gardens aflame with buds and blossoms, each leading to arches, beyond which were more gardens, more fountains, all aligned to recede perfectly beneath each other, it was a supreme masterpiece of Islamic architecture. But Islam wasn't around in Solomon's time. Christianity had a thousand years to wait in the wings, too. I felt a twinge of sorrow for Parnian's foolish enthusiasm.

"Different Solomon, I think, Hassan."

He looked surprised.

"This one not Sullyman," he said. "I show you Sullyman fountain soon."

"Really?"

"Yes, yes. First look at Nasruddin Shah bathing house." He lowered his voice as if about to impart bad news. "This is where the Amir Kabir, he was murder-ed."

Ghossam and Reza suddenly brightened. It was obviously one scrap of Persian history dear to their hearts.

"Stab heem," Ghossam announced.

"Why?"

"No like heem."

"Maybe we stab you too, azzhole," cackled Reza, slapping my back. "You don't mind me making fun of you, do you?"

"Yes."

"Too fucken bad. I like it."

DEATH BY WATER

The bathhouse was a warren of gleaming white, low-vaulted rooms with walls and snoozing ledges covered in cerulean tiles, and an exquisite Italianate marble on the floors. Reza insisted on being photographed in the limestone tub where Amir Kabir, chief minister to Nasir-ud-Din Shah, had been stabbed to death. The sordid history of Iran's late royal dynasties held little interest for me, but apparently one of their more notorious members had once been exiled within these walls.

People have been exiled to worse places than Fin Gardens, I thought, overwhelmed by a formal beauty and architectural harmony that was not too formal, and not too rigidly harmonious, either. Flowerbeds were irrigated by smaller channels that splashed down into the larger ones, these in turn leading through arch after arch into ever-widening pools, each with a large central fountain within a square or rectangle of smaller ones. Shah Abbas the Great, pride of the Safavids, loved beauty—that much was certain—but whatever he built was either for his own pleasure or his own glory. The thought of him sitting behind these walls with his harem and sycophants enjoying the cool waters, the fragrant shade, and the delicious fugue in ceramic and stone, while his people toiled in the burning fields outside, subsisting on a diet that made them old at thirty-five — this was a melancholy thought.

Too melancholy. By the close of the Qajar dynasty, and not a hundred years after Nasir-ud-Din's own death, Ayatollah Khomeini's revolution brought the two and a half millennia of Iranian monarchy to its final end. It should have happened two centuries earlier.

Looking around, however, I could see that parts of the garden were far older than the Safavids or Qajars. Indeed, there were inscriptions recording the presence at Fin of Yaqub ibn al-Layth al-Saffar ("the Coppersmith"), founder of the ninth-century Saffarid dynasty. His son, Amr, caliph viceroy of Khurasan, Isfahan, Fars, Seistan, and even Sind, is also known to have visited Kashan for the Fin waters.

"*Kohnay*, very old," Parnian admitted.

But where was King Solomon's fountain?

"Sullyman fountain in private place," Parnian explained, pointing to another high wall opposite.

A ROYAL FOUNTAIN

For the first time I could see how close we now were to the Sialk hill palace or temple. It was no more than a bow shot away. We had acquired the services of Meybodi by this stage, manager of the gardens, a man with many keys and a belly that had known many titanic meals. The twenty-fifth key fit a padlock holding together the halves of a mighty studded door, so dry with age it could have been kiln-baked.

Beyond was a courtyard leading out to an unruly garden where a large exterior pool led toward a smaller interior one, the structure covering it clearly from the earliest period of Islamic secular architecture, unadorned and pleasingly simple but still a model of proportion and harmony. Parnian rushed us past these pools, however, to the far end of this private garden nearest the Sialk hill.

"Sullyman fountain," he announced with pride.

Beyond the enclosed pool, which it fed via a bridgelike tunnel, was another pool surrounded by a wall of very ancient and massive stone blocks that had been either renovated or added to much later. Subtly elegant steps flanked by monumental stone structures one could only describe as early Indo-Egyptian in style led down to this pool.

"*Garm*," said Parnian, pointing at the water.

"What?"

"Warm," Reza helpfully translated. "He says the water's warm."

It was, too. Very warm, and saturated in salts. Yet clearly not dead like the Dead Sea, since I could see a crab scuttling after copper-colored fish among dense weeds. This was the original spring. I could see the spot where water was coming up through the bedrock below, rippling a central point in the pool.

"Tree towsand year age," stated Parnian, nodding to indicate the humility such a span of years required from mortals.

That was certainly King Solomon's time. And this spring must have once been connected to the Sialk complex visible just over its protecting walls. The lack of any solid evidence was frustrating. And where did the Zoroastrians fit in?

"I will show," Parnian said. "Not here. This Sullyman fountain. But there"—he pointed west—"in *kooh*—mountain—with the magic of Zardhushti the Sullyman make . . . ah . . . "

After much back-and-forth muttering, Reza finally decided that Solomon had made an altar for sacrificing animals.

"Maybe we sacrifice you there," he threw in.

KING SOLOMON'S MINE OF INFORMATION

Meybodi insisted we see his museum. Alone in one huge grimy display case was a curious little bronze pot with three legs. It resembled the mysterious Luristan artifacts—no apparent use urgent enough to justify the enormously skilled work—yet it had apparently been excavated locally. A number of fairly accomplished clay pots labeled simply "Prehistoric" also caught my interest. Amazingly intact, they were decorated with simple designs reminiscent of those found at the various Indus valley sites. Yet these, too, were discovered around the Sialk hill. No doubt the best booty unearthed here was now scattered around in what the author of *The City of Cupolas and Windwards* had termed "the world's famous and valid museums."

With Meybodi eager to explain every cobweb on display, and the sun making its usual swift descent outside, I had to zip past Kashan's Islamic cultural heritage—which comprised ninety-nine percent of the museum's collection—take a swift look at the stained glass wind palace on its roof, decline several offers of tea, and finally bribe Parnian's son with a folding microscope—which his dad immediately confiscated—to get us up to "Solomon's altar" before dark.

> And to Solomon (We
> Made) the Wind (obedient):
> Its early morning (stride)
> Was a month's (journey),
> And its evening (stride)
> Was a month's (journey);
> And we made a Font
> Of molten brass to flow
> For him; and there were
> Jinns that worked in front
> Of him, by the leave
> Of his Lord, and if any
> Of them turned aside
> From Our command, We
> Made him taste
> Of the Penalty
> Of the Blazing Fire.
>
> They worked for him
> As he desired, (making) Arches,
> Images, Basons
> As large as Reservoirs,
> And (cooking) Cauldrons fixed
> (In their places): "Work ye
> Sons of David, with thanks!
> But few of My servants
> Are grateful!"

> Then, when We decreed
> (Solomon's) death, nothing showed them
> His death except a little
> Worm of the earth, which
> Kept (slowly) gnawing away
> At his staff: so when he
> Fell down, the Jinns saw
> Plainly that if they had
> Known the unseen, they
> Would not have tarried
> In the humiliating Penalty
> (Of their Task).

> — The Holy Koran (xxxiv. 12–14)

This was the passage Parnian had referred to. It clearly concerns the building of Solomon's Temple, though, not his alleged "fountain" in Kashan. Yet it is, like most of the Old Testament stories retold in the Koran, fascinating for its differences from the Hebrew text as much as for its similarities. "Jinns" or genies, best known from *The Arabian Nights* tales, are supernatural beings, whose assistance to humans generally entails a nasty catch-clause. They originally come from a Zoroastrian tradition that went on to spread in folklore across Europe as far west as Celtic Ireland. Jinns became leprechauns, fairies, goblins, and elves. Here, however, they assist Solomon in his massive building projects.

Dr. Fathullah Mujtabai, Professor of Comparative Religion and Mysticism at the University of Teheran, director of the Great Islamic Encyclopaedia project, and one of Iran's most eminent scholars, told me that — because the Koran mentioned such things — it was quite possible to believe that all the gigantic construction projects of the ancient world, like the pyramids and Great Sphinx, had been assisted by Jinns, particularly since there is no other good explanation for how such feats of engineering were achieved.

During the building of the showy Temple, conceived by Solomon's father King David to house the Ark of the Covenant, Solomon controls the Jinns through magical powers. Old Testament accounts pointedly noted that Solomon's wisdom "excelled the wisdom of all the children of the east country, and all the wisdom of Egypt," besides that of the greatest other extant sages. This echoes the way that Moses' magical prowess was earlier shown to be a match for any of Pharaoh's court sorcerers. Both Koran and Old Testament, of course, ascribe such powers to the grace of the one God.

In the Koran, however, there is an ambiguity: the Jinns only seem to work for Solomon. Thus, when he dies, the knowledge is concealed from them so they don't down tools and float off the job. Long after his death, Solomon appears to be praying at the altar, but—a potent image—his corpse is merely propped up by a staff (to this day Indian yogis use a Y-shaped prop beneath the chin to support the body while in deep meditation).

In the Koran, God makes it clear that, powerful as they may well seem to be, Jinns are ultimately very stupid entities, since it takes an earth worm chewing through Solomon's prop to show them that he is in fact dead. Their task is presented as a "penalty"—presumably just for being Jinns in the first place—and they work "in front" of Solomon, meaning perhaps "under his direction," punished severely with "blazing fire" by God, however, if they try to escape their servitude.

Other details of the Temple match those in the Hebrew texts, although in a far more abbreviated, poetic fashion. The word "Koran" means "recitation," and it was just that: an oral recitation by the Prophet Muhammad, who could neither read nor write, copied down by scribes. This explains its repetitive nature and its often stunning verbal power, which one scholar describes as "language compressed and shattered by the force of divine impact."

Why, I wondered, is the wind "made obedient" to Solomon in connection with the work of the Jinns? which seems largely involved with fashioning items from molten brass: arches, images, ablutions pools, cauldrons. In 2 Chronicles and I Kings, this work is handled exclusively by a certain brass worker named Hiram: ". . . he was filled with wisdom, and understanding, and cunning to work all works in brass." He was not Hiram the king of Tyre, but he was sent to Solomon by him, just as the king of Tyre had earlier supplied David and Solomon with materials and craftsmen to build their royal palace. The craftsman Hiram, we're told—perhaps to avoid confusion—had a Tyrian father and either a Napthalite or Danite mother. Hiram is an abbreviation of the Hebrew *Ahiram,* meaning literally "My brother is on high," but it is also extremely similar to "Ahriman," the common version of the name for one of Zoroaster's two Spirits, who evolve into Ahura Mazda's two sons, Angra Mainyu and Spenta Mainyu. The former is soon known as Ahriman, the evil brother who ends up locked in the great cosmic battle with the forces of truth.

Furthermore, the brass worker Hiram features in one of the major and more esoteric psychodramatic rituals of Freemasonry that links him with the mysterious disappearance of the Temple's focal point—if not its *raison d'être*—the Ark of the Covenant. This substitution of Jinns for Hiram in the Koran would therefore seem to be more than simple cultural overlay, although the sheer quantity of work Hiram was responsible for certainly seems a superhuman feat.

The two vast pillars, twenty-seven feet high and eighteen feet in circumference, the huge ablutions "sea" fifteen feet in diameter, thick as a hand and capacious enough to hold "two thousand baths" of water, along with the scores of lions, oxen, cherubim, pomegranates, and various floral designs decorating, supporting, or just standing in the teeming outer courtyards of the great Temple, were all cast in brass by Hiram personally, we're told.

But, like the enormous winged figures overlaid with gold that Solomon himself apparently made for the "oracle" to hold the Ark, all these objects also break the Second Commandment: "Thou shalt not make unto thee any graven image, or any likeness of any thing that is in heaven above, or that is in the earth beneath . . ."

Yet God in the Koran makes no comment on the blasphemous nature of the "images" that He clearly mentions—and which Sunni Islam vigorously forbids. They don't seem to bother Solomon's Lord either, which is stranger since he was the one who first forbade them.

Although "a month's journey"—as the Koranic sura terms it—is a reasonable assessment of how far winds can travel in a day, the Koran was dictated in a land where mighty wind and dust storms reach speeds that could frequently amount to a year's journey in a day. It would be an unnecessary quibble if it were not connected to the Jinns, the images cast by Hiram in brass, and the fact that Persia was then also exactly a month's journey from Jerusalem. And a month was precisely what I had allotted myself to follow the Magi on that same journey.

TEMPLE?

Solomon and his Temple were much on my mind as Ghossam broke the bad news to his Paykan that we were heading yet again up the western slopes of the Zagros mountain range. They hadn't enjoyed the experience much in Saveh when we headed for the castle, and doubted if a change of location would make a difference.

Source of so much European mysticism that was imported home by the Knights Templar, rulers of Jerusalem, the great Temple of Solomon has for centuries fascinated people who believe, as others believe about the Great Pyramid, that secrets were embedded with sacred geometry in its architecture: that it contained a Message. A model of the Temple in eighteenth-century London drew thousands of curious visitors daily for over a year. Freemasons, partial inheritors of Templar rites it would seem, have much other lore in their arcane ceremonies concerning the Temple's construction, besides the one involving Hiram. And much Masonic imagery also relates to the Great Pyramid. Why, as many have asked, were stone masons once considered so important that a secret society was formed around them, and indeed continues to this very day?

The greatest of all European buildings, Chartres Cathedral—itself intimately connected to Bernard of Clairvaux and the Templars—contains numerous references to the Temple, including one relief carving quite clearly showing the Ark of the Covenant being carried from Jerusalem to the Queen of Sheba, or Saba, in Ethiopia. This, curiously enough, is an event only described in Ethiopian religious texts (see the Kebra Nagast, trans. E.A. Budge; and also *The Sign and the Seal* by Graham Hancock; Doubleday; London, 1991), although one would have thought that the disappearance of the single most mysterious and important object in the entire Bible—the Ark and the stone tablets of Moses' Decalogue it contained—would be mentioned, if not explained, in Hebrew texts. It is not. The fact that the Temple's "oracle," its sanctum sanctorum, no longer contains the sole thing that made

King David decide to build the structure in the first place, and then—since the Lord decided David had too much blood on his hands for such a holy task—caused Solomon to execute his father's plans, must have struck someone as troublesome. But apparently it didn't.

And the Temple remained—destroyed, rebuilt, destroyed—as the great symbol of Jewish faith for a millennium without anyone ever alluding to the vanished Ark. Indeed, the Temple most closely resembles another ark—Noah's—whose dimensions are so copiously described that it becomes impossible to believe such a vessel existed. There is not a parallel in history for a structure of such importance of which there are no reliable eyewitness accounts. The detail in the biblical accounts makes it all the more suspicious that not a trace of the Temple remains by the time it is "rebuilt" five centuries later: who could have carried off such monumental brass works? No reliable original ruins have ever been found to this day (the Western or Wailing Wall is merely a section of Solomon's palace walls and Herod's Temple). And, according to orthodox archaeology, Solomon's Temple, from its biblical description, bears no resemblance to any other major temple yet excavated or recorded. When I reached Syria, I realized orthodox archaeology was wrong about this.

When the building was finished, Solomon seems to have had his doubts about the Temple's value, though: "But will God indeed dwell on earth? Behold, the heaven and the heaven of heavens cannot contain thee; how much less this house that I have builded?" (1 Kings 8: 27) After reading of the stupendous expense and effort that went into its construction, you cannot help but feel that Solomon should have considered asking himself this question earlier on. But he exhorts, begs, pleads, cajoles—and finally sacrifices 144,000 sheep and oxen to his Lord, a mountain of carcasses that, unsurprisingly, "the brasen altar that was before the Lord was too little to receive."

After letting him sweat over the fate of his petition for a few weeks, however, Yahweh eventually admits to Solomon the he has taken note of all the prayers and offerings, and that he has "hallowed this house, which thou hast built, to put my name there forever; and mine eyes and mine heart shall be there perpetually." There is, however, a caveat to this promise: Solomon has to behave, as his father David before him had, with "integrity of heart, and in uprightness, to do according to all that I have commanded thee . . ." Should he fail in this, Yahweh says sternly, and, most of all, should he do the unthinkable and turn to worship other gods, then the entire land of Israel and all its people will be banished from his grace. The Lord also reveals a fear and distrust of women still prevalent among men throughout much of the patriarchal East, and his high opinion of David is clearly unaffected by the king's acts of murder and adultery that biblical scribes recount.

As for the Temple, if Solomon fails: "at this house, which is high, everyone that passeth by it shall be astonished, and shall hiss; and they shall say, Why hath the Lord done this unto this land, and to this house? And they shall answer, Because they forsook the Lord their God, who brought forth their fathers out of the land of Egypt, and have taken hold upon other gods, and have worshipped them, and served them: therefore hath the Lord brought upon them all this evil" (1 Kings 9:7–9).

After building Yahweh the finest temple he had ever seen—not to mention the only proper temple ever dedicated to him—it seems unlikely that Solomon would drift off to join another cult. Nonetheless, the consequences of failing to keep his pact with Yahweh were still quite a responsibility, but there was no reason to doubt that if anyone could achieve such unwavering all-round good behavior Solomon could.

Until he couldn't, that is:

> But king Solomon loved many strange women, together with the daughter of Pharoah, women of the Moabites, Ammonites, Edomites, Zidonians, and Hittites; of the nations concerning which the LORD said unto the children of Israel, Ye shall not go in to them, neither shall they come in unto you: for surely will they turn away your heart after their gods: Solomon clave unto these in love. And he had seven hundred wives, princesses, and three hundred concubines: and his wives turned away his heart. For it came to pass, when Solomon was old, that his wives turned away his heart after other gods: and his heart was not perfect with the LORD his God, as was the heart of David his father. For Solomon went after Ashtoreth the goddess of the Zidonians, and after Milcom the abomination of the Ammonites. And Solomon did evil in the sight of the LORD . . . Then did Solomon build an high place for

Chemosh, the abomination of Moab . . . And likewise did he for all his strange wives, which burnt incense and sacrificed unto their gods.

And the LORD was angry with Solomon . . .

—1 Kings 11:1–9

But not *so* angry, apparently, that He carried through with his original dire threats. "I will surely rend the kingdom from thee," says this angry Yahweh, adding that he won't, however, rend the kingdom during Solomon's lifetime "for David thy father's sake: but I will rend it out of the hand of thy son." However, Yahweh even qualifies this already much-diluted threat, saying that he won't even rend *all* the kingdom away from Solomon's son "but will give one tribe to [him] for David my servant's sake, and for Jerusalem's sake which I have chosen." In short, the Lord's bark is uncharacteristically far worse than his bite in this case. He'd smitten people with far more dire punishments for infinitely more trivial sins in the past—or even, like Job, for no reason at all.

It also seems fairly clear that Yahweh places little value on the Temple. Besides being abandoned for other gods, loyalty to King David and David's city is all that really concerns him here—although his attitude toward David during the king's life can only be described as ambivalent at best.

GOD or god?

This is a far more parochial deity than the Creator of the Universe speaking. Indeed, Yahweh here appears to be just another local god like the numerous "abominations" he virulently despises and to whom, he warns Solomon, women invariably turn men's hearts. After a glance at comparative mythologies, it is hard to see what Yahweh imagines makes him so different from the competition at this stage in the history of Judaism. It is a far cry from the God of Genesis, who destroyed the entire world when its inhabitants displeased him. That, however, was long before there was a god of Israel. And when there was, the faith is more properly termed henotheism—the worship of one god amongst many—than monotheism.

But Yahweh would not be specifically identified as the Creator by a Jewish writer for nearly five hundred years after Solomon's time, when the nameless prophet known as Second Isaiah celebrates him thus (Isaiah 45:5–8) in a torrent of spectacular poetry which also represents the first imprint of those Zoroastrian doctrines that were to transform the Jewish faith during its renaissance after the Babylonian Exile.

WISE GUY

As a man famed for his wisdom, Solomon is not portrayed as being especially wise, either. And his father David was hardly a model of "uprightness" and "integrity." The mystery surrounding Solomon's accession to the throne remains unsolved, too: he was not the first-born — in fact, he was the fourth son of David's seventh wife — and, after much rancor and infighting, it is only Yahweh's support, of which everyone has to take David's assurance, that settles the issue. If the vanished "Book of the Acts of Solomon," referred to in 1 Kings 11:41, ever shows up, we may learn more. But from the information we do have, it appears that Solomon seized the throne after a coup; and it also appears that, given the immediate dissolution of a united monarchy during his son's lifetime, his reign was a disaster.

The first ten chapters of 1 Kings, however, are intent on establishing a picture of King David's son and heir as great and glorious, wisest of the wise, richest of the rich, his reign peaceful and prosperous.

Initially this seems to have been true enough. His marriage to the Egyptian pharaoh's daughter brought a much-needed alliance with Egypt, not to mention an inevitable knowledge of Egyptian culture and architecture that no Old Testament author dares mention. And Solomon's subsequent extension of the treaty his father David had made with Hiram, ruler of the Phoenician city of Tyre, further brought Israel into the mainstream of Oriental commerce. As part of his dowry, Pharaoh handed Solomon the Canaanite fortress of Gezer — which the Hebrews had never managed to conquer, but which an Egyptian army had recently waltzed through apparently without a hitch. Most significant, though, was the partnership Solomon embarked on with Hiram, which allowed him to share maintenance of a vast fleet of oceangoing ships that traded not just the Mediterranean but also, from near what is now the Red Sea gulf port of Aqaba, set out on three-year-long voyages to India, Sri Lanka, and possibly even Indonesia. The Hebrew words *tukkiyyim* (peacocks) and *qophim* (apes) used in descriptions of cargo returning on Solomon's ships, for example, are probably derived from terms in languages of the Malabar coast region in southwest India.

This prototypical success story reaches its legendary climax in 2 Chronicles 9:4 when the impossibly rich and beautiful Queen of Sheba arrives and is stunned by the unparalleled glory of Solomon's kingdom. It literally takes her breath away: "There was no more spirit in her." Ancient Ethiopian accounts—in the Kebra Nagast or "Book of the Glory of Kings"—have to complete the legend for us, however, with Menelek, illegitimate offspring of Solomon and Sheba, removing the Ark of the Covenant for safe keeping during the chaos that followed the ignominious end of Solomon's reign: if, that is, there ever was an Ark. But these particular Old Testament authors are obviously concerned with keeping the bad news for last. This would be a trite explanation for the inordinate amount of space employed to describe in excruciating detail the great Temple's construction, but having to justify Yahweh's failure to protect his kingdom could not have been an easy task.

A closer reading reveals, however, that the Temple was really little more than an appendage to Solomon's palace and its outbuildings, upon which thirteen of the total twenty recorded years of construction work were expended. The king's temple-building spree was not restricted to the monument on top of Mount Zion either, because he built at least one temple to "strange gods," on the Mount of Olives (2 Kings 23:13), a little east but still directly opposite the one for Yahweh; a palace for the daughter of the Egyptian pharaoh (but to Egyptians in 1000 B.C., palaces and temples were the same thing); and, as we were told above, he made adequate provision for his tribe of wives and concubines to worship their own deities in an appropriate manner. The eclectic range of religious structures springing up and the profusion of pagan rites going on around Jerusalem at this time must have resembled a Near Eastern Spiritual Convention.

The writers try very hard to make us believe that this pagan sexathon went on when Solomon was extremely old—read "senile"—but things had in fact begun to slide quite early in his reign. For instance, after Joab's death (1 Kings 11:21—or in other words when Solomon was still at his youthful peak) the Edomite prince Hadad, who as a child survived an appalling massacre of his people, was back and ruling on the throne of Edom; and Rezon the Aramaean had firmly ensconced himself in Damascus. These two events alone would have wiped out Solomon's control over the vital overland trade routes. Then, to pay off debts, he had to actually turn over territories in Galilee to king Hiram—who wasn't even very happy with the generous deal.

Next there were internal troubles to contend with, troubles that were partially connected with a sly attempt to abolish tribal loyalties. In order to move on with his grandiose building schemes, Solomon divided up the country into districts, but on an unequal basis that had the north complaining of being subject to the south. Basically the men of Israel—the north—were obliged to contribute forced labor in Lebanon for one month out of every three, but the men from Judah—the south—managed to avoid making such altruistic contributions of their time. In 1 Kings 11:28, we learn that Jeroboam, son of Nebat, was in charge of "all the forced labor of the house of Joseph," and he stirred up a revolt against Solomon which failed so miserably that he had to hide out in Egypt. Jeroboam returned after Solomon's death, however, to rule over the northern tribes—who had had enough of Judaean monarchs and their exactions by this time—and effectively brought his earlier revolt to a successful conclusion. To rub this humiliation in further, Jeroboam even established two competing temples to rival the one in Judah, his own "king's sanctuary" at Bethel and another at Dan (1 Kings 12:25–33). This gives us reason to believe that Solomon's Temple, since it *was* subordinated to his palace, may also have been designed as a "king's sanctuary," more personal chapel than public place of worship.

LORD OF THE AIR

Of Solomon's fabled reign, we thus have a fairly familiar picture on the surface: spectacular court, miserable, overworked, and underfed masses grumbling about funding it. It seems very far from the kind of righteous life that Solomon promised Yahweh he would live. But there appear to be two different Solomons, or at least two sides to the man: one the stuff that myths are made on, the other the stuff that fuels popular revolutions.

None of the Old Testament authors here could have been fabricating their accounts to flatter the king—ultimately they don't flatter him anyway—because they were all written long after he died. What we seem to have is an attempt to salvage something from an apparent disaster, to construct noble and glorious legends for future generations. But this makes it still more puzzling to find a pervasive conviction about Solomon's superhuman wisdom that is so widespread it not only extends to crediting him with the authorship of the Song of Songs, Proverbs, Ecclesiastes, the apocryphal Book of Wisdom, his own Odes, and even some Psalms within the Jewish tradition, but it also extends out, spreading his fame into Persian, Arabian, Islamic, and Ethiopian traditions. It cannot be a simple case of overcompensation.

The classic story of Solomon's shrewdness in judging over which two prostitutes is the real mother of a disputed child may even be adapted from Arabian folklore, which lauds an eleven-year-old Solomon for handing out far wiser judgment than his father in a matter of damage by trespass. The same may also be true of the queen of Sheba tale. In Arabic literature she is known as Bilkis or Maqeda, daughter of the Jinns and more beautiful even than the houris of paradise.

In the Talmud, Solomon has a magic carpet sixty miles long and sixty miles wide, upon which he could fly off at dawn for breakfast in Damascus, and then have supper in Persia. On one of these journeys he was apparently scolded for his excessive pride by no less a person than the queen of the ants. He is also recorded possessing a magic ring, engraved with the name of God and containing four jewels that were given him by four angels, who assumed the forms of a whale, an eagle, a lion, and a serpent. These jewels gave Solomon power over various aspects of the natural world. The one given him by the eagle-angel gave him control over birds and animals, for example, and the entire ring made him lord of the spirit world, and of the winds and waters.

The Talmud maintains that Solomon's seal, like his father's shield—the Magen David, now Israel's national emblem—was a six-pointed star, though in Western legends Solomon's seal is the "pentacle," the *Drudenfuss* or "Druid's foot" with which Faust, inscribing it on his threshold, protected himself from Mephistopheles. The five-pointed star eventually became common in the lore of Western magic, which is still considered "white" if the star's single point is at the top of the symbol, and "black" if the two points, imagined as devil's horns, hold the upper position for ritual purposes. Both Zoroaster and Solomon, curiously, assume the status of occult masters in Renaissance mysticism. Jesus, we should remember, is as much a direct descendant of Solomon as he is of David—according to Matthew—and it is, in fact, the five-pointed star of Solomon's seal rather than David's more famous six-pointed star that eventually becomes the emblem of both Jesus' birth and the significance of his messianic role.

Talmudic tradition further adds that on the steps to Solomon's throne there were mechanically operated figures of animals and birds. To help the king climb up toward his regal seat, for example, an ox on the lowest step held out its foreleg, and on the sixth and highest step there were eagles to raise him aloft and gently lower him on the throne itself.

Islamic traditions also mention Solomon's magic ring: he once even lost it, apparently, and the rebel angel Sakhr managed to get hold of it, reigning as king himself for forty days while poor Solomon roamed the earth penniless and in rags. Fortunately, Sakhr dropped the ring in the sea, and Solomon was then able to recover it from a fish that had swallowed it. The latter part of this tale is very similar to an extremely ancient Egyptian account relating to the court magician of Pharaoh Cheops, who is popularly credited with building the Great Pyramid. Solomon's magic carpet is described in Muslim lore, too. Once Solomon flew to Mecca for a pilgrimage upon it, sheltered from the heat of the sun by a canopy formed of living birds. The only bird missing was the hoopoe, and, fearing this affront to the king's majesty would earn him punishment, it was the hoopoe who, trying to make up for his insult, told Solomon about the incomparable beauty of Bilkis (or Maqeda). Then, of course, there is also the story of the Jinns who helped Solomon with his Temple. In short, there's too much in external sources that bears no resemblance to the biblical material—like Jesus' birth.

What we have here, it seems, is not two different Solomons so much as two competing and utterly opposed theologies slugging it out: an arcane mystical tradition and a more mundane history involving Israel's state religion. Only one wins in the end, however, and victors always get to write their version of history. But the struggle between these two truths—the direct, inner mystical experience, and the outer, politically oriented national faith—continues far beyond Solomon's time. It was what brought the Magi to Bethlehem.

MORE FUEL FOR THE PYRE

> And Solomon loved the LORD, walking in the statutes of David his father: only he sacrificed and burnt incense in high places. And the king went to Gibeon to sacrifice there; for that was a great high place: a thousand burnt offerings did Solomon offer upon that altar.

—1 Kings 3:3–4

In Hebrew there is another word reminiscent of Ahiram, Ahriman, and Ahura Mazda: *Ahimaaz*. It means "My brother is angry," but is also a name. The most prominent biblical Ahimaaz was son of Zadok, whose name derives from *zedek*, "Justice." King David (1 Chronicles 16:39) makes Zadok high priest in service of the Ark. This numinous object was then being kept where Solomon made his sacrifice, at Gibeon, a word derived from the Hebrew for "height." In a sense, the Ark—or the Law it contained—was the altar upon which true sacrifice was made: one sacrificed the base, animal flesh of earthly desires to bring the Self into harmony with spiritual laws. Traditionally, the Zadokite high priest anoints the Davidic prince. Both are messiahs—"anointed ones"—yet the priest must sanction the prince's authority, just as John the Baptist does when he "anoints" Jesus.

There is a legitimate process of biblical interpretation known as the "pesher." Ostensibly, it entails using the meanings of names to add a greater, more generalized and symbolic level on top of the basic narrative, while also finding a more specific and personal history within it, thus making a text relevant in time—on two levels—as well as prophetic or even timeless. Similar qualities give great poetry its ineffable power and eternal relevance.

It is clear from work by biblical and Dead Sea Scrolls scholars like Professor Barbara Thiering that many biblical passages work simultaneously on more than one level when the pesher technique is applied. Frequently it also makes indescribably trite or monotonous passages— such as the Old Testament's notorious genealogies—visible in an entirely new and often revelatory light. It can easily be applied translingually, since all of the languages encountered between Persia and Israel share many common roots, and the possibilities for puns and wordplay were and still are endless.

"Sialk," for instance, contains both a Hebrew word transcribed from Egyptian meaning "pool" (as in *Shihor*, "Pool of Horus"), and an assonance with the Hebrew for "vulture," *aiah*. In "Kashan" we find *ashan*, Hebrew for "smoke," as well as the Persian asha, "truth, order, justice." The smoke of sacrifice or incense was viewed as an offering to heaven, and, of course, the real meaning of sacrifice was an alignment of the human will with eternal truth, order, and justice by overcoming the individual ego's petty desires.

Consider a religion with two brothers as opposed deities, one representing Justice or Truth, the other Evil or the Lie. Consider that this religion is focused on ritual offerings made to a sacred fire, whose smoke visually represents these offerings being carried up to the god. Then consider that the same religion does not cremate or bury its dead— viewing these practices as defiling the elements—but instead leaves corpses in high places for vultures to devour.

When pushed too far the cliché becomes an archetype. What happens to coincidence under the same conditions?

> When he saw creation all around, and the throng of angels around him
> that had come forth from him, he said to them,
> > "I am a jealous God,
> > and there is no other God besides me."

But by making this announcement, he suggested to the angels with him that there is another God. For if there were no other God, of whom would he be jealous?

. . .

This is the number of angels: in all they number three hundred sixty-five. They all worked together until they completed each limb of the psychical and material body. There are other angels over the remaining passions, and I have not told you about them. If you want to know about them, the information is recorded in the Book of Zoroaster.

—from The Secret Book of John ("The Teaching of the Savior") Nag Hammadi Codex II

In this gnostic text—familiar to Nietzsche—John "the brother of James (the sons of Zebedee) went up to the Temple, [when] it happened that a Pharisee named Arimanios came over to him and" asked where the teacher he had been following was. John replies, "He has returned to the place from which he came." To which the Pharisee says, "This Nazarene has deceived you badly, filled your ears with lies, closed your minds, and turned you away from the traditions of your parents." John walks away deep in thought, asking himself questions about the "Savior" and his teachings, questions to which he has no answers. Then a figure with several different forms—at once child, father, mother—appears within a blinding light and proceeds to deliver one of the most profound discourses in all of Christian literature.

Ahriman is the Zoroastrian Satan, the "Spirit of the Lie." Was the Pharisee named "Arimanios" by coincidence?

A HIGH PLACE, AN ALTAR

I first realized that this journey with the Magi toward the Nativity was not going to be as straightforward—on any level—as I had once imagined it would be when Ghossam turned out of the fourth zigzag in an almost perpendicular road and I suddenly saw, perched alone high on a hill, a Zoroastrian fire altar in almost pristine condition after more than two thousand years. With the deepening shadows creeping in from higher mountains to the west, and a panoramic view down over the wide plain twelve miles back to Kashan, the altar's situation of remote isolation was eerily similar to the "Castle of the Fire-worshippers" back in Saveh, which lay almost directly north along the same serrated purple ridge.

Reza grumbled angrily and slumped in the car with "Chickadee," Ghossam, and his Zagros Slims, while Parnian and little Amir Hussein scuttled after me up toward the recondite structure.

It was square with four large slightly-widening arches opening out to the cardinal directions. On the roof was a smaller square platform upon which perched a slightly conical dome. Three steps led up to the eastern arch. Inside, the structure seemed curiously larger, with four small windows now visible in each side of the platform supporting the dome—perhaps to help smoke escape? Apart from a circular indentation in the center of the floor there was no trace now of the throne where the Bahram, king of sacrificial fires, had been ensconced. Long ago priests must have removed it to another location. Looking up, I found that the interior appeared less sectioned than the exterior, a huge vaulted chamber leading straight up to a dome made of stone bricks laid with extraordinary skill against eight bronze rods that curved up toward the center, forming a perfect eight-pointed star.

Most casual visitors would have probably assumed the place was Islamic, largely because of its dome. Without the gaping arches it could also have been a major contender for Marco Polo's tomb of the Magi. Yet the more I looked, the more grand and ancient this massively subtle architecture seemed, like the older areas of "Solomon's fountain," or the temple associated with the Great Sphinx at Giza, and even like the Great Pyramid itself. They were all part of an age that found its beauty not in elaborate ornamentation but in the booming chords of harmony, proportion, and—particularly—the stone itself that created them. There was a true grandeur about this huge, simple square with its dome and splayed arches. It seemed to be standing guard up here, too, watching over a world that sorely needed someone or something to watch over it these days.

All around, especially down below the southeast side, were the remains of ancient walls of rough-hewn stone slabs, in places revealing what must have once been sizable chambers. It had been a complex of dwellings, possibly even the remains of a temple of some sort, or a public area where people could watch from a distance the rituals taking place beneath the eight-pointed star of the smoke-filled dome towering above them.

While twilight deepened and a menacing north wind began to blow, I conjured up an image of the fire flickering amid those soaring arches. Turbanned figures wearing masks like surgeons, to prevent even their breath from defiling the sacred symbol of God, were illuminated by the dancing orange light. Rhythmic intonations made their bodies bob back and forth in time, as they placed their offerings on the tongues of flame, watching them borne up to heaven in rivulets of fragrant smoke.

"Too much old this place," said Parnian.

I had quite forgotten he was there. Clinging to his chunky waist, Amir Hussein's teeth chattered from the chill swooping in from those indigo mountains that clamped shut their jagged jaws on an old jaundiced sun without us noticing. Shadows went from phantom stalactites to shapeless hordes of hooded warriors now, their ghostly capes flapping about our ears.

Reza hollered something through the Paykan's window, blasting its horn.

"Too much cold?" I asked father and son.

They nodded gratefully. Much as I wished to sit far into the night and let the stones tell me their tale, I told Parnian to go back to the car, and then with numbed fingers I quickly took some measurements. The main structure with its four arches, excluding the platform and dome, was exactly thirty feet square and fifteen feet high at its base. From the base to the central point of the dome was also thirty feet, meaning that, if the area around the dome were filled in, the whole altar would be an exact thirty-foot cube.

Only months later did I find that the sacrificial altar standing in the courtyard before Solomon's Temple also measured, converting biblical cubits at just over half a yard each, thirty feet square and fifteen feet high (2 Chronicles 4:1). In addition, I discovered later still that the great Temple's *debir* or Holy of Holies, where the Divine Presence was said to dwell, and where the high priest performed the Day of Atonement service, was a thirty-foot cubical chamber.

Had I known it then, however, Reza would have been on his way to

Yazd far more quickly than he even wanted to be. It is obviously not possible to understand the Magi and their journey without understanding the religion they presided over. The last remaining bastion of Zoroastrianism left in Iran is the desert city of Yazd; and so I decided to digress from the Magi's route to Bethlehem in order find out what, if anything, today's Iranian Mazdeans made of Polo's story. And, for that matter, all the other stories I'd been accumulating myself since arriving in Iran.

Chapter Six

THE LAST OF THE ZOROASTRIANS: YAZD

*He presented to them a closed box, desiring them not
to open it till their return home. After having
traveled a number of days, however, they were curious
to see what was in the box, and opened it, when they
found only a stone, which was meant to express that
they should remain firm in the faith which they had
received. They did not understand this meaning, and,
despising the gift, threw it into a well, when
immediately a great fire came down from heaven, and
began to burn brightly. When they saw this wonder,
they were quite astonished, and repented that they
had thrown away the stone. They, however, took a
portion of the fire, carried it to their country, and
placed it in their church, where they kept it
continually burning. They revere it as a god, and use
it for burning all their sacrifices; and when at any
time it goes out, they repair to that well, where
the fire is never extinguished, and from it bring
a fresh supply. This is what all the people of that
country tell, and Messer Marco was assured of it by
those of the castle, and therefore it is truth.*

—Marco Polo, *Travels*

*Yes, although Thou are the First One, I realized
Thee to be (ever) young in mind, Wise One, when I
grasped Thee in a vision to be the Father of good
thinking, the real Creator of truth, (and) the Lord
of existence in Thy actions.*

—from the *Gathas* of Zoroaster (c. 1000 B.C.)
(Yasna 31.8)

THE GOOD RELIGION

"The original word of false religion is that evil comes from the creator": I came across this sentence in my notebook as the Paykan hurtled toward Yazd. It was a quotation from *The Teachings of the Magi*, a book translated by R. C. Zaehner [London, 1956, p. 94]. It had been recommended to me long ago by Dr. W. Y. Evans-Wentz, who was the pre-eminent authority on Eastern mysticism at Oxford when I was an undergraduate. He spent years studying in India and had translated *The Tibetan Book of the Dead* and numerous other texts. His college was opposite mine and I used to attend a weekly seminar held in his rooms. Eventually I managed to get invited to drop in for tea alone once or twice a term. He was less academic about his interests in eastern mysticism when he talked privately; and one thing he said several times over tea, but which I had forgotten for years, came back to me some hundred miles from the last true bastion of Zoroastrianism left in the world.

"Without Zoroaster there would be no Christ. He was the bridge, and the Romans burnt it," was what Dr. Evans-Wentz had said.

I knew nothing of Zoroastrianism at the time, understanding only that its prophet had attempted to preserve the purity of ancient Vedic wisdom of India and bring it to the West, so the statement merely puzzled me. Twenty years later, however, it began to make a lot of sense. Of all the noncanonical Christian texts I pored over, none provided so much endorsement for Marco Polo's Nativity tale as the Syriac document known as the Arabic Gospel of the Savior's Infancy, where, as I mentioned earlier, I read this astonishing passage:

> And it came to pass, when the Lord Jesus was born at Bethlehem of Judaea, in the time of King Herod, behold, Magi came from the east to Jerusalem, as Zeraduscht had predicted; and there were with them gifts, gold, frankincense, and myrrh. And they adored him, and presented him their gifts. Then the Lady Mary took one of the swaddling-bands, and, on account of the smallness of her means, gave it to them; and they received it from her with the greatest marks of honor. And in the same hour there appeared to them an angel in the form of a star which had before guided them on their journey; and they went away, following the guidance of its light, until they arrived in their own country.

These Magi, unlike any others, come "as Zeraduscht had predicted." Zeraduscht is of course Zoroaster. Here the visitors also receive a gift—different yet just as humble as the one in Polo's tale initially seems—but in this case they are evidently thrilled to get it. The star in this Arabic infancy gospel is also identified as an angel in disguise, something no other text mentions, either. It was the kind of missing-link version of the Nativity that I had always—if vaguely—hoped might exist, one unambiguously connecting the Magi with Zoroastrianism.

Many Syriac texts—written in an Aramaic dialect Jesus would have been able to understand himself—were, unsurprisingly enough, destroyed by the Roman Church. Among these is thought to have been an all-purpose gospel source, a single text created by combining all the elements from Matthew, Mark, Luke, and John together. This explains much, but it does not explain the presence of Zoroaster in this infancy gospel, which must have been written by someone well versed in the Mazdean scriptures.

In his hymns, the *Gathas*, Zoroaster himself predicts that some time after his death there would come "the man who is better than a good man," the *Saoshyant*—a word literally meaning "one who will bring benefit." It is this Saoshyant who will lead humanity in the last battle against evil. The Magian priesthood, developing this teaching further, produced the generally held belief that the Saoshyant would be born of the prophet's own seed, miraculously preserved at the bottom of a lake. Near to the dreaded End of Time, it is said, a virgin will bathe in this lake and be impregnated by the prophet's seed; in due course she will give birth to a son, named Astvat-ereta, meaning "He who embodies righteousness," and reflecting Zoroaster's own words: "May righteousness be embodied."

Despite his miraculous conception, therefore, the coming Savior of the World will still be a man, born of human parents. In this development of the Saoshyant belief the Magi thus did not betray Zoroaster's own teachings about the vital role to be played by humankind in the great cosmic struggle. Like kings and heroes, the Saoshyant is thought of as being blessed with divine grace, which, according to later literature, "will accompany the victorious Saoshyant . . . so that he may restore existence . . . When [he] emerges from the lake . . . this messenger of God . . . will drive the Lie out from the world of Righteousness."

The gift of the swaddling band—and possibly the original symbolic intent of the "swaddling clothes" or bands in Luke—can be linked to the distinctive badge Zoroaster gave to his followers. Adapting the old Vedic Brahman tradition of men wearing a sacred thread over one shoulder which was knotted for them by a priest during their initiation and is never untied, Zoroaster decreed that the sign of membership in his religious community, but for both men and women, would be a thin cord worn as a girdle, passed three times round the waist and knotted at back and front. After initiation—which took place at the age of fifteen—and every day for the rest of their lives, believers must untie and retie the girdle repeatedly when praying, its three coils likely intended to signify the thoughts, words and deeds by whose sum they would be judged after death. If the swaddling band is intended to represent Jesus' initiation girdle in the Syriac Nativity—since the Savior would be considered "pre-initiated" from birth—the Magi would indeed have regarded it as a gift of immense value.

That the star is really an angel also adds an unmistakably Zoroastrian touch to this part of the story. We owe the whole idea—and inexplicably revived popularity—of angels to Zoroastrianism, particularly the concept of guardian angels.

Zoroaster was unquestionably an historical rather than mythical personality, although no one can agree when precisely he lived, the dates ascribed by various scholars ranging bizarrely from 10,000 B.C. to 300 B.C. A series of hymns called *Gathas* are the only writings attributed to him that have survived in the body of Mazdean scriptures, yet in these exceedingly beautiful verses his humanity as well as his divinely inspired vision are both equally evident. He taught of one supreme God, Ahura Mazda, the Wise Lord, source of all goodness and righteousness, creator of the universe and everything in it. But unlike other religions—where someone eventually, after much deep thought, invariably asks: "So, who created Hitler?" or words to that effect—Zoroaster dealt with the question of a good Creator and the presence of evil in his creation from the start.

In its first stage of existence, Ahura Mazda's universe is in an immaterial or spiritual form, yet it still instantly contains two entities or spirits, two primal beings with free will who each make a deliberate choice, according to their proper nature, between good and evil. The act prefigures the identical choice each man and woman will have to make in this life. As long as the creation remains in its spiritual form it is safe from Angra Mainyu, the evil spirit—who later becomes Ahriman. Spenta Mainyu is the good spirit, and involved in his God's work of creation, whereas Angra Mainyu is the force of counter-creation. In the prophet's own terms these roles are more like the making of "life" and "not-life" (that is, a perpetual death). The addition of choice in this primal process, however, changes the passive antagonism between the two spirits into an active one. Before the Creation, as in Vedic philosophy, there is only Eternity, an utter stillness and silence and absence of time—thus also of movement—in which only God is.

With Creation, though, time suddenly begins, along with movement and, inevitably, the choice inherent in every action. According to the vision which Zoroaster claims revealed this to him, God knows that the moment his creation moves from the spiritual to the material the evil spirit will attack it, because it is good, and it will thus become a battleground for their two forces. But in the end, God also knows he will win the cosmic struggle there and be able to destroy evil, achieving a universe which will be wholly good forever.

Zoroaster's rarefied cosmology—as such things tend to do—became increasingly embellished with the passing of time. Eventually, this embellishment would cause serious problems. First, the two spirits came to be regarded as Ahura Mazda's two sons, though, which merely created the minor problem of God being Satan's dad. Thus Spenta Mainyu, the good spirit, gradually became completely fused with Ahura Mazda. On one hand, this made the supreme God suddenly disappear from the scene, and on the other it made Spenta his own father—with Satan for a brother. Ultimately, though, it left them both without a father, giving the appearance of two gods, a good one in a constant state of war with an evil opposite number. Feuding brothers—such as Cain and Abel—are a common theme found in numerous faiths originating in the Near and Middle East, linked to the idea of the heavenly twin: a kind of double each individual creates in the next world through his or her actions in this one, the result being either beautiful or like Dorian Gray's portrait.

To avoid the impossible-to-grasp absolute nondualism of the Rig-Veda, or the vague endlessness and lack of urgency of karma and reincarnation, there is no way of explaining creation that can avoid including a personified force of evil separate from the good force of a creator-god.

Zoroaster had already conceived of divine entities—six holy Immortals—each really representing a quality or attribute of God, like Justice, to assist the Creator and explain how the Eternal and unknowable can operate among the ephemeral and undesirable down here. Thus it's easy to see why Zoroastrianism is considered dualistic, although, and fundamentally, it is most definitely not.

Ormazd and Ahriman are not rival gods, but rather the inevitable consequence of spirit descending into matter—the two anodes between which the current of life flows, in other words. Unquestionably, this attempt to express the true nature of inner states did, all the same, produce at least one genuinely dualistic spin-off religion: Manichaeism, the faith of the third-century Persian prophet Mani—whose pessimism about the inherent wickedness of this material creation has deeply influenced Christian thought. The ascetic movement, for example, and Milton's sexy portrayal of Lucifer in *Paradise Lost*, are both obliquely indebted to Mani's teachings, which claim creation is the devil's work: Lucifer is Lord of this world.

Manichaeism has tended to make a major come-back when this world looks like something only Lucifer could have dreamed up, too: it was widespread after the Goths sacked Rome, for instance, and it's around in various forms now. Being officially branded a heresy, however, it tended to fulfill its own prophecies: inasmuch as Manichees believed the world was evil, so the Church vindicated this belief by torturing them to death for believing it in the first place. Zoroastrians, however, viewed Mani's pessimism as an appalling act of cosmic ingratitude and an abomination, believing themselves in the goodness of creation and all the marvels it contains, from starry nights to gourmet dinners. In the purest form, it is an extremely attractive faith, which is why it was marginalized by the religions that based much of their theology on Zoroaster's original teachings, then claimed it as their own unique revelation.

The prophet's system of divine emanations, as one might expect, gradually subdivided uncontrollably. The result became those angelic hordes which so fascinated medieval theologians: precisely how many, for instance, might be capable of dancing on the head of a pin? There was soon such a multitude—like the Hindu deities which pullulated out from one absolute and indivisible Eternal Something—that a few gnostic Christian texts suggest readers watching "Swan Lake" and "The Nutcracker" performed simultaneously over one corner of a pin cushion refer to Zoroastrian literature if they really need to know all the performing angels' names.

Only cabalistic Judaism—which today most closely resembles Essene Mysticism—gets into angelology with any enthusiasm, but other Zoroastrian ideas pervade orthodox thought in both the Bible and Talmud on many levels. The purity and dietary laws of the Jews as well as the ritual meals, the prayers with their tying of cords, and the celebratory feasts, can all be traced to the profound influence exerted by Zoroastrianism on Judaism during the Babylonian exile. Reasons change, yet forms remain remarkably similar. And these forms originated in Vedic India, from whence Zoroaster and the Magian priesthood transported them west. Although the Persian faith was a wholly unique revelation, it was housed within the framework of the oldest religion on earth.

It is in the Nazarean-Essenes and the Christian (and later Muslim) sects evolving from them that the influence of Zoroaster is most obvious and all-pervasive. He is the only founder of a world religion who was both priest and prophet, which perhaps explains why his religion is the earliest dogmatic and proselytizing one in the world, too, and thus the model for all later varieties.

Zoroaster terms himself *manthram*—one able to compose mantras, or utterances of power—which is comparable to the *logos* or "word" embodied by Jesus in John's gospel. Just as the Holy Spirit descends like a dove into Jesus immediately after his baptism, so Zoroaster's original vision occurs after he emerges from a river ritually purified to be led by a shining being into the presence of his God.

The Ahunvar is to this day the first prayer taught to every Zoroastrian child, and is what the Lord's Prayer is to Christians—and possibly even what the Lord's Prayer once was. Composed by Zoroaster himself, thus in the ancient Gathic dialect he spoke, the exact meaning of its lines after possibly more than 3,000 years has been the subject of much tiresome debate by the handful of scholars who have had any interest in the matter. Here is a conflation of the most recent translations:

"God is as much the desired Master as the Judge according to Truth, Order, and Justice. He is the source of all good things, of life itself. To God is the kingdom, established as a refuge and protector for the poor." The word translated as "poor"—*drigu*—is the origin of the Persian "Darvish" or "Dervish"—a name still used for certain (whirling) sects of Muslim Sufi mystics—and it had a specific and special sense, meaning a pure, devout, and humble person, a true follower of Zoroastrian doctrine: a believer. It is also identical in meaning to the Hebrew *ebionim*, translated as "Ebionite"—the term used by the Essenes of Qumran to describe themselves—and both terms are reflected in "Cathar"—derived from the Greek for "pure"—as well as in the Templar title, "The Poor Knights of Christ and the Temple of Solomon."

Almost as old as the Ahunvar prayer is the Zoroastrian creed, a declaration of faith clearly required by the faith, in its early and difficult days, of each new convert: "I profess myself a worshipper of God, a follower of Zoroaster, rejecting evil, accepting divine doctrine; one who praises the Archangels, who reveres the Archangels. To the Lord God, the good, infinitely rich in treasures, I ascribe the source of all things that are good."

I use the word "God" for "Ahura Mazda" here because the meanings are identical yet the effect on most readers would be utterly and unnecessarily different.

This creed is the first formal profession of a monotheistic faith known, and, like the previous prayer, it cannot fail to sound familiar to contemporary Christians.

ANCIENT STARS

The Arabic infancy gospel, which binds Christianity to Zoroastrianism inseparably, also contains another interesting departure from the canonical New Testament. Only Luke mentions an incident in Jesus' life between Nativity and baptism: the story of Mary and Joseph bringing their son to celebrate Passover in Jerusalem when he was twelve years old (that is, the year in which he would become a man). They lose Jesus among the crowds and eventually find him debating knowledgeably with the temple Elders. Verse 51 of the Syriac text, however, gives this incident considerably more flesh:

> And a philosopher who was there present, a skillful astronomer, asked the Lord Jesus whether he had studied astronomy. And the Lord Jesus answered him and explained the number of the spheres, and of the heavenly bodies, their natures and operations; their oppositions; their aspects, triangular, square and sextile; their course, direct and retrograde; the twenty-fourths and sixtieths of twenty-fourths; and other things beyond the reach of reason.

But not so far beyond the reach of this writer's reason that he is unable to present a detailed and knowledgeable summation of the intricacies involved in what amounts to the classical astronomy upon which was based all ancient astrology—something which had very little to do with contemporary horoscopes and far more to do with the movement of vast cosmic cycles, the precession of the equinoxes, the arrangement of celestial bodies, and the effect of all this on the nature and quality of human existence. Language still contains many vestiges of astrological precepts: people are "mercurial" or "jovial"; countenances are "saturnine"; sexually transmitted diseases are "venereal"; and the arts of war are "martial" to this day. The ancient world is still closer to us than we think.

And the ancients lived in a holistic, interconnected universe: "As above, so below," in the words of Hermes Trismegistus, the "thrice great," the god Thoth—a figure often associated with Zoroaster by the Greeks and Renaissance mystics. Everything in the mundane sphere had its counterpart in more rarefied realms. Thus the star of the Magi could easily become a form assumed by the angel assigned to their case. Just as Matthew describes Joseph's nightmare warning being delivered by "an angel of the Lord," whereas God himself takes time out to appear in the Magi's own dream.

Most Westerners lost the ability to see that the parts make up a whole after the seventeenth century. The result has been self-evidently disastrous, which is why there is such urgency in fields as disparate as ecology and physics to return to a philosophy where causes are no longer isolated from effects. "You are what you do" was and is the essence of a teaching that both Jewish Essenes and Zoroastrian Magi became engaged in a battle to preserve from corruption, as spirit submerged into matter and the conflict between Truth and the Lie escalated towards all-out war.

THE MAN WHO SAID HELLO TO KHOMEINI

"Na'in," said Reza, as we sped past a large green sign reading NA'IN. "Big city for carpets, Na'in. Very famous."

"And valid?"

"What, azzhole?" He leaned over the seat and flicked his tongue at me like a snake. "Hey, maybe you get some nice juicy Zoroastrian woman tonight. Eh!"

I confess there were times when I wanted to do him harm.

Na'in appeared to be scarcely more than a large deserted village. Everything was shut for the night, but what few stores the place seemed to possess did not sell carpets. In fact, Na'in was, for Iran, unnaturally lacking in any vendors, let alone carpet vendors. I pointed this out.

"Famous for carpets," Reza repeated, with less certainty.

I could tell he was hungry, because he lit himself a cigarette without noticing that he already had one alight in his hand. He now pretended he had lit it for Ghossam, who responded by puffing at the one Reza had given him only minutes before, returning to lean possessively over his steering wheel and peer through the windshield into a feeble cone of light with which the Paykan punched its way through the inky darkness all around us.

"Azzhole!" Reza held the spare cigarette over his shoulder.

I pretended not to notice.

"Hey! Smoke?"

"No thanks."

He proceeded to smoke both cigarettes, acting as if this had been his intention all along.

At the edge of a town called Bafaran, he finally saw the salvation he'd been anxiously awaiting.

"Ghossam!" he yelled. "*Khorak!*" Then he turned to me like a child at Christmas, saying, "Food! Look!"

It was freezing outside and the air felt drier. We were well into Iran's central desert plateau now, which in places rose some three to four thousand feet above the northwestern plains. I stood basking in the sudden silence and gazing up at the sea of starlight through which a fat crescent moon cruised like a neon barge.

The Magi would have probably started heading west toward Susa back at Na'in, along what is now the Isfahan road. Kashan was once almost equidistant from both major centers of the early Archaemenid kings (the first Persian dynasty), who spent their summers at Ecbatana—yet to be excavated since modern Hamadan stands on its site—and their winters at Susa, imperial capital of Persian Emperor Darius I. Yazd, which still lay some hundred miles away to the southeast, had probably not even existed then.

The central desert is an inhospitable place, one where few Iranians have ever freely chosen to live. It was for this very reason that the Zoroastrians had gradually relocated themselves here. They feared persecution from Muslims during the centuries that followed the Arab invasion of Iran in A.D. 637, although the official policy was one of toleration. With the assassination of Yazdegerd III in 651, however, the Sassanid dynasty ended and there would be no stable indigenous government in the country until the rise of the Safavids 850 years later. But Yazdegerd was the last Zoroastrian monarch Iran would see. Islam was its new master.

Ghossam and Reza were sitting at their table already munching on bulbous spring onions, radishes, and cucumbers when I came in from the cold. There were only three other customers in the vast incandescent hangar that was a restaurant, and they were sitting *on* their table. Admittedly, their table was slightly lower than the one Reza and Ghossam had chosen. These customers looked more like Afghanis than Iranians, too, with rough wool caps rolled to form a thick brim, and baggy pants tapered at the ankle but possessing a crotch low and capacious enough to house a set of bagpipes. Cross-legged, elbows on knees, they ate furiously from a communal platter the size of a shield.

"Fucken Israelis!" growled Reza, as I sat down.

"What?"

For a moment I thought he was referring to the other diners.

"Fucken Israel. Nothing but motherfucker trouble-makers."

Ghossam nodded grimly.

I gathered that they'd learned from the waiter some news involving yet another diabolical assault on Islam by Israel. What it was precisely, however, I couldn't get Reza to tell me. I felt that it was somehow my fault. We ate in silence.

Our waiter, a gaunt and rather sepulchral figure with a mustache composed of hairs that were more like tendrils or quills, wore a tuxedo jacket from the 1920s over striped pajama pants from beneath which protruded yellowed long johns. On exceptionally dainty feet, that were swathed in the remnants of three different pairs of socks, he wore what appeared to be ladies' evening slippers in gleaming black plastic with simulated gold buckles. He liked to serve with his thumbs a good inch into the food he was serving. His thumbnails proved to be nearly an inch long themselves and curled like a falcon's beak. Earlier on, it seemed likely, he had been doing something intimate with an old and oily machine.

The soup had a very unusual taste, as I remarked to Reza.

"Zoroastrian piss."

"That could be it . . . and peppermint toothpaste."

After I'd given up trying to chew a kebab threaded with beef-flavored India rubber, I noticed the waiter's spectral presence at my side holding out what I assumed was the bill. Reza normally grabbed all bills since he felt my money was safer in his pockets, but I took it without meeting resistance this time, finding, however, a mangled old black-and-white photograph showing a horde of several hundred people who appeared to be fighting each other.

"What's this?"

Reza spent two minutes translating my question. Then the waiter spent five minutes explaining something in a thin, eerie whisper.

"It's a photograph of him with Imam Khomeini," Reza eventually told me.

I squinted into the mob, looking for Khomeini.

"I don't see him."

"Who?"

"Khomeini. Or the waiter."

Reza relayed this information, then the waiter, tugging at his pajama legs to prevent the knees bagging out a foot farther than they already had, squatted down beside me. Very carefully, he took the photo, smoothed it out over the grease stain on his worn sleeve, and pointed with a tortoise-shell thumbnail at a group of faces the size of freckles in the lower right-hand corner. Taking the photo again, I bent closer. It was just conceivable that the shadowy figure with more space around him than anyone else could have been Khomeini.

"Ah-hah! *Balay!* Yes, yes. Imam Khomeini!" I whooped.

The waiter retrieved his picture, nodding sagely and standing.

"I am . . . hello . . . imam . . . me," he announced.

"I could see. How lucky. When was that?"

"Fucken firty-fife yearth-go," mumbled Reza through a mouthful of rice. He swallowed. "He was wounded in the fucken war. In the head. Say something nice, azzhole."

I said something nice and the waiter bowed politely, gliding off with a look of enormous satisfaction on his face.

"Did you phone that Mr. Yazdani?" I asked.

Sam Sadatian, a Zoroastrian member of Iran's parliament, whose business card read "Foreign Relations Committee, Islamic Consultative Assembly," had given me a contact—Mr. Yazdani—to look up in Yazd (there's a distinct site-tenacity about Iranian names that only Indiana Jones and Tennessee Williams seem to possess in our culture). He had phoned Yazdani, pillar of the Zoroastrian community, telling him to expect us tonight. It was late and I thought we should perhaps call to say where we were.

"We phone when we get there," Reza replied.

"He might be waiting up . . . or in."

"So let him fucken wait."

"Phone him."

"No!"

"Then I will."

"Go ahead."

He knew I'd never get beyond the local operator, if I even got that far. His lack of respect for minorities was, I suspect, partly bred into him and partly exacerbated by his habitual all-round lack of respect for everyone—starting with himself. There were times when I felt sorry for him . . . although these times invariably occurred when I was also nowhere near him.

OLD MOVIES

It was midnight before we hit the outskirts of Yazd. I could see why it was called a desert city. Sands blew in beneath the harsh sodium glare of streetlights sparkling like solidified fragments falling from the lamps themselves. Flat and unrelievedly bleak at first, the city gradually asserted itself, with trees becoming more and more frequent, boulevards growing wider, single-story bungalows huddling closer together, then springing up into houses and eventually even small apartment blocks. It was exciting, being among the last devotees of Ahura Mazda left in the land of his prophet. But not very exciting. I looked out for signs of fire temples, altars, Zoroastrian shrines, yet saw only the usual portraits of Khomeini and his successors plastered on walls and in shop windows. There was something different in the air, all the same; something secretive and ancient. It turned out to be kerosene vapors from a leaking trailer tank.

"Arghah! Ghossam!"

Reza had seen a phone booth.

He jumped out and was soon deep into an exceedingly belligerent conversation, even banging the receiver against the booth's wall a few times to emphasize his point.

Oh, no, I thought. Not *again*. Reza hung up savagely and paced back to the Paykan.

"Mag-mag-mag-mag-mag!" he said, laughing hysterically.

"What?"

"Mag-mag-mag-mag-mag, mag-mag!"

"Fine . . ."

"That's what the person said, azzhole! Some fucken Zoroastrian language: mag-mag-mag-mag-mag . . . Give me some change."

Fortunately, it had been a wrong number. The Zoroastrians had, though—or so I'd heard—developed a hybrid language of their own to prevent Muslims from understanding private conversations.

Mr. Yazdani met us in an old Peugeot with one door and three seats missing. In his late fifties, balding with close-cropped gray hair, he had a sardonic smile and inordinately bright eyes. While slender, he gave off an aura of physical strength that had something dangerous about it: like a martial arts maestro. Yet, talking to Reza, he adopted a stance and air of mock servility—as if by habit. I hoped he'd arranged a hotel and was going to take us straight there. It was very late, and I did not feel like staying in someone's house. He had in fact arranged a hotel, I learned, but he also first insisted that we come to his house. His family had been waiting for us to arrive since six P.M. Food was ready. Very ready. I offered to accompany him, but he showed me that the Peugeot only contained a driver's seat—the way cars do on assembly lines—except this assembly line had been twenty brutal years long, judging by the ravages of time and Iranian driving that had gnawed, pocked, scarred, hammered, and bleached the vehicle's body.

"I speak English," Yazdani whispered urgently, when Reza had returned to Ghossam's car, "but not when *he's* around. Understand?"

"Of course."

I gave him a knowing look. We had a secret, which seemed to please Mr. Yazdani. It made me feel I'd walked through a cinema screen into the movie. It was old, too, this movie—black and white, or really washed-out sepia. Possibly street lighting caused this effect, or had the government cut off color in Yazd?

Our grumbling Paykan followed the one-seater Peugeot around a main square reminiscent of provincial southern France, then down some prosperous-looking boulevards and into a warren of narrow streets and high-walled windowless houses. Yazdani drove as if he were trying to lose us, not guide us.

"Maybe he has daughters," Reza speculated. "Big juicy ones, eh?" He paused. "Except they don't shave, Zoroastrians. I hate that . . ."

In unnecessarily graphic detail, he then related an experience he'd had with a Jewish landlady in Boston. It was the first time he had ever seen pubic hair on a woman.

Streets were either covered in wind-blown sand now, or they *were* sand. The Paykan and Ghossam leaned left, leaned right, right then left, as we closed in on Yazdani like high-speed cops. There was no escape. There would not have been any escape for pedestrians in our way, either, but not a soul was out on the streets of Yazd at 12:45 A.M. No people, no colors: was there a curfew as well? All these windowless houses we passed, I now noticed, had various versions of what were clearly updated "windwards" on their roofs. But no cupolas. Desert architecture, desert city. Deserted.

MY DINNER WITH ORMAZD

Yazdani's front door was around four inches thick, and steel-plated on the inside. It was more like a Manhattan apartment door, with four deadbolt locks and three security chains. No one would be getting through this portal uninvited. Who did he need to keep out so conclusively?

We were shown through the hall, then into a sort of antechamber with frosted glass half walls and a table, at which sat two attractive young women, who nodded shyly in greeting. Leading off this space was a large L-shaped sitting room, where a ten-foot-long coffee table held enough food for fifty. At the far end stood two mighty bookshelves crammed with huge old leather volumes, every available gap stuffed with papers. A nearer group of low Danish do-it-your-shelves held five or six video players and a host of other electronic gadgets, some with wires leading to a gigantic television set.

Another, older woman poked her head around the door, saying something that did sound a bit like "mag-mag-mag-mag-mag," to which Yazdani nodded graciously in assent. Only then did it occur to me that our host's daughters—as the younger women proved to be— were the first unveiled females over ten I had so far seen in Iran. Zoroastrian women were famous for their beauty, I'd read somewhere, and because of this they also apparently flaunted their exemption from the veil, which did not exactly please their Muslim counterparts. But since no man could see that much of women he wasn't related to anyway, how did anyone know the Zoroastrians were more beautiful? It was one of those national clichés that persist no matter how little truth they contain: like the stupidity of Poles or the superiority of French restaurants.

Reza, however, was beside himself with agitation over the sight. His years in the U.S. were now far, far away. For him, this was like coming across a couple of hot babes in their underwear. His behavior, of course, became acutely embarrassing. For the first time, also, I saw him and Ghossam through someone like Yazdani's eyes: they looked like corrupt, brutal undercover cops, Islamic Vice Squad.

The room was dominated by two enormous framed pictures painted upon engraved mirror-backed glass. One showed the Prophet

Zoroaster alone, sunburst nimbus behind his head, right index finger pointing up to heaven, a scepter in his left hand and a broad golden sash around the waist of flowing robes. With the cascade of reddish hair and beard pouring from beneath his regal turban, he resembled an Anglo-Saxon warrior Moses or a crusading Druid. The other picture was in the same mirror work but oblong, divided into three segments by arches like a portable Hindu shrine. There was a kingly figure on the left paying obeisance to a big chalice-shaped altar of fire in the center, and another image of Zoroaster on the right virtually identical to the one in the adjacent picture. Only the flames of the altar, the prophet's face, hair and gold sash had been painted over the glass here as well, creating the rather spooky effect of suspending them in a reflection of the room. I had seen this kind of work before. Lots of it.

"Are they from Bombay?"

Yazdani smirked, turning to Reza, who translated.

"He said yeah. Brought them by mule a hundred years ago."

"Who did?"

"Who fucken cares?" he said, lighting up a Zagros for himself and Ghossam.

Yazdani said something in a plaintive voice.

"Azzhole don't want us to smoke in here," Reza announced scornfully. "C'mon, Ghossam, let's go outside and fuck his daughters."

They went off to the street for their smoke, and Yazdani flashed his bright eyes, saying, "You like to drink something?"

"Drink?"

"Al-Kool. Do you?"

"Alcohol" is derived from an Arabic term that once basically meant "eye-liner."

"I've been known to. Sure. What do you have?"

"Wine, vog-kar, whatever you are want . . ."

Wine and vodka turned out to be the whole range available, though. Not really expecting any eighteen-year-old Laphroig in central Iran, I settled for vodka. Yazdani grabbed a flimsy decanter that looked like a five-dollar souvenir from Venice, pouring clear liquid into matching souvenir goblets. I felt like a schoolboy smoking an illicit joint in the washrooms. Alcohol had quickly become a novelty. It was quaint. It was also, I felt, some sort of spiritual litmus test on Yazdani's part. But this was hardly a problem: a drink was exactly what I needed after yet another Longest Day with Reza, so I knocked it back. And then very nearly sprayed it out again all over Yazdani's face. It tasted like 200-proof country grappa, felt like burning gasoline, and, as it hit the stomach, I could feel my entire body saying *No thanks, pal, not in here you don't.* My eyes began to water and I hastily peeled a nearby orange, shoving it into my mouth to keep both this "vodka" and the recent dinner beneath it where they were.

"Good, yes?" Yazdani asked.

"Phew, yes! Haven't had a drink in a while. Man. . . . Yep, that's good stuff. Where did you get it?"

"My wife, she know the secret of making vog-kar from the syrup. More?" He unplugged the flimsy decanter.

"Maybe later. What's the wine like?"

What "syrup" was his wife using? Napalm?

Poor bastard, I thought, thinking this voodoo moonshine was vodka. No wonder his eyes sparkled. The stuff surged through my pipes like molten lava.

The law regarding alcohol in the Islamic Republic states that only Muslims are forbidden to drink it. The religious minorities who use alcohol—and, like the Armenians, even use it in religious rites—are allowed to *make* it, but not sell it or even transport it. Every Zoroastrian family knew how to make at least wine by now, or at least imagined they knew.

"I thought Zoroaster was against alcohol?" I asked, recalling that he was.

"Against aboose, against big drunk-ness," Yazdani corrected. "In my faith all good things of earth are permitted. It is sin not to enjoy everything God he is provide for us."

"I like that."

I hoped Ahura Mazda did not number voodoo vodka among the "good things of the earth" that he was currently providing.

"You stay here tonight," Yazdani then said urgently. "We talk. Not in front of *them*, though. *Komiteh*, yes?"

I shrugged. I don't think Reza would have passed a medical for Girl Guides let alone Komiteh, but I wasn't sure where Islam stood on the ethics of psychological testing. He did have a cousin in the Komiteh—whom he occasionally set on people who bothered him. That I knew, because he'd made a point of telling me, presumably in case I ever thought of bothering him.

Reza's cousin also did a brisk business in selling items confiscated during spot checks on suspicious homes. IranPop CDs and cassettes and foreign magazines were his specialty, but he did well with women's lingerie and cosmetics, too, apparently. Liquor he handed in to the authorities, however: he had principles.

"I'll probably go to the hotel," I replied. "I'm exhausted."

"I have gwest room. You are always safe in the Zoroastrian house. Mudge better for you here."

"No, really. I wander around at night, too. Insomnia. I'd bother you."

"Not at all. You wander. Sit here, sit there, read. As you will. Always you safe in the Zoroastrian house."

He sounded like a new-home-builder's ad.

"Thank you. I'll think about it."

We heard Reza and Ghossam thudding back into the Zoroastrian house.

"No talk now," Yazdani whispered. "All right? They are bass-turds."

He was having problems with a bottle of wine whose plastic stopper had been cocooned in wire and melted wax to prevent fermentation from firing it through the cellar ceiling. Wax peelings were all over the floor by now and the wire was not cooperating. He went off to fetch something.

"You see those cheeks, man?" croaked Reza. "All whores, the Zoroastrian womens. Sheet!"

"I'd watch it if I were you, Reza. They understand English."

"Who fucken cares what they understand!"

I looked over at Ghossam for support, but he was blank as usual, as befitted a major comedian's straight-man. They were both edgy though, almost afraid in this infidel environment, it seemed, with its forbidden images of a pagan prophet flashing from the wall.

Considering how Zoroastrians had suffered at the hands of their ancestors, they had good reason to be afraid. But it was not this, I sensed, that scared them. It was the unknown and arcane religion brazenly ruling over this house with its strange gods. More superstitious than really religious, they had obviously absorbed just enough Islamic scripture to believe that these people worshipped demons and were doomed to hell—but before that they were still up to no good here. The academics and mullahs I'd met were invariably tolerant, well-informed men, respectful of Zoroastrianism and conscious of the debt their own faith owed its national predecessor. But the masses were ... well, like masses. And people like Reza resembled Mississippi rednecks half a century ago: behind the cruel jokes and snide remarks lay genuine malice.

Yazdani returned with a pair of pliers and renewed his assault on the wine bottle, making an extraordinary mess before he managed finally to pry off its stopper. He poured me a tumbler of cloudy pale pink liquid redolent of old damp wood. It tasted like moldy, grape-flavored Kool-Aid in vinegar: the kind of home-made wine that you're obliged to admire because it's a friend's first attempt. Except it's usually his last attempt, too, fortunately. When you know how wine is supposed to taste, you can at least tell that whatever it is you've produced in the basement from grape sludge and yeast is not wine. Poor Yazdani had spent his life under the impression that this colloidal suspension of mildew and dead fruit was what the fuss was about, was what poets had virtually deified, and what high-brow clubs and whole encyclopedias were devoted to.

"You fucken junkie," whispered Reza, as I sipped from the glass. "You drink that fucken junkie sheet!"

He was genuinely shocked, indeed so shocked that he even tried to mask the shock in mockery. In the Islamic Republic, drinking alcohol in front of devout Muslims is probably about the same as lighting up a cigar in a crowded California cancer hospital elevator. Except Reza was hardly devout.

It made me determined to drink more even if it killed me.

Yazdani indicated that we should make a start on the thirty platters of food displayed before us. Moments later the woman I took to be Mrs. Yazdani staggered in with a tray larger than her front door on which were piled five more steaming cauldrons of stewed poultry, peas with yellow things, big lumps with other yellow things, the roasted carcass of a small creature that appeared to have been slaughtered with a lawn mower, and about three hundred oranges.

I wondered how Reza felt about infidel food, but I shouldn't have bothered: food was *food* to him. I felt bloated from our earlier dinner, but he acted as if this were the first meal he'd seen in months. As he attacked a haunch of the mangled carcass, I said,

"Didn't think you ate pork, Reza?"

He froze, meat and bones splayed from his jaws like a still from *Teenage Cannibals*. His eyeballs peered down at the creature diving into his gullet.

"Just kidding."

"Oo-wazz-ull!"

Yazdani was busy connecting wires amid his bazaar of electronic gadgets. Then he plugged in a videocassette, speaking to Reza.

"Eeth goan foh oohn id-joh ape aworrara-eenth."

"Pardon?"

"Wideo," Ghossam translated. "He has wideo of the Zardhushti prayers rally for you watching."

"That's what I fucken said, azzhole," Reza complained, the galleon of food through whose hull he'd been speaking now visibly sailing on a tide of peristalsis down toward whatever gaped within him where others have stomachs.

Zardhushti prayers rally?

On the monumental television screen appeared, back to front, the kind of numbers you get on film leader. Then grandiose chords of symphonic music shuddered out, very far from their right speed, and an image so blurred it could have been anything in red and orange appeared. Unlike the music, it went into focus briefly, proving to be a large bonfire. Then the camera wobbled drastically, revealing what closely resembled a brick wall like another dimension behind the one where the bonfire was—although in focus.

"The Sacred Fire of Ahura Mazda," boomed a voice like a drunken Winston Churchill promoting Britannia's Empire.

"Wotha-fuck ithissheet?" burbled Reza behind a bolus of poultry legs, peas with yellow things, and bread.

I finally realized that what we were viewing was in fact a sixtieth-generation copy of a sixteen-millimeter movie that had been shot with a video camera while it was actually being projected onto a creased bed sheet hanging from a brick wall.

The movie had been made some time in the late sixties, judging from the sideburns and bell-bottom pants sported by a few 400-pound playboys who featured in it prominently. The director had also obviously been watching too many avant-garde Italian films—or, alternatively, had never seen or directed *any* films before this one. Long stretches of painfully out-of-synch soundtrack filled five-minute pans across blurred landscapes, or over hordes of people milling around at what looked like a crowded garden party in Tibet. One two-minute interlude even showed traffic on a highway. Every now and then, Winston Churchill would utter some mighty truth, his momentous, lurching sentences laden with words like "timeless," "eternal," "ancient," "primordial," "venerable," "ageless," and "immortal," backed up by "since the dawn of time," "before the age of our earliest ancestors," "when the planet was young," and so on.

It was like a pioneer infomercial for Zoroastrianism—I kept expecting a 1-800 number to flash up—vending the faith, presumably via a major annual festival, as if it were something between *Woodstock* and *The Ten Commandments*. Parts resembled old newsreel footage from Haight-Ashbury's Summer of Love. Some people even held joss sticks and wore love beads or head bands, and a great many of them did not look remotely Iranian. Fat Greek pop stars and hare-brained British aristocrats in floral kaftans ate from heaped paper plates, lounging on the steps of what seemed to be a temple built into rock face. A man in a yellow bathrobe and a Tolstoy beard smiled a lot. One self-consciously pretty girl reappeared so frequently and for so long that she must have been the director's main squeeze, or was by the time the editing had been completed. If editing had even occurred. . . .

At one point Winston delivered a rather stirring invocation to natural forces, springs, crossroads, and Ahura Mazda. It reminded me of Prospero's penultimate swansong in *The Tempest:* "Ye elves of hills, brooks, standing lakes, and groves. . . ."

But this was not impressing me on the whole. Or anyone else. Reza and Ghossam had long ago embarked on a conversation that amused the hell out of them. Mr. Yazdani was reading a newspaper. I got the distinct impression that his preposterous video was a facade, so I moved over to sit nearer him. As I did, he turned up the already thundering volume cascading from a virtual wall of crackling cathode ray.

"They cannot hear me," he said from behind his newspaper.

I had my back to them, and, not that I cared, they could not have been able to hear me either, even if they had stopped roaring and braying with laughter and I'd used a bullhorn.

"That is our temple in wideo. Near here but far from *them*. I will show you."

"Eh?"

I could barely hear him.

I asked about the Saveh castle. Yazdani confirmed it dated to around 500 B.C. but insisted it was just a temple.

"Why so remote and impregnable?"

Because what went on in it was not for the eyes of strangers, seemed to be the answer. But remote and dramatic places were part of the faith, too, he added. They helped you appreciate the beauty of God's creations. I sensed he was just guessing about the castle. It didn't sound as if he'd ever actually seen it himself. I pointed out that the temple currently looking like Seurat-on-mescaline an inch from my nose looked nothing like the Saveh one. This, Yazdani whispered, was because it was built much later. Ah-hah! One of Yazdegerd III's daughters, refusing to renounce her faith and fleeing from Muslim hordes, had run toward the mountain, which opened up to protect her. It was the tale Dr. Mort had told me. The temple had been constructed in this same mountain—which made it mid-seventh century A.D. It was as if the Zoroastrians had returned to their early minimalist architecture—where man provided an altar and nature handled the temple—as the faith entered its twilight. But, like the Saveh "castle," this Yazd temple so skillfully blended the natural rock with man-made structures that it was difficult to determine which was which—particularly in this psychedelic pointillist vision.

"They always watching us."

"Who?"

"Muslim. They move near our houses. They lizzen in on phone line—that is why I use this." He indicated a cordless telephone by his chair.

I hated to point out that cordless phones were even easier to tap than regular ones. Any short-wave receiver could pick up conversations a quarter of a mile away. I also seriously wondered if years of drinking his "vodka" had perhaps induced a wee tad of paranoia. But the line between paranoia and caution is very fine, and being a member of a religious minority that comprised something like 0.06 percent of the total population in a revolutionary Islamic theocracy would make anyone overcautious. "A paranoid is someone with all the facts," as William S. Burroughs once observed.

I asked Yazdani if any Parsees ever visited the old country from India. Apparently they did. There was no difference between his form of worship and theirs, he claimed—although experts seem to disagree with him totally on this.

"Recently," he added, "a Russian scientist from the Azerbaijan told me he is finding evidences of Zardhushti religion beneath ice in Siberia. Before Ice Age our religion has exist. See?"

Picturing woolly mammoths in turbans cavorting around sacred fires, I tried to get a few more details about this astounding revelation—such as what exactly the "evidence" was, who the scientist was, and where this anthropological breakthrough had been published.

"It is vact," was as close as he came to answering. "Scientific *vact.*"

"Did Zoroaster ever visit Siberia?"

"Of courze."

I thought it wise to change the subject. What about Marco Polo's story?

"We have the manuscriptizz no one else has," he replied obscurely. "With truth no one else has writed down there in them. Christian religion we regard as vorm of Zardhushti religion." He sighed with the weariness of centuries. "Once there are temples all over Persia, you know? Yes. Persian empire extend to Vinland and to Vrance. Yes, it is true."

Why had historians never mentioned this?

"It is vact. Ideas they are like the empirezz, no? Ideas spread vurther than map, yes? In Vrance you have guitar people, yes?"

"*Guitar* people?" I could only think of Johnny Halliday.

"*Gattarre* people. The Pobe is burning them."

"Who? The Pope hasn't burnt anyone in years . . ."

"This is long time bevore. Gattarre people, they get burned, towsand of them, for saying pobe religion wrong and evil."

"You mean *Cathars*, yes?"

"Of courze."

I poured myself a shot of Napalm.

RIVALS

It was to Herodian estates in southern France, where the Cathar heresy thrived a millennium ago, that several Bible scholars—including Professor Barbara Thiering—claim Jesus' family fled after events around A.D. 33. Numerous myths, legends, and rumors have sprung up over the centuries linking this area of France to a mystery cloaking the truth about Jesus—a mystery that vanishes into itself the closer it gets to the mysterious life of Jesus himself. It is this end of the mystery that Marco Polo's Magi finally shed light on by opening a window in the walls between Zoroastrianism and Judaeo-Christianity, and then a door that leads into the ancient ideals for a perfect human society expounded and practiced in Vedic India. The light that floods back through illuminates equally the Cathars and others closer to our end of an imposed puzzlement.

Catharism's own origins appear to have sprung from a mixture of Manichaeism—the dualistic doctrine of Mani—several gnostic mystical doctrines, and dense accretions of Zoroastrianism. The rise of Manichaeism, however, proved to be as much of a problem in its homeland as it was to be in Roman Catholic Europe.

The son of a Parthian nobleman, Mani experienced his first vision at the age of twelve, and by the time he was twenty proclaimed himself the fulfillment of the work of Zoroaster, Buddha, and Jesus. An impassioned and deeply committed prophet, he roved the world, preaching from Babylon all the way to China. Having access to the royal Persian court, Mani received the favor of the Sassanian monarch Shapur I and converted numerous influential nobles and statesmen. His status in the court continued until the last days of Bahram I, when a faction of the Magian priesthood, led by one Kartir, grew nervous of his success, opposed his teachings, and began plotting his downfall. Mani was executed by being flayed alive, in Persia around A.D. 276— just when Rome's persecution of the Christians was in full swing. But the influence of his teachings continued, particularly in the eastern reaches of the Roman empire, using various different names and formulations.

Under the emperor Justinian—who had the Nativity mosaics featuring Persian Magi installed at Ravenna and Bethlehem—Manichaeism was decreed a crime punishable by death. But earlier, during the appalling confusion that reigned supreme as the Roman Empire was brought to its knees by northern Barbarians during the late fifth century, the belief that Satan, not God, controlled the physical world had suddenly seemed an eminently reasonable working hypothesis. Thus Manichaeism under various guises spread like wildfire, only to submerge and resurface in the Gothic land once called Moesia, now Bulgaria, during the tenth century. By this time it had accumulated more mystical baggage collected during its seven-hundred-year trip from Persia.

Yet Roman orthodoxy felt sufficiently threatened by the Cathars to want them off the planet. In 1181, Pope Innocent III managed to put together a Crusade against the heretics with an army 30,000 strong. Countless numbers were tortured into confessing heresy, then consigned to the flames of the stake. Others died after prolonged sieges or in pitched battles. But the fortress at Montségur, repository of the legendary Cathar treasure, the "lost" gospels, and perhaps the Holy Grail itself, held out until March 1, 1244—the year Muslim armies captured Jerusalem—defended by a hard core of five hundred believers. This last stand strongly resembles the Roman siege of Essene Zealots at the desert fortress of Masada in A.D. 73. The Cathar treasure was supposedly lowered out to safety by rope. It then vanished forever. Perhaps. Three hundred Cathars chose to surrender and face the consequences. The remaining two hundred were burned alive by the noble forces of the Roman Church. And with the war on Catharism, the Inquisition was born. Many would now argue that this failed to destroy heresy but succeeded in destroying the Roman Church's ambitions for total control of Europe and then the world.

BEDTIME

"Lezz go, azzhole!" complained Reza.

Predictably, the video ended with a virtual earthquake as Richard Strauss' *Also Sprach Zarathustra* simulated the moment of Creation, and the sun set over bonfires, loving couples, and a flock of large birds . . . followed by descending numbers on film leader in reverse.

Yazdani mumbled something in his servile voice.

"He wants you to stay here and fuck his daughters," my minder translated.

I rolled my eyes pointedly, telling Reza to thank Mr. Yazdani kindly for his offer, but I did not wish to impose on his hospitality. Reza managed this in three words.

As we reached the Paykan, Ghossam groaned dramatically. Chronic indigestion, I thought, but it was not. The driver pointed at his front right tire, shaking his head in disbelief. The tire looked as if it had melted into a treacly pool on the sandy road. A flat.

"Sheet!" Reza consoled his buddy. "How could fucken *that* happen?"

"Maybe because the tire should have been thrown away five years ago?" I suggested.

Ghossam was already burrowing in the trunk, flinging out pieces of a jack and some wrenches. Mr. Yazdani came over to offer his condolences, reacting with exaggerated sorrow at the sight of the dead tire, but flashing his twinkly eyes at me. Did he have something to do with the puncture? I wondered.

Deciding to take the incident as an omen, and unwilling to wait through yet more trauma surgery on the Paykan, I told Reza I would stay at Yazdani's after all. He glared at me furiously, then pretended he was joking.

"You fuck his Zoroastrian daughters. Then he keel you and burn you on the Ahuuuurah Mazdaaaah fires," he told me, adding more curtly, "Better you come with us."

"See you in the morning," I said, walking back into Yazdani's house.

"Make heem very angry," Yazdani stated in a satisfied tone, turning his deadbolts and slotting in his chains behind us.

You're always safe in a Zoroastrian house.

I hoped this wasn't one of those ironic proverbs.

"Now we can talk," said Yazdani, pulling the stopper from his Venetian vodka decanters. "They repord everyting."

"What is there to report?"

He filled two goblets, handing me one.

"They like us gone."

He was already fairly gone by now.

I tossed my vodka into a flower pot when he looked away.

There appeared to be no concrete grounds for his paranoia about Islamic authority—apart from a history of persecution that technically ended in 1882 with the repeal of a tax on Zoroastrians. They were before then generally referred to as *gabars*, "infidels," and obliged to wear undyed white wool garments, forced to ride mules not horses, which they even had to dismount if a Muslim rode by. That sort of thing.

Yet during the struggles for reform in the late nineteenth century it was Muslim sects like the Ba'hai that were made scapegoats and purged, not the Zoroastrians, who were admittedly marginalized as a presence in Iranian society all the same.

Since the Islamic Revolution, however, there seemed to have been no serious incidents of persecution that Yazdani could name. As I could attest myself, they were represented in the Majlis. It was not enough representation, Yazdani complained, but considering they were a minority of possibly less than 40,000 in a country of over 60 million, the last of the Zoroastrians could hardly expect much more. I understood his fears, but in reality they amounted to little more than the fears of, say, Koreans in New York. There were petty incidents, occasional brutality, name-calling, idle threats, problems between children, and a sense of general discrimination—but nothing to indicate a looming holocaust.

What there was, however, I sensed increasingly as we spoke, could best be described as a communal malaise, a mass depression caused by the unspoken knowledge that everyone was clinging to something whose time had passed, clinging to it sentimentally and also out of pure habit.

Yazdani's knowledge of his faith and its place in history was pitifully bare. It was his identity that concerned him, not his religion. Behind all he said lurked a hopeless nationalism: Iran for the Mazdeans! It was not going to happen.

Before long I decided that it was futile trying to keep the conversation on the topic of Zoroastrian history, let alone Marco Polo's Magi, so I claimed weariness. Yazdani invited me to look through his library whenever I wished, then showed me to the guest room.

It was bare, almost Zen-like. This and the silence were a delicious relief.

Lying in the dark for a while fully dressed, I thought over the events of a very long day. Exhilaration replaced weariness. When the house was sound asleep, I returned to the sitting room and started to look through Yazdani's bookshelves.

"Without Zoroaster there would be no Christ. He was the bridge and the Romans burnt it . . ."

Chapter Seven

A Zoroastrian Notebook

Now these two spirits, which are twins, revealed
themselves at first in a vision. Their two ways
of thinking, speaking, and acting were the better
and the bad.
Between these two ways the wise choose rightly,
fools not so.
And then when these two spirits first met, they
created both life and not-life, and that there
should be at the last the worst existence for the
followers of the Lie, but, for the followers of
Truth, the best dwelling. Of the two spirits, the
one who follows the Lie chose doing the worst
things; the Most Bounteous Spirit who is clad in
the hardest stones chose truth, as do they who
will willingly come with true actions to meet
Ahura Mazda.

—the Gathas of Zoroaster
(Yasna 30. 3–5)

He created man to have dominion over the earth and
made for him two spirits, that he might walk with
them until the appointed time of his visitation;
they are the spirits of Truth and the Lie. In the
abode of light are the origins of Truth and from the
source of darkness are the origins of the Lie.

—The Manual of Discipline, one of the Dead Sea Scrolls

According to Pliny, the great philosopher Hermippus, who lived during the third century B.C., had studied some 2,000,000 verses composed by Zoroaster. Tabari and Masudi, the Arab historians, claim that Zoroastrian texts were copied on 12,000 cowhides. In the Indian Parsee tradition, the prophet wrote twenty-one Nasks or volumes, and we're told these dealt with religion, philosophy, ethics, medicine, as well as various other sciences. Of two copies known to exist, one was burned by Alexander's armies and the other sent to Greece, where it was translated, then seemingly lost. No one knows which Greek work may in fact be the translation, though, but one most certainly is—and possibly several are—since the Nasks covered what was thought to be the entire range of human knowledge.

It was no trifling spiritual culture that the Magi emerged from, but rather one that still towered in wisdom above the others of its day—which is perhaps why those others became so intent on marginalizing it once the means were within their grasp. What took the Magi to Bethlehem was not anything remotely like superstition, and certainly no symbolic renunciation of their so-called pagan ways—as their presence at the Nativity was presented by the Church.

The ancient mythic difference between Christianity and Zoroastrianism is said to be that the latter granted Evil an eternal origin but denied it an eternal existence in the future, depicting its end as a melting into the effulgence of limitless unending light; while Christianity reversed man's condition, denying to Evil an eternal source but granting it an iron, unalterable immortality. Yet Truth cannot differ from Truth. The journey of the Magi was, in a way, an attempt to make sure that the Lie did not become an ersatz Truth.

THE PROPHET

Nothing is known of Zoroaster the man beyond his vision itself, whose light, in Mary Boyce's beautiful phrase, "obliterated for him his own shadow upon the earth." This vision has survived in seventeen of his hymns, the *Gathas*. It is, however, worth repeating the traditional account of the prophet's life—since there is no doubt that he lived one, and lived it under very human conditions, too.

According to tradition, Zoroaster lived "258 years before Alexander," which is taken to mean before Alexander the Great's invasion of Persia in 330 B.C., and, owing to confusion over whether the dating refers to his birth, death, or the beginning of his mission, places him somewhere in the fifth or sixth centuries—making him a contemporary of the Buddha and Pythagoras, among others. One legend even has Pythagoras studying at the feet of Zoroaster; another postulates that Zoroaster was in fact the Buddha; and another associates him with Abraham.

Avoiding the more overt embellishments on the few facts that exist about his life in the internal evidence of the *Gathas*, it would seem that Zoroaster experienced the first of several potent visions when he was thirty. His subsequent teaching clearly aroused considerable hostility, since he was forced to flee the region of his birth for the area that is now much of Baluchistan on the southeastern borders of Iran—implying possibly, but not necessarily, that he was originally from one of the western provinces. In exile, however, he converted a local ruler, King Hystaspes or Vishtaspa, becoming a figure of some importance in the affairs of court. Most accounts have him married with a daughter and two sons. Tradition also generally agrees that he was murdered at the age of seventy-seven.

That's it.

With so little hard evidence from which to work, some scholars go with the tradition just to have a background, others work with what little evidence there is to produce a background. The phrase "some scholars" is also misleading: there are perhaps four scholars of Zoroastrianism who merit any serious attention. Out of these four, who disagree with each other entirely on almost every issue, there are two major British scholars—Richard Zaehner and Mary Boyce—who dominate the field. They have been slugging it out for thirty-odd years now, and can often seem like Ormazd and Ahriman themselves: because only one of them can be close to the truth. Few areas of scholarship virtually demand that one takes sides, yet here—unless the tradition is accepted at face value—one is forced to get in line behind either Zaehner or Boyce.

Since Mary Boyce bothered to live among the Zoroastrians of Yazd for some years, and since she comes at the subject with more intuition and sympathy, we're going to take her side. Richard Zaehner, a leading Vedic authority, traps himself with conventional chronologies and, ironically, cannot thus make the essential connection between Zoroaster and the Vedic Religion as significantly as Boyce can. Without this connection, Zoroastrianism is made as if to appear from a void and already denied a future. It is also denied a past by Zaehner. He also chooses to accept Zurvanism as a development of Zoroastrianism, rather than as the spin-off cult it surely was.

The most ancient compositions in any language, it would seem, the hymns of the Rig-Veda constantly refer to Truth as the indivisible unity of all creation, warning that language itself can and will fragment the universe, drawing the curtains between humanity and absolute reality. Zoroaster's teachings, arriving when Vedism had been splintered through the prism of Hinduism, can thus be viewed as a first attempt to deal with a new or partial kind of reality imposed by the divisive effect of language on the human mind and the concomitant disintegration of a just and harmonious society. His message is an objective truth as something seen through a glass darkly, yet it is also one that is initially determined to halt the process of fragmentation that had turned the nondualistic purity of Vedism into Hinduism's bewildering polytheism, where what had been purely spiritual became more and more obscured by coat after coat of pure emotion.

Mary Boyce is cognizant of this, aware that the language of Zoroaster's hymns, the *Gathas*, is archaic and close to that of the Rig-Veda—therefore about 1700 B.C. onward—and portrays the people of Zoroaster's tribe as a Stone Age society. She thus hazards a "reasoned conjecture that Zoroaster lived some time between 1700 and 1500 B.C.": 1,200 years earlier than the traditional view, and placing him around the time of Abraham.

Zoroaster refers to himself in the *Gathas* as a *zaotar*, a fully qualified priest. Training for the Indo-Iranian priesthood at this period began at about the age of seven and was carried out orally. There was no knowledge of writing. Indeed, the *Gathas* were not actually committed to writing at all until during the third Persian empire, ruled by the Sasanian dynasty—around the second century A.D. In other words, they survived orally for nearly two thousand years.

Zoroaster further describes himself in his hymns as a *vaedemna*—"one who knows"—an initiate possessed of divinely inspired wisdom, which implies that he continued seeking higher knowledge from those who could teach him after his priestly training was concluded. Like the Buddha and countless other masters within the Vedic-Hindu tradition, Zoroaster spent many years in a wandering quest for truth. These years seem to have made him acutely conscious of the suffering endured by those unable to defend themselves in a violent, lawless, tribal world, and he became filled with a deep longing for justice, for a divine law to be established for strong and weak alike, so that order and tranquillity could prevail, and all men and women be able to pursue a life of goodness and truth in peace.

Then, at the age of thirty, he experienced his great revelation, which opens this chapter, after ritual purification in the waters of a river—in much the same way as Jesus received the Holy Spirit after his baptism in the Jordan. Emerging from the pure element, water, Zoroaster saw a shining being on the river bank, and this being led him into the presence of Ahura Mazda, who was accompanied by five other radiant figures, before whom the prophet "did not see his own shadow upon the earth, owing to their great light." It was from this numinous heptad of deities that he obtained the transforming vision, and with it his life's mission.

This was the first of several occasions that Zoroaster saw Ahura Mazda in visions, or felt conscious of the divine presence, or heard its voice summoning him. His surrender to the greater will is then absolute; he announces to his God: "For this I was set apart as yours from the beginning . . . While I have power and strength, I shall teach men to seek truth, order, and righteousness [*asha*]."

The Indo-Iranian tradition would have easily accepted all of this, since it already held Mazda to be the greatest of the three Ahuras, or gods—much as Brahma was senior deity in the Hindu trinity—but Zoroaster went much further. In what can only be viewed as a reforming attempt to keep something of the original Vedic purity, he proclaimed Ahura Mazda to be the one uncreated God, existing eternally, and Creator of all else that is good, including all the other beneficent deities.

The terms "good" and "evil" are of course loaded, especially within the Judaeo-Christian tradition, which gives evil far more credit than it gets from most Eastern religions. In Hinduism, there is no real concept of a devil or a hell. Just as darkness is not the opposite of light but the absence of light, evil is viewed as a mere absence of good caused by ignorance and bad karma.

Zoroaster's terms are not "good" and "evil," but rather "truth-justice-order-righteousness" versus "the Lie." The consequences of following "the Lie" are certainly dire; but, being simply a lack of truth, the Lie has no substance or future, and certainly poses no ultimate threat to Truth, the war between them presented as a cosmic drama whose purpose is to strengthen Truth, not to question whether it will emerge victorious. These are fundamental differences, and in them there is much to explain the difference between Eastern and Western civilization. Zoroaster also does much to explain the relationship between Creator and creation, or how pure spirit operates within pure matter, by envisaging a system somewhere between the excessively anthropomorphised and emotional Hindu cosmology, and the overly complex and intellectual Jewish Cabala.

Zoroaster's doctrines were lucid and comprehensive, leaving little scope for "heresy" or schism in more important matters. Yet the Zurvanite "heresy" grew from one of the prophet's most striking innovations: the concept of history having an end. Zurvan, which simply means "time," was introduced as a father for the two warring spirits, but quickly assumed an importance that obscured Zoroaster's original doctrine. Rather than the field upon which the drama of creation unfolded, time became, in effect, both figure and field, both cause and effect. Zurvanism eventually imploded into the black hole of its own convoluted density, but nonetheless it was a profound and damaging heresy, which was greatly to weaken Zoroastrianism in its coming struggles with Christianity and Islam. "Ormazd and Ahriman are brothers," declared a Zurvanite polemicist; but this statement betrayed Zoroaster's fundamental doctrine that good and evil are utterly separate and distinct by both origin and nature. The heresy also diminished the grandeur of Ahura Mazda, once proclaimed as uncreated God, the only divine being worthy of worship, whose existence is eternal. Tiresome speculations and ridiculous myths also confused the original clear teachings of the faith. Moreover, the Zurvanites' increasing pre-occupations with time's inexorable decrees and with fate clouded over the fundamental Zoroastrian doctrine of the existence of free will, the power of each individual to shape his or her destiny through the exercise of choice.

The gulf between the two doctrines is in fact so wide that the toleration and survival of Zurvanism can only be accounted for by the fact that it gained some influential followers among the Sasanian royal family, who consciously maintained Archaemenid traditions in various ways. It is thus possible to suggest that the later Archaemenid kings set this example, and, seduced by certain Magian sects, established the heresy in western Iran. From here it went on to exert enormous influence on Essene and gnostic groups (for whom the concepts of Three Times, the remote First Cause, and the inferior nature of the Creator of this world, were fundamental doctrines). Once established, the continued assistance of royal favor evidently ensured the survival of Zurvanism for several centuries, and—despite persistent rejection by other factions of Zoroastrianism—it only disappeared finally a few hundred years after the coming of Islam.

THE PURITY

Few religions have been so ill-served by their own priests and followers as Zoroastrianism. The original clarity of Zoroaster's teachings makes it hard to understand why subsequent generations would have wished to tamper with them, especially when the result produced mere obfuscation. With the doctrine of the Three Times there is a symmetry to the process of Creation, not to mention an assurance that all the sorrows and strivings of the present time of Mixture are part of the battle against the Lie. Zoroaster thus not only saw a noble purpose for humanity but also offered humankind a reasoned explanation for everything endured in this life. It is not the Creator who is responsible for the sufferings of his creatures here: the Hostile Spirit brings on all afflictions.

The great affliction, of course, is death, which, during the time of Mixture, forces souls from this material world into a kind of spiritual limbo, where they await the end of time. According to Zoroaster, as each spirit departs it is judged on what it has achieved in this life for the cause of goodness. He was the first to teach that women as well as men, servants as well as masters, may hope to attain Paradise, for the old physical barrier of pagan days, the "Bridge of the Separator," becomes in his vision a place of moral judgment, where each soul has to depend not on its power or the value of sacrificial offerings made in the life left behind, but solely upon its own ethical and moral triumphs. Much like descriptions from the Egyptian Book of the Dead, the soul's deeds, words, and thoughts are weighed in the scales of justice, the good on one side, the bad on the other. If the good outweigh the bad, the soul is escorted by a beautiful girl—the personification of its own conscience—across the broad bridge and up into Paradise. But if . . . well, then the bridge contracts to the width of a razor blade, and a hideous old hag tackles the soul as it tries to cross, seizes it in her scaly arms and hurtles with it down to hell, "the dwelling place of Worst Purpose." Zoroaster seems to have invented the concept of hell, a place of torment presided over by Angra Mainyu, where the wicked endure a "long age of misery, of darkness, ill food, and the crying of woe." Hell: even the food is bad. There is also a sort of purgatory, for those few whose good and bad balance out, where they suffer a bleak, gray existence, devoid of either joy or sorrow.

Just as the pure Vedic concept of heaven is a place where the good are punished, as it were, so Zoroaster's Paradise is not a realm of complete bliss. Such a state cannot come during the time of Mixture, and souls there must wait for the final reward until Separation arrives, when—in the words of a third-century A.D. Zoroastrian Pahlavi text—all the deities and humankind will be together, and "every place will resemble a garden in spring, in which there are all kinds of trees and flowers . . . and it will be entirely the creation of Ormazd." Ahura Mazda's name contracted across the centuries along with his role.

Zoroaster was the first to teach the doctrines of an individual judgment, Heaven and Hell, the future resurrection of the body, the general Last Judgment, and life everlasting for the reunited soul and body. These doctrines went on to become familiar articles of faith to much of humankind, through the extensive borrowings by Judaism, Christianity, and Islam; yet it is still in Zoroastrianism that they have their most complete logical coherence, since Zoroaster insisted both on the inherent goodness of material creation—and thus of the physical body—

and on the unwavering impartiality of divine justice. According to the prophet's teachings, an individual's salvation depended entirely on the sum of his thoughts, words, and deeds, and there could be no intervention, whether compassionate or capricious, by any divine being to alter this. Thus, belief in the Day of Judgment had its full awful significance, with each man having to bear the responsibility for the fate of his own soul, as well as sharing in responsibility for the fate of the world. It was a noble and strenuous gospel, one which called for both courage and resolution on the part of those willing to receive it.

THE PRIESTS

Later Zoroastrianism becomes crowded with lower hierarchies of the *yazatas* or spirits and *daevas* or demons, much as Christian theology became preoccupied with the names and functions of archangels and angels, devils and demons. But as late as the ninth century A.D., it is apparent that the prophet's original philosophy was still understood by the priesthood.

It is also evident that Zoroaster was teaching a philosophy, not starting a religion. Indeed, he was more intent on ridding Iran of its debased post-Vedic beliefs, denouncing blood offerings and at least one aspect of the *haoma* or *Soma* ritual. In order to do this, it seems, he retained and elevated the fire sacrifice, making flame the symbol of Truth and Order, of God's essence manifest in the cosmos.

It was the Magi, not Zoroaster, who turned the teachings of his *Gathas* into a religion. Magians, as they're also known, were the priestly caste of the old religion—Iranian Brahmans—and it would seem that their reception of the religious reforms implicit in Zoroaster's teachings was understandably mixed at first. In fact, one sect of Magians probably murdered him—if he was murdered. And the priestly caste appears to have remained divided even after adopting— or co-opting—Zoroaster's philosophy, this division or divisions affecting the course of not just the new religion but also of Iran's history, much of which was directed behind the scenes by a priesthood more powerful than the monarchy. It is at the point where Zoroastrianism probably entered it fully that Iran's history also starts to affect the history of Western civilization. With the empire of Cyrus the Great, the doctrines of Zoroaster spread rapidly, reaching out as far as the borders of China to the east and westward throughout the Mediterranean world. Though not as visible or boisterous as other faiths, Zoroastrianism's influence was still profound enough in its own subtle way to remain in one form or another in all the places it ever reached to this very day.

※

Chapter Eight

THE FIRE TEMPLE

Overcome doubts and unrighteous desires with reason, overcome greed with contentment, anger with serenity, envy with benevolence, want with vigilance, strife with peace, falsehood with truth.

—*The Teachings of the Magi*

THE END OF THE WORLD

It was some time after dawn when I awoke, slumped over Yazdani's books. I wiped a trace of drool from the page that had been my pillow and crept up to bed.

We had 374 years, nine months and eleven days left, according to *Dr. West's Tables of Zoroastrian Chronology*, some of which I found printed in reverse on my cheek when I later went to wash. The history of the world was the history of God's conflict with the devil. There were four periods, each of three thousand years. In the first two periods God and the devil prepared their forces, in the third the battle began, and in the final period the devil would be conclusively defeated.

Dr. E. W. West had calculated 9630 B.C. as the beginning of the first millennium of Zoroastrian time, when the Fravashis—the primary ideas of the "good creation"—were formed, remaining "insensible and motionless for 3,000 years." In 6630 B.C., the spiritual body of Zoroaster was "framed together, and remains 3,000 years with the archangels, while the primeval man and ox exist undisturbed in the world, because the evil spirit is confounded and powerless." In 3630 B.C., the evil spirit rushed "into the creation on New Year's Day," destroying the primeval ox and distressing "Gayomart, the primeval man." Here a note added cryptically that "Z. appears to remain with the archangels for 2,969 years longer." Had something gone wrong? According to Dr. West, Zoroaster was not born until 660 B.C., the same year that "Vohumano and Ashavahishto descend into the world with a stem of Hom [*haoma* or *Soma*]."

The tenth millennium, naturally, did not begin until 630 B.C., when Zoroaster went "forth to his conference with the sacred beings on the 45th day of the 31st year of Vishtasp's reign." This conference went on for two years, wrote Dr. West. Not much then happened until 591 B.C., when "About this time the Avesta is written by Jamasp from the teaching of Z." Jamasp had been Vishtasp's chief minister and one of Zoroaster's first converts. Eight years later, however, in 583, "Z. passes away, or is killed, aged seventy-seven years and forty days, on the 41st day of the year." Ten years after that the "arrival of the religion is known in all regions."

For something supposedly worked out two and a half millennia ago, this was not bad. According to Zoroastrian chronology, time began around the end of the Last Ice Age, which is generally agreed to be circa 10,000 B.C.—so you can't argue with 9630 B.C. This first quarter is essentially the ascent of contemporary humankind, and takes us through the so-called Hunter-Gatherer Period. The second, 6630 B.C. on, covers the Neolithic revolution and the widespread development of agriculture. The end of the first two preparatory quarters, and thus the beginning of God's conflict with the devil, takes us to 3630 B.C., pretty much the recorded start and simultaneous zenith of Sarasvati-Indus-Valley-Vedic India and Old Kingdom Egypt—that is, the dawn of religion and civilization in the forms that we now know them. The entire third quarter covers the gradual decline of Vedic-Hindu India and Egypt and the dissemination of their spiritual science around the world.

The last quarter, the period of intensest battle between God and devil, thus began with the traditional date for Zoroaster's enlightenment. This tenth millennium—630 B.C. to the end of A.D. 368—also included the birth of Buddhism, Jainism, Confucianism, Judaism and Christianity, as well as the philosophies of Plato, Pythagoras, then Plotinus, the Gnostics, and neo-Platonists. It saw the final collapse of Egypt, then the rise and fall of the Assyrian, Babylonian, ancient Persian, Greek, and Roman empires. The ancient world vanished entirely.

The eleventh millennium began in A.D. 369. As far as I know, however, the only significant event of 369 entailed the Picts and Scots getting driven out of Britain by Theodosius. But surrounding decades definitely mark the ascendancy of the northern Barbarians that soon led to the final sack of Rome, as well as the start of a "Holy" Roman Empire based in Byzantium which effectively destroyed the teachings of Jesus and re-created Christianity as an imperial religion and political tool of mass control. This period also saw the beginning of Manichaeism in Iran and its spread into Europe, along with the rise of the mainly Zoroastrian Sasanian Dynasty, which would reign until the Arab invasion in the eighth century, a point marking the permanent decline of Zoroaster's influence and his faith. The rest of the millennium saw the rise of Christian Europe, the birth of Islam and its concomitant empire stretching continuously from Senegal to India and discontinuously from Indonesia to the Philippines. Toward the close of this thousand years there were the Crusades, the age of the great Cathedrals, the end of Confucian rule in China, the Black Death, the Mayan golden age, the seeds of the Reformation, the last widespread resurfacing—with the Cathars—of Gnostic-Manichaeism until its hybrid modern form as one of the mainstays of our new age, and of course the waning of the Middle Ages.

Thus the final millennium began in 1369, just as bubonic plague had finished reducing the planet's population by a quarter, an event whose social and economic repercussions ushered in first the Renaissance and then the modern era, of which the rest of course is history.

The end of Zoroastrian chronology's fourth and final period—in fact the end of time—should therefore come before or perhaps at the stroke of midnight on 31 December 2368. One assumes that God will have defeated Satan a little earlier, because otherwise those last days will be nerve-wracking Dr. West, however, for reasons he does not explain, states that the last millennium will end with 2398 — 12,030 years since time began. Perhaps this bonus thirty years is so that whoever is around then can briefly enjoy a devil-free world?

I'm sorry that I'll probably have to miss it, I thought, drifting off to sleep, reassured that the devil would at least be finally defeated, but still wondering what happened after that. The world, it was nice to know, belonged to God himself. Thus Zoroastrians did not believe matter to be evil. Indeed it was the devil, not human beings, who was in an alien and material world. The devil could have no material form, apparently, but remained in the world parasitically, struggling in vain to destroy God's work. Get a *life*, I urged him, yawning . . .

HE'LL BE BACK . . .

> Just as there was an incarnation of Lucifer in the flesh and an incarnation of Christ in the flesh, so, before only a part of the third millennium of the post-Christian era has elapsed, there will be, in the West, an actual incarnation of Ahriman: Ahriman in the flesh . . . The Ahrimanic incarnation will be greatly furthered if men fail to establish a free and independent spiritual life and allow it to remain entangled in the economic or political life . . . To the Ahrimanic power a free spiritual life would denote a kind of darkness, and men's interest in it, a burning, raging fire . . .
>
> —lectures by Rudolf Steiner in November 1919

"They will be soon here," Mr. Yazdani informed me. "Watch. I am right, you will see."

He meant Reza and Ghossam, Ahriman's little helpers.

Mrs. Yazdani, inquiring if I would like breakfast, proceeded to ferry in another dinner—or perhaps the same dinner—until the table resembled a restaurant buffet lunch counter.

"Eat vastly," Yazdani urged me. "I have arrange for you to meet our high priezd at the temple."

"Fanff-few."

"Pardon?"

"Thank you."

"No, no. Eat!"

As we stepped out beneath a flawless sky of Dufy blue and dazzling lemon chrome sunlight I was ready to peel off a few layers of clothing, until I noticed that the air was still several degrees below freezing. But Yazd looked so different by day: massicot and ocher, sand and plastered mudbrick everywhere. The color had been turned back on. It felt more like Morocco than Iran for a moment.

The Peugeot must have mysteriously sprouted an extra seat overnight, but just as I was about to sit on it the assiduous Paykan swerved into sight amid clouds of dust, horn tooting, engine coughing, and a head thrust through the passenger window yelling,

"You get the juicy Zoro-cheeks, eh? Har-harrr!"

"See?" said Yazdani, depressed.

"He's unique. Iran should export him."

"Ex-*cute* heem."

THE LOWER HIGH PRIEST

The temple was not far from Yazd's central square, secluded from the street in an immaculately maintained garden behind high walls. It had clearly been constructed within the last fifty years, and from outside it looked more like a school or community hall. I was, after all, expecting something *from the dawn of time . . . when the earth was young*. I thought we were going to visit the temple in last night's video, and thus also expected mountains at the very least.

When Yazdani unlocked a door at the end of a high-walled side street, I assumed that it led to his office or storeroom—that he needed something he kept there. A map? The high priest? The door, however, opened into a little oasis of unrestrained flora, a secret jungle of malachite and jade greens spattered with crimson, orpiment, Persian and

Prussian blue, cadmium, carotene, and heliotrope. Buds glowed like fairy lights, burst into flaming stars, or hung with the majesty of planets in their leafy void.

"What a beautiful garden, Mr. Yazdani."

"Our communi-dee take mudge care with it," he whispered.

"Fucken weeds," grumbled Reza. "What he do, azzhole? Brainwazz you all night?"

"No, this is love . . ."

We skirted the community center, arriving at its main entrance. This was definitely a temple, although it looked more like a set facade from *Cleopatra* that had been grafted onto the community center. A flight of six steps led up to six pillars supporting five basket handle arches above which lay the busiest entablature conceivable. A jutting frieze of guttas and rounded dentils soared to a cornice of half-relief Hom flowers drooping in splayed arches on either side of a prodigious sort of acroterion showing an anthropomorphic Ahura Mazda with twenty-foot wings extending on either side of him, his robe fanning out in segments exactly like tail feathers. In the precise center of these colossal wings was a chrome yellow hoop held beneath his left elbow and framing a peace-sign-like pattern in three groups of three bands on his robe, the upper shaft invisible behind a broad drooping sleeve. In his outstretched left hand he held an identical but far smaller hoop resting above the wing he faced and supported against the spread palm of his right hand. Curling down on either side of his robe beneath the wings were two snaky tendrils.

It was almost identical to the friezes above many Egyptian temples, where the figure of God would have usually been replaced by a solar disk supported by serpents between the same huge wings. The sun was Ra, Light, Truth, and God, ruler of the solar system. The flying serpent symbolized the conquest of duality: serpents don't fly, and alone, wriggling on the ground, they represent the lower nature, dual, divided, deadly. This symbolism was already ancient when the Book of Genesis borrowed it. The vulture and cobra of pharaonic crowns similarly represented not just the union of Upper and Lower Egypt but the perfected man, the royal man, the being who has unified his lower and higher natures and transformed himself.

Here Ahura Mazda had become a phoenixlike bird—which is reborn from its own ashes like the great cycles of the year, life and death, astrological ages, precession of the equinoxes, and so on. The phoenix is another major Egyptian symbol. Here it assumed the place of the sun god, who was still present, though, symbolized by the yellow hoop. But the smaller hoop was more puzzling. The moon perhaps? or the lesser spirit of the Lie? That both were held by the god's left arm and hand, however, the smaller one guided by his right, seemed to suggest his easy control over both with the base, material or left side of his nature, the one that here literally faced the world (the Latin *sinistra*, "left," gives us "sinister"). And there was no question that the serpents were still present in those two curling yellow tails, which even looked as if they emerged from beneath God's robe to form the two yellow circles. All was azure or turquoise and chrome yellow: sky and sand, heaven and earth—the colors of Egypt, too.

But God's stylized beard and pill-box hat showed the profound influence of Assyrian winged sphinxes as well; although they were human-headed winged beasts and this was quite clearly not an angel but a bird with a human torso, something quite unique in world mythologies. Yet the overall look of this image was proof enough alone for me that there had been far more of Egypt than India in later Zoroastrianism.

"It is beautiful, yes?" asked Yazdani when Reza was out of earshot.

"What are those circles?"

"It is design."

"Yes, but . . ."

I gave up.

An old hobo clad in a threadbare overcoat, with a few tattered sweaters beneath it and a frayed orange wool toque pulled down over his ears approached us—probably wanting a hand-out. Yazdani spoke to him, beckoning Reza over.

"This is the fucken high priest."

"Sure, Reza."

"Honest," he said, stifling a giggle. "It's Ahuuuura Mazzzzda's high priest. It *is*!"

"Tell him I'm deeply honored to meet him."

I extended a hand and the high priest of Ahura Mazda allowed me to hold for half a second what felt like a stiff, frozen leather glove.

"He wants to show you the temple," Reza announced.

"Tell him I'm—"

"Yeah-yeah-yeah . . ."

There were double doors on either side of the veranda's rear wall beyond the pillars. Only one door on the left seemed to be open. Inside I found a lobby that reminded me of an old public library or small local museum. A huge mahogany display case contained an equally huge hand-written volume opened to reveal two pages of neat Persian script and a tempest of festering brown, cloudlike stains that suggested the book had once spent some time under water. Opposite this and framed in the same gleaming wood was a near-life-size oil portrait of Zoroaster. Posed exactly the same way as the etched-glass paintings in Yazdani's home, the prophet's details were, however, a little easier to study here.

The main feature of this lobby, as Reza forced me to see by literally dragging me away from the painting, was a six-by-six-foot square of inch-thick plate glass, concealed behind shutters that the high priest had just opened. Beyond the glass, in a bare room lined with large marble tiles, was an urn about five feet high with a diameter of four feet, cast in solid bronze or brass. It stood on a stone altar identical to the one in Kashan but in miniature and without the dome. This in turn stood within a square formed by a deep grove cut into the marble floor. The urn was shaped like an inverted bell with two handles linked by a thick stem to its base, which was an identical bell a third of the size. Protruding from the urn were the smoldering ends of two logs: the sacred fire of Ahura Mazda itself.

The high priest spoke in a crackly old voice.

"He says cup is three thousand year old," Reza told me, bored.

"Cup?"

"What the fucken fire's in, azzhole . . ."

The high priest spoke again.

"But the fire's only fifteen hundred years old."

"Only?"

"They keep it burning 'cozz they don't have any matches. How should *I* know why these azzholes do what they does?"

Three thousand years old! Looking at the monolithic piece of bronze or brass casting, I could not help thinking about the vessels cast by Hiram—or the Jinn—for Solomon's Temple.

"Where did the ur . . . *cup* come from?"

"He says maybe Persepolis. He doesn't know."

"And the fire?"

That definitely came from Persepolis, lit from a very special source of fire in the fourth century A.D. and kept burning ever since, even during its long journey from the old capital to Yazd. Perhaps it had been lit originally during the reign of one of the later Zoroastrian kings, Bahram IV? Bahram was also the name for the "king" of Zoroastrian sacred fires, the one used for major rituals like the Hom sacrifice. Was the fire named after the king, or the king after the fire?

"He say king had same name as fire. This is the King Bahram Four fire, he says—whatever that means . . ."

"Ask him if the urn came from King Solomon's Temple."

"He doesn't know . . ."

Reza went to light a Zagros, but was quickly informed he couldn't do this in a temple.

"Fucken *fire*-worshippers and you can't fucken smoke! *Azzholes!*"

I asked if it were possible to take a closer look inside the fire shrine. It was certainly not possible. Only the priests were allowed there, and even they wore surgeons' masks to prevent their breath from polluting Ahura Mazda's sacred flame.

Beyond the shrine, out on the far side, I could see an area with seats, obviously where the congregation sat. I wasn't allowed in there, either.

There was something profoundly impressive about this huge vessel with its one-and-a-half-thousand-year-old fire. Even the glowing embers seemed different from those of ordinary fires. Alone in its chamber, the symbolic urn emanated a grandeur and majesty that defied expression. Something sacred dwelt in that shrine, something belonging more to its own holy realm than this one.

Q & A

"He will answer your questions now," Reza informed me.

The old high priest and I sat on the top step below the teeming portico and its winged deity.

"What's his name?"

"Hormouz Farkhani."

I asked about festivals, hearing the main ones were at harvest time and spring, which in Iran coincides with New Year's Day. I would have been surprised to find Zoroastrians did not have festivals at harvest and spring, attempting to probe further about other holy days and what took place.

"There is different ceremonies in different cities."

"Ask what goes on at these ceremonies."

"He says there is some refreshment served and the people they watch plays."

At first I thought Reza was not translating properly, but a glance at the old high priest suggested otherwise.

"What are the ritual prayers?"

"He says there is the praying and the praising and also the asking for forgiveness."

I requested an example of such prayers.

"He says he cannot translate them."

"Why?"

"He's too fucken stupid . . ."

Next I inquired about *Hom* or haoma. It took ten minutes for the high priest to work out what I meant.

"It is a flower."

"I know *that*, Reza! What effect does it have if eaten?"

"It is the . . . er . . . evergreen bush."

"What narcotic effect does it have?"

"He says they read the Zoroastrian scripture to the flower. Then they beat it up . . ."

"Beat it up!"

"They are pounding it until juice come out." Reza winced.

"*What effect does it have?*"

"He say it heal the spiritual and physical pain."

"How?"

"He say it is like acetaminophen."

"Yeah? So why don't they just use aspirin for their ritual?"

"He says Hom plant is sacred to them."

"Why?"

"Because they read it the Avesta book and plant listens then becomes sacred."

"Oh really?"

I changed direction and asked how someone became a Zoroastrian priest, what the qualifications were.

"He says person should be a Zoroastrian."

"Tell him I find that highly unusual."

"But he says it is not essential."

"What isn't?"

"To be Zoroastrian."

"Oh. So what qualifications do you need, then?"

"He says person should do some good doings and read some Zoroastrian books."

"That's *it*?"

"He says yes."

I was beginning to lose my temper. I told Reza to ask him about the symbolic meaning of certain animals in Zoroastrianism, starting with the lion. The high priest seemed baffled, and much explaining was apparently required before I got any answer.

"He say good to drink and also they give as offering to the fire."

"They *drink* lions and sacrifice them on the fire!"

Reza was starting to creak with mirth.

"See," he explained, "lion in Persian is *sheer*—which is same word for 'milk.' I think he talk about milk, no?"

"Well, explain what I mean, then!"

"He says no meaning."

"Lions have no meaning? I see. Ask him about bulls."

"He says the Hindus worship bulls, but he doesn't."

I inquired about Gayomart—the Zoroastrian Adam—and the primeval ox, asking how he interpreted this.

"He says he doesn't have enough information on this."

"Ask him if he's sure he's the high priest."

"I think he's the fucken gardener," Reza confided.

For the first and last time I was inclined to agree with him. We moved on to rams.

"He doesn't think so."

"He doesn't think so *what*?"

"He says there is ram statues in Persepolis from the King Rustam."

"Who the hell was King Rustam?"

"He says big king of Persepolis."

"You sure, Reza?"

"It's what the azzhole says."

"Tell him he might mean Naksh-e-Rostam, which is a *place* near Persepolis, not a king. Is that what he means?"

"He still goes on about King Rustam."

We moved on to the significance of springs, wells, and water in Zoroastrianism.

"He says you must keep clean the water for health."

"Amazing! What *spiritual* significance does it have?"

"He says angel Mittra preserving it."

"What?"

"The fucken water!"

"Who's this Mittra?"

"The Ahura Mazda have six angels, he says. One is Mittra."

We moved on to Marco Polo's Magi. The high priest had never heard this story, or so he claimed. I told him that the Three Kings had been connected with the three sons of Zoroaster by Mary Boyce. What did he know about this?"

"He says that childrens will always tell not believable stories."

"Children? What children?"

"He says those boys who tell you Zardhushti son is kings."

"What bloody *boys*, Reza?"

"Hey, azzhole, you said some crazy boys told you this kings sheet."

"O Lord! *Boyce*, not boys! Mary Boyce. She lived here for two years. He must have met her."

Reza yelped with laughter, repeating "Merry boys, I thought you saying merry boys."

"Tell him she's a famous professor from London University."

"He says London best city in entire world."

"Well, he's wrong about that. What about Zoroaster's sons?"

"He say Zardhushti, he have only two son, one daughter . . ."

The high priest interrupted him.

"He says he can name the three Zardhushti sons for you if you want, your highness."

"I thought he said there were only two sons?"

"He did, azzhole. But he knows the names of three of thems."

The names proved to be Easad Vastar, Orvatad Nar, and Khorshid Chehr—at least this was how Reza suggested spelling them. Since no other scholars agree on spelling—or anything—in Zoroastrianism, they might as well stay as they are.

"What's the meaning of the word 'Yazd'? Ask him."

"He says it is name of this city."

"For Chri— Does it *mean* anything?"

"He says used to be Easad."

"Like the son's name?"

"Same."

"What does that mean?"

"He doesn't know."

"Ask if he's being deliberately evasive or whether he knows less about Zoroastrianism than you."

"Fuck off."

By now a considerable crowd of local youths had gathered at the foot of the temple steps to watch my interview. Obviously there was not much in the way of entertainment available out here in the desert. Yazd had only been linked by a proper road to the rest of Iran a few years back. Still no one visited the place unless they had to, though.

"He says he does not have enough information."

"He doesn't have *any* information! Ask if Zoroastrians are persecuted in Iran."

"He says no. All live in peace now for one hundred and fifty years."

"Does he feel obliged to say that, or is it true?"

"True, he says. No tax now and equal for—"

"One hundred fifty years."

I presumed he meant the "gabar" tax, repealed in 1882. Next I had Reza inquire about the concept of a messiah in Zoroastrianism.

"He doesn't know."

"Ask him again, clearly: messiah, Saviour, Hidden Imam, second coming of Zoroaster, God incarnate. Every religion's got one, tell him . . ."

"Bushida, he says."

"What?"

"They wait for Bushida."

"Can he elaborate a tad?"

"Same as twelfth imam, he says. Bushida will make all religions equal."

"The twelfth imam would presumably do that by making all religions Islam, wouldn't he? Ask him."

"He cannot say. He has no information on this."

"Ask why he thinks that Zoroastrianism was once such an influential religion and is now so . . . minor."

This took some explaining.

"We don't advertise the way we should, he says."

I thought of Yazdani's video. The high priest was right, although "evangelize" was probably what he'd told Reza.

"Where's the oldest surviving temple?"

"He doesn't know. But he says oldest fire is here in Yazd."

"The one we just saw?"

"Yes. He says that is oldest fire of Zardhushti remaining now."

"Thank him for being so incredibly helpful and informative."

THE DRAGON SLAYER

Reza needed lunch, so it was relatively easy to lose him by saying I wasn't hungry. Yazdani and I left the temple grounds through the same back gate, finding the high priest clambering onto an aged red moped out in the alley. The machine sounded like an irate hornet trapped in a soda can as it moved away in a zigzagging path with the old man clinging to its handlebars and lurching from side to side as if his transportation had a will of its own.

"Is he really a high priest?"

"Very old man," replied Yazdani, shaking his head as if this extreme age had been an unexpected twist of fate.

"Yes. But is he the high priest? Or even the low priest?"

"Of courze, yes. He is high priest now vor since I am small boy."

"He does not appear to know much about Zoroastrianism, though. Have you noticed that?"

Yazdani's eyes glittered as he sighed deeply, saying, "He is veared to speak in front of *them*."

I didn't buy this. Surely *they* would expect a high priest to be slightly well-informed about his own religion? But I could tell from Yazdani's expression that I just didn't *understand*. He was right. I didn't understand what the Zoroastrians had to be so secretive about. They weren't pretending to be Muslims, after all. There were no priest-holes; they did not turn their framed kufic scripts of Koranic quotations or photographs of the Ka'aba to face the wall every Friday night, as Jews in Spain did with crucifixes during the Inquisition. Everyone knew they were Zoroastrians, and anyone could pick up a book and discover what they believed and how they believed. Why the secrecy?

"They wish to destroy uzz," Yazdani replied. "They want uzz gone away."

The real answer, I suspect, was that secrecy had become a way of life with them, and also become a source of power—their only source of power, really. The Zoroastrians of Yazd knew that Muslims were, deep down, a little afraid of them. Reza certainly was. After all, they were associated with magic and strange practices. Persian history was filled with tales of Magians possessed of strange powers, of mythical heroes fifty feet tall who slayed demons in the name of Ahura Mazda. And the greatest period of Iranian history was when Zoroastrianism ruled over the land and its emperors ruled over an empire stretching from Egypt to India. Thus no Iranian Muslim could view the followers of Zoroaster as exactly underdogs or interlopers.

"Was there a King Rustam?" I asked Yazdani.

"Rustam? Yes, but not king." He laughed to himself. "He was hero of the legends. He keel the White Demoon. Through the graze of Ahura Mazda the god, Rustam is having strength of ten men and keeling the dragoons . . ."

"Dragoons?"

"The big dragoons with the vire breathings and the snake body."

"Dragons?"

"Yes. Rustam he keels them, and he is taller than one house."

TOWER OF SILENCE

I made Reza and Ghossam take me out to the *dakhmas*, the "Towers of Silence," after their lunch. I could tell that the prospect of visiting Zoroastrian burial sites bothered Reza. He complained about vultures and corpses all the way there.

The sky's limpidity was suddenly transformed by dense, congested clouds, brownish in color like a sulfurous fog. They intensified the light now confined low on a horizon serrated by the same mountain range that every Zoroastrian structure we had seen lay near. The day grew ominous, threatening, and this epic lighting effect made it feel as if the world had prepared itself for some portentous event.

"Sky like this when the Imam Khomeini he die," said Ghossam fearfully.

"Maybe he's about to return?" I suggested.

"He find you azzhole Zionist spy here," snapped Reza, "and he eat your balls while you wear them."

"Not *halal*. He couldn't. Just like eating pork."

"Then I fucken do it for him."

The *dakhmas* were beyond the edge of town on two nearly identical hills rising up above a curious collection of new concrete structures that resembled ancient Nubian mudbrick houses, with domes and huge covered arches. There were also windwards, I noticed, but not attached to any buildings; and one structure that looked like an igloo, merely a pointed dome flat on the sand. It seemed to suggest that what lay on the surface served something else underground.

"What is all this?"

"Top secret place," Ghossam replied knowledgeably. "Military."

There were no soldiers in sight. In fact there was not a soul in sight.

"All computer there. Not the people."

Yazdani had told me that these *dakhmas* were only 150 years old, but they were constructed over previous ones that he insisted were 3,000 years old—when Zoroaster, according to Dr. West, had still been with the archangels.

They reminded me of the abandoned artillery posts you still find dotted around Britain's coast, constructed for the expected Nazi invasion. Round, fortlike affairs, they were made from rough-hewn stones, many of which had considerable antiquity, supporting the theory that older structures had been demolished in order to build new ones. A crude, winding ceremonial path led up to what at first appeared to be an entrance that was now sealed. Reaching it, however, I saw that there was still a windowlike space open some six feet from the ground.

"What you see in there?" Reza asked nervously, after helping me clamber up and through.

"Oh my *God*! It's *horrible* . . . the bodies . . . the vultures . . . the *stench* of dead flesh."

I offered to pull Reza up, but he had backed away and was standing looking edgily from side to side as if expecting enemies.

"You are sick motherfucker," he told me. "Get outta there."

I moved back inside. There were no bodies or vultures, but saying so bought me a few Reza-free moments to feel the age of the place. A circular walkway like that on castle ramparts contained a broad pit filled with rocks. The entrance to the *dakhma* is sealed up after the body has been placed in it, leaving it open to the sky. No human being will enter again until the birds of prey have done their job. Bones are removed for burial and stones are piled over whatever remains exist. There is nothing repulsive about the practice at all, bizarre as many seem to find it. People bury each other in earth, fire, or water all over the world, but only the Zoroastrians and the Tibetans still use the element of air. The practice is called *excarnation*, and has been known from Neolithic times and from some American Native tribes. Dead flesh is unclean: why defile the good earth with it? goes the theory.

The interior was silent, too. A tower of silence. Yet it was the silence of peace, not a calm before the storm. As at the Zoroastrian mountain structures of Saveh and Kashan, the view from the tower was spectacular. Again, the whole valley and plain were visible to the north, south, and east. Always the same mountains behind, somewhat dejected though, as if they offered something no one needed any more.

THE NOBLEST CITY IN THE PERSIAN EMPIRE

Reza and Ghossam had an unusually urgent need to pray after this brush with Zoroastrian death. We drove to the city's main mosque, its

Jama Masjid, which was smack in the center of town and almost excessively major, its entrance alone like the pylon of a vast suspension bridge or industrial power plant. Two minarets soared up into the amethyst twilight over a fifty-foot Tudor arch that contained a twenty-foot ogee arch, all bathed in blinding white light. To match this entrance the rest of the mosque would have needed to be forty times larger than it was. The entrance was the point, though—since this "point" was obviously being made for the benefit of people who would never pass beyond that incandescent arch.

A thriving shoe-shine-cum-shoe-minding business operated just outside the arch. We left our footwear with a man whose hands were like black patent leather and wandered into a courtyard far older than its entrance.

It did not take long to see that the mosque had once been a huge Zoroastrian temple. Inside the older Mazdean arcades everywhere were the telltale X-over-P shapes, too: the mosque had also been a Christian church at some point. This co-opting is not necessarily an aggressive gesture, either, although it is invariably assumed to be. But it need not imply the attempt to superimpose one faith over another by erasing the previous structure and decoration. It doesn't in Egypt, where the work of successive pharaohs is constantly presented as one tyrant blotting out another, yet is in fact a conscious physical demonstration of flux and change around an unchanging truth. The fire-temple-church-mosque metamorphosis can, if we're generous, also be viewed merely as the facade of shifting attitudes around an eternal core. After all, there has only ever been one Truth.

> Yasdi is a beautiful and noble city, with rich manufactures. The people make silk cloths called by its name, which the merchants carry into various countries. They all adore Mohammed.

—Marco Polo, *Travels*

As I've noted, nowhere in Iran would this last statement have been less true than in Yazd during the late thirteenth century. It is truly curious that Polo seems not to have noticed he was in the Zoroastrian stronghold.

To Sir John Mandeville, a few decades after Polo, Yazd was the "noblest city in the Persian Empire." He'd also been informed that no Christian could stay there for long and not die: "and no man knows the reason for this." No man knows the reason Mandeville thought so highly of Yazd, either. But he probably confused it with Kashan—a case of reversed-itinerary common in those whose traveling mostly takes place at the local library. I wondered how long "for long" was when the average lifespan fluttered around thirty-two, though. One reason Christians might have been dropping like flies in Yazd, though, was Mr. Yazdani's "vodka"—if it had been brewed back in the fourteenth century.

THE LAST SUPPER

We dined at Yazdani's house again, the conversation this time staying well clear of the controversial—almost preposterously so. Around ten P.M., the son of a friend of the family from Pakistan dropped in. Wide-eyed and affable, Jamshad Gustausp was not afflicted by the paranoid reticence of his Iranian relatives, but he also appeared to have little interest in Zoroastrianism. He'd traveled overland, so I asked if he had come through Afghanistan and if so how that was these days.

"Quite hectic."

Considering the civil wars that had reduced the country to total chaos, this seemed an understatement.

It transpired that he had taken the southern route, however, through Baluchistan and into Iran near Zahedan.

"I am having wife with me," he explained.

"I understand."

Since we had been on the topic when he arrived, I asked if he was aware of any agreed-upon date for Zoroaster's birth.

"Eighty-five hundred before Jeezy-Krist."

"Eighty-five hundred B.C.!"

"Some they are saying two towsand before the Jeezy-Krist."

"Every time I ask this question I get more confused."

"What is wrong with Zardhushti religion?"

"Wrong?"

"Yiss."

"Nothing. I think it's great."

"What is wrong?"

"What do you mean?"

"Everywhere we have troubles."

Yazdani furtively passed me a note reading "Thiy are watching us." I nodded discreetly.

"You will come carry cheese," stated Jamshad.

"Cheese?"

"You will come?"

"Oh . . . To Kara-chi, not 'carry cheese'?"

"Thank you."

"When you will come?"

"Next year?"

"Good. You will send me your books, please."

He wrote down his address.

Yazdani, who had polished off a decanter of his "vodka" over the evening, cornered me as I emerged from the washroom.

"You will not vorget us?"

"No. How could I?" My eyes watered in his breath.

"We are izzolated, you see?"

"Yes."

"With no vriend and eyes in the walls. *Eyes*, you know?"

"You need anything, you write, okay?"

He wanted to say more, but it was clear that he was not sure what more he wanted to say.

We set off for Isfahan that same night. The city wasn't there when the Magi passed through, but their route still took them past the site of a settlement that was to be Isfahan. I felt less certain about this part of the trip. In some ways, I'd found out more about the Magi and their connection with Christianity than I'd ever expected to find; but in others, I did not feel I'd found what I was looking for. As they headed west, away from the familiarity of their homelands, I imagined they, too, felt as uncertain as I did about what awaited them.

Chapter Nine

REZA'S EDGE:
ISFAHAN

After having traveled a number of days, however, they were curious
to see what was in the box, and opened it, when they found only a
stone, which was meant to express that they should remain firm in
the faith which they had received. They did not understand this
meaning, and despising the gift, threw it into a well . . .

—Marco Polo, *Travels*

W e did not get far. The Paykan blew another tire. No one even
seemed surprised this time. There was no spare left and finding someone to fix a tire around midnight in Yazd was not easy. But nothing difficult is ever impossible in the Orient—only simple things there seem
to aspire to that lofty condition.

Toward Na'in we ran into a blizzard, an avalanche of swirling galax-
ies which immediately vanished without a trace as we headed due
west, once more back on the route of Polo's Magi.

"City of Jews," was Reza's sole comment on our destination.

Queen Shushan-Dukht, Jewish consort of the early fifth-century
A.D. Sasanian monarch Yazdegerd I, seems to have settled a colony of

Jews in a suburb of the city called Yahudiyeh. Was this what my minder meant?

"They still there."

Little is heard of Isfahan until Sasanian times, although it was a sizable Bronze Age settlement, and there is even some evidence to suggest that the later Archaemenid kings had begun to use it as an alternative summer capital. Nebuchadrezzar is reputed to have first settled Jews there, although little evidence exists to support this legend. But it was the Arabs who, after capturing the place in 642, made it the chief city of the great central province they called Al Jibal, "the mountains," but which had once been most of the former country of Media. Developed by the Seljuk dynasty, after its Turkish founder Togrul Beg captured the city in the mid-eleventh century and made it his capital, Isfahan was one of the few cities to escape destruction by Ghengis Khan's Mongols. In 1388 it fell into Timur's brutal hands, however. He spared the inhabitants initially, but after they revolted Timur ordered the slaughter of some 70,000, fashioning one of his infamous cautionary towers from their skulls. It was not until 1598, when the Safavid Shah Abbas the Great made it his capital in place of Kazvin, that Isfahan entered its golden age. Abbas zealously set about transforming a low-key provincial town into one of the largest and most beautiful cities of his day.

The outskirts did indeed make the place seem vast still in my day. What I wanted to believe were flaming torches blazing high on jeweled watchtowers turned out to be, of course, the fires from oil derricks. Isfahan's eastern limits border onto heavy industry. The whole province is now the industrial heart of Iran, particularly rich in steel mills, refineries, silk and synthetic textile weaving, pharmaceutical manufacturing, and the base of what are officially termed "Defensive Industries."

Reza awoke from a fitful two-hour slumber as the Paykan thumped onto an airport runway-sized boulevard.

"Isfahanis are tricky," he announced, resuming his last thought. "Big liars in business. This was fucken Jewish town."

"Fifteen hundred years ago, though."

"Ach!" he coughed violently, lighting up Zagros Slims for everyone and slamming in "Chickadee, chickadee, chickadee." "They still here.

Isfahanis richest people in Iran now." He looked to Ghossam for confirmation of this fact.

"Too much money," Ghossam agreed dutifully. "Big liars."

As we hit the downtown core the city certainly looked more opulently mercantile than even Teheran did, with splendid store windows displaying carpets, fabrics, ceramic work, and antiques of every description. At four A.M. the streets were not even totally deserted and a few juice stands still operated. Possibly, I considered, Isfahanis, being so "tricky," were early risers, not night owls. Ghossam pulled up outside the Toos Hotel, which was next to a juice bar bedecked with images of Mickey Mouse wearing a blue turban and a curious green robe. The artist had run into problems with Mickey's ears here, however, obliged to make the turban run diagonally between them.

"Martik Barberian," cautioned Reza. "Right?"

"Right. Sausages."

"Tooth problem."

"What?"

"You hold handkercheeve over mouth, azzhole. Bad tooth. Cannot speak, yes?"

My room was a massive wood paneled Victorian chamber with five single beds and seven tables, along with various built-in niches and drawer units. Everything was encrusted with what resembled ocher dust or dried mud. I went to open the theaterlike cascade of curtains, succeeding only in tearing a foot-long gash through one of them. A curious trench gaped between the windows and the room from which a suffocating gale of hot air blasted, explaining why the curtains were just this side of being ash.

Reza burst into the room, followed by a frayed and down-at-the-heels version of Luciano Pavarotti holding a tray of tea.

"Fucken bastard," hissed Reza.

"Who? Him?" I indicated Pavarotti, who threw down the tray and left.

"Manager."

The manager had apparently told Reza that he knew damn well I was a foreigner, but it was okay as long as I handed over my passport.

"So? I'll do it."

"No fucken good."

212 ⚓ In Search of the Birth of Jesus

Reza would lose face if I did this, I eventually gathered. He refused to admit he had lied.

"So what's going to happen, Reza? Can I go to bed or not?"

"He said he call Komiteh so they can come investigate you."

"Fine."

It wasn't fine, however, according to Reza. They would come in an hour or so and interrogate me for the whole day. Maybe more.

"Waste everyone fucken time."

We had to move immediately. Reza wasn't against the Komiteh in principle, but he had other principles which he valued more highly than the preoccupations of his government.

Just around the corner was the Turist Hotel. Its desk clerk looked and acted like Dean Stockwell in *Blue Velvet*, his motions languid, opiated, precious. I handed over my passport even before Reza could open negotiations.

"He say room for you eighty dollars; for us ten dollars."

I was tempted to pay, but with Reza it was all a matter of principle. After half an hour, during which I had all but gone to sleep on the counter, we ended up with a "suite for three" for fifteen dollars. It took the desk clerk some twenty minutes to practice calligraphy on a huge form before we obtained a key to our suite, though.

The management obviously intended to do some renovation work, since the lobby and corridors were piled high with new paint cans and rolls of acrid-smelling carpeting, but, judging by the dust that had gathered over these intentions already, no one was in a rush to begin the actual work itself.

The suite was a long narrow room divided by a fifties-style partition of deep boxlike shelves that yearned for lava lamps and LP records. The place had in fact been recently painted, its walls recently papered, too—in a pattern that initially made them appear to be covered with revolting floral bathroom tiles. A large fridge hummed and shuddered beside a tiny table upon which a television perched precariously.

"This is nice, no?"

"Very nice, Reza."

"For fifteen dollars . . ."

"*Very* nice."

I realized he was embarrassed that I had been forced to move. Odd things bothered him—but because they bothered him not me.

Ghossam arrived ten minutes later carrying three polystyrene buckets, one for each of us.

"Special for Isfahan, this," he said.

"Thanks."

Inside my bucket was a kilo of what resembled grated frozen apple. It tasted more like grated frozen radish, however.

"Iss good, no?" Reza pitched a bale into his mouth.

"Mmm." I sat on the edge of the bed, picking at mine. Then I shoved the tub of frozen grated radish in the fridge, put on my jacket, and bid the boys good night.

"Where you go?" Reza sounded hurt.

"For a walk."

THE ONE-DAY DAWN

I strolled south down Chahar Bagh Avenue to the corniche of Zayandeh Rud—"the life-giving river"—where already scores of people were pouring across Pol-e-Allahverdi Khan, a sublimely beautiful bridge built on thirty-three arches by one of Shah Abbas' generals. Dawn was breaking and the jagged humps of mountains ruffling the sky's hem at the southwest edge of the city glowed carnelian and begonia.

Chahar Bagh—"four gardens"—had been Shah Abbas' idea to give his city an imposing southern entrance. In order to construct the mile-long and two-hundred-foot-wide boulevard, he had been obliged to purchase "four gardens." Down the center of two alleys, originally, there was a promenade with a watercourse featuring basins and fountains at intervals. The promenade still exists, a garden between polluted traffic-jammed roads, although the watercourse and fountains are long gone.

I continued east along the north bank of the broad river, soon reaching an even more lovely bridge, the Pol-e-Khwaju, built in the mid-seventeenth century by Shah Abbas II. It was designed as a weir as well as a bridge, and when the sluices were closed the level of the river could be raised sufficiently to create an artificial lake in front of all the palaces and pavilions that once stood on either side of it upstream. This was truly a fairy tale city, but like most such places, it seems, those it was built for led ugly, goblin lives. All in all, it was probably more attractive when the Magi spent a night here.

I turned back and strolled north along Chahar Bagh, window-shopping. Inlay was big here. Inlay was king. After a hundred yards I had seen almost every item capable of being reproduced in wood, then inlaid with mother-of-pearl and colored ivory displayed somewhere. There were stout telephones; a copse of five tuliplike desk lamps with curved stems; a frivolous attaché case; ash trays that would presumably burn if used; radios the size of closets; a small refrigerator for gypsies; clogs; knobs for stick shifts; millionaires' Kleenex containers; a spoilt brat's rocking horse; and even an impractical hat.

A huge bald man, who looked as if he'd been wiped out during the last stock market crash but still had his clothes and dignity, stood next to me before one window which was full of inlaid pipes. Every imaginable shape and size of inlaid pipe existed here, from things inspired by humming bird beaks to gaping receptacles resembling inlaid toilets and capable of holding entire bales of tobacco for dedicated marathon smokers. The man nudged me with his elbow. He placed the thumb of his clenched fist in his mouth and proceeded to suck it noisily. For a moment I thought I was the victim of an indecent proposal; then he nodded at the window and puffed on his thumb more forcefully.

"Pipes, yes? I know they're pipes."

"*Ah-gah,*" he said. "*Dood kashidan.*"

I skimmed through my *Simple Colloquial Persian*, and was soon saying "*Mahi doodi.*"

"*Gurusnay?*" he inquired, pointing to his very adequate belly.

Looking for this word, I noticed that *mahi doodi* in fact meant "smoked fish." I tried "*Sigaar kujaast?*" instead.

The man delved into roomy pockets, eventually producing a battered pack of Marlboros from which he offered me one as wrinkled and curled as an old worm. I declined, which puzzled the man. Only later did I discover that instead of "For smoking, like cigars?" what I'd actually said was "Where are the cigarettes?" The book's small type confused me, although nowhere near as much as it confused any Iranian I used it on. People were very good about this, however, willing to at least attempt working with what I gave them. (Even the infantry colonel at a military checkpoint whom I had unwittingly informed

"We're not here for dinner, take a half-day's holiday," had directed me to a good local restaurant rather than shooting me.)

A quarter of a mile up from the river I came across a mosque that took up the entire block. One side of its huge blue and yellow ceramic dome was covered in precarious scaffolding and broad, uneven planks that, from a distance, gave the appearance of sparse hair on the pate of a gargantuan blue head. I turned east down a smaller street here, soon finding myself surrounded by new and very Western-looking buildings. There were spacious sunken courtyards with fountains fronting modern arcades of stores, with curving concrete stairs leading up to office buildings and cafés. Many bookshops and countless young men in jeans, some accompanied by women with jeans and sneakers beneath their chadors, too, suggested that this was college country.

I looked in a few bookstores to see if they contained much, or anything, in English. In one, next to a vast tome called *Applied Engineering*, I thought I saw *The Satanic Verses*, but closer scrutiny revealed that it was *The Napoleonic Wars*. Judging by the wares on display, everyone in Isfahan was studying for an M.B.A.: Accountancy, Trade Law, Management Studies, Biotechnology, Applied Genetics, the Pharmaceutical Industry, and hundreds of variants on Computers and Tomorrow's Business lined the shelves that were not bulging with Korans, Commentaries, and theological tracts. There was, however, also a section of deluxe art books, most of them full-color facsimiles of illuminated manuscripts or collections of Persian miniatures. And deluxe they were indeed: five-color separations on heavy glossy stock, bound in leather embossed or tooled with gold leaf, most of them in elaborate cases of their own. I leafed through a leather-bound edition of Ferdossi's poems. Three feet long and two wide, every page a glorious color plate, it would cost four or five hundred dollars in the West at least. I imagined that even here it would be a hundred or more, and asked the price out of pure interest.

The manager, an intense, fine-featured young woman, seemed impatient with her chador's vagaries and kept irritably brushing it off her face. She could barely lift the volume. She peered closely at both end papers, then all over the six square feet of cover looking for a price. Settling on a pencilled mark several pages in, she prodded a calculator violently for some seconds, then held it up an inch from my nose.

"That is U.S. dollar price," she announced.

Green digits said 7.89.

"Less than eight dollars! Are you sure?"

"18,936 rials," she told me. "Divide by 2,400 is 7.89."

"Is this a sale price?"

"Yes, of course. We buy for less. It is business."

"No. I mean was it originally more expensive but now reduced to clear, as they say."

"No." Her expression made me feel seven years old and the class idiot. "It is a new book, in fact. Only just published."

I hauled over a smaller but thicker and equally opulent coffee table work on Islamic pottery, asking its cost, feeling certain it would be over $50, that she had miscalculated the previous book somehow. There was a major difference as well: this volume cost $4.34! The Islamic Republic viewed books like medicine and food—an essential commodity, a basic human right and thus something to be subsidized. And censored.

"You are Italian," the manager stated, shaking the shroud off her face to reveal a torrent of hair the color of highly polished old mahogany before covering it over again.

I denied this, telling her I was British, from Oxford, and in Iran to research a book. I wished I had brought my degrees, hoods, and robes along, because I felt an urgent need to dispel this notion that I was whatever she imagined I was: an import/export guy? a pilot? an oil pipeline troubleshooter?

"Oxford?" she repeated, less hostile now and less managerial. "So you pity us, do you?"

"Pity?" I was startled.

"Pushed back to the ninth century, treated like children, imprisoned in black sacks . . ."

"Every society has its down side. I don't pity Iran—that would be insulting—and inappropriate."

"What's the down side of your society?" she asked, absent-mindedly selling her only other customer a book without even looking at him.

"Social injustice, crime, oligarchs, urban nihilism, television . . ."

She laughed, throwing her head back like a wolf.

"We have *those* . . . But we are not free to complain about them. Or anything. Be honest," she said, as the door closed and we were alone, "you see someone like me—a walking tent—and you think 'poor thing.'"

"No, I don't. Should I?"

"Look," she said, opening the chador to reveal designer jeans and a brown silk blouse. "This is who I am." She refastened the chador. "Why should I be *this*?"

It made a change to have Iranian women complaining about their lot rather than trying to convince me they preferred it exactly the way it was—which had been my experience in Teheran, where a prominent female politician was currently lobbying for a chador Olympiad: athletic games geared to sartorially challenged women. Give Veils a Chance.

"Why don't you leave?" I asked.

"My parents. My country . . . And it is almost impossible unless you have money abroad. Who wants rials?"

"What about friends?"

"I have none now. You can't trust anyone."

"Why would you risk telling me all this?"

"I just wanted to talk to someone normally. The way people used to talk. I can't talk to a man here now without tongues wagging. I either marry or get a 'bad reputation' or keep to myself—or my mother's friends, who are dreadful gossips."

I pointed out that it did not seem like a normal conversation to me. It was angry and sad and she was more talking at me than with me.

She fell silent.

"You can't have a normal conversation until you're in a normal situation," I suggested. "I'd imagine it's not such a good idea to unburden yourself—even on strangers—here."

"Is it that bad?" she asked earnestly. "I mean, is that what I sound like?"

I was about to apologize when the door opened and two students—men—came in laughing. But some sixth sense told me that this was no genuine tragedy I'd been listening to, though. This was a difficult person, a person who would be difficult, would suffer wherever and however she was. There is an arrogance to the martyr's mind, a need to be more-miserable-than-thou in the martyrarchy.

"Browse," she muttered.

I did. Near several hagiographies of Husain the Martyr I found an interesting section. A four-foot-long shelf was labelled "Jewish Conspiracy," although it only held two books: proof of the conspiracy? Next to *The Protocols of the Learned Elders of Zion* leaned Henry Ford's *The International Jew*. Published by an outfit called the Islamic Propagation Organization, the *Protocols* was a small, two-hundred-page paperback retailing for around twelve cents. Immediately after the title page I found a map of the Middle East. Half the area was surrounded by a spotted serpent whose head rested just east of Damascus, its body curving up some hundred miles into southern Turkey, then down diagonally just east of the Tigris all the way to the Persian Gulf. It bowed back west at this point, sloping down through Saudi Arabia and reaching the Red Sea just south of Medina. From here it cut a forty-five-degree swath up through Egypt, reaching the Mediterranean some two hundred miles west of Cairo. The end of its tail hugged the coastline east and finally north, embedding itself a few hundred miles back into southwestern Turkey where it began.

The map was entitled "Dream of Zionism" according to its legend, which further elaborated "Map of 'Greater Israel,' " explaining that the serpent was the "proposed boundary of 'Greater Israel,' " that its triangular spots were the "Freemasons eye—'symbol of gewry.' " There followed a four-page foreword by the International Relations Department of the Islamic Propagation Council. In somewhat vague terms this foreword pointed out that Israel's occupation of the Gaza and West Bank, as well as its violent incursions into southern Lebanon, were transparent proof of a Zionist plot to take over the world. It struck me that the Falklands War was a more convincing example of incipient global hegemony than this. The foreword then offered a "famous statement" by Imam Khomeini: "If each one of the Moslems of the world pour a bucket of water towards Israel, the Israelite murderers will be drowned." I presumed Khomeini meant this metaphorically, although for all I knew he may well have decreed the formation of an aqua-Jihad Think Tank whose members were still struggling to work out the details involved in getting a billion people to toss a bucket of water towards Israel at the same time.

The next section was called "Some Opinions on the Protocols" and contained quotes, the most recent of which dated from 1948. Henry

Klein, identified as "New York Jewish lawyer," had then apparently written in his book *Zionism Rules the World* that "The United Nations is Zionism. It is the Super Government mentioned many times in the Protocols . . ." This might have seemed possible in 1948, when the U.N. had just begun, but in 1994 it was surely risible. The U.N. had enough trouble delivering food packages to starving Africans. Norman Jaques, a "Canadian MP," had apparently wondered in Ottawa's House of Commons on July 9, 1943, how "can any reasonable man deny the truth of what is contained [in the *Protocols*]?" Such a statement sounded highly unlikely coming from a British Commonwealth politician in the middle of World War II. Jaques, I later discovered, was in fact an ally of a French Canadian fascist named Adrien Arcand, who'd been imprisoned for the duration of the war because of his pro-Nazi views.

After this preamble came the Protocols in their usual form. I found it hard to believe "any reasonable man" could imagine that a conspiracy of Jews and Freemasons controlled Stalinist Russia where so many Jews were killed in gulags, let alone controlled the mosaic of chaos that existed there these days. Jews and Freemasons would do a better job.

Why did Iranians insult their own intelligence by keeping these silly tracts in print? "The Dream of Greater Israel" revealed in the *Protocols* did not even affect Iranian territory. It was only a problem for the Arabs they still so despised for having overrun the Persian Empire in A.D. 637.

Iranians were far too intelligent and sophisticated to extol the virtues of Nazism, and they did not share the old Arab maxim that "My enemy's enemy is my friend." Iraq, for example, was more hated than Israel. The late and despised Shah's father had been such a great fan of Hitler that the British ordered him deposed during World War II — which was in fact when his son had attained the throne. So why this anachronistic attachment to The Jewish Conspiracy?

"Khomeini believed in it," the bookstore's manager told me.

The two students had left and we were alone once more.

"Do you?"

"Of course not. I am obliged to carry certain official publications. Every book store is."

"Are they big sellers, those two books?"

"Foreigners buy them as souvenirs. Like you."

I protested that I was just browsing as instructed.

"But you'll buy them—just to show your Western friends how barbaric Iran is now."

"You know, your attitude to the West is more hostile than any mullah's—at least in my experience."

"Defensive. Best method of defense is attack—isn't that the phrase?"

"Yes, but the optimum method these days is regarded as diplomacy and negotiation. Unless you like wars."

She looked down, then paced across the store to rearrange some books. I couldn't tell if she was angry or embarrassed.

"So Henry Ford isn't on university reading lists?"

"Is he at Oxford?"

"We had problems with Nazis, not Jews."

"Oh? I thought you expelled them from Britain once?"

"Seven hundred years ago."

"It's still seven hundred years ago here. More."

"And there are still Jews in Iran. I met some in Teheran, in fact. One was a Member of Parliament."

"We don't mind them here," she replied, smiling. "It's in Israel we mind them."

"I think they'll leave Iran before they leave Israel, don't you?"

"You know," she said, looking serious and thoughtful suddenly, "the Archaemenid kings created Judaism as it is now by fusing it with Zoroastrianism. Then the Sasanians tried to do the same thing to Christianity."

I stared at her in blank amazement. Then I outlined the nature of my travels, asking for any assistance she might be able to give.

"Have you heard of the Mandaeans?" she asked. "They're sometimes called Nazareans, too. They claim descent from John the Baptist's followers."

What I knew about Mandaeans at that point could have been engraved on an eyelash, but the manager enlightened me. There were only two small communities of the sect left now, in southeast Iraq and just across the border in Iran. They believed their ancestors had fled east during the Roman destruction of Jerusalem around A.D. 70. Reclusive and secretive, the Mandaeans had a philosophy that blended Semitic, Persian, and gnostic elements—not so unlike that of the Cathars. But they were far more esoteric, it seemed, only their priests permitted to read the major religious texts. Their Absolute God is called "the King of Light," conceived as a formless supreme entity, and set over against the realm of darkness. Emanations from the King of Light created the world, and the most important such emanation is the savior, Manda d'Hayye ("the Knowledge of Life"), whence comes the sect's name.

I asked the manager why she thought Mandaeans were connected to Polo's Magi.

"They tell the same story to show that the roots of Judaism and Christianity lie here . . ."

She said there were two main sects of Jews in ancient Jerusalem. One practiced a pure and esoteric faith more like the eastern religions, and the other—Pharisees and Sadducees—was more concerned with worldly power. John the Baptist was a leading figure in the former sect, but his followers split, some following Jesus, John's chief disciple. Jesus' objectives were more political, seeking closer ties with Rome in order to edge out the Pharisees and Sadducees, who ultimately urged the Romans to arrest him for seditious activities.

"Yes," I said, stunned to find what was speculation in one part of the world considered fact in another. "That is slightly different from the version we were taught at Sunday school."

"This is what the Mandaeans say. But other Christian sects used to believe a similar story. The Koran also says Jesus was not crucified . . ."

"Are you a devout Muslim?"

She hesitated, then said, "No. Not devout. My grandfathers were Zoroastrians . . . so I suppose I must have infidel blood."

"Infidel blood. There must be a tremendous Zoroastrian influence in Iranian Islam," I suggested.

"Of course there is. Look at Khomeini: he saw Ahriman everywhere he looked . . ."

"Mainly in Washington, no?"

"No. Mainly in Israel. Like the Mandaeans, he believed that the orthodox Jews were followers of the Lie, the false worldly faith of Ahriman. But the real influence of Zoroastrianism went into Sufi Islam."

"What about Essene or Zoroastrian Christianity?"

"It more or less died out. Originally it was a sort of Sufi Judaism, but it became perverted by the Romans. Only a few sects of Jews and Christians still practice genuine religion."

"Is Islam 'genuine religion'?"

She laughed. "No organized state religion is *genuine*, is it? Faith is about the spirit, not politics."

"I can see why you find it hard to live here."

"It's hard to live anywhere, isn't it?"

Anywhere else I would have asked if we could meet again and talk further, but here the thought did not even enter my head. I got some more details about the Mandaeans from her, then stood in an awkward silence trying to find something useful to say.

"Good luck with your research," she said, probably to help me out. "Drop in if you're in Isfahan again."

"I—"

She cut me off with a cheerful "Goodbye."

I was a hundred yards away when I remembered the books.

"Goodness! I didn't think you would be back so soon."

I mentioned the books.

"Don't feel you are obliged to *buy* something. Our chat wasn't a sales ploy, you know."

"I know that."

"And I can't have dinner with you, in case you were thinking of asking."

"I know that, too."

This was definitely a difficult person. I felt sorry for the unsuspecting Iranian man she would no doubt marry one day. Darius the Great would have had trouble keeping up with her; what would someone like Reza do? She'd keep him in a kennel, though—when he wasn't running errands.

I bought the two deluxe art books and some twenty other paperbacks. The cost, including packaging and air freight to North America, came to $18.95. I can't even buy *one* of my own books wholesale for $18.95.

THE GREAT ABBAS

Back at the Turist Hotel it was lunch time. Reza and Ghossam were sitting glumly in the lobby staring into space. The same desk clerk sat in a catatonic trance, his eyes glazed over as if he'd just learned news of staggering importance.

"We wait for you, azzhole," grumbled Reza. "Where you been?"

He sulked all day like a rejected lover.

After an extravagant meal in a hotel that had an eight-foot-high silver teapot standing in its lobby, I was forced to tour the monuments that Shah Abbas the Great had left for posterity in order for posterity to realize how great he had been. Generally speaking, Europeans were more impressed by Abbas than Iranians ever were, probably because the shah went out of his way to impress Europeans as forcefully as he went out of his way to oppress his subjects. Chardin the jeweler was so impressed that he wrote "When Shah Abbas the Great ceased to breathe, Persia ceased to prosper." Chardin certainly ceased to prosper.

But far from toying with Christianity—as he fooled many a missionary priest into thinking he was—Shah Abbas was in fact constantly attempting to make Christian priests embrace Islam, as the Carmelite Father John Thaddeus observed in 1609. The Church could hardly hope to make much of an impression on a man who frequently and openly boasted that "he would have killed a hundred children in order to reign alone for a single day."

Knowing this also did little for my appreciation of Abbas' contributions to architecture.

"Fucken beautiful, no?" Reza announced, gesturing at the shah's summer pavilion or Chehel Sotun place.

The vast porch with its painted and mirrored ceiling was supported by twenty fifty-foot-high fluted columns carved from single trees. "Chehel Sotun," however, means "forty columns." The disparity is explained by the fact that the columns of the palace were reflected in a large pool that it faced, doubling their number. Alternatively, it is also suggested, forty was then used in Iranian literature simply to denote any large number. A large hand-painted notice board displayed a single sentence two hundred words long that explained in part "According to the historical documents the palace was destroyed by fire in 17th century and was renovated with mirror decoration in safavid era and asaresult the Mirror ornamention period was begun the isfahan museum is located in the main hall the cultural heritages preservation organization." [*sic*]

The glories of Persian miniature painting had one major shortcoming for Shah Abbas, it would seem: they were too small. To decorate the interior of his palace he had artists simply enlarge this traditional work, creating Persian miniatures the size of billboards. The result made me feel like an ant crawling across the pages of an art book. One entire wall sixty feet high was emblazoned with a battle scene depicting some thousand men and horses charging at each other with spears and sabers. It was so violently hectic that I could almost *hear* it.

Reza and Ghossam stood transfixed by the sheer violence entailed, as if watching a movie.

"Chop heem," the driver murmured. "Stab heem."

"Hack his arm off: look!" marveled Reza. Then, for my benefit, he added, "Big fucken bastard, these shahs."

Abbas the Great seemed fairly traditional as shahs went, though: virtually in league with Western powers against his own people. The Jesuit missionary Father Paul Simon writes:

The good treatment and favoritism afforded the Franks [i.e., Europeans] by the King of Persia is the more marked because, notwithstanding what the Christian princes have said to him, and notwithstanding the injuries inflicted on his people in Hormuz, he has never allowed the slightest injustice to be done to our merchants on their way overland to India, nor has he lost the respect he used to pay to Franks who came to this country, where some of them, and Italians too, have caused no small scandal, and committed many follies, such as to get drunk and when drunk to dash about the Maidan at a gallop, striking this and that Persian, and killing one or other of them, of which the city of Isfahan made complaint to the King—all the same the King did not wish them to be condemned to death because they were Franks, although he is very severe with his own people, even when they be governors and nobles of the realm . .

One can understand the slowly simmering resentment of the Iranian people to such a double standard. Imagine if British soccer hooligans abroad were granted diplomatic immunity by the European parliament.

There were no drunken Italians galloping around the Maidan assaulting locals when we arrived, however. The Maidan was Shah Abbas' showpiece, a massive open area surrounded by the city's four principle buildings: the Royal Mosque to the south, the Royal Bazaar to the north, the Shaikh Lutfullah Mosque to the east, and facing it the Ali Qapu Palace with its grandstand for dignitaries to view events like polo, executions, or archery contests in the Maidan. Now the place is called, naturally, Imam Khomeini Square, and the Royal Mosque has become the Imam Khomeini Mosque. Horse-drawn carriages, which looked as if they had just been teleported from Central Park, stood idle by the sidewalk, their drivers too disheartened by a fifteen-year downturn in tourism to bother soliciting trade. We parked next to a six-wheel Mercedes passenger van which had a large hand-written note pasted across its driver's side door. I asked about this note.

"It say," Reza translated, "eighteen kilo of opium was found in the back of this van."

"Why?"

"Police find it."

"No. Why park it here with the note?"

"So people fucken know, azzhole," he replied in exasperation.

There was something almost childlike about this three-dimensional cautionary tale. On the one hand, it would make owners of similar vehicles rather nervous, but on the other, it seemed to be suggesting to potential opium smugglers that such vans were ideal for concealing large quantities of narcotics.

The Imam Khomeini or Royal Mosque is the largest and most spectacular monument of Shah Abbas' reign. Its main problem is that it was designed to be the largest and most spectacular monument. Begun in 1611, when Abbas had been on the throne for twenty-five years—although he was still only in his early forties—its construction was marred by the haste with which the shah felt it should be completed. He was only dissuaded from tearing down the marble from another mosque to save time and money by mullahs who pointed out that such a precedent might result in the desecration of his own mosque in the future.

Yet, despite its extravagant beauty, Abbas' Royal Mosque was ultimately overkill. After ten minutes I felt as if I'd been force-fed for a
month by Julia Child. It was too much, and too much for the Cultural
Heritage Organization to preserve as well. Inner courtyards revealed
walls propped up by wooden buttresses and heaps of broken tiles waiting to be glued back in place. There was no sense of sanctity either.
Even in the sanctuary, which seemed far too well lit for inner contem-
plation. The mosque was about Shah Abbas, not God. The most
luridly extravagant temples in south India always contain at their core
a shrine of stark, simple, lamp-lit mystery, a still center where all the
images coalesce into one image, where all the noise and bustle vanishes into a single booming chord and an unadorned, timeless ritual.
Here there seemed to be no heart, no core. The center was everywhere
and thus nowhere at all.

Reza was profoundly irritated by my reactions. Bigger was better to
him, bigger was *holier*. I tried explaining that you could wear a flam-
boyant floral tie and be considered well-dressed, but not a floral
suit . . .

"We don't fucken wear ties in Iran, azzhole," was his response to this.

I couldn't handle any more acres of blue tiles, so I declined a visit to
Shah Abbas' other mosque on the Maidan's eastern side.

"Fucken people come from all over the world to see this mosques,"
Reza informed me. "Why not you?"

He told me I wouldn't even get into a mosque if I were on my
own—and should thus feel doubly fortunate that he was with me.

"I'll have to manage somehow without you soon," I reminded him.
We were nearing Iraq, where I would be heading next—to pick up the
Magi trail and find the last remaining Nazareans to see how different
their religion of Jesus looks from the form that now dominates the
world.

"You cannot be alone," he told me in a serious voice. "I spoke to
Teheran and they say Dr. Roberts doesn't go alone. You come back
with me."

"Who said this?"

"Government."

"Which part of government?"

"Spying department."

"Sure they did . . ."

"Honest. I tell you truth, azzhole. I have to bring you back."

A shudder ran up my spine. Was he telling the truth? (He could have been.) Was this as far as I'd get on the trail of the Magi? I couldn't believe that I had come all this way to be turned back now.

"Let me talk to them," I demanded, as we walked north toward the Royal Bazaar.

"They won't talk to you, azzhole."

"Then I'll just carry on as planned."

"First you settle your accounts."

"What accounts?"

"I will show you," Reza replied mysteriously. "We get some tea soon and I show you."

Reaching the north end of the Maidan, I looked back over its bland grassy expanse, trying to imagine the appalling scenes that had been played out there. Not twenty feet from where I stood Nadir Shah had ordered 5,000 of his subjects burned alive, or buried alive, maimed, mutilated, or beaten to death with red-hot iron bars. In this case their crime was not sedition, however—as it usually was. It was not being generous enough with contributions to the shah's personal coffers. Nadir rarely visited Isfahan, but he liked to make a forceful impression on its inhabitants when he did visit them. By the time he left in early February 1746, Isfahan's inhabitants were so impressed by Nadir that parents were selling off their children as sex slaves to soldiers for a few cents—with which they paid not for personal acquittals but merely the hope of some leniency in the nature and extent of their own punishments when the time came.

Most shahs during this period began their reigns with a traditional ritual known as killing off every conceivable rival. They ended their reigns in an equally traditional fashion—usually murdered by chief ministers before they got any crazier. Nadir Shah, whose self-confessed and sole interests were "war, a good melon, and a horse," in that order, once expressed amazement when a mullah informed him that there was no war in heaven. "How can there be any delights, then?" he inquired. Nadir was soon able to explore the issue further for himself.

MERCHANTS AND KINGS

The citizens of Isfahan must have been mightily relieved when Qajar monarchs decided to relocate the capital to Teheran. Few could have discerned any advantages whatsoever in living at the heart of Persia's empire. It was therefore not surprising to find that commerce and trade still interested Isfahanis far more than politics—which, however, still interfered with their business interests even now that shahs had been replaced by mullahs. Neither shahs nor mullahs understood business, as one Isfahani trader told me, because shahs stole whatever they wanted, and mullahs expected to be given whatever they wanted for nothing. This was history, not economics, the man explained, and his country had far too much history yet not enough economics. What Iran really needed now was a businessman at the helm. A politician at the helm would definitely be a good start, though, he conceded. Islamic law, I next heard, began with the rights of people, only working its way down to the punishments prescribed for those who'd forfeited their right to rights after first portraying the entire panorama of a just society. The mullahs, however, all too often concentrated entirely on the punishment end of the law rather than the rights that the law had not only established in the first place but also continued its existence solely in order to protect. For in punishment alone—not human rights—lay both the source of clerical power and the potential for clerical abuse of that power. I gathered that businessmen in Isfahan had seen mullahs abuse power more often than most other sectors of society had.

The Royal Bazaar of Isfahan, unlike Kashan's bazaar, was relentlessly geared to the tourist trade. There was not a frying pan or sink plunger for sale anywhere. The trouble was that the tourist trade had dropped off somewhat over the past fifteen years. Hussain, who sold antique rugs and military decorations from every army on earth, estimated that the number of tourists passing through the bazaar over the last decade was around eight.

"Eight?" I repeated.

"Or nine. We get many Chinese engineers, but they have only two dollars for buying the souvenirs."

And those two dollars were for a whole group of them.

He admitted that vendors also saw Italian engineers, who were rude and surly. There were Russian engineers, too: crude and stupid. He probably characterized Americans as rich and stupid—if he remembered any. I wondered how he survived, how anyone survived here. The answer was a knowing shrug: whatever survival entailed, it wasn't legal. Everyone certainly seemed to be surviving, though, and Hussain wouldn't budge from $250 for a seventy-year-old Turcoman rug I viewed as $50 cheaper—but which would have cost me $2,500 at home. I should have bought the damn thing, and I would have bought it had Reza not kept muttering in my ear about "Big thieves" and "Big liars." Only idiots purchased old carpets, he also told me. New ones were better. Everyone agreed new ones were better—except idiots.

Admittedly, the sight of a Westerner did cause some excitement among the bazaar's traders, who rubbernecked in their booths and stalls beneath the massive shadowy arches. Above flapped huge banners of Imam Khomeini, Father of the Revolution, though Distant Cousin of Commerce. Perhaps these banners were there in case any vendor ever temporarily forgot who to blame for the fifteen-year recession.

I managed to get rid of Reza by handing him some dollars to change on the black market, but he was back in minutes and scuttled a promising deal with Ali that involved a pair of eighteenth-century English dueling pistols. Ali, however, was not so easily put off. Shoving the pistols aside, he disappeared behind a ragged curtain and emerged seconds later with a Kalashnikov semiautomatic rifle which looked as if it had seen some heavy action in its day.

"No," I told him. "I like older, prettier weapons."

Next he produced a bolt action Enfield. By the time Reza dragged me away, I'd seen Lugers, Gatling guns, cross bows, something like a drainpipe with a shoulder rest and trigger, and a device with ten revolving barrels designed by someone who clearly scoffed at the idea of feeding six bullets by cylinder to a single barrel when you could feed ten preloaded barrels themselves to the firing pin. The thing must have weighed 150 pounds and been lethally accurate almost up to ten feet.

I dug my heels in by a counter upon which a crazed-looking individual was painting tiny camels on postage stamp-sized slivers of ivory. His nose almost touched the surface he worked on, and when he glanced up his eyes resembled bloodshot targets.

I inquired what he charged for these camels.

"One hundred Ammerkan dollar."

It seemed steep.

He dived beneath the counter and resurfaced with a bale of ragged pages upon which were glued slivers of ivory-colored Formica with camels painted on them.

"Theese ones only twenny Ammerkan dollar. But inverior works."

He was right. A studious ape could have painted them, but from a distance they looked just like the hundred-dollar ones.

"Did you paint these as well?"

He nodded. It was an interesting sales gimmick, being able to demonstrate irrefutably that customers merely got what they paid for. Maybe Isfahanis were "tricky" after all. I went to move on, but the painter asked me my name.

"I will give your name in Persian writings," he offered.

"I don't have time."

"No, no. I have all the names. What is your name?"

I told him. He dived below again, coming up with another bale, this time eight × ten sheets of elaborate, swirling calligraphy. He thumbed his way down the pile, then paused, pulling out a sheet in green, gold, and black.

"This is your name in the Persian: Ball Wiyam Robberse."

In fact the sheet read "God is Great" in Arabic. I pointed this out. The artist looked quizzically at his page.

"No, no," he then protested. "This Persian, no Araby. This your name. You have mistake. It is truth, I say."

I thanked him and walked on.

"You want buy some ofium?" he called after me.

Maybe it was his Mercedes van parked at the other end of the Maidan . . .

"Big thieves," Reza muttered. "Big fucken liars."

REZA'S EDGE

Back at the Turist Hotel I packed, and then agreed to have tea with Reza before heading—finally—for the bus terminal and the freedom

Iraq without Reza would provide. Ghossam had decided to rebuild the Paykan's engine—if it owned such a part—or at least was engaged in dismantling something complex and oily that he would presumably reassemble later. Reza seemed oddly formal and edgier than usual, opening his Samsonite attaché case on the chair beside him. I'd often wondered what he kept in this fat case. Five crumpled sheets of legal paper, three pens, two packs of Zagros Slims, a black comb, a pocket calculator, a BMW brochure, eight pocked aluminum strips of a prescription drug, and one very long yellow shoelace was the answer. He produced a pair of clerkly spectacles I'd never seen before from an inside pocket of his jacket, perched them on his nose, and smoothed out the five sheets of legal paper in a puddle of tea.

"Fucken sheet," he muttered, dabbing at the tea stains with a handkerchief.

Then he told me I owed him $600.

"For what?"

"You don't wanna pay is up to you." He sounded hurt.

"I want to know what I'm paying for."

On the paper were itemized lists of expenses. I realized now why he had insisted on paying for everything: so I would lose track of what had been spent. Perhaps.

"But it was my money you were spending," I protested.

"Look," he said, adopting the manner of a patient but fussy schoolteacher. "First day: lunch; Imam shrine, one tea and one cassette tape; newspaper; one cab fare; one lunch; box of cookies; cab fare; burger; cigs; cab; dinner; tea; acetaminophens; newspaper; camera film; poster."

And so it went on. Unfortunately for this scheme, I too kept accounts and receipts, and it was laughably easy to show him he was billing me for things that I'd paid for myself. By my reckoning, not only did I not owe him $600, he actually owed me $100. The news was devastating.

"I am fucken poor man," he complained. "You think I live in beeg house but wife and me we living in one room—basement room—very fucken damp and colds . . ."

"Rats?"

"What?"

"You probably have rats there, too, no?"

"No fucken rats, azzhole," he muttered, furious. "No car even . . . No children . . . no future . . ."

He next spent half an hour detailing his medical history, which included what sounded like schizophrenic hallucinations, a nervous breakdown after the war with Iran (but caused by guilt over not being eligible to join the army rather than shellshock or trauma), paranoid delusions (the world revolved around him), bleeding ulcers, and a zero sperm count.

"I need sperm medicine, cost thousand dollar one bottle," he wanted me to believe. "Not fucken available here even. I have to send money to Germany for it. Mostafa has much money, but me I have nothing."

"I thought you were partners . . ."

"No. He pay me a hundred a week—I mean, a hundred for one month . . ."

"You told me you were partners."

"I fucken not. I don't lie to you. We are school friends."

"You said partners."

"Listen," he sighed. "You don't wanna pay me is up to you . . ."

It went round in circles. Ghossam's fee mysteriously doubled from $40 a day to $80, too—which made him around 2,500 percent better off as a wage earner than Reza claimed himself to be—and gas, oil, repairs, tire wear, et cetera were proposed as "extras."

"Why?"

"Because he work too much hard. He drive up mountains for you, azzhole. Do damage to his fucken car."

"No one asked him to drive up mountains. He's a driver, anyway. But that car . . . that—"

"Listen. You don't wanna—"

"Yeah, yeah, Reza, I've got that. And I *don't* want to."

"Fine." He hung his head, carefully folding up the damp accounts sheets with staggering pathos. "I hope you have nice trip back to your home."

He made "home" sound like "earthly paradise."

"Thanks."

I offered to send him the sperm-boosting medicine he needed when

I got back to my earthly paradise. If he was trying to make me feel guilty he succeeded entirely. I certainly never asked for the $100 he owed me.

In the hotel's parking lot Ghossam stood beside a pile of engine parts staring at the Paykan.

"*Eshtebah*," he murmured.

I flipped through *Simple Colloquial Persian*. *Eshtebah* apparently meant "mistake." I turned to the chapter called "Domestic Issues."

"*Baayad hamishay baa aab pooshiday baashad*," I told Ghossam.

He looked perplexed.

"What?" said Reza.

"What did I say?"

"You said 'It must be kept covered with water.' "

It was supposed to be "Have you checked the oil?"

Next, instead of announcing my departure, I asked Ghossam to clean his ice-chest with divine sanction and a small valve. The driver considered this advice carefully before telling me "*Khoda Afez*," and offering a soft hug.

Reza came with me to the bus station. We sat in silence until the Ahvaz bus showed up.

"I miss you, azzhole," he said quietly, thrusting a plastic bag at me.

Inside was a black knitted mullah's skull cap. I recalled admiring a similar one back in Teheran.

"Thanks."

"My mother she make that for you."

I'm certain that Reza's mother had never even seen this cap, let alone made it, because her son had bought it himself from a stall outside the main bazaar earlier that very day. I'd watched him do it, assuming the vendor—who vended only black knitted caps—was also an unauthorized moneychanger, and even admiring Reza's subtlety in keeping up the man's front by actually haggling over and purchasing something while (my) money was changed. But it is the thought that counts—and this particular thought could be counted on to make me feel like Ebenezer Scrooge.

"Try it on."

I did.

"You look like fucken Jew."

"*That* should make the trip more interesting."

He laughed and we embraced formally, kissing cheeks three times.

"You remember you promise to send medicine," Reza said, as I clambered aboard the bus.

"You remember your promise to give me happy memories of Iran?"

Reza looked dubious but nodded.

"Well, you delivered . . . I guess it doesn't take much to make me happy, does it?"

"Azzhole!"

"That's more like it! *Khoda Afez.* Bye . . ."

I was finally alone with the Magi, who weren't much company, but then nor was Reza. From Isfahan they would have started heading through foreign territory in a region where nothing has ever been safe or entirely certain. Perhaps they felt now the same sense of urgency and impatience and just wanted to get the job done. There were still eight hundred miles of desert between us and Bethlehem.

Chapter Ten

THE MAN OF LIGHT: SUSA

Jesus said, "Let one who seeks not stop seeking
until one finds. When one finds, one will be
disturbed. When one is disturbed, one will
marvel, and will reign over all."

—The Gospel of Thomas, Logion 2

Khuzestan is a small part in southwest of Iran
which was a part of the great and independent
government of Elam in ancient times. One of the
oldest human civilizations which dates back to
8000 B.C. rose from this area.

The Elamites, Archaemenids, Parthians, and Sasanids
have also selected and built some parts of this
land as their winter capitals.

Because of its geographical importance, this area
was always subject to phenomenons, but after the
presentation of Islam, Khuzestan became habitable.
Right now with an area of 67,132 sq. kms. and a
population of 3,219,446 (1992), it is counted as
one of the important provinces in the country.
Because of the precedence of human civilization
in this area, so many ancient and splendid monuments
have remained in this land.

—Iran Today

Khuzestan—according to *Iran Today* at least—was presumably "subject to phenomenons" when the Magi passed through the area on their way to Bethlehem. No mention is made in the publication of the sort of "phenomenons" available two thousand years ago, but, as "phenomenons" go, the phenomenon of Saddam Hussein lurking just across a few hundred miles of mostly indefensible border would take some beating.

Instead of heading due west toward the setting sun's beacon, as I fully expected it to do, my bus forged south from Isfahan, eventually depositing me in a forbidding, windswept little desert city named Yasuj, less than a hundred miles north of Shiraz. At least the Magi were presumably in control of their transportation. I could virtually see them heading on without me, oblivious to my cries of protest. I spent a miserable night lashed by ugly freezing winds in the bus terminal here, since it was impossible to determine whether the first transport to Ahvaz left at 5:30 A.M. or 9:30 A.M. A man who looked like Charles Manson sat on the concrete right next to me—and not on account of any space shortage. Initially, I was grateful for the extra warmth. But he kept calling me "komrad," which I soon learned, besides "Marlboro?" was the only word we had in common.

"Komrad," he would say, nudging me awake. "Marlboro?"

Zagros Slims were Marlboros as far as he was concerned.

APOCALYPSE THEN AND NOW

The only viable southern road into Iraq runs from the city of Ahvaz, which I had once considered a strong contender for the ancient capital ruled by one of Marco Polo's "kings"—until I discovered the "Ava" not far from Saveh's castle. I suddenly felt glad to have shed this particular burden. There was little evidence of ancient grandeur around here now. Like many of Iran's oldest cities, Ahvaz is an archaeological palimpsest, generation upon generation building layer upon layer over the past, right up to present-day construction sites still repairing damage from the recent war with Iraq. The place could never be properly excavated unless its citizens abandoned their homes, which many had in fact seriously thought of doing after Saddam pounded them into dust. Some of the most savage fighting had taken place in this region, close to the prodigious Abadan refinery—and it showed. Iraqi troops and missiles were not the only incursions, either. A sadness had also invaded everything and everyone. Unlike the military intruders, however, this psychic one had not been driven out or its damage repaired. It had stayed on and was busy with colonization now.

Even the characteristic Iranian resilience seemed to have been worn down: people were weary, suspicious, even hostile at times. The few cab drivers who seemed to exist at all regarded my inquiries about crossing the border as a joke. One, however, at least offered to show me why his colleagues found the request so very droll that a few almost laughed instead of crowing or hissing like punctured tires.

Rain lashed at the windshield as we set off across a flat marshy plain. To the west a low mist hung over swamps that marked the edge of the Fertile Crescent—rich agricultural lands following the erratic course of the Tigris and Euphrates, rivers synonymous with those potent civilizations that had arisen in their nourishing embrace. Beyond the town of Hamid, where the road curved due south, a blurred landscape was littered with tortured metal remnants barely recognizable as vehicles: trucks, tanks, armored personnel carriers, cars, mobile missile launchers. It resembled a set for *Road Warrior*.

What looked like puddles were often three-foot potholes filled with water, and motoring became more like a proficiency test for stunt drivers. Thuds, rumbles, and flashes of light came periodically from the murky west, where a narrow band marked the point where mist ended and low swirling cloud began.

"Saddam," the driver explained, nodding toward the "phenomenons." He might as well have said "Satan."

Indeed, the whole area could have been a demons' fairground on the perimeter of Hell. It brought back with hideous clarity the time I had spent in Iraq covering the Gulf War. As in any war, civilians suffered more than soldiers—and the Iraqi soldiers had suffered more than adequately.

Ahead suddenly was a military road block. A lean, troubled fifteen-year-old in a sodden camouflaged parka waved us over into a muddy lay-by. He took my driver's worn and shredded papers, holding them in the rain until I thought they would completely dissolve; then he indicated me, muttering something in a weary little voice. The driver launched into an elaborate explanation that involved much shrugging and slapping of the forehead.

The soldier stared at me, more amazed than angry. He too slapped his forehead, saying "*Majnun*," then he waved us on.

Majnun means "madman"—but in a nice way.

"He say why you dance with the death?" the driver informed me.

I laughed—which seemed to confirm his worst suspicions.

The blaring of high-volume air horns behind us forced our cab off the road as a dozen or so heavy duty army trucks—some bearing loads beneath flapping tarpaulins, others holding grim-faced chain-smoking teenagers in full combat gear—roared past at top speed, their huge double tires as unworried by hardtop craters as they were by any other obstacles in their path. Like us.

As we snaked off again, the ground suddenly shook. At first I thought the cab had hit a series of savage potholes, but then several deafening explosions followed. These massive blasts were accompanied by blinding eruptions of bluish light that silhouetted mile-high twisters of black smoke blossoming out into monstrous flowers of evil. This glare ripped open the western horizon like a huge, grand theater curtain collapsing in flames. Immediately, not half a mile off, batteries of ground-to-ground missiles spat out screaming streamers that drew wavering lines of yellow light westward—as if some Wagnerian demigod or Titan would next scrawl a stave with fire and mark in red-hot boulders up there the opening bars of theme music for a last ride across smoldering air into the brief and final apocalypse.

"See," announced the driver, braking drastically. "Beeg problem for you."

I got the picture. If it was like this half an hour from the border, I was willing to believe that actually crossing the border here might well prove impossible. Big problem for me.

The driver did not wait for me to suggest that we should probably head back to Ahvaz. He'd gone to a lot of trouble to prove his point—and make three dollars in fare.

I looked behind to where the curtain of smoke, mist, cloud, and crackling light hung between Iran and Iraq. Two hours or so beyond it lay what had been Ur of the Chaldees, the birthplace of Abraham, the Patriarch acknowledged by Jews and Muslims as their common ancestor, a man so devoted to the one God that he was willing to sacrifice his beloved son, Isaac, for him. Isaac is often and wrongly termed Abraham's "only son," however.

ABRAHAM'S BOYS

Before Isaac had been born to his wife (and half sister) Sarai, Abraham had, at his wife's insistence, taken her Egyptian maid Hagar as a concubine when he was eighty-six years old. For much of his early life, Abraham had attempted unsuccessfully to fob his wife off on various Egyptian aristocrats. Sarai was "barren," we learn (she was also seventy-eight), and she wanted Abraham to have children no matter what it involved. But once Hagar was pregnant, she started to despise and resent her mistress. Sarai confided this new staff problem, and Abraham told her that Hagar—pregnant with his child or not—was still her maid and she should treat her as she saw fit. By the sound of it, Sarai dealt with Hagar so harshly that the poor maid fled into the wilderness, where an angel found her, telling her she would have a son and should name him Ishmael ("God hears"), because the Lord had heard her affliction. The angel, however, added a somewhat gloomy caveat: Ishmael would "be a wild man; his hand will be against every man, and every man's hand against him . . ."

Hagar returned to have her child in Abraham's household without any further trouble. When Ishmael was thirteen, the Lord appeared in person to Abraham—who was himself ninety-nine by then—telling him great things lay ahead for his descendants, and that Sarai would soon also bear him a son. Abraham literally fell to the ground and laughed his head off at this news, reminding God that Sarai was now ninety years old herself.

Why not be content with Ishmael? Abraham suggests reasonably. God repeats his promise, however, saying Sarai—now renamed Sarah—will bear him another son to be named Isaac, with whom God would make his covenant. Ishmael, on the other hand, would "beget . . . twelve princes, and I will make him a great nation"—but it is only Isaac who will have the special bond.

Sarah also laughs herself silly when the Lord informs her she will bear a child at the age of ninety-one. Then Abraham and Ishmael become the first men ever to be circumcised—which, considering their ages, shows considerable devotion in itself.

Once Isaac is born, however, Abraham generously gives Hagar some bread and a whole bottle of water before kicking her back out into the wilderness with their son. This gesture was just to make it clear which son would inherit, though—and no doubt it achieved its object. When their water runs out, Hagar and Ishmael—whom the author here appears to forget is no longer a baby—lie down to die, understandably dispirited. But another angel calls to Hagar, saying God has heard Ishmael's voice (a rare example of the Lord's humor, even if only a pun on the meaning of Ishmael's name) and he will indeed make him a great nation. Eventually. A well of fresh water magically appears, enabling mother and son to live in the wilderness, where Ishmael "became an archer" and, somehow, his mother also managed to find him a nice Egyptian wife.

Meanwhile, Abraham nearly kills Isaac to prove his loyalty to God, and Sarah, not surprisingly, dies soon after. When he is around one hundred and fifty, Abraham himself still has no intention of dying: instead he marries a teenage virgin named Keturah, fathering with her another six children. He finally dies at one hundred and seventy-five—"in a good old age," as the scribe jests—and Ishmael makes a brief and considerate reappearance to help Isaac bury their father. How far away could Ishmael have been to receive news of his father's death in time to attend the funeral?—especially when funerals usually took place within twenty-four hours.

Besides hearing that he died when he was only one hundred and thirty-seven, though after fathering the promised twelve sons, the rest of Ishmael's life remains a mystery in the Old Testament. His divinely favored half brother, Isaac, certainly makes no attempt to keep in touch with him. The brothers encounter each other only at the Patriarch's funeral—something I was to find of poignant relevance when I reached Israel.

The descendants of Ishmael, though, are traditionally those Arabian desert tribes to whom the Holy Koran was eventually given. Before Isaac won God's and his father's exclusive love, Abraham and Ishmael, according to Islamic scripture, helped restore and rebuild the Ka'aba in Mecca, the crude square stone shrine which, draped in black cloth, is now the spiritual heart of Islam.

Ishmael and Isaac are, then, two more brothers treated unequally and unjustly by this mysteriously capricious and insecure God. They prefigure many others, and the second son is always favored over the first. Some scholars believe this reflects the division of the kingdom in Judah and Israel during Solomon's time, when these texts were probably written down. Just as there are now two Chief Rabbis in Jerusalem, so King David had elected two high priests. But Solomon only kept the priest who had supported his bid for the throne, banishing the other. The northern kingdom of Israel formed itself around the outcast high priest and, writing its own version of the scriptures, probably viewed itself as a kind of favored second son. It's a good theory.

In Abraham's time, the blighted war zone through which I traveled back to Ahvaz was still sea-bed. The area formed part of the Persian Gulf, with Ur, now in the Tigris-Euphrates delta, then near the ancient coastline. Abraham and Ishmael would have sailed around the coast to reach Mecca—or the port near it—which was thriving as a trade center before records even exist.

Of the ancient land routes west now open to the Magi the most likely was from Susa to Ur and thence along the banks of the Euphrates to Babylon. I decided to head for Susa, Darius the Great's old administrative capital, where his own information super highway, the Royal Road, began. It ran for 1,677 miles all the way to Sardis on the west coast of Lydia, now Turkey—where King Croesus had invented coinage to replace barter—and nearly within sight of Greece. Darius' "swift messengers," mentioned by Xenophon, are not just the roots of an organized postal service, they are also direct ancestors of our much-vaunted Information Age itself. It was only by regularly receiving fast, reliable information from all across his vast empire that Darius was able to have, build, and retain such an uncohesive and fractious empire at all. But Darius did not own a monopoly on efficient communications. Another network of vested interests was equally adept at keeping itself up to date across vast distances, too. The influence of the great religious orders—Brahmans, Magi, Essene Priests, and Gnostics—can constantly be seen across the vast expanses between their respective bases, always unannounced, but no less potent and profound.

SHUSH

My bus had GOD IS GRATE neatly painted in huge red letters upon its rear. I was muttering the phrase to myself an hour later as we hurtled through the ragged outskirts of Susa, a good seventy miles from Ahvaz and just thirty from the Iraqi border. Susa is now known as Shush—which was what I felt like telling its weaving rapids of horn-happy motorists. Our bus driver acted like someone with a cruise control set at ninety m.p.h. who forgets he has no legal *obligation* to travel at this fixed speed indefinitely—particularly when road conditions warrant slowing by two thirds, or even stopping altogether. It was indeed great of God to spare so many lives.

A snowstorm of considerable talent was busy promising the earth that the best was yet to come: if we thought this was a snowstorm we hadn't even seen a snowstorm before. Besides snow, its great beating wings fired out rounds of white buckshot on every side, too. I took a direct hit on my front teeth, the pain streaming like darts up through my sinuses and scoring three treble twenties in my brain. Before long I couldn't tell up from down, let alone east from west.

Lost enough as I was, I still had no desire to become even more lost. I tried in vain to find someone willing to blend their Basic English Conversation with my Simple Colloquial Persian, and, striving to locate the remains of Darius' palace without assistance, ended up on a highway whose presence was announced by the sudden appearance of a truck stop called the "Yakh-dan Restaurant." It was open, too—although I only realized this Ramadan marvel fully while ordering a kebab and Iranian Coke. Although "Yakh-dan" apparently means "ice-box," the Coke was room temperature, and the room, thanks to a central wood-burning stove the size of a commercial furnace, was kiln temperature.

At the northeastern end of a fertile plain, Shush was prey to some evil winds blowing down from the Zagros mountains. Judging from the clothes worn by other diners—sheepskins, heavy woolens—the nights were probably colder than the days by a factor of ten. Perhaps "Yakh-dan" was the town's nickname rather than the restaurant's boast?

Thrashed by brutal, flapping gusts hurling snow and hailshot from every direction—including vertically—I reeled out, then headed back down a decrepit main street. After a hundred yards that required the energy of a mile to traverse, I noticed a bookstore featuring in its window several titles in English. Tottering like a sailor suddenly on dry land again after a solid year before the mast, I heaved at the door, fell inside, and dragged it closed behind me as if a pack of wolves were inches behind.

An elderly man with a white beard so long and glossy it could have been an Arctic wolf's tail looked up from behind a stack of books. After that crazy wind, the sudden silence and the musty aroma of old pages was disconcerting.

"Now I know why Dervishes whirl," I said, feeling the situation required some explaining.

The old man stared.

"The wind," I explained. "You know, whirling me around . . ."

"Over there," he announced, pointing at a wall of books behind him.

"You speak English. Great. That's great . . ."

"Over there," he repeated.

"What is?"

"Dervish. Sufi books."

"Thanks."

I walked toward the shelves he'd indicated, not wishing to offend him, and stood there pulling out a book at random. It turned out to be Fritz Meier's *Die Fawa'ih al-jamal wa-fawatih al-jalal des Najm ad-din al-Kubra* published in Wiesbaden, 1957. Furtively looking up, I saw Heinrich Leberecht Fleischer's *Ueber die farbigen Lichterscheinungen der Sufi's,* and various other similarly user-friendly titles. I felt like asking the old man if he had *The Celestine Prophecy.* Edging sideways, I noticed that this store had certainly stocked up on its Sufis, though. I tried to find an author not represented but drew a blank. For a while I wondered if the sign outside had read SUFI BOOKSTORE, but I eventually came to a substantial section on gardening. It was nice to be out of the wind and snow, so I browsed.

I'd reached *1001 Things a Boy Can Make with String,* when the opulently bearded man said,

"Do you not find what you want?"

He didn't sound especially hostile, so I told him why I'd come to

Iran. He continued filling out index cards while I spoke, and I assumed the subject bored him as much as it did virtually everyone else I'd discussed it with recently.

But when I reached the end he looked up and said "Suhrawardi, Ruzbehan of Shiraz, Najmoddin Kobra."

"Pardon?"

"You are familiar with these writers?"

I was by the time he had finished.

> After having traveled a number of days, however, they were curious to see what was in the box, and opened it, when they found only a stone, which was meant to express that they should remain firm in the faith which they had received. They did not understand this meaning, and despising the gift, threw it into a well, when immediately a great fire came down from heaven, and began to burn brightly. When they saw this wonder, they were quite astonished, and repented that they had thrown away the stone. They however took a portion of the fire, carried it to their country, and placed it in their church, where they kept it continually burning. They revere it as a god, and use it for burning all their sacrifices; and when at any time it goes out, they repair to that well, where the fire is never extinguished, and from it bring a fresh supply.

—Marco Polo, *Travels*

The people mentioned by the old man were all Iranian Sufi masters. Suhrawardi, who died young in 1191, martyred in Aleppo by vindictive mullahs, is best described as a neo-Zoroastrian Platonist. He set about reviving the Zoroastrian wisdom of pre-Islamic Iran, arriving at a theosophical system he called Ishraq—since he charted its origins to a light that came from the Orient, but not the Orient of geography. To Suhrawardi, and evidently the old man who told me about him, Persia's ancient sages were the guardians and representatives of the Eternal Wisdom, yet although they were called "Orientals" this term really referred to their orientation toward pure Light, which originated in a spiritual Orient. Suhrawardi, it seems, forged a link between the ideas of Zoroaster and Plato in a doctrine overshadowed by the name and wisdom of Hermes three hundred years before the Byzantine philosopher Gemisthus Pletho arrived at similar conclusions. The *Alter Ego* or "heavenly I" of Hermeticism, a sort of guardian angel figure, both eternal partner and companion, became in Suhrawardi's system some-thing called Perfect Nature. Suhrawardi's Perfect Nature is revealed in another thirteenth-century philosopher Najmoddin Kobra as a figure called his "Witness in Heaven," his "suprasensory personal Guide," "Sun of the mystery," "Sun of the heart," "Sun of high knowledge," or "Sun of the Spirit." To his disciples, Najmoddin Kobra would say, con-cerning his figure, "Thou art he."

What had all this to do with Polo's Magi, though?

"He who knows himself," the old man said, "knows his Lord."

It is perhaps the quintessential Sufi statement—if not the meaning of life.

Lahiji was the old man's name, I learned, as he scuttled off to the rear of the store, soon returning with what proved to be an edition of Marco Polo's *Travels*.

"Look," he said, finding the section with the Magi story. "You must understand the symbols."

Suhrawardi's theosophy, according to Lahiji, was as close to the orig-inal teachings of Zoroaster as you could get. At its core was the concept of *mundus imaginalis*, a kind of parallel world, the Earth of Hurqalya, the Heavenly Jerusalem, a world of light that was itself a mirror of a still-higher realm. In this world of light each person had another self, a self of light that was his or her true identity or Perfected Nature—but until this was realized it appeared as a guardian angel or spiritual guide.

The "square house carefully preserved" above the tombs of Polo's Magi, and their own perfectly preserved bodies, was a symbol of mysti-cal transcendence: they had merged with their Perfect Natures and were in Hurqalya, of which the square building, like Solomon's square holy of holies, was a microcosm. The tower or castle on its mountain in Saveh, near the dried-up salt lake, was the "Mountain of the Lord," where the Fravartis, angelic beings, watch over the Zoroastrian seed of the Savior, the Saoshyant to come. It was the *Mons victorialis*, the point from which the Magi began their journey.

St. Thomas supposedly visited the court of Gondophares, an Indo-Parthian king, whose territories included Arachosia, Kabul, and Gand-hara, the Greco-Buddhist center. There, the apostle was put in charge of constructing a royal palace but ended up in prison for spending the money entrusted to him on feeding and clothing the poor in the king's name. Then Gad, the king's brother, died and was taken up to heaven by angels who showed him the palace that St. Thomas had built there with his good deeds. Gad was miraculously restored to life and both he and Gondophares were converted to Christianity. The Armenian form of Gondophares is Gathaspar: clearly, Lahiji stated, the "Gaspar" of Polo's three Magi—the one name I'd never been able to trace. Both the area and the story also bear a strong resemblance to Zoroaster's visit to the court of Hystaspes, who was one of his very first converts.

The reason each of the Magi, visiting the child separately, see him as themselves is that he is their Perfected Nature, their heavenly twin. In a gnostic text called The Book of Thomas, found in 1945 at Nag Hammadi in Upper Egypt, "the Savior" says to Thomas: "Since it is said that you are my twin and my true friend, examine yourself and understand who you are, how you live, and what will become of you . . . For whoever does not know self does not know anything, but whoever knows self already has acquired knowledge about the depth of the universe."

The Magi travel west by night, through the symbolic darkness of ignorance away from the light of the east. But they return to the Orient when they reach their goal at Bethlehem, carrying the gift that the child has given them. The stone is the alchemical Philosopher's Stone, connected also to magnetic ore that indicates true north, and found in Suhrawardi as an image of the spiritual heart. The well into which the Magi unwittingly cast the stone is the symbolic depths, the dark night from which the soul's ascent to Light begins, the real exodus—a journey back to the Orient-origin.

It is an inner journey, though, as Najmoddin Kobra emphasizes so powerfully: "Know that the soul, the devil, the angel are not realities outside of you: you are they. Likewise, Heaven, Earth, and the Throne are not outside of you, nor paradise nor hell, nor death nor life. They exist in you; when you have accomplished the mystical journey and have become pure you will become conscious of that." This was the meaning of "pure" carried by terms like "Dervish" and the "Ebionim," which the Essenes of Qumran used to describe themselves in the Dead Sea Scrolls. The term "Essene" itself even derives from the Aramaic for both "healer" and "pious."

Kobra is referring to meditation techniques or *dhikr*, one stage of which he likens to a bucket being lowered into the well of the heart. "Ours is the method of Alchemy," he announces. "It involves extracting the subtle organism of light from beneath the mountains under which it lies imprisoned . . . It may happen that you visualize yourself as lying at the bottom of a well and the well seemingly in lively downward movement. In reality it is you who are moving upward."

Polo's Magi witness "a great fire [come] down from heaven, and [begin] to burn brightly" in the well. Then they repent throwing away the stone and they carry this fire back "to their country, and [place] it in their church, where they [keep] it continually burning." They also "revere it as a god, and use it for burning all their sacrifices." Whenever the fire goes out, they return to the same well, "where the fire is never extinguished, and from it bring a fresh supply."

Najmoddin Kobra writes: ". . . the heart is a light in the depths of the well of nature, like Joseph's light in the well into which he was thrown." Of water in inner visions he says if it "is clear and if suns or lights or flames are drowned in it, know that it is the sea of mystic gnosis . . . the color of ardent pure fire is the sign of the vitality of spiritual energy." Initially when the well is revealed it has a depth to which no depth perceived physically can be compared, but as the seeker ascends toward the light shining above, the whole well below is transformed into a well of light or of a green-colored light: "Dark at the beginning, because it was the dwelling-place of devils, it is now luminous with green light, because it has become the place to which descend the Angels and the divine Compassion."

There had always been a gap in the teeming profusion of connections between the Magi and Jesus, but this felt closer to what I was seeking, although it was not yet everything. The Magi were certainly Zoroastrians, but in Polo's story not all the components could be explained just in terms of Christianity and Zoroastrianism. There was another element present.

I asked Lahiji if he felt Polo's entire story was thus a parable. He shrugged, and I suddenly understood that it did not matter one way or the other. Whatever happened in the material world was of no consequence spiritually, and merely mirrored events in a higher, more permanent realm. In this sense, all spiritual stories—including the

Nativity and brief ministry of Jesus—only had any genuine reality on a spiritual level, whether or not they also had an historical authenticity. Spiritual realities could only be expressed through symbols, metaphors, and parables—or through their mathematical equivalents—thus looking for literal meanings was like floundering around in the darkness at the bottom of that well attempting to describe the place. You wanted to leave it, not know it better.

"Do the Mandaeans tell this story?" I asked, keen to know if there was any truth to what that other bookstore manager in Isfahan had told me.

"Yes."

Lahiji seemed surprised that anyone would think that the Mandaeans did not tell the story.

"Oh. Are there many Mandaeans left?"

"Yes."

"Oh. Where?"

It turned out that Shush was virtually Mandaean Central. And half an hour away, just over the border in Iraq, were more Mandaeans. But you had to be careful, however, that these Iraqi Mandaeans were not Yazeedis.

"Yazeedis?"

Lahiji frowned, but in an amused way. Yazeedis were a tribe of Kurdish origin, he explained, who worshipped the devil. They did not actually worship the devil, but from Lahiji's description of their practices they might as well have worshipped the devil.

"Is it possible to cross the border?" I inquired.

"Yes. Why not?"

I mentioned Armageddon happening not far south, but Lahiji's response made me feel as if I were complaining about slight drizzle or cold coffee.

Before long, I'd been invited to break the Ramadan fast with him and then meet some Mandaeans who would probably not mind taking me into Iraq with them when they next made the trip. Since they apparently made the trip a couple of times a week, this sounded hopeful. It also sounded as if they had a thriving smuggling operation going, although I did not dare ask what exactly it was they took into Iraq or brought back. I doubted if it was Mandaean evangelical literature, though.

A CHAT WITH THE VIRGIN MARY

[Jesus] said to them, "Whoever has ears should hear. There is light within a person of light, and it shines on the whole world. If it does not shine, it is dark."

—The Gospel of Thomas, Logion 24

Around thirty people appeared to live with Lahiji in the brand-new and palatial suburban villa to which we rode through a torrent of snow, hail, and sleet in his deluxe Paykan—a vehicle that worked. There were sons, daughters, sons-in-law, daughters-in-law, grandsons, grand-daughters, at least one wife, a mother and possibly a grandmother. None of the women was veiled, and no one found anything unusual in the patriarch bringing home a foreigner who must have resembled Boxcar Willie's nephew by now.

"Amir will take you to your room," announced Lahiji.

"My room?"

"You are my guest. You wish to wash and change, am I wrong?"

He wasn't, although everyone else in the house probably wished that I would wash and change, too.

Amir turned out to be Lahiji's youngest son. He had the scrubbed and groomed look of a prosperous doctor, but told me—before I'd even asked him—that he was a used car salesman.

"Paykans?"

"Pardon?" he said.

"I suppose you sell Paykans?"

"Good God, no! I sell the foreign cars only. Paykan is—how you say in United States?—pieces of shirt."

"More or less . . ."

"I told Father not to buy, but he is not listening to everyone, you see . . ."

"He seems to have been lucky, getting one that works."

"Ayaah!—piles of the crop, this cars."

I found it hard to believe that the house could contain enough bed-rooms for all its occupants let alone any guests, but I was wrong. My room clearly belonged to no one—empty closets, dearth of knick-knacks—and was also exceedingly spacious, with an en suite bathroom that looked as if it had never before been used.

Returned to the reception room half an hour later and somewhat renovated, I found everyone listening to a child who could not have been much more than four play Beethoven on a piano that resembled a coffin with legs.

Lahiji—or someone—certainly had interesting ideas about furniture. Nine people were crammed together on a sofa whose design reminded me of something from a Victorian opium reverie: quilted scarlet Willow Pattern silk with a frame of mahogany dragons curling round from the back to open their jaws as two arm rests and, in a pair of menacing scaly claws, to clutch wooden balls upon the marble floor. Nearby, a tiny man was half-consumed by the maw of a monstrous green velvet chanterelle mushroom with feet. Next to him a four-hundred-pound grandmother, smoking a huge pipe, perched upon a wicker cabriolet whose pencil-thin legs appeared to dangle from her buttocks like small vines. Two gangly kids shared a stark Wassily chair. A very beautiful woman had a gilded recamier upholstered in peach-colored satin all to herself. Seven men who could have been the same man at seven different stages of life, from twenty to eighty, sat in chronological order on a black leather sofa that creaked rudely whenever one of them moved. Lahiji himself was regally ensconced on a stately walnut armchair with cabriole legs and scroll feet that were enlivened by a profusion of acanthus leaf and cockleshell designs and other carved reliefs. There were also several white plastic sun-beds, all fitted with cushions covered in a washable fabric bearing the photographic images of six different Polynesian-style cocktails. I was shown to one of these sun-beds by Amir, sinking back onto its sighing Trader Vic's heptads of forbidden beverages.

The prodigy—a girl, I think—concluded her concerto to polite applause, then promptly burst into tears. Apparently a brother or cousin had eaten her candy during the performance.

"Ah-hah!" trilled Lahiji. "Guest has arrived. You like Beethoven?" he inquired, staring at me suddenly with bottomless eyes.

I nodded.

"Yes," he said. "Good. Beethoven is the sound of God."

"Even if he did say so himself . . ."

I sat next to another son named Mirza during dinner. He also could have passed for a prosperous medic, but he was employed by the Iranian postal service. Working with this information, I tried to fashion for small talk a statement that indicated my extensive knowledge of post office history, especially its origins with Darius the Great's "swift messengers."

"Swiss massagers?" Mirza repeated in a baffled tone.

I explained about Xenophon's history of Persia and the Royal Road.

"Telefon? That is Communications Ministry, not postal services."

"No—Xenophon, not telefon . . ."

Somebody else expounded on the relationship between xylophones and pianos for ten minutes. Mirza had never heard of Xenophon, it seemed. I'm not entirely certain that he knew who Darius the Great was, either—which in Shush seemed as improbable as a Parisian who'd never heard of Napoleon.

"My sons are idiots," Lahiji announced cheerfully. "Don't waste your time talking to them. It's true, isn't it?" he asked the vast table in general.

Several men, Amir and Mirza among them, nodded happily.

The pipe-smoking granny, I noticed, had removed her false teeth, which sat on a place mat grinning inanely at a loaf of flat bread. I wondered how she planned to deal with the haunch of mutton on her plate, only to find her sucking on it soon like a huge lozenge.

"You are interested in Mandaean faith, is it, Mr. Ball?" asked the man on my left.

"Yes. Paul . . ."

"I know. Ask me."

"Ask you what?"

"All things. I am Mandaean. Ask what you wish?"

His name was Nabat, and he looked more like someone who would be involved in off-track betting or hot CD players rather than esoteric religion. He was married to one of Lahiji's granddaughters. I asked him various questions he could not answer, deciding to get down to basics.

"Tell me about your scriptures."

"Only Nazareans and priests know this."

"I thought you were Nazarean?"

"Mandaean."

"Aren't they the same thing?"

Yes and no, was the answer. A "Mandaean" was basically a layman, it seemed, but a "Nazarean" was a member of the Mandaean elite—an archbishop, perhaps, higher than a priest and worlds away from laymen. Here the analogies ended, though, because the difference between Nazareans and Mandaeans was quite considerable: only the priests were ever allowed to see, let alone *read*, the sacred scriptures, for example.

"Why?"

Because they were just too sacred, seemed to be the answer.

"So how does anyone know what their faith actually consists of, then?"

Listening to the answer, I realized that Nabat was describing a situation virtually identical to Roman Christianity as it would have appeared to the masses in the early Middle Ages: everyone knew the gist of Christ's life story, but the details were concealed in texts written and read in a language none but the priests understood. Nabat did, however, know a hymn, which he recited in a dialect reminiscent of Bob Dylan on helium. He then attempted a translation which went something like this:

"One day big Light was from inside Light and in mirror the river Jordan his double emerge. Then the water was made in breath. And river Jordan flow in Light and breath water come down everywhere, everywhere this come down. Then power of Light made itself visible and got bigger and much bigger. Then Crown made itself firm and was surrounded by wreath of leaves named myrtle which surrounded it. Myrtle leaves grew well and the trees they helped carry weight of the fruits. God spoke inside them and wound all their truths on the kings from the beginning of it all right up the end of it all."

"Yes. Now what does that mean?"

"Only priests understooding the Mysteries because these Mysteries are too much important, yes?"

Who knew if mysteries were still important?

"My uncle is a zebra," Nabat informed me proudly.

"A zebra?"

Ganzibra was what he'd said, I finally gathered, and a ganzibra turned out to be something like a Nazarean scribe—humble enough a profession in the hierarchy but nonetheless one also privy to the secrets of the priesthood. Most of them.

"You like meet him?"

"Would he like meet me?"

"He happy for meet Mr. Ball."

"Does he live nearby?"

"Yesh. One whore's the driving."

One hour's drive in this case was half an hour beyond the Iraqi border, however. I told Nabat that I did not have an Iraqi visa. This statement caused problems, but it caused problems because someone translated the word "visa" for Nabat as "visor"—so we spent five minutes discussing appropriate headgear. When the confusion was sorted out I found that not having an Iraqi visa was viewed about as seriously as not having a spotted bow tie. Nabat didn't even have a passport, he declared triumphantly, suggesting such things only caused trouble— I'd be better off tossing mine away. Without this passport, I learned, he traveled to and from Iraq several times a month.

"Why?"

"Some business."

"What kind of business?" I felt I should know.

"Import-export business."

"Importing what? Exporting what?"

"Some things."

"Ah. Like what?"

"Pishtashoo nuts, meloons, dates, other thing . . ."

Do not take riches from a man you do not know, lest it only add to your poverty. If God has ordained that you should die in your poverty, so He has appointed it. But do not corrupt your spirit because of it.

—Dead Sea Scroll, number 4Q416

"Of course not," said Lahiji, as we sat talking after dinner. "They buy and sell alcohol and weapons . . . and they are spies."

"Great. Spies. Who do they spy for?"

"Whoever pays. Israelis probably."

My hair stood on end. Surely I could find better company in which to travel across the Iraqi border?

"No, no. This is not a problem for you."

If this was not a problem for me, I wondered what Lahiji considered could be a problem for me.

"Listening to their nonsense," was the answer. "They have brains in their knees. I will tell you about their religion, but first you will sit with me."

Since I was already sitting with him I assumed this was some sort of idiom meaning "first you and me will chat some more" or "hang out awhile." But it was not. Lahiji bade me follow him to a distant wing of the villa, where he unlocked the door to a room with a high white cupola, bare walls, and a terracotta-tiled floor upon which were scattered numerous small firm cushions. Besides these, the room's only other furnishing was a large candle burning without the slightest movement of its flame within a round glass case.

"The devil laughs at all our threats," said Lahiji, ushering me in and seating himself cross-legged on a cushion. "But what frightens him is to see a light in our heart."

I too sat, staring at the candle, its flame still yet moving, consuming and consumed. This was a Sufi form of meditation. I'd once practiced it before at a weekend retreat in Gloucestershire run by the late J. G. Bennett, one of Gurdjieff's chief disciples and in some ways his inheritor.

The form may have been similar but the substance turned out to be very different. In England the single light had seemed to connect itself within to that vague point of radiance, of colors and forms on that screen of visualization in the forehead between the eyes. Here, however, it was far more a thing of the heart, and also far more star than candle flame. It behaved the way stars do when you stare at them: shooting down toward the inner cosmos like an incandescent wire, then receding into the walls of the universe, streaming back again, withdrawing, the needle of eternity embroidering on time's fabric, the universal's imprint on the particular. As above, so below: here was a thread of light stitching into my heart's little night those same diamond mysteries patterning heaven's great dome — that bejewelled inner skull of the universal mind.

It was a peaceful, tingling feeling — the one you often tend to get in rooms devoted to a search for the Self. Lahiji sat behind me, his presence tangible yet impersonal.

I thought of the Magi following their star to find the divine child who was their own perfected natures, their true selves. Then the thread coalesced and its tiny pulsing orb became a light impossibly far above me at the mouth of a tunnel . . . or a well. It was a light I could only ever reach, however, if it came down in a blinding flash to melt away the thick fog of darkness, to banish the black light of shadows that were almost solid and hung as viscous shrouds obscuring my self from me — like the cocoon's coils that prevent a butterfly dreaming of its glorious destiny in the skies after crawling through a drab eternity as one mere worm.

I was no longer sure if my eyes were closed or open. I moved the lids but still could not decide what was closed and what was open. Dull blue light began to brighten, then with a roar like subatomic thunder there was a waterfall of etheric fire cascading down on me. I felt myself swimming up through it at the same time, emerging in a fountain of white flames, their spray cool and quenching. I intuitively understood this was the spring that had bubbled up beside Mary in the verses Aya-tollah Khazzari had quoted from the Koran back at Fatima's shrine in Qom — the last time I had visited the cosmos, back when my journey was just beginning.

Mary sat convulsing with the agony of labor, leaning against the shaft of a palm tree that also began to convulse, spurting the seed of its dates high into turquoise air. Some fell upon her lap, others plunged like meteors into the pool all around me. The pocked water hissed and spat out steam as the burning seeds fell in iridescent trails all the way down to the unknown depths of the sunless well.

"Ah!" gasped Mary, clutching her huge belly, "would that I had died before this! would that I had been a thing forgotten and out of sight!"

Squatting on her haunches, she screamed, blood flowing out and catching fire as it poured into the flaming pool. She sank back, her spine merging with the palm-tree's shuddering trunk, which lent her strength so that, after one more howl of pain she bit into a huge ripe date and the baby slid out in a torrent of honeyed light. He was laughing, not weeping, and I kept thinking he was not a baby but a man like me; yet when I looked closely he was just a bald, wrinkled little thing wrapped in the abstract tartan of blood and slime.

I tried to call out to Mary, whose milky light enveloped her baby in a shimmering veil. I had questions, but I had no voice. Then she turned to me, serene, bathed in golden mist, saying, "I have vowed a fast to

God Most Gracious, and this day will I enter into no talk with any human being."

Lightning flashed through a cloudless sky and thunder rolled from east to west.

Then I was gazing up from the bottom of the well again at that pinpoint of white light hopelessly far above. But I soon understood I was in fact gazing down into basalt waters that—although it was broad daylight—reflected a single star. I felt the hot breath of a camel on my neck, finding I had pulled up a bucket of water for the beast, which nudged me aside to drink greedily.

You can see prominent stars in daylight from the bottom of mine shafts and wells. Aristotle mentions the phenomenon. The shaft reduces the sun's glare, revealing the heavens it normally conceals by day. There were shafts in the Great Pyramid that served such a purpose. And there was the old legend I'd heard but never traced of the Magi losing sight of their star and, while stopping to water their camels, seeing it reflected in the bottom of a well and realizing that they finally stood in front of the very house where the promised messiah lay.

A fierce mental wind now arose. I turned to see a cave within which vague figures stood wrapped in veils of pure silvery-white light. I had to shield my eyes, seeing black and white light at the same time. Twisting gusts tore up the sand and lashed me with it. Then another force began tilting the ground itself, and I clung to the lip of the well for support, feeling myself too heavy to hold on for long but striving all the same, my feet running aimlessly against the black slimy walls in an effort to slow my inexorable descent.

Yet, as a deep, droning chant echoed all around, it occurred to me that I no longer knew which image was the reflection and which one the true star. I might be floating up to the light instead of falling into an endless darkness—where the light's double would always be unattainably far away no matter how far down after it I journeyed. How could I tell? What sort of hell was pursuing a reflection for centuries, only to find—and probably when it was too late—that you had to spend as many centuries again retracing the path even just to reach the spot where you had started following it the wrong way? And would that little glimmer of light still be there then? Or would the night have finally perfected its darkness?

A cluster bomb of vertigo and primal dread erupted inside me. I suddenly heard myself repeating the psalmist's phrase: "Yea, though I walk through the valley of the shadow of death, I will fear no evil: for thou art with me; thy rod and thy staff they comfort me . . . Yea, though I walk . . ."

But the words seemed jumbled: "Art thou for evil, no? Fear will I death, the shadow of the valley—walk I though, yea? Death of the shadow valley I will fear . . ."

Overriding this goblins' babble there came a rich, booming voice:

"Know that the soul, the devil, the angel are not realities outside of you; you are they. Likewise, Heaven, Earth, and the Throne are not outside of you, nor paradise nor hell, nor death nor life. They exist in you; when you have accomplished the journey and have become purified you will become aware of that . . . aware of that . . . aware that . . ."

An urgent tattoo of blood beating on my eardrums was the only sort of thunder I could now hear. I was in a quiet, warm room, not a dank well full of hostile echoes. A benign gloom sparkled everywhere, illuminated by a faint golden vapor that flowed out from the motionless flame of a single candle like the quiet, blissful thoughts of a god. No star, just the candle, so white and solid in its landscape of time.

And Lahiji standing over me, gentle as a mother at the crib.

"Sometimes we take a wrong turn in there, no? We should not venture far without a guide, I think. Yes?"

I took a deep breath and shook myself awake.

"Yes, indeed. I thought I was never coming back for a moment there. And a moment there isn't the—"

"But you came. We take some tea now, yes? Then go out to meet the less stupid Nazarean. You wish to do it?"

FAMOUS GROUSE

Usually with such treks into the subconscious universe—to employ a neutral term—one is surprised by how much time has passed. Tottering back to my cocktail-cushioned sun-bed in the hectic sitting room, however, I was astonished to find that barely twenty minutes had elapsed since we'd left. This dinner party in a chair museum still in progress seemed like a childhood memory.

What was it with Lahiji and all these chairs? I wondered idly, still dazed.

"Very important to human history, chairs," he explained. "Big effect on psychology. They're anthropomorphic, you see. Important positions are even named after them: the Throne, for example. Head of a board or committee is called the Chair, isn't he?"

"Or she . . ."

"Cultures that have no chairs are not hierarchical, yes? But the man who sits in the Peacock Throne is clearly more important than the man who sits on a . . . a . . ."

"Stool?"

"Exactly. 'Stool' is also a word for excrement, yes?"

"To doctors . . ."

"And look how we name the parts of the chair!" he exclaimed, as if discussing the architecture of the seven heavens. "Like ourselves, no? It has a head, a back, arms, a seat, legs and feet. Agah!"

"Yours might," I complained, constantly forced to wedge my arms somewhere to prevent them dangling over the sides of my armless sun-bed.

"Why name the parts thus, hmmm? It names what it numbs, see? Take my chair: only the head is missing. Rest of body is relaxed—back, bottom, arms, legs, feet—only head does not rest anywhere. Do you see? This is a chair for the man who has to keep his brain awake."

"What's mine for, then? The man who has to keep his arms awake?"

He laughed heartily. I did not find chairs as fascinating as he obviously found them, but I could find a good many holes in his theory. What about Ottomans, for instance? (Were they really the basis for a empire?) Why did Formula One racing cars have bucket seats and not just heads but head rests?

"Brain must be paralyzed for a man to drive such a car," Lahiji replied. "Then he is lowered in the bucket seat down into the well of ignorance." He smirked more than smiled.

He had given this chair business more thought than I thought it was worth. I was also never quite sure whether or not everything he said contained at least two or three meanings. This is the problem with Sufis: anything can mean everything, and everything frequently means anything you want it to mean. Or not.

I felt rather feeble-minded after my fifteen minutes of eternal labor in the well of ignorance. Although I wanted to meet the "less stupid Nazarean" Lahiji had promised, I didn't have the energy now to inquire when this meeting might occur.

The pipe-smoking granny caught my eye and said something utterly unintelligible in a voice that made Leonard Cohen's seem positively girlish, while waving her pipe stem in the direction of an armoire inside which a Holy Synod could have hidden.

I sought Mirza's assistance.

"She asking for you to have the vissy."

"The vissy?"

"Ayah-hah," he apparently replied.

"What exactly is the vissy?"

"You have, Mr. Ball. You are the good guest of we Father and you must be having every hospital alley, also your designs."

"Huh?"

By now he had hauled open the armoire's portals, revealing some hundred bottles of Famous Grouse scotch "vissy." I was willing to bet that Nabat had some intimate relationship with this prodigious stash.

"You wanting sodomite?" asked Mirza.

"What?"

"Sodo-sodomite," he yelled impatiently, waving a bottle of club soda at me. "Sodomite and the eyes?"

"Please. Half sodo in it, no eyes. Thank you."

"Yesh. You come well."

"Thanks, I'll try."

The drink had a curious soapy taste and specks of what could have been tea leaves floating in it. I decided not to risk blindness or death by drinking counterfeit Famous Grouse from Iraq, and poured it into a flower pot, from where it dripped steadily through the air vents of a stereo tuner. Who knew what secret weapons Saddam was sending Iran's way these days?

The prodigy, who had fallen asleep like a cat beneath a chaise longue, was now hauled out for another recital looking as dazed as I felt. She launched nonchalantly into a piece that many competent pianists would have needed two extra arms to play at all well. Nabat tugged me by the sleeve into a corner. His breath was now perfumed with fermented malt and his eyes could have used a rubdown with Windex.

"You got the dollar with you, yes?"

"Some."

"Good. I do spezzal for you." He fumbled around his jacket pockets, finally producing a worn greeting card-sized envelope. "Loog," he urged, opening the envelope an inch to reveal several color photographs.

I went to take them but Nabat snatched the envelope from my grasp, saying, "Nod show this peoples, yes? Loog this ways." He demonstrated how he could look through the photographs without removing them from the envelope, then handed me the package. "Loog good," he urged. "Yes. Spezzal for you."

Fully expecting to see blow jobs, gang rapes, no-holds-barred rutting, I was quite startled to find images of an immense pig being roasted on a bowed spit over an open charcoal fire pit. These were followed by pictures of wild-eyed men sitting on kelims and cushions in some kind of old tent. They all had shiny dripping slabs of roast pork in their hands, between their beards, and plastered over everything south of their nostrils, from shirts and chest hair to grimy toenails. Each man clutched a bottle of (ersatz?) Famous Grouse. The final photographs showed these same men sprawled untidily on the cushions. They looked somewhat cross-eyed and blurred at the edges now, understandably, but they still had their bottles of Famous Grouse with them all the same, and at their feet lay a platter the size of a satellite dish. It contained what looked like the aftermath of a showdown between some sort of cow and thirty starving jackals. Next, the men were attempting with mixed results to squint over their own bellies at the belly of a female belly dancer, who resembled Elizabeth Taylor and was decorated like a Christmas tree.

"Good, yes?" asked Nabat breathlessly. "Porg, agaah! You like the porg, yes? And the Vamoose Gruse vissy? Good, yes? And then the daassing, yes? Good daassing-grills, yes? You like?"

"Quite a party, Nabat. Some belly dancer . . ."

"You give for the five toosand dollar to change for the rials, yes? Then you come for grills daassing and the porg eatings as Nabat spezzal gwest. Good, yes?"

"One problem: I don't have five thousand dollars, Nabat."

"Not problem. You give the four toosand. Same, yes?"

We got down to one thousand; then five hundred. It seemed impossible to convince him that, since I was about to leave Iran, I did not want a trunk full of rials. And even if I did, I would pay to avoid his dancing piggies' pig-out.

Fortunately, Lahiji whisked me away before Nabat had devised another angle to avail himself of my cash.

"Big idiot, this Nabat," Nahiji pronounced.

I told him wild horses couldn't drag me into Iraq with Nabat.

"Think, think!" he shouted. "You are much safer with a big idiot than with some smarty-pants. What danger could Nabat perform? Border guards don't bother with big idiots but the smarty-pants worry them."

I wondered where he'd picked up a term like "smarty-pants."

Just as the story of the Magi was wedged in between mighty opposing forces so, in suddenly feeling that I'd arrived close to a genuinely inner version of their truth, I, too, was painfully aware of being wedged between some of the most hostile nations on earth. Not all borders feel like demarcation points between national dreams. But the point where Iran begins to segue into Iraq literally felt like the gulf at the end of the world, with its one-way toll bridge leading to a country called Hell.

THE ROYAL PALACE OF DARIUS THE GREAT, KING OF KINGS, ETC.

Every known form of precipitation seemed to be tumbling down on us as Lahiji and his deluxe Paykan negotiated a series of ever-shrinking lanes that soon had more potholes than hardtop. One moment it was snowing; then an avalanche of hail hit the roof as if someone had emptied a ton of gravel from an airplane; and suddenly it started to rain so heavily the windshield wipers only made it up thirty degrees before collapsing back under the sheer weight of water they'd accumulated, leaving us in a submarine. Before long we were back to snow, however.

The cycle repeated itself several times before the weather gods made up their minds, settling for a nasty mixture of snow, hail, and freezing rain to which they added a fog that could acquire the density of cotton candy when it needed to. Our headlights could only penetrate six feet through the stuff, causing Lahiji to hit the brakes every fifty or so yards and open his door to check that we were still on a road—or planet.

Stupendous, biblical gusts of wind joined the party, buffeting the car so violently I thought we'd driven over a precipice when the first blast hit. These winds soon vanished, though—probably deemed counter-productive by Climate Central since they swept away the fog in their path. After a particularly savage pounding from some apprentice ty-phoon, I looked up to see terraced foothills that reminded me of a tea plantation in Darjeeling.

I asked Lahiji what was grown up there.

"Memories."

I nodded, thinking "memories" were some kind of flower, like pe-onies—until I realized they weren't.

"Memories?"

"Those 'terraces' are the outer walls of royal palace of Darius Great."

The way he pronounced the words sent shivers down my spine. I asked him to stop for a moment, hoping I might see more than glisten-ing mud slopes.

MEMORIES ARE MADE OF THIS, OR THAT

In a way, memories *had* been planted at Susa. Excavations had un-earthed an unusually rich hoard of treasures here, especially inscribed steles and clay tablets: the kind of treasures scholars treasure most, be-cause they add to knowledge and not just rich museum collections. The French even dug up the original stone stele of King Hammurabi's legal casebook. It was already nearly twelve centuries old when Cyrus the Great finally toppled mighty Babylon in 538 B.C. Cyrus added it to the loot he hauled back in triumph to Susa.

Darius generally seems to have had things carved in stone if they weren't true—like his billboard autobiography on the rock face at Behistun. His subjects must have been sick of the phrase "Saith

Darius the King," which begins almost every paragraph he ever dictated.

References to Darius' laws exist in various Babylonian and Akkadian tablets, however, and on some royal inscriptions. Differences with Hammurabi's law are not exactly striking. The Babylonian lawmaker stressed that "the strong should not injure the weak," for instance; yet Darius had quite another view altogether, deeming it essential for society's well-being that "the stronger does not smite nor destroy the weak." Loosely defining the term "injure" hardly revolutionized jurisprudence—indeed it virtually legitimized any injuries to "the weak" as long as the "weak" weren't beaten or actually destroyed in the process.

Darius also had a talent for stating the obvious as if archangels had just announced it from on high: "Of the man who speaks against the truth, never do I trust a word . . . What is right I love and what is not right I hate." This was not exactly an astonishingly novel concept of idealized human behavior even in the fifth century B.C.

But all Darius had to do in order to draw up a legal code, evidently, was to list his own deeds and then outlaw them. Civilization itself may well have hinged upon an agreement that "the stronger does not smite nor destroy the weak," but Darius did not let this lofty thought interfere with, say, the fate of Fravartish, a Median tribal leader whose forces he crushed. After the defeat, Fravartish had his nose, ears, and tongue cut off and his eyes put out—before Darius displayed him to his followers as a (barely) living illustration of the new Persian law in action. The three thousand people Darius had crucified in Babylon probably weren't especially impressed by any radical changes in the nature of crime and punishment or the quality of Persian mercy, either.

Admittedly, Darius did put a Zoroastrian spin on Hammurabi's laws, but he also put a Zoroastrian spin on himself. Anyone not getting the hint that Persia's new king might be Zoroaster's second coming—if not the Savior himself—had never been anywhere near Persia.

"Saith Darius the King: At Susa a very excellent work was ordered," reads a cuneiform clay tablet dug out of Susa's foundation box, "very excellent it was. Me may Ahura Mazda protect, and Hystaspes my father, and my country." In that order. Most excellent the palace may have been, but the purpose of this tablet—and in the usual three languages—was to prove that Darius was most excellent. "Downward the earth was dug until I reached rock in the earth . . ." Darius the Great was even handy with a shovel: what a guy! The rest of the text, however, is a geography lesson on the Archaemenid empire that reads like someone dropping designer brand names: "The yaka [teak] was brought from Gandara and from Carmania. The gold was brought from Sardis and from Bactria . . . lapis lazuli and carnelian . . . was brought from Sogdiana . . . turquoise was brought from Chorasmia . . . silver and copper were brought from Egypt . . ." Ornamentation from Ionia, ivory from Ethiopia and India, stone from a village in Elam, stonecutters from Ionia and Sardia, the goldsmiths were Medes and Egyptians, the bricklayers were Babylonians. And so on. Even if true, the message was not information, it was power. And the medium—a royal palace—was that same message in three dimensions.

What justice really seems to have meant to Darius was making sure that no one else behaved the way he did. The law that once would have kept him from power—if not jailed him for life—was now tabulated and ruthlessly enforced to keep his enemies from power or in jail and him on the throne. This regal principle was strenuously developed and refined by most of Iran's kings over the following two and a half millennia, until, in 1979, an eighty-year-old theologian and cleric ended Iranian monarchy forever.

It is surprising how many historians have been taken in by Darius' tactics. Build a few great palaces, leave a few hundred inscriptions extolling yourself and your many achievements—your front row seat in posterity is all but guaranteed, or so it seems. Until posterity changes its priorities.

"Like every king," one writer declares humorlessly, "Darius was especially fond of taxation. His taxes were usually fair . . ." His taxes were indeed usually fair, except when they were outrageously unfair. In fact, the same writer notes that the case of Persia itself was an example of Darius' taxes being unfair. Quite an important example, too, I imagine, and one which must have irked Darius' non-Persian subjects considerably. Few of these could have considered his taxes "usually fair" when Persia proper paid no tax at all. Would citizens today find federal taxes fair if they learned that government employees were totally exempt from all taxation and, moreover, used tax dollars collected from others to build themselves luxurious homes?

Darius was very far from fair, usually, but, to be fair, he never aspired to be fair. He made the laws; he didn't have to obey them as well. The larger and more opulent his palaces—those symbols of power—the greater his aura of power. The first pharaohs of Egypt, on the other hand, poured their nation's wealth into temples and probably lived themselves in more modest mud brick dwellings, of which nothing now remains. In this emphasis, though, lay the strength and potency of a civilization that survived almost unchanged and continuously for over three thousand years. It would be surprising if an astute man like Darius had not learned this secret of national success when he became the first to conquer Egypt, as it stumbled around in the twilight of its long life. He certainly realized that destroying temples, persecuting priests, and generally waging war on the religion itself was a big mistake—his predecessor Cambyses had made it, supposedly cursed with madness after he slaughtered the Apis bull. Darius went in the opposite direction: worshipping Egyptian gods when in Egypt, and even sponsoring his own royal cult—of which he was overly fond. He restored many temples, too, adding to others or embellishing existing work—in the tradition of Egyptian rulers. This concern with the beliefs of subject nations exceeds any expediency or necessity. Excessive interest in other religions was not just limited to Egypt, either. Darius soon announced his intention to make good Cyrus the Great's legendary promise to the Jews—made after conquering Babylon and ending the Captivity in 538 B.C.—by rebuilding Solomon's Temple in Jerusalem.

THE "SECOND" TEMPLE

The supervisor of this ambitious project was Zorobabel (or "Zerubbabel"), a Jew who features prominently in the books of some Old Testament prophets, and also in one of the more fanciful Exilic texts—omitted from many Bibles—known as *The First Book of Esdras*.

Esdras depicts Zorobabel as one of three courtiers who are also close friends of the Persian king-emperor. To amuse Darius one night after a long dinner party, the three friends propose a debate on the subject of "Which is more powerful: Wine, Women, or the King?" The most entertaining and convincing argument will win its exponent any favor he asks from Darius. Zorobabel follows two eloquently persuasive pitches for Wine and Kings, launching into a promising argument for the superior power of Women that suddenly and inexplicably veers off into a discourse on Truth, a discourse steeped in Zoroastrian doctrine. Although this mid-stream change of topics is like whipping out a twelve-bore shotgun to end a fencing match, Truth still beats out the competition, and Zorobabel gets to ask of Darius any favor he wishes. He requests the rebuilding of Solomon's Temple. Josephus, the ex-Essene Jewish historian, repeats this story uncritically.

Some less unorthodox Old Testament books—particularly Ezra—present Zorobabel more prosaically as an official representative of the Persian court, sent to supervise the Temple project. His name also appears in lists of prominent Jewish nobles returning from Babylon when the Captivity or Exile is over—although it would seem that he left Babylon for Persia long before he returned to Jerusalem.

In the New Testament, however, both Matthew and Luke include Zorobabel in their genealogies of Jesus' ancestors—all of whom are, of course, direct descendants of King David. Except that Luke traces his blood line through David's lesser son, Nathan, not through the royal line of Solomon, as Matthew's more traditionally Jewish gospel presents him.

Zorobabel is an exceedingly curious and curiously important figure, one whose mystery is compounded by both the key role he plays in rebuilding the Temple and the ambiguous treatment he receives at the hands of biblical authors in both Testaments. The prophets finally let him disappear without even mentioning this odd disappearance or his name again. During the rebuilt Temple's opening ceremonies, for which he is conspicuously absent, there's not so much as a casual reference to poor old Zorobabel, although few people had more right or reason than he to be there celebrating this most auspicious occasion.

ZOROBABEL THE VANISHING MESSIAH

In fact, though—and proof is abundant—Zorobabel is the Davidic Messiah of the Jews. His partner in rebuilding the Temple is Joshua, the son of Jehozadak, who himself becomes the first High Priest of the Jews—a clear indication that his own genealogy is the Zadokite or priestly line descended from Aaron. The relationship between these two men is exactly the same as that between Jesus and John the Baptist. Zechariah (4:11–13) even defines the role they will play as joint leaders of the community after the exile: ". . . a government divided equally between priest and prince." They are equal, but "priest" still comes before "prince"—unlike the situation Solomon created, banishing one of his father's two high priests and assuming both roles himself, a situation which eventually tore the kingdom in half, with northern Israel forming itself around King David's old high priest. Furthermore, Zechariah continues, they are "the two anointed ones who stand before the Lord of the whole world." He is not referring to Darius, but is he referring to God or just *a* god?

Later (6:11–13), Zechariah also mentions Zorobabel's crowning as Davidic ruler—except it is Joshua's name we now read in this section. After Zorobabel's (apparent) death the messianic expectation became concentrated in the priest or Zadokite; and what is termed by some theologians an "inspired rereading" of the text caused Joshua's name to replace that of Zorobabel. "Stalinesque historical revisionism" would, however, be a more accurate description of this textual tampering. Any Jew 2,500 years ago would have known that Joshua could not possibly have become the princely Davidic ruler: his job is control of the temple and cultic activities. Besides, only Zorobabel has applied to him— by the prophet Haggai (2:23), for example—the language of royal messianism: "[Saith the Lord, I] . . . will make thee as a signet: for I have chosen thee." Haggai (1:11) also makes it clear that the Covenant made "between God and every living creature of all flesh that is upon the earth" (Genesis 9:17) has been broken. But, through the work of Zorobabel and Joshua—that is, the rebuilt Temple—God's covenant, which has never been broken spiritually, will be restored physically, too. This emphasis on a material symbol for what is only a spiritual process of unification seems to be—according to the prophets—Judaism's downfall.

Haggai describes Zorobabel first as "the son of . . . the governor of Judah," and later as the "governor of Judah." His father, Salathiel (or She'alti'el), also appears in the Matthew-Luke genealogies, of course, and thus, like his son, is cut off from the royal blood line by Luke—the most suspect gospel. Luke was St. Paul's close companion and thus in opposition to the "Jesus Movement" later headed by James, the brother of Jesus. The term "governor of Judah" in fact means the hereditary title of Davidic king-messiah. Gubernatorial positions are no one's birthright. Through Haggai (2:22), God tells Zorobabel ". . . I will overthrow the throne of kingdoms, and I will destroy the kingdoms of the heathen . . ." This is the reinstatement of an ancient ideal: nations ruled by priest-kings, or a priest in conjunction with a king, rather than a king with puppet high priests—or the abhorred Egyptian emperor-gods that would come again with Roman times. These are the "kingdoms of the heathen" and the "throne of kingdoms" Haggai's God predicts he will "overthrow," perhaps. But Darius was a god in Egypt—as Alexander would be; hence their title "The Great."

Thus, and interestingly, Joshua assumes both roles after Zorobabel's death, arousing sorrow, possibly—at the failure of the princely messiah's mission—but no hostility. When Jesus later attempts to do the same thing in reverse—presenting himself as king-priest—after John the Baptist's death, he arouses a frenzy of hostility from both the orthodox Jewish establishment and a section of the Essene theocrats, as well as the occupying Roman leadership. This backlash evidently included the crucifixion of at least three men directly involved, and marked the beginning of the end for dreams of a Jewish empire.

The Temple project began—as idea at least—according to most biblical sources, in the second year of Darius' reign in the sixth century B.C. It was obviously something close to his heart. The restoration to office of the Zadokite priest and the Davidic king—which the Temple's reconstruction could easily have proceeded without—was evidently something else high on Darius' busy agenda, too. He certainly devoted an inordinate amount of time and money to it, both of which commodities could have been better employed back in Persia.

The highly controversial Dead Sea Scrolls scholar Professor Barbara Thiering has recently suggested that the "Persian overlords . . . imposed on [the priest and king] . . . the condition that the king must give up his primary military role." She further adds that "Kings could become the center of rebellion, and the Persians soon went further and abolished the kingship altogether." Yet these statements do not take into account events occurring within the Persian court during the various periods she refers to here. Nor do they consider the significance—related again to John the Baptist, Jesus, and the Jewish leadership—of a pattern repeated in reverse, a pattern whose design is first apparent in the third chapter of the Book of Genesis, then recurs as if a fugue of ideas throughout every major story or episode in Judaic scripture. Its essence—feuding siblings—is the central tenet of Zoroaster's philosophy.

THE SON OF A STAR

Persian rulers were the only powerful allies that Jewish Zealots resisting Roman occupation seemed to have had. Indeed, Persian armies were on their way to provide reinforcements for Simeon Bar Khochba's troops during the second Jewish revolt—beginning in A.D. 132—when they were waylaid in a battle with marauding northern tribes. Had they reached the Zealots in time Simeon might well have beaten Rome's legions. He had done it before. Earlier in this highly organized and well-financed revolt, Simeon managed to defeat a force of nearly 12,000, effectively ridding Israel of all occupying troops and even reinstating Judaic rule in Jerusalem.

The Zealots' last great leader was also hailed as a Messiah by the renowned Rabbi Akiba; and Simeon's adopted nom-de-guerre, Bar Khochba, means "son of a star," a term related to another Old Testament prophecy evidently concerning two messiahs: "the star" and the "scepter" that shall come to Israel's rescue—both of them from David's line, too. According to recent work by Dr. Robert Eisenman, another Scrolls scholar arousing the ire of Christian orthodoxy, Simeon was directly related to Jesus' family. Persian military support for the Zealots here does not thus seem to indicate disapproval of Jewish kingship. Quite the reverse.

Professor Thiering further undermines her own theory in a letter she wrote to me in February 1994. While mentioning research by K. G. Kuhn which "established the connection between Iranian religion and the Qumran literature" as long ago as 1952, she goes on to state that the "term Magi in the New Testament is partly a kind of nickname, but partly has a genuine connection with the true Magi. The people we are meeting in the Hellenistic period were primarily Samaritan Jews who kept the Essene solar calendar. They had developed their interests in calendar, medicine, and manipulation of superstition while they were in Babylon during the Exile, so there was indeed a genuine link with Zoroastrianism . . . But they were Diaspora Essenes who had formed one of the ascetic orders who came together under Herod the Great to start a mission to Diaspora Jews . . . that . . . after some seventy years split into Christians and Jews, with the Magians staying on the Jewish side, deadly enemies of the Christians . . . Their leader, Simon Magus, was the Antipope." She concludes: ". . . we are dealing with fashionable cultists who were thought to represent Judaism, but teaching that they themselves were incarnations of gods, and circulating an exotic mix of Hellenistic and Eastern thought . . . This Jewish-Samaritan sect had a strong hold in places like Asia Minor. Acts 19:19 speaks of the public burning of the Magian books under Christian influence. The Christians were in direct competition with them, and in fact were a reform group that had once been with them in a single organization."

Thiering, however, ultimately promotes a rationalized version of Jesus' life that ends up with St. Paul emerging as the hero. Ironic as it is, considering the hostile reactions from Catholics to her work, she is the sole "unauthorized" Scrolls scholar to thoroughly condone the Pauline heresy. As brilliant as many of her interpretations are, Thiering's major shortcoming is her inability to realize that the "Eastern" gnostic, or Magian, or Nazarean Essenes were not superstitious fools: they opposed Pauline Judaeo-Christianity for the very reason that, by removing doctrines and practices regarding the subjective experience of "Truth," it would end up as little more than the secular humanism Thiering herself seems to have arrived at—besides creating a society governed increasingly by political or personal expediency rather than eternal spiritual values and truths. Simon Magus's claim to be a god— or God—must be viewed in the same light as Jesus' statement that "my Father and I are one." Information on Simon, remember, comes down to us from hostile sources.

Yet Professor Thiering's work, looked at through "Eastern" rather than Western or Pauline eyes, oddly reinforces the contention that Persian Zoroastrian Magi exerted a most powerful and profound influence over the development of both Judaism and Christianity, as well as—later—Islam. Indeed, so powerful and profound was this influence that without it, beyond all doubt, Judaism would have disappeared after Nebuchadrezzar destroyed Jerusalem in 586 B.C., and neither Christianity nor Islam would have ever existed—or, at least, existed in the forms we know today.

HOUSING GOD

In Darius the Great's resurrection of Judaism, however, we can see the ancient world slipping imperceptibly toward modern times. The inscription on clay tablets found in Susa's foundation box suspiciously echoes the words of God to the prophet Zechariah regarding the rebuilt temple (Zechariah 4:9): "The hands of Zorobabel have laid the foundation of this house; his hands shall also finish it . . ." Three verses earlier we find: "This is the word of the Lord unto Zorobabel, saying, Not by might, nor by power, but by my Spirit . . ." Professor Thiering uses this passage as evidence that the "Persian overlords" were reinstating a princely messiah but minus military capability; yet it could be interpreted just as easily as an indication that priestly and princely roles were to be combined—something Darius was certainly attempting to do for himself both in Egypt and in Persia.

Joshua, the priestly messiah, is as ambiguous a presence in Zechariah as Zorobabel. The Zadokite is shown at one point (Zechariah 3:1–2) standing between "the angel of the Lord, and Satan . . . at his right hand to resist him"—a quintessentially Zoroastrian image—with God then saying to Satan: "The Lord rebuke thee . . . even the Lord that hath chosen Jerusalem rebuke thee: is not this a branch plucked out of thy fire?" This last verse also serves the dual function of presenting both Joshua and Jerusalem as something denied, or saved from, Satan's fire, as well as something emerging like grace from Ahura Mazda's sacred fire—with the "branch" or "brand" representing barsom rods, the sticks or wands that Zoroastrian priests use during their sacrificial rites at fire altars. "Branch" is, in addition, a messianic name used for Zorobabel by Zechariah a little later on (Zechariah 3:8); it was also employed by the prophet Jeremiah (23:5) for a coming Savior who sounds anything but passive and priestly. In Hebrew, "branch" is *zemah*, but the Greek term is *anatole*—the word Matthew uses when referring to the achronychal rising of the Magi's "star," something I will get to in the Epilogue. Simeon Bar Khochba's choice in surnames therefore contains a pun that any Jew or even Roman would get: the "son of a star" was also son of a "branch taken out of David."

The Book of Zechariah is predominantly a high-pressure sales pitch for the proposed rebuilding of Solomon's Temple, which makes it seem suspiciously close to Darius' own propaganda campaign. Like Darius' inscriptions, God's pronouncements are inevitably preceded by the phrase "Thus saith the Lord of hosts . . ." The prophet also invokes Solomon whenever he can do so subtly, too.

In a vision that concerns a giant flying Torah scroll, for example, the measurements of the scroll are precisely those of the inner shrine in Solomon's Temple (Zechariah 5:2)—which is where Zechariah would like to see the "word" or "spirit" of God come to dwell again. "Solomon's altar" at Kashan, as I found, has those same measurements incorporated in it.

But this drive toward the institutionalization of religion—which is what the Temple represents—did not receive unanimous approval.

The much misunderstood term "Antichrist," best known from the New Testament's apocalyptic Book of Revelation, in fact refers to anyone presenting himself as both prince and priest. Zorobabel is an "Antichrist," as is Darius. The Roman emperor-gods were Antichrists, too, and—some television evangelists will be happy to learn—so are all the popes. Oddly enough, though, an Antipope—like the Magian leader Simon Magus or the one elected by Frederick Barbarossa—would in effect be the opposite of an Antichrist, which is not, however, necessarily the same as being a true messiah. "Pope" derives from a term meaning "Father," and it refers to Abraham, "Father of all Jews."

It was to Abraham that the mysterious Melchizedek "king of Salem" appeared (Genesis 14:17–20) after a victorious battle. Melchizedek is also, we're told, "the priest of the most high God," and in this capacity he "brought forth bread and wine . . . And he blessed him, and said,

Blessed be Abram of the most high God, possessor of heaven and earth . . ." After this, Abram presents the priest-king with a tithe of all his battle booty. The action seems intimately linked with what follows immediately in the next chapter (Genesis 15), where God appears to Abram in a vision urging him to fear not, for "I am thy shield and thy exceeding great reward." Abram then complains about his zero sperm count, which will make his heir another man's child. The Lord "brought him forth abroad, and said, Look now toward heaven, and count the stars, if thou be able to number them. And he said unto him, So shall thy seed be."

Reza would have settled for two boys.

Then the Lord makes his covenant, granting to Abram's descendants all the land from the river Nile to the Euphrates—basically the map called "Dream of Zionism" I'd seen in a hate tract back in Isfahan. However, talking Ishmael into account, Abram's descendants got what was promised, and more.

But who was this enigmatic Melchizedek, a priest-king from Salem? Some scholars believe the city mentioned is Jerusalem. But, while there are several other Salems to pick from, I think we must accept here that Melchizedek is king of what *Salem* (or *Shalom*) means in Hebrew: he's king of peace in the sense of integration, wholeness. He's the "royal man," one who's conquered and unified his upper and lower natures, becoming perfect. Such men are called kings. He's also the only high priest in the Old Testament whom no one seems to have ordained. In the Psalms (110:4) he is a figure of David, who is, in turn, himself a figure of the priest-king messiah.

Yet in the Epistle to the Hebrews, chapter seven is entirely devoted to employing Melchizedek (whose name means "my Lord is Justice") in an attack on Jewish priesthood and the Law. A prophetic figure of Christ, Melchizedek has "no father, mother, or ancestry" according to this epistle. Therefore he's outside time, like a Son of God, exercising an eternal priesthood, one thus superior to that of the Jewish priests. Not only are the latter mortal, but in the person of their ancestor Abraham they gave tithes to Melchizedek and received his blessing. Like Melchizedek, Jesus is not of priestly descent but is described by the Pauline philosophy as "a priest of the order of Melchizedek" (Hebrews 7:11–19). This settles the question of Jesus' right to a priestly role.

By assuming Abraham's title, the popes of the Roman Church are thus also asserting their supremacy over Jewish priesthood as well as the legitimacy and ultimate superiority of the Melchizedek order and thus Pauline Christianity. St. Paul was a polemical propagandist of genius, one must admit, and he convinced everyone with such theological *tours de force*—everyone, that is, except those who, like James, knew better because they knew the truth through experience, not faith.

POET, ANTICHRIST, BUT NOT REALLY ISAIAH

That poetic genius, the unknown prophet called in scholarly circles Second Isaiah—since, though written two hundred years later, his work closely resembles that of Isaiah and is often included as chapters forty to sixty-five in Isaiah's own book—can also be called an Antichrist, since his opposition to the Temple in Jerusalem voices the most central issue of all here: the dangers inherent in natural philosophy becoming institutionalized religion, of priests becoming kings—or, worse, kings becoming gods. It is worth quoting God's words as related by the unknown prophet (Isaiah 66:1–4) in full, because they appear elsewhere and pointedly: when Solomon has completed his Temple and wonders whether God can dwell in it; and again, most notably, in a passionate speech given by Stephen (Acts 7:49)—a follower of Jesus' brother James, who opposed the Pauline faction—just before he is martyred.

> The heaven is my throne, and the earth is my footstool: where is the house that ye build unto me? and where is the place of my rest? For all those things hath mine hand made, and all those things have been, saith the Lord: but to this man will I look, even to him that is poor and of a contrite spirit, and trembleth at my word. He that killeth an ox is as if he slew a man; he that sacrificeth a lamb, as if he cut off a dog's neck; he that offereth an oblation, as if he offered swine's blood; he that burneth incense, as if he blessed an idol. Yea, they have chosen their own ways, and their soul delighteth in their abominations. I also will choose their delusions, and will bring their fears upon them; because when I called, none did answer; when I spake, they did not hear: but they did evil before mine eyes, and chose that in which I delighted not.

Solomon, as we have seen, sacrificed 144,000 sheep and oxen at his Temple's altar just to get God's attention. Yet apparently God would have seen 144,000 bloody corpses of men and dogs piled up for his approval. Curiously, however, it is the unknown prophet who also refers to Cyrus as the messiah (Isaiah 45:1) (not Darius, who later wanted the role), partly for freeing the Jews held captive at Babylon, and partly for promising to rebuild the Temple. He is careful, though, to make it very clear that his God is not the one worshipped by Solomon. Indeed, it is in this unknown master's soaring verses that Yahweh is first celebrated as the Creator of the Universe and everything in it—in just the same way as Zoroaster had celebrated Ahura Mazda: "I am the Lord, and there is none else. I form the light, and create darkness: I make peace, and create evil. I the Lord do all these things" (Isaiah 45:6–7).

The original prophet Isaiah—a great poet in his own right, too—was also a consummate statesman in the court of King Hezekiah, where he was not afraid to pour scorn upon the pagan ritual sacrifices going on outside in Jerusalem's Temple. He also approves of making an alliance with the Assyrians—to oppose the Egyptian threat in this case—just as Second Isaiah approves of a close relationship with the major Eastern power of his day: Persia. Solomon formed an alliance with Egypt; it seems that those opposed to Solomon and his apostasy always found the East—or something in it—more attractive than anything offered by the West. Like the sun, religions have always moved from east to west, before, in some cases, returning to the East.

Much as he craves it, though, Darius is never presented as a Messiah by any of the prophets. Zorobabel gets that part, and something goes drastically wrong when he plays it. That "something" is also directly related back to Solomon—and, in a curiously prophetic way, onwards five centuries to Jesus, too. This "something" is strongly hinted at in the Old Testament and in an enigmatic story in one of the Dead Sea Scrolls. In both cases a crisis arises out of events directly related to the construction of a new Temple in Jerusalem.

In broad terms, what happens here is a mirror of what occurs with Jesus and John, where the Davidic Messiah assumes the role of the priestly one after his death. In both cases there is a somber sense of unfulfilled promises, failed expectations. This also probably ex-

plains why Luke deprives Zorobabel of his royal Davidic ancestry—
and thus doing, deprives Jesus of his, too. The only canonical gospel
apparently used by the Essenes and Jewish Christians at all was
Matthew.

The Dead Sea Scrolls, as we are now finally able to read them, in
both published and in-progress translations, reveal a bitter conflict between rival factions and the warning of a coming schism that would
rend the religion in two. This conflict appears partly to revolve around
leadership of Jerusalem's Temple, which the Qumran Essenes
shunned (claiming it had been defiled by the installation of a Roman
idol), and whose high priest's authority they refused to recognize. The
Temple had only recently been rebuilt—by Herod, in this case—just
as it had been at the time of Zorobabel's rise and vanish. Darius' motives for rebuilding the Temple, it would appear, have much in common with Herod's; and the Persian's seem to originate in Egypt, where
Darius probably first understood the importance of temple building.

He built no significant temples in his own land, or ever expressed interest in building any; although, as his rock-carved billboards show, he
was eager for his subjects to know of his great devotion to Ahura
Mazda. He never mentions the prophet Zoroaster, however, probably
because he was trying to usurp his place as God's right-hand man. This
puzzling omission continues through the Archaemenid dynasty (sixth
century B.C.), as well, and even beyond into the Sassanian era, where it
includes inscriptions by the great high priest Kartir—who engineered
the murder of Mani.

ACTING GLOBAL, THINKING LOCAL

"Darius could not have temples without Magi," said Lahiji. "And he
was scared of the Magian power. He falsely accused a high priest of
murdering Cambyses' brother, the heir, and instigated a massacre of
the most powerful Magian sect. How could he build temples for the
Magi when he feared them so much?"

Magi, like India's Brahmans, were the priestly caste and officiated at
all religious functions, Zoroastrian or otherwise. *Religion*, not reli-

gions, was their business. They were already powerful enough as it was, and to build temples that Magi were inevitably going to control would have merely undermined the king's own power. If they were a sufficiently potent force to make feasible Darius' claim that one of their number had usurped the throne, then they were obviously also sufficiently potent a force to be capable of such an action. Like Brahmans, however, Magi were on top of the caste hierarchy: they controlled rulers, and rulers governed. Only when this traditional order came under attack by those wishing to replace priests with kings would Magi have had any reason to seize thrones themselves.

According to Lahiji, Darius wanted to institute a system like that of the Egyptians or Israelites, where the king was both secular and spiritual head. To this end he was gradually importing into Persia the trappings of Egyptian religion—like the winged image of Ahura Mazda I saw in Yazd—as well as cultivating the gratitude and respect of Diaspora Jews, who had previously termed Cyrus "messiah" and "God's shepherd," incorporating him into Hebrew prophecy. Darius was apparently banking on this Jewish sanction to bolster his own divine right as king and priest. Moses, after all, had himself been an Egyptian prince, and the Exodus can be viewed as an attempt at a sort of religious reform staged during the long twilight of Egypt's decadence.

By building up his spiritual credentials in Egypt and Palestine Darius was further undermining the Magi back in Persia. Just as restoring and embellishing Egyptian temples and rebuilding the Temple of Solomon—while doing nothing for the religion of his own people—threatened orthodox Zoroastrianism with absorption or, at best, marginalization by the faiths of potent neighbors. The Egyptian temples certainly also served as palaces by Darius' time—the two functions were indistinguishable—and, as we have seen, Solomon's original Temple had probably been little more than a private chapel adjoining the royal palace. The words for "temple" and "palace" were, of course, interchangeable in Persian, Hebrew, and Greek—a legacy from the time when the ruler was God's surrogate on earth, a symbolic role that was often more burden than privilege, and at times more dangerous than glamorous. The priesthood were the real rulers, just as today's world leaders are frequently mere front men—even fall guys—for the anonymous consortiums whose power is not subject to the capricious whims of an electorate. Presidents come and go, big business comes and grows.

With Darius, however, this question of accommodations worked the other way round: his palaces were also temples—as all palaces were eventually to become in the modern world (even when the "palaces" housed only art or artifacts). The great New Year's Day celebrations at Persepolis were parodies of the old religious rituals, with Darius standing in for God's high priest—if not God.

"But what does God want with religion?" asked Lahiji. "Darius served no God but his own greed and lust for power."

"What about Khomeini?"

"Here we do not discuss Imam Khomeini," he replied pointedly. "Which is perhaps your answer, hmmm?"

It wasn't, in fact. For the first time it suddenly occurred to me, amid all this talk of the struggle to retain theocracies in ancient Persia and Israel, that Iran was now the only theocracy on the planet since the Dalai Lama fled Tibet. And Israel was not far from theocratic rule each time the balance of religious parties in the Knesset got shuffled about. What's more, Israel today would never have existed without the theocratic nation that vanished two millennia ago. Iranians were also just as obsessed with Jews and Israel as they were under Darius—except for very different reasons. Love had turned into hate, as it can do. And the more things changed, the more determinedly they remained the same. Perhaps time is after all merely a device to prevent everything from happening at once—or the illusion that prevents us from seeing that in fact everything is happening at once. For time really dwells within the vastness of Eternity—where all things exist simultaneously without any past or future: as that most ancient of all texts, the Rig-Veda, tells us so pointedly.

THE LAST OF THE MANDAEANS

We finally reached a ramshackle compound, with a crumbling mosque-like building in its center cowering beneath rain-driven slaps from the branches of ragged pine trees. A volley of hailstones the size of grapes nearly fractured my skull as I ran behind Lahiji to a darkened porch. Cloud artillery fired down barrages onto old stones and wood. It sounded like a biblical plague of tap dancers. The huge gnarled wood door possessed a knocker slightly larger than a salt spoon, its tenuous clicks no match for the clattering orchestra of castanets and Fred Astaire multiples tuning up on every suitable surface. Lahiji kicked the door instead, shouting out "Yahi-ah!" at the top of his voice.

It did not look as if anyone had been home for years, but I assumed the old man knew what he was doing.

"His name is Yahia," he explained, perhaps in case I thought he was taking yodelling lessons and needed to practice.

"What is he exactly? If he's here, that is."

"Nazarean high priest."

"Is that fairly important?"

"No. It's not an important religion, though. In fact," he chuckled to himself, "it's probably the least important religion on earth."

And the competition in this area is fierce.

"How many Mandaeans are there?"

"Lots of Mandaeans. It's Nazareans that are the problem. Can't have a religion without priests—especially a religion where only priests are allowed to read the important scriptures."

"How many priests are there, then?"

"Perhaps five . . . or six—and the youngest is eighty-five."

"How old is this Yahiah?"

"Too old. He must be well over ninety, but he's not sure."

A mysterious outbreak of plague in the nineteenth century had apparently killed off virtually all of the Mandaeans' priests: not a good omen for the faithful, one would imagine. The community regrouped, though, forming another hierarchy, but a marked lack of interest had resulted in no one being ordained now for over sixty years all the same.

"You'd think someone would be curious to read the secret scriptures, wouldn't you?" I suggested.

"Not if they're like their other scriptures . . ."

"What are they like?"

"They don't make a lot of the sense."

"You could say that of most scriptures . . ."

"Not like these ones. These really do not make the sense. They are not enigmatic—is that the right word?—they are just nonsensical. One text is called The Thousand and Twelve Questions, although it contains nowhere near a thousand and twelve questions . . ."

The rituals were also apparently so complicated—with astonishingly detailed prescriptions given for all of them, and dire consequences promised to both initiate and priest for incorrect performance—that no one now dared undertake them for fear of failure. The simple handshake—known as *kushta*—is very important to Mandaeans, for instance, with a two-hundred-page text devoted to the sole prescribed method for shaking hands.

"Like people," Lahiji sighed, "religions can get lost, too."

To him, the best of the Mandaean faith, as well as the best of Zoroastrianism, could be found in the teachings of his Sufi masters.

Without warning, the door slid open to reveal a troll holding an oil lantern.

Yahia was well under five feet tall and wore what can only be described as a filthy old potato sack tied at the waist with a greasy length of rope. He had not given much thought to his hair or beard recently—or perhaps ever. Both were a smoky gray color and matted into clods in places, which made sections of hair on his head stick out like twisted roots, while parts of his beard resembled a mangled felt bib. Strict Nazareans were apparently not allowed to cut their hair, but they were allowed to *comb* it . . .

Yahia's nose was a small, plump country sausage. His moustache poured from its nostrils, giving the impression that his head was stuffed with horse hair like an old sofa. He had skin the color of boiled beef, and it was not so much lined as buckled, with some sort of muscle problem going on around his lower eyelids. They sagged in little bloodshot folds that made his jaundiced eyeballs seem in danger of rolling out from their glistening sockets. A potent aroma wafted from him, too, part stale urine, part rotten vegetable matter. In a voice that could have belonged to a cartoon rat, he said something to Lahiji and beckoned us in.

We ended up in a room that reminded me of a Victorian subway tunnel, with a damp flagstone floor and curving walls of gray brick. It contained many freestanding bookshelves crammed with musty volumes and yellowed bales of paper. There was also a child's desk upon which a six-foot-high pile of documents perched; two grim wooden chairs; and about a hundred yards of galvanized zinc drain piping in six-foot sections stored against one wall. What I took to be a very thick door mat proved to be a bed, with two brown horse blankets and a yellowed pillow no larger than a paperback novel on it. Behind a tattered green shroud was what looked at first glance like part of a limestone cave festooned with budding stalagmites. It proved to be a kind of altar completely covered with the pooled remains of about a hundred thousand white candles, from which protruded bits of brass and the tips of several empty picture frames, as well as some string and a few dozen knives and forks. In an alcove nearby was a bowl of round dark green things that I think were oranges purchased in 1925.

Yahia made Gandhi seem positively hedonistic.

He started speaking at me, waving a dusty green bottle with no label.

"Will you have some wine he has made?" Lahiji translated.

"Why not?"

Yahia shuffled about in circles, lifting up rags and sheaves of paper, rifling through drawers, and eventually locating a pewter goblet which he handed me. It was not in fact pewter, I realized, but glass that had lain untroubled for half a century. The Nazarean pulled out a disturbing cork and commenced pouring greenish liquid into my goblet. He had fingernails like bear's claws, and an old piece of mystic twine was tied around his wrist. All the while he spoke, unbothered by my protests of incomprehension.

"He thinks you are in the Turkish army," Lahiji informed me.

"Why?"

"Because of your boots. He wonders if your troops could repair his roof."

"They don't do roofs . . . or windows."

I asked if Lahiji could see what the high priest knew about Magi before he harpooned me for being a Roman legionnaire or a Mongol.

The two men embarked on an exchange that lasted fifteen minutes, during which Yahia continued to pour his wine over the floor. The stuff tasted like fennel and shampoo.

"What's he saying?"

"He says that John the Baptist was Hibil-Ziwa."

"I'd always suspected that myself. Who the hell was . . . thingy?"

"Hibil-Ziwa was a Savior who entered the world of darkness and de-stroyed the evil spirits so that the faithful could obtain liberation before the end of the world."

"So was Hercules. Ask him about Jesus."

"Don't."

WHAT GOES AROUND GOES AROUND AGAIN

Mandaeans regard Christianity and rabbinical Judaism as false reli-gions that, along with the negative influence of planets and stars, im-pede the soul's release from bondage. Avoiding anthropomorphic terminology, they describe the Absolute as a formless entity known as the King of Light, or Lord of the Greatness, or the Great Mana. The King of Light has to deal with the Zone of Darkness, and for this pur-pose he generously created the world with a series of emanations, of which one of the most important is the Savior, Manda d'Hayye, the "Knowledge of Life," whence comes the name of the sect.

All created things have their heavenly counterparts. Even the cosmos is shaped like its creator, the archetypal Being. Physical limita-tions are unreal, unconnected to a human being's true nature. Man-daeans assert that the soul is in exile down here, a speck of light stranded in matter. The body, like all matter, springs from the plane-tary bodies, but life and breath come from the divine world of light.

Yahia certainly looked like a soul in exile to me.

After an hour we were into the celestial phallus and the cosmic womb, with starry trees wreathed in myrtle leaves and heavenly seed spilled into rivers. Then it started to get really interesting. There was much symbolism concerning springs of water and date palms among which the Great Mother hides. Then there was a well called Sumqaq in which could be found the Great Nest of Darkness. It resembled Las Vegas during a power outage.

John the Baptist preached the true faith, but Jesus, his chief disciple, went astray, floundering in the waters of materialism. The Magi had traveled to symbolically repatriate the faith, as Yahia saw it.

From what I could gather, the Mandaean faith was a salad of Jewish Cabalism, esoteric Zoroastrianism, gnostic Christianity, Sufism, Tantra, Madame Blavatsky, and the Lord of the Rings. Its symbolism had become ludicrously abstruse, too, and there was a marked penchant for lengthy descriptions of diabolical punishments that would befall the faithful for the most trivial of errors. All of this had combined to make the faith thoroughly unattractive. This may explain why it hasn't ordained a priest since 1933, let alone made any converts.

Yet it was one more piece in the four-dimensional puzzle, and, isolated since the fall of Jerusalem in A.D. 70, the Mandaeans had still retained a little something of the flavor of pure Essene Judaism, the faith that Jesus preached and practiced. It was also the faith from which Paul and his followers created a religion for the Roman Empire, a religion that would ultimately destroy classical Judaism, and then go on to threaten monotheism so profoundly that Islam sprang up to man the barricades. And all three faiths share the guilt for edging out the religion of Zoroaster—from which they had taken their most important and radical beliefs—because they knew it was inherently capable of overshadowing them all as the major World Religion.

With no congregation to trouble him, what did Yahia do with his time? I wondered. Mandaean rituals were so demanding, however, that it was apparently all he could do to keep up with his own sacred obligations. Occasionally, old-timers would drop in to consult him about some topic or other, I learned, and a number of Muslim families placed enormous faith in his ability to drive out evil spirits. He probably confused these evil spirits into submission if his exorcism rites were anything like the rules governing handshakes.

As we tried to leave, Yahia began exploring a theory that St. Thomas the Apostle was actually Zoroaster. It resembled the theory that Zoroaster was actually the Buddha and Mahavir, or alternatively that the Buddha was actually Zoroaster and Mahavir. By now I was beginning to believe there had been dozens of people spanning three millennia who were all Zoroaster. It was like hearing that Shakespeare's plays were not written by Shakespeare but by another man whose name also happened to be Shakespeare.

The parallelism of portentous tales was, however, something I started to think more carefully about. Darius clearly worked on being compared to Zoroaster. The early Christians worked so hard at making their faith acceptable to pagans that by the time they'd finished Jesus shared Hercules' biography and even had much in common with Alexander the Great, from virgin birth heralded by Magi, through (symbolic) heroic conquests to death at thirty-three. Christianity became so acceptable to pagans in the end that pagans adopted it—because it was pagan, or neo-pagan. Did the Jewish scribes also deliberately mirror Persian history? or were tales honestly confused by embellishment? Perhaps, however, comparisons between Jewish history and that of the Persians or Egyptians were really attempts to make a macrocosm of a fragmented little tribal microcosm—to make a "great nation" from scratch.

The Mandaeans had not attempted to compare themselves to anyone, however. They had absorbed everyone instead—which was probably a mistake. Even Yahia wasn't entirely sure now how many Saviors he should expect.

Contrary to the consensus in what little exists to be read about Mandaeans, however, they do not regard Jesus as a false messiah so much as a failed messiah. And even this failure seemed couched in terms of a cosmic drama: he was supposed to fail, thus in failing he succeeded in his mission. It was a curious statement, yet the more I looked at the repeated pattern of failed princely Messiahs from Solomon through Zorobabel to Jesus, the more I sensed myself close to heart of the matter, a beat away from the reason Persian Magi were at the Nativity.

UNTO US TWO SONS ARE GIVEN

Yahia then announced—as if observing a change in weather—that Jesus had escaped crucifixion, as the Koran rightly said he had (I assumed he felt obliged to add this for the theocrats back in Teheran), and then had lived for some time right here in Shush among his cousin and erstwhile partner John the Baptist's followers. From here, apparently, Jesus eventually traveled to India—where he died.

I had heard the legends of Jesus in India—who hasn't?—so was not unduly surprised. What I was told next, though, definitely surprised me unduly.

The Mandaeans subscribe to the belief that Judas Thomas was Jesus' twin brother—as the Celtic and Egyptian Christians did—it seems, but they also believe that it was this Judas, not Iscariot, who was crucified. Why? Because his resemblance to Jesus was sufficient to fool Pilate—who knew what Jesus looked like and was legally obliged to witness the Roman punishment of crucifixion when meted out by Jews—and because Judas Thomas had been instrumental in a rift among Jesus' followers that ultimately brought down the crucifixion sentence. Sibling rivalry, perhaps?—which in identical twins can take on bizarrely stressful forms.

Jesus, the old Mandaean troll patiently continued, had then posed as Thomas for the rest of his life to avoid the taint of his failure as messiah interfering with his work. He had enacted the drama, played the role: now he wished to get on with his life. I could understand that. Actors don't have to die for real—unless of course they want to—and failed messiahs rarely find a future as gurus.

The writings attributed to Thomas—his "book" and his "gospel"—were in fact written by Jesus, I was told: something few were privileged to know, apparently, but which certainly accounted for their widespread popularity among the Eastern and Celtic churches, as well as the various "heresies." Jesus-Thomas had continued to preach wherever he could that was beyond the reach of the Roman-Pauline church, ending up in Madras, where he was finally burned to death by ungrateful Hindu priests. St. Paul was the great villain of the piece, seen by the Mandaeans as a fanatic and a Roman agent. The rest was a more familiar version of theological history. If Yahia was an example of what happens to those who denounce the Pauline doctrine as heresy, I thought, it's hardly surprising that few ever consider the matter.

CHRISTIANITY: A REAPPRAISAL

Thomas certainly plays an odd role in Christian history. Even his name is odd. It's not a name, in fact, but a sobriquet meaning "Twin"—just as Peter would be "Rocky" today. Sometimes he's referred to as "Thomas the Twin"—which is like saying "Twin the Twin"—and at other times he appears to possess another name,

"Thomas who is called Didymus." But since "Didymus" is just Greek for "Twin" this means he's known as "Twin who is called Twin." If this isn't deliberate obfuscation, then it's accidental obfuscation. Someone doesn't like Thomas. He's barely allowed any space in the canonical New Testament: once he says something stupid, and the other time he asks if he can put his fingers in Jesus' nail wounds. Yet his own alleged works were a huge hit everywhere but Rome for several hundred Christian years. And he also does for Christianity in the East what Paul did in the West. If Thomas achieved half of what he claims to have achieved during an evangelizing stroll from Palestine to India, then he towers above any other saint. The gnostic texts attributed to him also contain more genuinely profound philosophical advice on a page than most entire canonical gospels can manage to fit in, when not narrating a rather pointless story about a "Prince of Peace" who comes to "bring a sword," is rude to his mother, prone to fits of violence, and dies achieving absolutely nothing: which is why no one but the authors seems to care much about him. Contemporary chroniclers are unusually silent about any "Jesus of Nazareth."

St. Paul then writes his own gospel—coyly termed "letters"—about someone also called Jesus but bearing no resemblance to the Jesus we've been reading about in the four gospels. Jesus' brother James is allowed a "letter," too, but only a two-pager. Nonetheless, he still manages to denounce Paul's version of Jesus' teaching—faith, obedience to rulers—as heretical Roman claptrap.

Then comes the so-called Revelation of someone else called John, but probably not any of the Johns we've so far encountered, since he lives on a Mediterranean island and appears to be stark raving mad—or possibly writing in code. It has nothing to do with anything that the gospellers or Paul have been telling us, and seems purely intended to frighten the hell out of its readers. Somewhere in this prose poem by Wagner and Hieronymous Bosch, this so-called Revelation, Jesus makes the odd appearance, but doesn't seem to be either of the two Jesuses we've so far encountered, closing the New Testament with a That's-all-folks non sequitur about showing up again sooner than anyone thinks. After two thousand years this loses some of its impact, of course. Even most theologians now suggest the book is "symbolic."

All the same, this bolus of enigma and contradiction is what the

Roman orthodoxy once felt adequately conveyed its message. It's hardly surprising the Church discouraged civilians from reading the Bible themselves and even resisted its translation into a language any-one *could* read for themselves for as long as was possible without arous-ing undue suspicion.

In bite-sized selections, the New Testament seems to be a wise book. Read from Matthew to Revelation, however, it makes about as much sense as Mandaean theology. Most astounding is that the world's largest and most influential religion is based on material that wouldn't even compel a handful of acid-heads to form some minor cult if it were published today.

Yet something lies in it—like Polo's Magi tale—and that something is clearly what we can read in Thomas or many other books "unfit" for the canon. Here at least are works that can stand up against Vedic, Buddhist, or Taoist scriptures: that is, they contain spiritual and philo-sophical guidelines for those whose hearts thirst for something more tangible than faith.

MAGI TO THE RESCUE

Via Lahiji, I asked the weary old Mandaean priest about the Magi again. Yes, he replied, Matthew's gospel was accurate—it was the only one of which this could be said. Persian astrologers had observed a major event in the heavens and knew that it held great significance for Israel. Magi had traveled from Iran, arriving two weeks after the birth, to perform rituals and bless the two children.

"The what?"

Hearing about Jesus and a twin brother, I still had never stopped to think what this would do to the Nativity story—not to mention reli-gious art . . . or carols.

The Magi's astrological skills had, however, allowed them to foresee the potential dangers ahead. They informed those Nazarean-Essenes with whom they were in regular contact, and then made sure that Mary and Joseph escaped to Egypt, where Jesus and Thomas were raised by Essene Magians while their parents returned to Israel.

"Good, no?" asked Lahiji, almost convincingly.

There had been two Magi, after all: one for each child (no one wanted to give the myrrh?). Earlier, Yahia informed us knowledgeably, one of the same men had attended the birth of John the Baptist: clearly a far more important occasion—and thoroughly misrepresented by that scoundrel Luke. John's mother wasn't as old as Isaac's had been, because the phrase "advanced in her days" merely meant she followed the Essene solar calendar rather than the orthodox lunar one—so making appointments with her was a problem because next Thursday was a week Saturday. Basically.

The Persian priesthood had always tried to sway its country's rulers to help those they viewed as brothers in Israel and elsewhere. They even raised armies to assist the Jews resisting Roman occupation. It did not work out, though, the old priest sighed. It never did. The only kingdom worth fighting and waiting for was, after all, the kingdom of heaven.

At least he wouldn't have long to wait for that.

As we were leaving, he called out something.

Lahiji translated: "Just symbols, remember . . ."

"What?"

"It's all just symbols," he says. "Life, death, twins, wars. You believe what you want to believe. Believe in the happy things, my brother. We must make this world happy. I think Christmas is a happy time, too, no?"

"Yes . . . Sometimes."

"Yes, yes. It is a happy time. And the world must be happy."

> You are pure spirit
> but imagine yourself a corpse!
> pure water which thinks
> it's the pot!
> Everything you want
> must be searched for—
> except the Friend.
> If you don't find HIM
> you'll never
> be able
> to start
> to even
> look.
>
> —Sana'i

"Was that of any use?" Lahiji inquired as we thumped back in his deluxe Paykan through straightforward heavy snow.

"Yes, in fact."

"Where they went wrong—these Mandaeans—was in failing to see the content beneath all the form . . ."

Where I went wrong was in agreeing to accompany Nabat and his crew of smugglers and spies into Iraq the following day.

Chapter Eleven

⚶

THE DEVIL IN IRAQ

The vines gleamed in the waters.
Here mighty ones were established.
Yonder the waters are clear
And your counterparts exist and are glorious.

Shine forth! Let your radiance appear,
Great spirits, and come!
Instead of concealing it, let your radiance
And the brightness of the King shine forth;
Bring your perfume and invigorate us!

—Hymn of the Great Mother from Mandaean scriptures

At dawn, we piled into a Range Rover that looked as if it had roved many ranges in its time. Along with the Mercedes, the Range Rover had been the vehicle of the rich during the late Shah's time; now both were vehicles of the Komiteh. Generally. The sky was like blood-stained concrete, thick and heavy, sitting low as if flattening the world. Nabat and his crew could have been supporting this roof of viscous vapors with their heads. They were subdued, almost disoriented, synapses not firing properly. A night of ersatz Famous Grouse obviously took its toll.

We drove north for about fifteen minutes, then, just as the low marshy land began to develop humps that were the toes of the Zagros foothills, we turned at a junction and headed due west for nearly half an hour. Next we took a road that went due south. One more turn, I thought, and we'll be back in Shush. At a town called Robut I noticed a sign reading BAGHDAD 350. It indicated the opposite direction to which we were traveling. Five minutes later, we passed through Cham Hendi, which appeared to be a gas station, and half a mile beyond it we crashed into the side of the road. The Range Rover bounced like a kangaroo, its roof colliding with my skull several times. The crew yo-delled joyfully, as Nabat wrestled with the wheel and navigated around a graveyard of dead trucks that resembled a rusty village buried in mud. Only then did I realize that we hadn't crashed, that Nabat intended to drive off the road. Now at least we were heading more or less toward Iraq. Soon we encountered more truck wreckage, strewn over a vast area. I was wondering what kind of spectacular crash could have hurled a truck so far from the road when I noticed a section of wing from an F-16 fighter jet.

"Hair plane!" Nabat shouted, weaving around it. "Big wars here!"

"Saddam," someone elaborated.

"Ayaah! Beeg dee-mon, the Saddam," another commented.

I asked where the Iraqi border was.

"Hah," came the reply.

"What?"

Apparently we'd crossed the border a minute back.

"Are there no guards?"

"Hah, guardizz iss here."

"Where?"

Within fifteen minutes, bucking and bouncing, we came to a dirt road and turned northwest onto it, roaring off more evenly. A sign read KUWAIT 15.

"Kuwait!"

Everyone laughed.

"Not same Kuwait like the Saddam war," explained Nabat.

"Hah!" someone added. "The Saddam, he go *this* Kuwait no problem."

Behind us a siren suddenly screamed. I turned to see, not a police car or military vehicle, but a red Ferrari with a detachable flashing blue light on one side of its roof.

"Ayaah!" groaned Nabat, slowing and pulling over near a little stream.

"What?" I asked, terrified. "Who is it? Police? Army?"

"Hah," Nabat sighed. "Armies."

"What should I do?"

Nabat waved my anxiety aside like a fly, fishing in his pockets for a wallet the size of a dictionary.

The Ferrari quickly overtook us, braking hard and sliding to block our exit. From it jumped two Iraqi officers in immaculate uniforms. One looked like Cary Grant and wore brown Gucci loafers. He sidled over to Nabat's window, smiling. The two men shook hands and soon were laughing raucously. The officer gave the rest of us a cursory glance, nodding amicably. Then Nabat pulled several U.S. hundred-dollar bills from his vast wallet and casually handed them to the Iraqi, who stuffed the cash in his jacket pocket without even looking at it. After more banter, both men yelled,

"*Khoda Afez!*"

The officer returned to his Ferrari and in seconds was a speck on the horizon.

"Beeg thiefs these man," commented Nabat.

"Ayaah!" everyone agreed.

"Is the Ferrari standard Iraqi army issue?"

"They get from Kuwait—real Kuwait—when they war there. Now beeg thiefs. Make too much monies from these border."

"Ayaah!" came the chorus.

Looking at the bleak lunar wasteland from the springy warmth of our vehicle, I suddenly didn't envy the Magi bumping and shivering their way west on beasts of burden.

HIBIL-ZIWA THE BAPTIST

At Kuwait we picked up a gravel road that possessed a pocked, buckled sign tied back to its post after apparently having been shot down at some point. It read BAGHDAD 300. Ten minutes later, having overtaken a military convoy a mile long on a two lane road without—miraculously—encountering any oncoming traffic, we turned down a side street in a swamp town named Manzilliya, pulling up outside a sprawling mud brick wall surrounding a compound of low stone and concrete structures.

"Uncle house," Nabat explained. "He is zebra. Come."

The crew began to unload some cardboard boxes that had been concealed beneath a tarpaulin in the rear of our vehicle. One man levered off wall panels, revealing a rack of long narrow items wrapped in oily rags. If they weren't guns, they certainly looked like guns.

Someone within was tugging at the compound gate violently. Suddenly, its hinges detached from the wall and we entered through the gap this created to one side, finding an eight-year-old boy with the face of a middle-aged man.

"Uncle," Nabat told me, embracing the tiny figure.

The man took my hand, saying, "You much welcome, friend."

Judging by its exterior, you'd have had trouble renting out the main house as a garage. In real estate parlance, it was a fixer-upper. But, leaving the crew to unload their "exports," we passed through a gloomy mud room and, leaving our shoes behind, down three stairs and through a steel plate door into something from the pages of *Architectural Digest*'s Sicilian edition. Brass chandeliers and wall sconces holding candle lightbulbs blazed down upon gold velour wallpaper, repro gilded consul tables, and a carpet patterned with giant red and purple flowers on a powder-blue background. It was so soft and thick you almost needed snow shoes to walk without sinking.

Thick plastic slip covers protected all the furniture in a living room that, had it become a person, would have been the ghost of Liberace. I sat on a rococo sofa of gold brocade, feeling its protective coat buckle beneath me. The ganzibra uncle—whose name was Zachariah—perched on the rim of a spindly armchair, only his toes in contact with the floor. Nabat heaved open a pair of crimson velvet crisscross curtains framed by a heavy draped swag. Behind them were ornately carved double doors, and behind these was a deep cupboard containing three shelves packed with Famous Grouse bottles and two shelves teeming with Alsace glasses. He grabbed a bottle in one hand and three green-stemmed glasses like flowers in the other, opening the scotch with his teeth and pouring a good two inches into each glass before handing one to each of us.

"Vissy!" he announced, throwing down an inch of his.

Zachariah followed suit, and I had little choice but to gulp down a mouthful of mine. It tasted like rubbing alcohol flavored with nicotine and coffee; but it burned like Drano.

"*Sum-Yawar!*" gasped Nabat, holding his glass aloft in toast.

"*Sum-Yawar!*" his uncle repeated lustily.

Sum-Yawar, I later learned, was Shem, Noah's son, who is regarded as the guardian of Mandaean wisdom after the Flood.

"So," I began, as soon as my eyes ceased to water, "Nabat tells me you are a ganzibra."

"Hah," Zachariah concurred.

"What exactly does a ganzibra do?"

"It is like small priest."

He certainly was small. I inquired if the role was more scholarly, more scribe-like.

The word "scribe" caused problems, instigating a five-minute debate between uncle and nephew in some sort of a dialect that I found utterly impenetrable.

"Write," I threw in, to be helpful. "A scribe is a kind of writer."

"Viper?"

"No, writer. A man who puts down language on paper with a pen. Or word processor . . ."

"Would bro-cess her?"

"No."

I mimicked someone typing, then someone writing with a pen.

"Ah, ah! Yezz: bright-her?"

We got there, but Nabat then informed me that his uncle could hardly be a writer since he had never learned to write . . . or read.

"So what does he do as ganzibra?"

He had memorized the scriptures, I eventually learned, by listening to his father recite them. Now he was helping his own son to do the same. It was a tradition.

Once there were other roles for the ganzibra, but, like the priests, they had all but ceased performing rituals in case they made any errors. The punishment for getting a ritual wrong was "Sumqaq"—the "Great Nest" or "Well of Darkness."

I asked what the major Mandaean scriptures were called and what they consisted of. Zachariah mumbled sorrowfully to Nabat for some minutes.

"He izz not allow to tell you."

"Oh."

"He go to Sumqaq if he telling you."

"Well, I wouldn't want that . . ."

Presumably to change the subject and avoid the possibility of banishment to Sumqaq, the uncle asked what the purpose of my journey was. He kept nodding as I told him, as if he were intimately familiar with the subject.

"Not go with the Yazeedi," he eventually said.

"Huh?"

"Uncle say," said Nabat, "that you must be care full for the Yazeedis on you travel."

"Ah. Yazeedis. Yes, yes."

"Yazeedis, they worshipping the Shaitan."

"So I hear."

"Always they saying they Mandaean peoples but not being Mandaean peoples. Yazeedis, they too much fool the foreigners."

I inquired what the Yazeedis did to those foreigners they fooled.

Both men shrugged helplessly. Clearly, nothing was too bad for Yazeedis to do to helpless strangers.

"Where are they based . . . as it were?"

"They everywhere," Nabat exclaimed. "Beeg problem for you."

I inquired if Yazeedis were considered to be a bigger problem for me than Saddam's Republican Guard.

Both men laughed.

"Soldiers, you giving some monies, yes? But the Shaitan, he not needing monies—he need *you*," Nabat informed me gravely, as if I were unaware of Satan's needs.

After much goading and prompting, I learned that Mandaean scriptures predicted the current decline in the faith, pitying those believers and Nazareans who lived during such times. Their garments would be black, the Great Father had apparently announced, and they would never rise to the Great Light because of the errors they would make in performing sacred rituals. I also discovered that any one not baptized on *"Kansia uzahlia,"* New Year's Eve, was deemed cursed and sentenced to seventy blows from a cane. On the other hand, Zachariah announced, every person who is baptized at the appointed time can consider himself baptized seventy times—which was clearly a good deal more beneficial than being baptized just once. Following New Year's Eve, there was a thirty-six-hour period of seclusion—part of *Kansia uzahlia*—when all members of a Mandaean family had to remain within doors. During this period, it was believed, the spirits who normally protect running water were absent and the water was considered to be under an evil spell. Thus Mandaeans are forbidden to touch any flowing water during these thirty-six hours, whether in ditches, irrigation channels, or rivers. This reverence for flowing water was very Zoroastrian in nature.

I asked if the belief was connected to John the Baptist—who was known to Mandaeans as Hibil-Ziwa.

A frenzy of incomprehensible debate followed. I gathered that talking to outsiders about Hibil-Ziwa was a bigger no-no than screwing up rituals. There seemed to be a place even worse than Sumqaq for those who broke this taboo. So bad was this very bad place that it appeared not to possess even a name. Since it seemed so unattractive, I wanted to ask what the appeal of the Mandaean faith was—what kind of deal did it offer the faithful that no other religion did?—but I had no desire to offend people who could make my life very difficult if they wished to do so. For instance, how would I get to Babylon without them driving me to one of the towns along the Tigris river where I presumed there were main roads and buses?

GNOSTIC REMARKS

By the time lunch was served both Nabat and his ganzibra uncle were as drunk as owls, having emptied the entire bottle of Famous Grouse and close to half of another bottle. Zachariah kept embracing me and exclaiming his deep admiration for all things British. I made the mistake of confessing that I was really from Wales and then creating a flippant analogy between the plight of the Welsh under English domination and that of the Palestinians in Israel. Admittedly, I was not exactly sober by this stage either, and it was still only 11:45 A.M.

Over a lunch that could best be described as roast meat with roast meat, Zachariah held forth on the wickedness of the Jews for an hour. Since he made no distinction between events in Jerusalem two thousand years ago and events in Israel now, I was never entirely certain which Jews he was talking about. Indeed, with a theocratic government in Iran, and a government often dominated by wanna-be theocrats in Israel, with a bloodthirsty tyrant like Saddam dreaming of a new Babylonian empire in Iraq, and a brilliant but fierce warlord still running what had been parts of Assyria, past and present again suddenly seemed oddly conflated across the entire area.

Eventually we got round to the subject of Thomas. Because he firmly believed that Jesus had assumed the identity of his twin brother after the latter's crucifixion, I realized, almost everything Zachariah confidently announced that Jesus had said derived in fact from the Gospel of Thomas—which, of course, the uncle believed Jesus had written himself. For instance, the uncle proclaimed Jesus personally told his disciples that John the Baptist was the messiah. Months later, I discovered Logion 46 in the Thomasine gospel:

> Jesus said, "Among those born of women, from Adam until John the Baptist, there is no one so superior to John the Baptist that his eyes should not be covered (before him). Yet I have said, whichever one of you comes to be a child will be acquainted with the Kingdom and will become superior to John."

It was not quite the same statement that Zachariah had made, but it was certainly close—if somewhat cryptic. Gnosticism is nothing if not cryptic much of the time, though, and Thomas' gospel is unquestionably a key gnostic text. Its influence was once extensive and can be found in the literature of numerous Western mystical schools, in much European poetry, the paintings of Leonardo Da Vinci, and even in the plays of Shakespeare.

The Mandaeans were considered to be the last surviving Gnostics—believers that salvation comes through "knowledge," not just faith as Pauline doctrine holds—when anyone considered there were any Mandaeans left, that is. Outside of Christianity, however, this belief is scarcely true. Most Eastern faiths maintain that direct knowledge of

God—and/or Self—is the only true religion. Elsewhere in Thomas, Jesus accuses the "Scribes and Pharisees" of holding on to the keys of the "Kingdom" and not letting anyone else open the door—while also not opening it themselves. It was again the argument against in-stitutionalized religion versus natural philosophy, which was the reason that the Magi had traveled west to help avert a catastrophe that would in effect lock the gates of heaven forever. Priests, not kings—let alone bankers—were supposed to be the caretakers of this world.

The Gospel of Thomas contains much that recalls both Zoroastrian and Sufi imagery and theology, too. Logion 13 even has a statement about stones and fire that is strongly reminiscent both of Persian Sufi mystical verse as well as Marco Polo's account of the Magi throwing the stone Jesus gave them into a well—Sumqaq, presumably, "the Well of Darkness." In it Jesus asks three disciples how they would de-scribe him. Simon Peter says that he is a "Righteous angel"; Matthew terms him a "Wise philosopher"; but Thomas tells his "Master" that he is incapable of describing him. Jesus replies:

> "I am not your master. Because you have drunk, you have become in-toxicated from the bubbling stream which I have measured out."

Then Jesus takes him aside and tells him three things. The disciples ask him afterwards:

> "What did Jesus say to you?" Thomas said to them, "If I tell you one of the things which he told me, you will pick up stones and throw them at me; a fire will come out of the stones and burn you up."

I tried asking Zachariah about Jesus' other brother, James the Just or Righteous, but he seemed reluctant to discuss this issue. Later, reading the Gospel of Thomas, it occurred to me that this reluctance probably stemmed from references that make James seem equally important a figure as John the Baptist:

> Then the disciples said to Jesus, "We know that You will depart from us. Who is to be our leader?"

Jesus said to them, "Wherever you are, you are to go to James the Righteous, for whose sake heaven and earth came into being."

—The Gospel of Thomas, Logion 12

Melchizedek says as much of Abraham when he blesses him.

On the subject of St. Paul, however, Zachariah showed no diffidence. Paul had been commissioned by the Romans to destroy the true faith by corrupting it with pagan doctrines and making it a tool of subjugation and oppression. He removed the inner quest for knowledge and replaced it with faith—which was meaningless without knowledge. Faith enabled the Romans to do exactly what Jesus accused the Scribes and Pharisees of doing. It was, Zachariah announced, what had prompted Moses to break with the Egyptian religion, which had become corrupted by pharaohs who no longer practiced the "knowledge" themselves and prevented anyone else from practicing it.

Was he saying, I asked, that the Egyptian religion had once been the same as the religion of the Jews?

"Only one Truth, is there not?" he replied.

"Were Mandaeans the same as Essenes, then?"

Much translation and elaboration was required before the answer to this came:

"There was true religion and false religion. Jesus is called the Nazarean, no?"

"Yes."

"Then Jesus was Mandaean, no? And disciple of Hibil-Ziwa, no?"

Jesus, according to Zachariah, had endeavored to hold the true faith together after John the Baptist's execution, but "demons" were too powerful. The hard-core disciples of John had decided to flee after James the Righteous was executed—which was probably in A.D. 62— and they were given refuge by Persian Magi, who also practiced the "True religion." Jesus, too—though now as Thomas—had been protected by Magi for some years, during which he wrote the Gospel of Thomas as well as, I was astonished to hear, the Gospel of John. Although, examining John's gospel later, I noticed remarkable similarities between it and Thomas, particularly in the emphasis on inner knowledge. John is the most "gnostic" of the canonical gospels, but it still delivers the standard life-death-resurrection dogma of orthodox

Roman Christianity. Interestingly, the oldest fragment of the New Testament to have been found so far contains that part of John's gospel where Pilate asks Jesus, "What is truth?"

"Romans, they changing these book," Zachariah responded to this observation. "Real book tell of Thomas his death—but in secret way."

Jesus had been high on Rome's Most Wanted list, it seems, and had to maintain the idea that he'd died. After Persia, he returned west, living near Damascus in Syria before finally being forced to travel beyond the reach of Roman forces. Nabatean priests and Magi had helped him, arranging safe passage along the trade routes. Jesus had resided in Basra and Palmyra briefly before crossing through Mesopotamia, spending some months in Susa, then moving from Magian stronghold to Magian stronghold—places where any Essene Jew apparently would have been always welcome—until he reached the Indus Valley. Here, Brahmans, who maintained close ties with the Western mystical orders, initiated him into their deepest mysteries before escorting him to the relative safety of India's southwestern coast— not the southeastern coast where others have speculated he ended up, near Madras.

Was this information contained in the secret Mandaean literature? I wondered aloud. But the reply consisted of knowing smirks and silence.

BUYING IRAQ

After lunch and more Famous Grouse, Nabat made a final valiant effort to relieve me of some dollars, imploring me to reconsider the pig roast and belly dancer.

"A night you never forgetting," he promised.

I wondered where he'd picked up this ad-copy line, which he repeated several times. After I'd refused him so forcefully that he backed away—perhaps fearing violence—he reluctantly agreed to drive me into Ali al Gharbi, on the banks of the Tigris, where I'd apparently have no trouble getting a bus to Al Hillah, nearest city to what now remained of Babylon.

Uncle Zachariah had passed out on a plastic covered sofa, snoring robustly and looking like a dissipated preteen. So I was unable to say goodbye to him.

> They said to him, "Tell us who you are so that we may believe in you."
> He said to them, "You examine the face of heaven and earth, but you have not come to know the one who is in your presence, and you do not know how to examine this moment."

—The Gospel of Thomas, Logion 91

Driving a Toyota with Iraqi plates now, Nabat had his nose virtually pressed against the windshield and kept rubbing his eyes. A freezing drizzle appeared to hang over the road like filthy net curtains, but I realized that Nabat probably attributed this poor visibility to the Famous Grouse clouding his brain.

"Maybe you should put the lights on?"

He switched the radio on instead.

About an hour later, we crossed the Tigris River on a hazardous little bridge and reached the outskirts of Ali al Gharbi. The place was a dreadful shambles of ruined slums and makeshift dwellings fashioned from old army tents and corrugated tin. Only when we'd reached its crumbling core did I realize that the place had not decayed naturally but had been heavily bombed or shelled, or both, by the Iranians, perhaps, or by the Americans more recently—or by Saddam himself, during one of his frequent drives to stamp out dissent.

Nabat, now hung over and weary, dropped me at what he claimed was the bus terminal, barely able to bid me farewell between yawns and groans. There was not a bus in sight, but there was something resembling a ticket office-cum-waiting room, in which several men and women chatted or dozed on wooden benches. Kerosene vapor clogged the stifling air, and the tin roof put every sound on reverb.

"*Salaam-aam aleikum-kum*," I heard myself say to the haggard old fellow slumped across his counter.

Instead of the expected "*Aleikum wahsalaam*"—more reflex in Arab countries than courtesy—the bus official stared at me in blank amazement, then said, "*Buon giorno, Signor.*"

I was more than happy to be thought Italian, developing a heavy Roman accent to veil the meagerly stocked shelf of my vocabulary. Before I could ask the man if he'd accept American dollars—because I had no Iraqi currency—he asked me in a furtive voice if I had any dollars. Guessing at the fare, I slipped him a ten-dollar bill, receiving a three-inch stack of tattered Iraqi dinars in change. I eventually estimated that the fare had been two cents. U.S. dollars were worth around a hundred times more than they had been the last time I was in Iraq, during the Gulf War.

Sitting on an empty bench, I fantasized about buying up property in Iraq, biding my time, becoming a real estate tycoon of the post-Saddam era—when tourism would boom and Americans doubtless flock to visit their devil's old lair. This daydream had progressed to me time-traveling back two thousand years and buying up most of Jerusalem, when squealing brakes and a blaring air horn announced the presence of a bus. The vehicle was almost entirely enveloped in mud, which gave it the comic appearance of a giant chocolate artifact.

Back out in the freezing damp air, I woke up, wondering if I'd inhaled too much kerosene vapor.

"Al Hillah?" I kept yelling at various people, indicating the bus.

Some nodded yes, some shook their heads, some shrugged.

"You go the Bab-lon, yesh?" said a throaty voice behind me.

I turned to find two fat, moon-faced pirates.

Sami and Ramzi were twin brothers, I soon learned, just as I learned that the bus was not going to Al Hillah—that, indeed, no bus would be going there today. But Sami and Ramzi personally would drive me there, for a few dollars. First, of course, we would have some coffee. Iraqis are, ironically, exceptionally friendly people on the whole, and I quickly decided that—besides the desire to acquire dollars—there was no harm in these two bloated rogues.

I told them I was studying early Christian history and was especially interested in the Mandaean faith. It explained—I hoped—why I was in the area. Hearing this, though, they both smiled so broadly that a dentist would have had nightmares enough to last a lifetime.

"We are Manda-hiya peoples," Sami (or Ramzi) proclaimed jubilantly.

Probing this statement, I found that they knew Nabat and his uncle—and his uncle's father and son. The tiny ganzibra was a big man in their community, revered for his wisdom. Had he shown me the ancient scriptures? Had I not seen their church?

"No, in fact."

Nabat had been so drunk, I assumed, that any thoughts of giving me a guided tour must have been drowned in the well of Famous Grouse.

A SNACK IN THE GARDEN OF EDEN

"Come, friend," Ramzi (or Sami) announced. "We go our church, then—fssssst—drive Al Hillah. Yesh?"

It seemed a reasonable offer, so I readily agreed.

They drove a thirty-year-old Cadillac, repainted matt black, its chrome replated to look like gold. The backseat was like a leather Chesterfield, and I reclined in lordly fashion in its great, springy embrace, reviving my daydreams of an Iraqi real estate empire. Then I recalled with sudden horror the warnings I'd received from Lahiji and Zachariah about Yazeedis—Yazeedis who posed as Mandaeans to fool strangers . . .

By now we were speeding south, having crossed back over the Tigris and turned onto a main highway. There was no point in demanding them to let me out here. Sweating with fright, I decided that a direct approach was best.

"Are you . . . er . . . are you Yazeedis, by any chance?"

Sami or Ramzi—whoever wasn't driving—looked over the front seat at me, his face reflecting more concern than menace.

"You know Yazeedi people?"

"I've heard about them, yes. Are you?"

"It is same as Manda-hiya religion."

"That's not what the Mandaeans think."

"Too much lies they saying about Yazeedi."

"So: are you Yazeedis?"

They slowly nodded in unison.

I assured them that I was very open-minded when it came to religion. People had the right to believe whatever they wished to believe. The Yazeedi religion was probably very wonderful and—like many faiths—much maligned by those who did not understand it. I was certain *I'd* find much to admire in it . . .

"You say truth, friend," agreed Sami (or Ramzi). "Yazeedi peoples very small. Not have the power like the Muslim peoples or the Kristy peoples. So much troubles we having with them, yesh?"

"No doubt. All religious minorities face persecution."

"Yesh, friend. Yazeedi peoples not getting the good government job, not getting the good medicine care, not getting . . ."

"The good wife," the other brother added.

"Yaaah! No girl marry the Yazeedi, yes? I tell you, friend, Yazeedi womans not safe to walk on the lonely . . ."

"Yaaah! Always they getting the rope from Muslims men . . ."

"Rope?"

"Yaaah! Some time the tree or the four mens roping . . ."

"Oh," I said, as the translation kicked in. "Rape. Muslims rape your women?"

"Always they roping . . ."

"And *qadi*, he doing nothings for the punishing."

A qadi is a judge.

"But is it true that you worship Satan?" I eventually dared ask.

The answer was anything but direct, yet amounted to a resounding YES. Except Satan wasn't Satan any more, it seemed. Satan had been pardoned by God for his trifling sin some time ago—it hadn't made headline news—and was now in charge of the world. That's why the Yazeedis worshipped him. Sami and Ramzi implied that I, too, ought to worship Satan, considering his position in worldly affairs. What point was there worshipping entities without the power to handle your requests where they mattered? I wanted to ask why Satan, being so influential, had not established the Yazeedis in a more comfortable position in Iraqi society, but thought better of it.

Just beyond a tiny town called Shaykh Juwi, the Cadillac swerved off the road down a muddy track barely above the marsh on either side of it. "Our church there," I was told, Sami (or Ramzi) pointing through mist and snow flurries toward some kind of mound.

I had the sickening feeling that all this pleasant banter had been the same as those lavish meals the fatted calf receives during the weeks before its ritual slaughter. *You are in a Cadillac with devil worshippers*, I told myself, *heading through mist and snow in the middle of nowhere to their satanic temple*. It seemed quite preposterous to believe that all these two Yazeedi pirates wanted was to give me a guided tour. Yet somehow I couldn't work up enough fear to impel me to take drastic actions. I felt the same way during the Gulf War, when I'd been arrested by Iraqi soldiers and locked in a freezing basement for twenty-four hours. Not once did I think any harm would ultimately come to me. Possibly I'm just stupid.

The mound turned out to be a sizable outcrop of rock, nearly fifty feet high at its peak, some hundred feet long, and thirty or so wide. Trees surrounded it, even extending off into the lower marshlands, where they seemed to gradually dwindle, becoming first saplings, then mere shrubs before vanishing into the glistening mud.

"Look like a big rock," one of the Yazeedi brothers informed me, indicating the big rock, as we climbed from the Cadillac onto very pliant soil.

I agreed that it did closely resemble a big rock, wondering what form a Yazeedi blood sacrifice might take these days, and expecting the earth to gape any minute and disgorge a horde of hooded fiends with knives and hatchets. An especially robust variety of sleet now fell from bruised and thrashing clouds, feeling like an avalanche of knitting needles on my skull.

"Yaaah!" Sami (or Ramzi) exclaimed, covering his head. "The Shaitan, he too much please you come."

If a lashing with sleet was Satan's idea of a warm welcome, I hated to think what he dumped from the middle air on those he wasn't pleased to see.

The brothers scuttled on tiptoe toward the shelter offered by the rock face, urging me to follow as they proceeded on around it. Like many enormously fat people, they possessed surprising small and dainty feet, moving on them so nimbly that they could have been almost floating over the ground.

Reaching the other side of the big rock, I saw what resembled a state park's picnic area: rough wooden tables with benches attached to them, much old garbage strewn around, a pit containing the charred and sodden remains of a fire. But Sami (or Ramzi) directed my attention to the rock.

"This our church," he said, quite proudly.

No longer uneven natural stone, the surface had been carved smooth and embellished with crude designs—mainly buckled stars of

David and lumpy swags of drooping fruit—most of which framed a massive old wooden door set into what still seemed to be solid rock.

"Look like big rock, yesh?" repeated Ramzi (or Sami). "But not rock. This church, see? Secret from the Muslim and Kristies, yesh?"

"Definitely. No one would ever know it was here."

I felt certain, however, that there wasn't anyone in the area who didn't know it was here. It seems impossible to have secrets in the Orient—which is why so many there profess to have secrets. What lay beyond that door?

"Church," I was told, as if I hadn't been listening.

I wondered if there were images of Satan, an altar, pews or just rugs, and so on.

"Yesh, friend," Sami (or Ramzi) replied. "Big carvering of rock of the Shaitan. Very good to look with the eyes."

I wondered what Satan looked like since he'd been pardoned by God. Did he still have horns and a tail, for instance? Cloven feet?

"Come, friend. You will see." Sami (or Ramzi) produced a bunch of keys and gouged with several of them at the door's rusty old lock until one managed to turn.

"You will see Shaitan church now, friend," his brother affirmed, as the door was pushed scraping and squealing to reveal a rectangle of utter darkness that, after a pause, emitted a torrent of eclectic odors, from frankincense to ancient urine.

"Wait, wait," Ramzi (or Sami) urged me, as if I were about to bolt past him into the perfumed void. "First I am making some lightings."

I very must doubted if Satan's church was wired to the national grid and could be illuminated with the flick of a switch, so it came as no surprise to hear Ramzi (or Sami) stumbling about inside and apparently colliding with metal and wood before producing a scraping noise, striking three matches before one actually stayed alight, then igniting the wick of a hurricane lantern, which he waved triumphantly.

"Come, come," he urged.

His brother and I stepped through the door. Ramzi (or Sami) was moving about now in the gloom lighting other oil lamps. For a moment all I could see were luminous freckles suspended in a night that smelled like the Vatican's septic tank. Gradually, though, forms emerged, shapes coalesced, and I could make out the walls of a chamber that had clearly been a natural cave enlarged by human hands to form a crude rectangle of space some sixty feet long and twenty wide, with ledges and hollows smoothed out wherever they occurred. As a result there were too many ledges and hollows.

At the far end, where Sami (or Ramzi) was now lighting candles in quick succession, I saw a somewhat mushroom-shaped monolithic altar standing in a gaping, shell-like alcove with three melting stone steps leading up to it. Behind this altar rose up what I took at first to be an artistic chimney stack. But as light seeped upward like luminous dye through oil, I saw that this chimney was in fact a sort of giant python or cobra carved in full relief from the rock face.

I walked toward it, over scraps of carpeting that squelched beneath my feet in places. There was no furniture of any description in the entire chamber. Upon the altar, some fifty-odd candles now blazed, held in old bottles, ink pots, narrow tin cans, an aspirin jar, battered machine parts, or just stuck into the relief map of aged wax covering the entire surface and the many unidentifiable objects that had been placed upon it over the last few centuries. Below the right-hand corner, however, I noticed a fairly new and very pink blob of bubble gum.

The wavering light from this ghoul's birthday cake made the carved snake's mighty torso seem to undulate on the wall, as if writhing free of it. The creature had faded markings in ocher, red, and green bands. Around its puffed head hung gaudy chains with semiprecious stones twinkling in them. Some kind of crystal had been set into its eye sockets, creating an illusion of alert prescience that was somewhat undermined by a mouth that seemed clamped shut and a jaw line that managed to convey the same idiotic expression of servile joy worn by Dino, Fred Flintstone's pet dinosaur.

"What is that?" I asked Sami and Ramzi, still staring up at the stone reptile.

"This the Shaitan," one of the brothers replied, his voice clearly astounded that I should have to ask such a moronic question.

Right, I thought. Who else could it be?

"He still looks like the devil to me."

"Yesh-yesh, friend. Is still look like the Shaitan in Bible book Ganeeshish."

"Ganeeshish?"

Eventually I found out he was talking about the book of Genesis.

"Is the serpent in Genesis Satan, then?"

"You know the Ganeeshish book?"

"Yes."

"Ganeeshish say the Shaitan come as big snack," Sami (or Ramzi) replied confidently, the matter settled. "Then the God, he too much angry with the big snack Shaitan, yesh? But soon forgoove heem, yesh? God too much good, is it? He see that the Yeeve she bad, not big snack."

"So God realized it was all Eve's fault, did he?"

"Womens no good, is it? Always the lying to mens, yesh?"

"Yaah!" his brother agreed, seemingly from recent personal experience. "Always the lying to the mens and making the *zigzig* with hushband good friend, no? This is truth."

"*Zigzig*" is Arabic slang for copulation.

So Yazeedis were misogynists, were they? I wondered to myself, wondering also what was in for me next at the feet of the rehabilitated Satan.

THE TONGUES OF MEN, WOMEN, AND ANGELS

> And the Lord God said unto the serpent,
> "Because thou has done this,
> thou art cursed above all cattle,
> and above every beast of the field;
> upon they belly shalt thou go,
> and dust shalt thou eat
> all the days of thy life:
> And I will put enmity between thee and the woman,
> and between thy seed and her seed;
> it shall bruise thy head,
> and thou shalt bruise his heel."
>
> —Genesis 3:14–15

All the serpent had done, of course, was urge Eve to start history by becoming the first autonomous human being. God was against this idea, but the serpent assured Eve that, by eating the forbidden fruit, she and her partner (who is also effectively her brother) would not die but rather their "eyes would be opened, and ye shall be as gods, knowing good and evil." Compared to Zoroaster's succinct vision of creation and the birth of Truth and the Lie, the account in Genesis is ambiguous, to say the least. Even the neo-Zoroastrian account contained in the Dead Sea Scroll known as The Manual of Discipline appears to have been written by someone eager to communicate an insight or some direct knowledge. Genesis, however, is poetry, pure emotion, designed to evoke fear and wonder, not to impart wisdom—although Cabalists would disagree, deconstructing and decoding the text with their magical tools, using the letters, not the words, to create a numerological message of Truth. But this was not an exercise most members of an oral culture would have ever dreamed of performing. And the poet of Genesis was composing for an oral culture, for illiterate nomads. Its audience—most of them—could not choose but grasp only the poetry, the primal emotions evoked.

The serpent had been a key Egyptian symbol. Crawling over the dust it represented the lower nature, earthbound, base; but with wings it represented the higher nature, a human soul elevated by wisdom. This Yazeedi serpent—their Satan—neither crawled nor flew, but appeared to be in the process of rising up from the earth. There was no doubt, at least according to the poet of Genesis, that God had decreed a hostile relationship between Eden's serpent and women. Yet without the serpent and Eve, the Bible and history would end with Adam and his companion roaming mindlessly around the Garden of Eden. But there is a paradox here, too: what was the serpent doing in the Garden? What sort of Paradise was it that God had created if it contained Evil? However, when God the Mother gave way to God the Father, partnership became patriarchy, reverence for the life-giving force turned into fear of death, the chalice became the sword—with which men wrote history in blood.

History really begins, according to Anastasias and other early Christian writers, with the rebellion of the archangel Lucifer. He is cast out of heaven and damned. But his crime was merely the refusal to worship Adam. Considering the first man's lowly condition, and Lucifer's elevated status, his refusal is understandable enough and certainly cannot be regarded as sin. He is punished, therefore, for something he has not yet done. Why would God wish to test the submissiveness of the archangels anyway? If he were so uncertain about their devotion, could he not have devised a less absurd test for it? And if God valued blind obedience above all things, he was quickly and radically refuted. For as soon as Lucifer falls he appears as the serpent and seduces Adam and Eve into disobeying God. But there is a difference between the myth of Lucifer's fall and the story of Adam and Eve. The story is simply a rational invention, a legend constructed for humankind's edification and for pedagogical purposes. The Hebrew Bible, it should be remembered, was being canonized around the same time that the New Testament gospels were written. Thus, in effect, one version of Jewish religion was in the process of being frozen in nature for ever, and another version was reacting against the way this process was excluding what it considered itself to be the real truth. The Magi truly can be termed midwives at the symbolic birth of what they certainly viewed as a bulwark of an ancient and eternal truth against floodtides of what they would have considered to be the biggest lie of all: the supremacy of faith over direct inner experience of God.

The apocryphal Lucifer myth, however, contains a formidable and fundamental truth, similar to the tale of Prometheus: the rebellion of a creature against the indelible fact that he is a created being and is constantly reminded of this derivative nature. No matter how absurd and doomed to frustration the archangel's rebellion may seem, in the rebellion Lucifer feels the solidity of his own existence. In the moment of revolt he suddenly *exists*, rejoicing in the consciousness that he is no longer a non-being, that he no longer exists merely in relation to God.

The serpent promises Eve that if the couple eat of the fruit they will "be as gods, knowing good and evil." There are two manuscript versions of the Creation—probably created, respectively, in the divided kingdoms of Israel and Judah during Solomon's time—one using Elohim, the plural, for God, the other using the singular Yahweh. This latter thus presents the serpent's promise as "ye will become as *God . . .*"

What is inherently wrong about knowing good and evil? Obviously, these distinctions have no place in Paradise, since Adam and Eve are immediately cast out of the place. But as soon as they have the knowledge, we read, they look at themselves, their own nakedness, and see it as Evil. They came to an illogical conclusion. Even if jumpsuits and overcoats had fallen from the skies, presumably, Adam and Eve would still have no place in Eden. The story would thus seem to imply that the danger lies not in knowing good and evil but in failing to be aware of their inherent differences, their separate qualities.

Since the story of Adam and Eve is the history of humankind, that history must inevitably consist of the search for the means to regain Paradise. After God casts the pair out, he places an entity wielding a flaming sword at the gates of Eden—as if Adam and Eve are liable to attempt to force their way back in. The paradise was a partnership; what lay beyond its gates was a patriarchy that would attempt to subjugate the female, to present the tomb, not the womb, as life's reality. Worship of the Goddess is always termed a "fertility cult," its image of a pregnant woman ridiculed. By the same token, however, and using its own central symbolic image, Christianity could justifiably be called "a death cult." Except when Madonna sits behind the altar, like Isis with her child.

THE KEYS TO THE KINGDOM

Lucifer exists in a state of magnificent solitude. He is the ego separated from eternal unity, the self without the Self. Jesus says he is "one with the Father"—there is no difference between his will and the universal Will—and it is this state that all mystical philosophies aim to attain. Obedience to the Law means a merging of the individual will with the eternal Will, the very mechanism of existence and creation and eternity itself. Love, in the Platonic and Christian sense, is the selflessness that achieves this same goal, whereas self alone is lovelessness. The failure of Judaeo-Christianity and Islam to clarify this central issue is not the fault of the founders and prophets of these religions, but rather the fault of those who institutionalized what was an inner quest into an outer tool of subjugation and control. Key to this control, of course, was withholding the central truth of the power of the individual in relation to the divine by obfuscation and deliberate falsification of scriptures. To effect institutionalization, it was necessary to create a hierarchy of mortal intermediaries between humankind and God: a priesthood that was really a bureaucracy.

Neither the original Brahmans, the Magi, nor the Nazarean-Essene sects constituted a priesthood in this go-between sense. They were teachers who taught individuals how to pursue their own inner path to knowledge, not spiritual legal counsel, not advocates who plea-bargained your case with the Judge. Nowhere in the Torah or New Testament, or in the Holy Koran is there any sanction for such a priesthood. Outside of Roman orthodoxy, the early Christian monastic tradition—which was entirely non-hierarchical—kept the ancient traditions alive for several hundred years before the orthodox Church finally managed to crush "heresy," driving it underground. Only with the discovery of the Nag Hammadi gnostic texts and the very recent "liberation" of the Dead Sea Scrolls from Vatican control are we finally able to regain the original teachings of the Western version of that mystical tradition which has managed to survive almost intact in the East. Unlike the orthodox canon, these gnostic scriptures often sparkle with clarity when dealing with what are essentially subjective issues of a personal relationship between man and God. For example:

> God allowed evil to exist, woven into the texture of the world, in order to increase man's freedom and his will to prove his moral strength in overcoming it.

Even Homer is aware of what is and what is not:

> "O alas, how now do men accuse the gods! For they say evils come from us. But they themselves, by (reason) of their sins, have sufferings beyond those destined (for) them."
>
> —Odyssey I. 32–34

And, again, Najmoddin Kobra's irreducible summation:

> Know that the soul, the devil, the angel are not realities outside of you; you are they. Likewise, Heaven, Earth, and the Throne are not outside of you, nor paradise nor hell, nor death nor life. They exist in you; when you have accomplished the mystical journey and have become pure you will become conscious of that.

In all of the above quotations, the responsibility for an individual's life—and indeed for the fate of the world they inhabit—is placed firmly in the hands of that individual. There is no mediator, no blind faith, and no external forces involved. Najmoddin Kobra promises—to those who pursue it diligently—a knowledge of Truth in this world, not a vague future paradise beyond death. The message is that we are God and (our) creation. With the gift of free will each individual can put wings upon the serpent of his basest nature, his selfish self, elevating it, transforming a static vacuum, a black hole of endless desires and greed, into a blazing star—that emblem of beauty and truth the Magi followed, appropriately, in search of a perfected being.

WHAT MADE CAIN ABLE?

The actual Fall occurs, not in Eden, but later, according to Genesis 6, when the "sons of God" suddenly find earth girls appealing and apparently start cohabiting with them. This is too much for God to bear, and he petulantly destroys everything he has created—which he'd once viewed as all "good"—with the exception of Noah's family and their floating zoo. This Fall is of course prefigured by the falls of Lucifer and Adam and Eve, and then the cursing and forced exile of Cain. In every case, however, it is the assertion of independence from God that moves God to wreak his terrible vengeances; and the "sons of God"—whoever they may have been—finding earthlings and their proud autonomy attractive, elicit the most terrible of all vengeances, the first and most effective genocide.

The story of Cain and Abel is strange and impenetrable, but it most definitely constitutes the continuation and consummation of the Eden Fall story—and yet another example of siblings treated unequally. The incident hinges around God's "respect" for Abel's offering of the firstlings of his flock and his marked lack of respect for Cain's offering of the fruits of the earth (Genesis 4:2–5). Abel is a herdsman, Cain is a tiller of the soil, a farmer. Not even the remotest hint is offered in the Bible about the reasons behind the Lord's preference for Abel and his scorn for Cain. It is this very lack of rationality that results in the slaying by Cain of his brother.

It inevitably seems that, just as Eve was tempted by the serpent for no apparent reason, so Cain was affronted disdainfully, and for the sole purpose of provoking their very natural and human reactions, in which they thus ensnare themselves. With Cain, however, the story is even more ambiguous. Having condemned him to wander the earth as a wretched outcast, God appears to be moved by Cain's plea that the punishment is too heavy, that he will surely be murdered (by whom?—Adam and Eve, the only other people on earth?), and the Lord—possibly realizing he had made a mistake in preferring Abel—"set a sign for Cain, lest anyone finding him should smite him" (Genesis 4:15). This has, of course, been interpreted as an even worse punishment: eternal life in misery. Yet if such were the case, why—with absolutely no explanation for it—do we next hear of Cain building a city (for whom?) in the land of Nod and raising (with whose daughter?) a family there?

This now seems to be a parable of civilization: the city builder slays the nomadic herdsman. To Cain and his descendants, who invented the tent, musical instruments, and tools to cut brass and iron (Genesis 4:20–22), we apparently owe the foundations of modern civilization; just as we appear to owe not just our very existence but our autonomy as beings to Eve. In Eve and her son, therefore, lie the roots of freedom and progress. The question thus becomes—just as with the question of good and evil—what are the real natures of freedom and progress? What are they worth?

Adam and Abel—poor and pathetic figures—are the first hit-and-run victims of humanity as its juggernaut gains momentum. They are good and innocent, but they lack will, initiative, and the creative spark. Eve and Cain are parallels in this respect, becoming the driving forces of history. Yet it is Cain who is the true father of humankind, and Cain's spiritual ancestor is Lucifer. This inequality in God's treatment of siblings can, I believe, be traced to the teachings of Zoroaster. The sons of Ahura Mazda are Angra Mainyu, spirit of the Lie, and Spenta Mainyu, spirit of Truth and Righteousness. One forms to counter the other; thus, presumably, Spenta Mainyu is the second son—the favored one. On the inner level, our lower natures and bodies are born before our spirit enters us: Zoroaster is the only founder of a major religion to have pronounced that the soul enters the fetus after three months in the womb. The Essenes, coincidentally, went through a second and final marriage ceremony only when the woman was three months pregnant. It was complications surrounding this ritual—which Mary and Joseph seem to have ignored—that gave rise to the widespread rumors that Jesus was illegitimate. In fact, his status fluctuated—according to evidence in the Dead Sea Scrolls—depending on who was high priest of the community and how that particular man interpreted the marriage rules. This stigma cast a shadow over Jesus' rights as legal heir to the Davidic crown.

DEVILS IN DISGUISE

As William Blake observed, the Bible can be interpreted as the story of each person's life and the struggle to regain the innocence of the lost paradise, but through transcendence—with consciousness and knowledge. In its universal aspect, therefore, the Book of Genesis shows the innocence that succumbs to temptation every day, everywhere; and it shows the triumph of the murderers and builders of cities over the meek and humble. Living at the other end of freedom and progress from the poet of Genesis, we are perhaps more able to see the folly of their attraction. Lucifer and Cain might appear to turn their personal tragic flaws to their own advantage, but appearance is not reality. Freedom without divine laws results in, to paraphrase Shakespeare, humanity preying on itself like monsters of the deep; and progress has brought us to the brink of doing to the world what God promised he would never do to it again himself.

In the beginning it may have seemed more difficult to disobey God—or the immutable Law governing the universe—but now it is more difficult to obey, to rein in the ego and its desires until the self merges with the Self, until—in an image from the Vedas—the raindrop realizes it is the ocean surrounding it. In Hebrew, the word "Satan" means "the Accuser." As the Gnostics knew, the devil is just the serpent without wings, and the serpent is both life and life's potential. To crawl in the dust or fly, to be or not to be: these are indeed the questions. But to the Magi, or any mystics, the answers are self-evident: fly, *be*, because the outcome of Truth's battle with the Lie is preordained. Truth will win. Free will is the tool that enables humankind to participate in its own liberation; yet in Eternity nothing has ever happened at all.

Such concepts are a hard sell to the masses, admittedly, but why sell any truth that is not true in their place? And it's said that when you attain direct knowledge of truth all questions cease, melting into bliss and a light that is not the opposite of darkness, that casts no shadow.

RENDERING UNTO SATAN

Asking Sami and Ramzi questions was out of the question. Yazeedis were clearly a backwater of religion—possibly deposited by the receding tides of Manichaeism—and their shallow pool contained little in the way of dogma and less than nothing of theological history. There did not even appear to be any scriptures, and the brothers had trouble describing what went on in Satan's temple—although Sami (or Ramzi) did recall a prayer that he translated something like:

> O Satan, punish our enemies
> And pour the gold of their coffers
> Into our worthy hands.
> For we worship you as the true Lord
> And the guardian of this world.

Ramzi (or Sami), however, disputed this rendition, offering his own, which amounted to a list of requests for much-needed items, like Mercedes cars, beautiful women, and amazing luck at card games.

"You now give offerings for the Shaitan?"

"Yesh," the other brother heartily agreed. "Mudge luck for you if giving the offerings to Lord Shaitan. *Guaranteed.*"

I thought of Faust, saying, "What should I offer?"

"The one hundred American dollar," the duo almost chorused.

It struck me as reasonable, considering the kind of offerings Satan had required in his heyday. I pulled a one-dollar bill from my pocket and inquired via sign language where Satan wanted his offerings offered. The brothers barely resisted the temptation to announce that Satan's offerings usually went into their pockets, indicating instead a kind of old paint can on a tripod next to the altar. And so I performed my first Satanic ritual.

As Sami (or Ramzi) snuffed the candles and blew out the oil lamps, I heard the rattle of tin and the rustle of paper. He had not realized that it was only a one-dollar bill when we reached Al Hillah and said our farewells—which was perhaps why there were none of the usual whining objections when I handed over five bucks for the ride. Had he assumed no one would dare cheat Satan, and thus taken the one dollar for one hundred? To an illiterate Arab, all American bills must look the same, after all. I imagined the apocalyptic punch-up that would ensue when some Muslim moneychanger tried telling these Yazeedis they were only one percent as rich as they believed. It would be yet another defeat for Satan, whom God seemed to have hoodwinked yet again. As Lord of the World, he must be pretty depressed with Sami and Ramzi and their pals as devotees. They were not exactly the legions of Hell we earthlings worry about—but then Satan wasn't exactly the Devil any more, either. Other rulers of the world seem to have acquired that position.

BY THE RIVERS OF BABYLON

Al Hillah was very dark as the Yazeedis and their Satanic Cadillac sped away, no doubt cackling about their big score. It had taken us nearly three hours to drive across the fertile plain between the two rivers that had led the literal-minded Greeks to call the land Mesopotamia—"between two rivers." Al Hillah in the province of Babil was less than fifteen miles from the Euphrates, to the west, and less than ten miles from Babylon, to the northwest. It had little to recommend it to the tourist, and even less to recommend it to the tourist with no visa. For a while I thought the place was some sort of vast military headquarters. Anyone who wasn't a soldier was either under nine, over ninety, or a woman. Nine out of ten vehicles were painted with swirling matt desert camouflage, and there were tanks and missile-launchers casually parked in front of restaurants full of khaki-clad diners, as if some craze for army surplus had gripped the population.

I soon realized, however, that I was less likely to be stopped for questioning here than anywhere I've ever been. With half the Iraqi army in town, everyone felt thoroughly secure. Foreign spies would have to be insane to wander around Al Hillah. I, too, felt quite mad here—barely able to stop myself howling with mirth, in fact. First the Yazeedis, now—for all I knew—Saddam's new mission control center . . .

Thus unhinged, I breezed into the Babilu Hotel, waved a British Library I.D. card that had expired in 1978 at the desk clerk, and without a hitch obtained a four-room suite for the equivalent of three dollars—which, I learned too late, also included breakfast and dinner. I should have bought the hotel.

> Jesus said, "Two will rest on a couch;
> one will die, one will live."
>
> —The Gospel of Thomas, Logion 61

An hour later, I was saying *Buon giorno* to waiters and fellow diners in a nearby kebab joint and knowledgeably indicating items on a handwritten Arabic menu—which, I soon found, amounted to three dinners and two desserts—then embarking on a pleasant but confusing conversation in broken English with four army officers, who soon invited me to join their table. Italians were a common sight in Iraq—they're a common sight everywhere no one else is welcome, come to think of it. They were engaged in engineering projects, I discovered, feeling fortunate that this fact had not impelled any Iraqis to learn much Italian. The soldiers had guzzled their way through two bottles of arak already, so their ability to speak any language was not that impressive. I did, however, gather that Saddam himself was believed to be in town, that most Iraqis would like to kill him personally, that he was insane, and also sadistically gay. This latter piece of information did not come as the surprise I would have expected it to be. I could suddenly picture Saddam in leather chaps, vest and cap with chains prowling along the bar of a dive like the Mineshaft . . .

BABYLON REGAINED

There was a sense of panic about my journey now. Reza had made Iran difficult, and the fear of all those unpleasant things that could happen to a North American in Iraq was beginning to hover like a genie over my path. I just wanted to reach Bethlehem, like the men in whose footsteps I was following once had, perhaps. The desire to linger, to explore, seemed irrelevant all of a sudden. My notebook reflects this urgency, its daily jottings more fragmentary now, less concerned with the minutiae of both past and present. I finally understood Marco Polo's tale to mean that the Savior himself needed saving, as much from himself as from those who would destroy him, and the Good Samaritan, in this case, was represented by two good Persians. The work that lay ahead consisted only of finishing the journey, and then returning to a library to travel in other ways and other directions.

Following the Magi's path, or the one I'd assigned to them, I passed what had once been Babylon, and was, it seemed, also to be Babylon again. French architects and building supervisors had been reconstructing ancient Babylon for Saddam Hussein. They had kept on working throughout the Gulf War, someone named Gilles told me.

"Why?"

"We were not allow to leave."

Every brick of the new Babylon was apparently stamped with the legend "The Babylon of Nebuchadrezzar rebuilt during the reign of Saddam Hussein."

"Reign? Well, I suppose . . ."

Nebuchadrezzar sounds as if he was deeply into S & M, too.

"Ee come ear often and stay dare all alone," Gilles announced.

"Who?"

"Saddam." He indicated a somewhat Stalinesque structure that was supposed to be the exact replica, the twin palace of Nebuchadrezzar II. "Day say ee walk around all night talking wizza ghost of Nebuchadrezzar. Day plan 'ow day capture zee Jews again, per'aps?" He laughed unconvincingly and too loudly.

It looked like time to get back to Paris for some R & R. Working for Saddam was clearly S & M.

Of the real Babylon there was little to be seen, and what little there was looked less impressive than Cairo's slums had after the recent earthquake. The mighty had certainly fallen, although Saddam was doing his best to raise them up again. Better this, I thought, than rebuilding those towers of human skulls Saddam's favorite Assyrian and Babylonian heroes were so fond of erecting whenever an opportunity presented itself.

Once the largest city in the world, Nebuchadrezzar's Babylon, most of which dates to between the late sixth and early fifth centuries B.C., covered 2,500 acres. The Euphrates River, which has long since shifted its course, used to flow through it, with the oldest section of the city—parts of which dated to the twenty-third century B.C.—on the eastern bank.

I walked west from the Marduk Gate, past the Greek theater that Alexander the Great had built with rubble removed from the Etemenanki, the great ziggurat which lay to the southwest, and was also associated with the Tower of Babel. Nothing now remains of it but a depression called Sahn. From the partly reconstructed Ishtar gate, with its enamelled bulls and dragons, I walked nearly a mile north to where Nebuchadrezzar's palace had been. Alexander, who planned to make Babylon the capital of his empire, died in this palace in 323 B.C., aged thirty-three. His body was shipped back to Egypt—where he'd been declared a god—for burial in a crystal coffin.

Standing on the mound called Babilu, which is all that remains of the place within whose walls the course of so much history was determined, I gazed back south through bitterly cold drizzle and mist at mighty Babylon. Even in their Captivity, the Hebrews could not have failed to be impressed by what must have been a magnificent, orderly city, crossroads of trade and culture, with quays and warehouses on the Euphrates loading and unloading cargoes coming from or going to the farthest reaches of the known world. It was here that the fusion of Magian Zoroastrian ideas had planted the seed that was to grow and transform henotheistic Judaism into the vast banyan tree of a monotheistic faith with seemingly separate shoots, still deeply connected by their roots, however, which would sprout into Christianity and Islam, whose branches and leaves would also, regrettably, shade the sun and veil the heavens from most of the world for two thousand years.

Our Magi must have stopped here, although by then Babylon was well into its decline, overtaken in geopolitical importance by Seleucia on the Tigris, capital of the Seleucid Dynasty—winners of the power struggle between Alexander's generals after his death. A Seleucid ruler transferred part of Babylon's population to his new city in 275 B.C. To the Magi, at the twilight of the old millennium and the ancient world, Babylon must have seemed an emblem of past mistakes they were about to bury forever—or hoped they were. In fact, though, it was the emblem of an even more misguided future.

Crushed by Cyrus the Great, then Alexander, Babylon had been the first great city on earth to be ruled by the will of men, not God. Although the golden idol of Marduk had been removed by the Assyrian warlords to prevent the conquering kings of Babylon assimilating his power for their own ends, the action proved futile. In the mid-seventh century B.C., civil war broke out between the Assyrian king Ashurbanipal and his brother who ruled in Babylon as a kind of viceroy. The city finally fell to Ashurbanipal in 648 B.C., but only after a siege creating a famine that drove Babylonians to cannibalism. It was the city itself, not Marduk, that conferred power upon its rulers. Like Lucifer, Babel and its tower were an affront to God, a manifestation of human autonomy, and even a threat to retake Paradise by force. And Paradise cannot be regained that way.

FALLING OUT OF LOVE

> And the Lord came down to see the city and the tower, which the children of men builded. And the Lord said, "Behold, the people is one, and they have all one language; and this they begin to do: and now nothing will be restrained from them, which they have imagined to do. Go to, let us go down, and there confound their language, that they may not understand one another's speech." So the Lord scattered them abroad from thence upon the face of the earth: and they left off to build the city. Therefore is the name of it called Babel; because the Lord did there confound the language of all the earth: and from thence did the Lord scatter them abroad upon the face of all the earth.
>
> —Genesis 2: 5–9

This, remember, happens to the generations of Noah, immediately after the Lord has made his covenant, his solemn promise never to destroy the world by flood again. He keeps his promise, of course, but it is reminiscent of a wife beater who swears he'll never lay hands on his woman again—and throws boiling oil over her instead. But *Bab-el* means "the gate of God": does this imply that in some way language—therefore thought—plays a crucial role in both blocking the route to and regaining Paradise? The principles behind meditation—the control of thought—would seem to indicate so. And in Hebrew "Zorobabel"—another failed Davidic messiah—and "Zoroaster" can both mean, for all intents and purposes, "the rock of the Gate of God," the foundation upon which an entrance to eternal Truth can be built.

As is often also the case in the Holy Koran, God speaks in the Bible here in the plural, and he performs a function that would later be ascribed to Satan, "the Accuser": he makes human life more difficult. There are few clearer examples in the Bible of the real nature of Evil, the Gnostics' conception of its purpose: to strengthen Good by trial and suffering. What does not kill us makes us stronger: *Also Sprach Zarathustra.*

MUSTAFA CAMEL

From Babylon, I traveled northwest along the banks of the Euphrates, taking a series of dismal bus rides that avoided the dangers of Baghdad and eventually deposited me at Al Hadithah, some fifty miles from the Syrian border. After a miserable night in a subzero flea-pit hotel, I decided to proceed on along the same highway, again following the Euphrates. Some two hours later I was at Anah, the last major Iraqi town before the border. I knew the border was basically closed, but I had imagined—back in Iran—that I could bluff my way through. After all, I had a Syrian visa.

But I did not have an Iraqi one, and it suddenly struck me as extremely foolhardy to attempt an exit from Iraq without one. This was not, after all, some no-account border post: it was the one on the main highway from Iraq to Syria, the ancient trade route that only now parted company with the Euphrates where President Assad's new dam—much like President Nasser's older one at Aswan—created Lake Assad, much as the Aswan dam created Lake Nasser.

Thus, it was at Anah that I purchased my first camel. I'd originally dreamed of making the whole trip by camel—just as I'd dreamed of buying ancient Jerusalem—but I suppose I'd always known that such a dream would have been the Mother of all Nightmares.

Anah was a taut and frenetically active little town, full of Bedouin traders and a mélange of ethnic groups, all of which spoke of the eternal supremacy of commerce over politics. I'd lived with Bedouin in Egypt, and been smuggled through Iraq by them during the Gulf War. It was comforting to see so many here, since I knew full well that these most independent of seminomadic peoples were no respecters of borders or laws or politicians. They respected only business and their own tribal codes. Their word was their bond, and all it usually took to get their word was an arrangement involving cash—preferably in U.S. dollars. They also never asked questions: if you wanted to pay them to take you from A to B, they wouldn't dream of inquiring why you wished this service. In fact, I wanted to go from Anah to Abu Kamal, ten miles inside Syria, where a highway led to Aleppo (or Halab, as it's known now), but a minor road also went due west, following the old trade route across the desert to Palmyra (or Tadmur).

I approached Hikmat in the souk, as he sipped tea in a café that appeared to have been scooped from solid rock—a portable cave. Money doesn't always swear, and it talked quite efficiently to Hikmat, a weather-beaten edifice of a man dressed as if he'd plundered a clothing museum: kaffiyeh, track pants sneakers, abaya, Afghan goatskin vest, red T-shirt, double-breasted pin-stripe jacket, and bandolier of bullets well concealed beneath these layers.

He took me to Nuri, a younger but less perceptive version of himself, who had apparently raided the same clothing museum—but ended up with what no one else wanted. Hikmat relieved me of some cash, telling Nuri in excruciating detail—twenty minutes' worth of it—exactly what was required. An hour later I had purchased a camel for an astounding $600 and was riding behind Nuri—who owned a proud and irascible beast of his own—southwest into the Great Syrian Desert upon which Anah bordered. Six hundred dollars would have bought the town, I kept thinking, reassuring myself that it was not just a camel I'd bought, but safe passage out of Satan's lair.

THIS LAND IS MINE

By nightfall—and sleet fall—we could well have been ten feet from where we had started. The landscape hadn't changed at all. Hoping we'd crossed the border—as I had with Nabat back in Iran—I was dismayed to learn that we were nowhere near the border. And Nuri wanted to stop for the night.

"*Here?*" I squeaked, squinting around at rocks, stones and scrub—but no sand.

Nuri had followed a curiously erratic route, zigzagging for no apparent reason. But since my camel—now named Mustafa—seemed incapable of doing anything but follow Nuri's confident mount, I had little choice but to trail behind. No doubt I'd bought a lemon, but at least it worked—it even ran, but only when Nuri's camel broke into the occasional canter itself.

I dismounted, tying Mustafa to a rock—as Nuri had done with his beast—and attempted to protest this unexpected halt. Nuri was far from stupid, but he was also far from rocket science. In the old days, perhaps, he would have been termed a "simpleton." It wasn't possible to argue with him, I realized, because he only did what was currently programmed into him, and I had not written the program. As I reluctantly unhooked my knapsack and stuff pack from Mustafa's tattered saddle, Nuri gestured around himself at the bleak, crepuscular wilderness, saying,

"Land-iss mine . . ."

"Yes," I replied, marveling at the Bedouin feeling for territory, at their innate sense of where they belonged and what belonged to them. "Yes. *Your* land . . ."

"Land-iss *mine*," he said, more forcefully, sweeping his arm in an arc at all ahead.

"Yes, yes. The great Bedouin desert. Where your people have lived for *thousands* of years."

He seemed angry now, repeating the gesture and the phrase.

"*Land-iss mine!*"

Oh Christ! I thought. He's going loony on me. I started to clear an area of small rocks and stones, where I planned to attempt sleep, when I discovered, after scooping away some gravel, a round black cylinder of metal. About to call Nuri and ask him to take a look, it suddenly struck me that his proprietorial announcement was nothing of the sort.

"Right," I said. "Here's one, Nuri! Isn't *this* a land mine?"

He plodded over and peered down, lighting a match.

"Ah! Land-iss mine," he agreed happily.

No wonder we'd been zigzagging.

I could have had it as a pillow—for a second. Always trust a Bedouin, particularly when you have no choice but to trust one. An old British diplomat once confided this useful piece of information to me. It's worth remembering.

Chapter Twelve

～✺～

THE MUSEUM OF SYRIA

Jesus said:
"Blessed is the lion
Whom the man devours,
And thus the lion becomes a man;
And cursed is the man whom the lion devours,
And thus the lion becomes a man."

— The Gospel of Thomas, Logion 7

By dawn we were in Syria. I think. Nuri seemed fairly certain that a shallow gully we'd traversed marked the border. Since Syria's eastern border alone spans some thousand miles, from Turkey through Iraq to Jordan, I was not expecting a wall or fence, let alone a billboard welcoming visitors. The Bedouin wouldn't take kindly to someone erecting walls and fences across their traditional routes. Even seminomadic peoples have a strong sense, not of ownership so much as their rights to travel freely over the land. It's true that most Bedouin now—whether in Iraq, Syria, Jordan, or Israel—have identity papers, indicating a base more than a homeland. But in my experience, such documents usually have less value than an expired British Library I.D. card. Only Israeli police or military seem to bother with the charade of demanding to see them. After a few years in some Bedouin's pocket, an identity paper is generally less legible than a Dead Sea Scroll fragment—indeed, it could well *be* a Dead Sea Scroll fragment.

Nuri's promised "tent," when we reached it, might have been made from whatever was left on the original bolt of fabric used for the Shroud of Turin. The size of a spacious kennel, it smelled of wet rat and looked as if a platoon of mechanics had been wiping their hands on it since the French Mandate. The way Nuri had been announcing its existence for half the journey, though, this tent should have been a portable silk palace. I was wistfully picturing tribal rugs, fat tapestry cushions, an urn of coffee waiting, with a haunch of spiced lamb roasting on a spit over glowing charcoal, while gazal singers crooned and houris pirouetted . . .

Instead, Nuri made a fire the size of a Frisbee from pieces of dried camel dung scooped from one of his saddle bags. From a corner of the tent he produced a rusty tin can, tipped what looked like soot and gravel out of it, filled it from an old army flask with water already the color of tea, into which he threw a handful of tea leaves and sugar from a supply apparently kept loose in a trouser pocket, then finally put this tin and its contents in his snapping, odorous little fire. We sat watching it for half an hour until the water managed to emit steam rather than actually boil. I was so cold by now my bones felt like icicles and my teeth were castanets.

Wrapping a truly horrible old rag round the tin, Nuri removed it from glowing dung, sniffed in connoisseurial fashion the curling vapors writhing over its jagged lip, and then passed the brew to me.

"Chee," he explained, miming the art of drinking.

From a jacket pocket he next produced several smashed pieces of bread, handing me three large shards. They were as brittle as pumice stone.

"Bregg vast," Nuri announced contentedly, ferrying his own outsized croutons into the little cavern lined with jaundiced stalactites and stalagmites normally hidden behind the black waterfall of a mustache that rippled when he spoke.

I'd often wondered whether he even possessed a mouth at all but had learned to simulate speech by whistling through his huge nostrils into the tributaries of hair streaming out of them.

"*Shokran gazeelan*," I told him. "Thanks very much."

"*Aafwan*."

The tea and bread in fact tasted amazingly good, as outdoor meals of crap can. We passed the tin can back and forth in silence, staring from the shadows of our greasy canvas kennel out at a bleak gray wilderness of stones and mud, as hot liquid thawed out aching muscles and numbed limbs. The weather boffins had come up with a new strain of snow, by the look of it. It fell in microscopic flakes like a mist of talcum powder, penetrating the skin's pores, then coating your bones with ice. When supplies ran out up there and a fresh batch had to be prepared, microsnow was replaced briefly by torrents of freezing slush. I found it impossible to imagine the desert being unbearably hot—or even warm.

"*Baard*," Nuri commented.

The word means "cold."

"*Fock*," he added, pointing up at Weather Control.

I agreed: "Fuck them. Quite right, Nuri. *Enough!*" I shouted at the churning charcoal fog. "Dump it on Riyadh! Give it to someone who needs it, you bastards!"

Nuri looked puzzled, scrutinizing the clouds to see who I was yelling at, then frowning at me.

He'd probably said "*Foq*"—which means "above"—not "Fuck," I realized later.

MUSTAFA'S MINE

Nuri's camel had been tethered to a rock near what looked to me like a dead gorse bush, but which clearly looked to him like breakfast, since he'd eaten it bare an hour later and was burping contentedly. Mustafa, who was quite a wretched spectacle in this evil dawn light and actually had icicles dangling from patches of fur, was still straining to chew up the little puff balls made of toothpicks that appeared to be lying around loose but were actually growing from whatever lay beneath the stones around them. Occasionally, he gave his colleague the odd wishful glance, his big felt lips sagging in an expression of abject misery.

While Nuri said his prayers, kneeling upon a brand-new pink nylon mat he'd plucked from another pocket, I roamed around the area until I found a big, tasty bush. The thing was more tenaciously rooted than I'd imagined it possibly could be, so I had to smash and hack at it with sharp rocks. By the time I was able to hoist the bush free and bear it back, I felt positively Cro-Magnon with achievement. It was another victory in the war between early humanoids and nature to chalk up on the cave wall.

Holding the bush behind me like a surprise bunch of flowers, I proudly produced it when I reached Mustafa, presuming the sight would be a camel's equivalent of chef Wolfgang Puck himself materializing with a steaming platter of munchies. But Mustafa sniffed the bush from a foot away, then looked at me balefully before closing his eyes and snorting through quivering nostrils. I left the bush at his feet, but, although he occasionally opened an eye to see if it was still there, he kept his face averted from my offering, as if deeply offended.

Nuri came to look at the situation, still rolling up his prayer mat, which he used to point at the bush, at the camel, and at me, while assembling a vocabulary sufficient to convey the idea that no camel would eat such bushes, because such bushes made them very sick. Such bushes were poisonous. What kind of idiot would feed his camel a poisonous bush? What was the matter with me? Didn't I know anything?

By the time he'd finished, I no longer felt Cro-Magnon; in fact I no longer felt like any kind of man, let alone a caveman. I felt a bit like a cavewimp, though, or caveduce: Cro-Moron. Nuri even managed to communicate that only the tribe idiot would cut down an edible bush to feed his camel (I assumed from this that no tribe would even contain someone stupid enough to try feeding camels poisonous bushes). Killing a bush was depriving other camels of food in the future. It was like theft—maybe murder. Bushes grew again after camels nibbled them. Didn't I know that?

"*Aaseff, aaseff,*" I kept saying. "Sorry, sorry."

"*Diffle,*" I heard him growl several times.

Tifl means "baby." I've often wondered whether he meant that I was like a baby, or that not even a baby would be so stupid. Or both.

Out here, I was the simpleton.

We rode off in silence. Even Mustafa had lost all respect for me, I sensed, bristling when I attempted to use the reins. Nuri again zigged and zagged—to avoid the kind of land no one wanted to call "mine"— often pausing to survey the lunar wasteland ahead before deciding if it merited zigging first or just more zagging. Soldiers use serious equipment for such vital decisions; I wondered what seventh-sensory gimmick Nuri owned for the task. I hoped it functioned.

Near the crest of a low hill, Mustafa suddenly stopped, sniffed the air voraciously, steam blasting from his nose like a kettle. He uttered an eerie, yodeling whinny, then veered away from Nuri's current zig or zag with uncharacteristic sprightliness, almost dancing toward a patch of bushes that lay some hundred yards off: a wayside banquet, presumably. I could hear Nuri yelling guttural imprecations behind, but it was all I could do to avoid being hurled from the saddle.

Then there was a flash of light followed by a deafening bang like a huge firecracker going off beneath me. A hail of sand and small stones blew in my face, then fell all around me in a blue cloud of cordite fumes. I jumped from the saddle, smashed my knee on something very hard, and scrambled frantically through the rubble of rocks. Nuri had dismounted and was running over, still shouting. I turned back to look at Mustafa. He stood stock-still, his big eyes bulging and rolling. As the foggy pool of dust and smoke beneath him cleared, I just had time to notice the bloody shreds of sinews, flesh and bone, dangling where most of his right front leg had been, as he keeled over, fell with a muffled thump on his side, and lay amid the icy rocks twitching and intermittently letting out a thin, dreadful scream through bared teeth. It was a piteous sight and sound.

"Land-iss mine," stated Nuri, matter-of-factly.

This real estate was really Mustafa's, though.

I'd always imagined that land mines packed a far more explosive wallop. Apparently not. Although, looking at Mustafa's leg, I'd probably have felt the wallop was explosive enough had I trod on the mine myself—or used it as a pillow.

As shock kicked in and panic surged on waves of fear from my chest up to my brain and even into my hair, Nuri calmly slit Mustafa's throat with an improbably small knife. The camel gurgled noisily and thrashed with three legs in a last urgent horizontal run, before subsiding into a still, silent pool of steaming blood.

I assumed I was in for yet another diatribe of humiliation from Nuri, yet the Bedouin said nothing, stoically engaged in practical matters like removing Mustafa's saddle, blankets, stirrups, reins, and so on. It made me feel worse than stupid: I felt completely useless. I went to help him, and, there being nothing I could do—besides get in the way—I started piling up rocks around the camel.

"*Limaaza?*" Nuri grunted. Why?

I'd also assumed we were going to leave the late Mustafa where he was. *Stop assuming things here*, I soon told myself, wondering if the Magi had ever run into such mishaps. "Some wise men came from the East . . ." It all sounds so straightforward, doesn't it?

ABU KAMAL?

A few hours later, feeling as if someone had taken a baseball bat to everything below my waist, I clung to Nuri's abaya as his camel carried both of us, along with my luggage and Mustafa's corpse, through a more benign and desertly desert into the outskirts of Abu Kamal. The name of the place cropped up with irritating frequency—on signposts, storefronts, posters—reminding me constantly of the limp mound of ratty fur that Nuri's haughty mount now wore like a huge old fox stole around the base of its neck. Abu Kamal, eh? Yes, yes! All right!—I *had* a camel but now I don't . . . *Okay?*

What Nuri planned to do with Mustafa's mortal remains, I wasn't sure, and I had no intention of asking him. Maybe there was a miracle-working vet in town?

Bumping and rolling down a dusty main street, we were suddenly overtaken by a speedy jeep, which then pulled in front of us recklessly and stopped. Two soldiers got out. One had blond wavy hair, the other ginger hair and a freckled face that made him look like a nine-year-old kid hooked on heavy steroids.

The pair started shouting at Nuri, and Nuri started shouting back— which struck me as a big mistake—often slapping Mustafa's sad little belly to emphasize a point. This went on for ten minutes before I even felt that the soldiers had noticed me. When Nuri dismounted and began to prod Ginger in the chest, while all three men yelled back and forth at one another even more angrily, I thought I'd better get down, too.

Without warning, however, the argument simply dissolved into handshakes and pats on shoulders, its harsh, guttural tones now almost croons. The soldiers began tapping Mustafa's corpse to illustrate their points next, but gently, as if commiserating with Nuri over his devastating loss.

"Papers!" Blondie suddenly demanded, extending his hand at me without turning away from the others.

I excavated my passport, with its Iranian-issued visa, placing it with various letters in the soldier's hand. He turned, glancing through the documents so quickly he couldn't possibly have taken in a word of them. Then he thrust them back at me.

"Breeteesh?" he asked, staring at his grimy thumbnails.

"Yes. Sir."

"Brinch esh die?"

"Huh?"

The word "die" was all I caught.

"Brinch esh die," he repeated. "You are know?"

"Die? Just because I don't have an Iraqi visa?"

It seemed so unfair. I wondered whether we were still in Iraq, at some other Abu Kamal, perhaps?

Blondie paced over to his jeep and rummaged around inside it. On the windshield was a flag sticker that could have been Iraqi, Jordanian, Palestinian, or Syrian. The Ba'ath Party ruled in Baghdad and Damascus—the way socialism runs both Sweden and North Korea—its emblem not just nearly identical in both countries, however, but nearly identical to two other national flags as well. Something must be done about this serious confusion, I thought idly. It could be lethal.

The soldier soon paced back, not with the shotgun or handcuffs I was expecting, but with an Arab newspaper. He carefully opened the paper, folding it to a certain page, which he held up an inch from my nose, revealing a large photograph of Princess Di—probably taken years ago when she was still young and blissfully ignorant.

"Brinch Esh Die!" the soldier repeated.

"Oh, Oh, Oh, yes!" I virtually sobbed with relief. "Princess Di?"

"Naa'am. Brinch Karlesh big vool, is it? Leef the Brinch Esh Die vor the Gaam-illah?"

"Oh, Oh Ohhh! Prince Charles and Camilla? Yes! Big mistake . . . to leave Di for her? Right!"

"Hah! Gamm-illah: loog like gaam-eel, is it?"

"Camilla . . . Looks like a camel? You're too kind, too kind. We say she looks like a Rot—a dog, in fact . . ."

Blondie thought about this.

"Dock?"

"Dog. *Woof, woof!*" I growled and barked.

Both soldiers slapped their thighs with mirth.

"Loog like dock!" they kept repeating.

"Bud zound like gaam-eel, the Gaam-illah?" Blondie eventually asked, clearly not certain if "Camilla" and "camel" did sound similar in English.

I assured him his facility with language was incomparable, then we all suddenly fell silent, looking at poor Mustafa, whose bruised dry tongue now dangled obscenely from the side of his mouth and was attracting much interest from flies.

"You mudge vell come to Syria, Breeteesh vriend," said the soldier gravely. "Breeteesh goot. Brinch Esh Die goot."

"Thank you. Very much. Sir."

"*Aafwan.* I am weesh you goot time in the Syria."

"Thank you."

Much time was next taken up with a lengthy form which Ginger and Nuri filled out together. I assumed that it concerned me, but Nuri was eventually presented with it and folded it into a pocket without comment.

"*Maa'aaz Salaam-ah,*" said Blondie, shaking my hand formally. "Me name Mustafa."

You couldn't get away from poor Mustafa in Abu Kamal.

"*Maazalaamah,* Mustafa. Thank you. Goodbye . . ."

The jeep sped off, and Nuri and I continued on our way. He seemed noticeably cheerier, but I failed to understand what his original argument had concerned, despite numerous attempts at asking him.

Like a sliding roof, the churning gray clouds above looked as if they'd suddenly been pushed back into Iraq, unveiling a flawless sapphire sky in which beat the warm yolky heart of some newly renovated and expansively generous sun. Its light felt like warm, kind hands holding my cheeks. *Syria! What a great country!* I thought. *Fabulous people, unbeatable weather* . . .

As we proceeded on our leisurely way toward the center of Abu Kamal, Nuri engaged in various conversations with passing pedestrians and motorists, some of whom seemed to know him, all of whom were clearly eager to hear what Fate had done to poor Mustafa. Since everyone glanced my way at some point, nodding sagely, I assumed that all of Abu Kamal would soon know Yankee Doodle Dunce had come to town — not riding on his camel.

LOST HORIZONS

A few miles to the northwest lay Mari, a vast and thriving city five thousand years ago, ruled by kings with names like Lamgi-Mari and Zimri-Lim. The site was discovered in 1933 when some Bedouin, looking for a suitable stone to cover a tomb, dug up instead a seven-hundred-pound statue, which, we're told, they immediately reported to the authorities. This seems an unlikely story. But the French ran Syria in those days, and the French were as interested in ancient treasures there as they were when in Egypt. Before long they had excavated a vast temple to Ishtar, finding numerous statuettes as well as spectacular mural paintings, the best of which are now, naturally, in the Louvre. Next came the discovery of Zimri-Lim's palace, which contained three hundred-odd rooms, courtyards, storage areas, and a library stacked with twenty thousand cuneiform tablets — many of them recounting the somewhat dull saga of a character called "Nani the Pious." Piety rarely makes good subject matter for stories. Zimri-Lim ruled Mari from 1782 to 1759 B.C., but beneath his palace was found another one, dating to before 2350 B.C. Beneath this there were two more palaces, one on top of the other, their origins well into the third millennium.

But relations between Syria and her eastern neighbor weren't any better then than they are now, and whatever went on in Mari clearly bothered that pioneer of jurisprudence, Hammurabi, because the

Babylonian monarch reduced the city to rubble forever around 1760 B.C. No king ever ruled in Mari again.

Yet the people carried on, picked up the pieces—as they always do. Only kings and their grandiose building projects attract the ire of other kings and their huge armies. And people had now lived in this area for at least two hundred generations. Obviously it provided.

THE CRUCIBLE

The Arabs call Syria "the land of Shem," who was of course Noah's second son—"Sum-Yawar" to the Mandaeans, the man who preserved their mysteries after the flood. Damascus is in fact *"Dimishq ash Sham"*—Shem Town—and the astonishingly fertile area around the city is even associated by many with the Garden of Eden itself. Among this "many" is the Prophet Muhammad. He buried his daughter Fatima—wife and cousin to Ali, the first Shi'ite Muslim—just outside Damascus. Understandably, the shrine attracts many Iranian pilgrims, flown in these days on charter flights and subject to special security measures during their stay in Syria.

Reza had told me this once—it seemed long ago—as a bus crammed with veiled Somali women nearly collided with us on the airport road in Teheran. They'd done the Shi'ite shrines in Iran, he said, and now were off to Damascus. He added that everyone in Iran with a shred of intelligence knew damn well that the shrine in Syria was a fake. The Prophet would never have buried his daughter in Syria. But what did Somalis know? They were "fucken Africans."

Shem's descendants became the Canaanites, whom many Syrians to this day claim as their ancestors. But the two soldiers Nuri and I encountered—Blondie and Ginger—would have a hard time selling anyone their Canaanite origins. There were a lot of French and British troops stationed in Syria during the first half of this century; and there were a lot of assorted European troops stationed here during the first part of this millennium, when Syria was virtually Crusader Central. If Blondie and Ginger didn't have a Brian and Pierre in their family trees, they probably had a Sir Gottfried and a Sir Roger lurking somewhere up amid the foliage of more remote branches.

.　.　.

If Iran was Gateway to the West for everyone east of its borders, then Syria was Gateway to the East for everyone in Europe and North Africa. Besides the Mongols—or perhaps because of them—there was usually far more traffic heading east. Gateway nations always have similar histories because of their geographical predicament, fluctuating from being someone else's imperial doormat, to creating their own belligerent empire. Thus a graph charting the Assyrian empire's fortunes over a millennium has more peaks and troughs than the Dow Jones Index during its most troublesome periods of financial fright.

In Iran you see foreign influence in the development of Persian culture, just as you do in the last twilight centuries of ancient Egypt's three-thousand-year life. But in Syria you generally find foreign *presence*, not influence—imposing presence, too. Egyptians, Greeks, Romans, Medes, Persians, Akkadians, Canaanites, Amorites, Aramaeans, Arabs, Hittites, Nabateans, early Christians, Crusaders, Jews, Turks, Soviets, Islamic orthodoxy and Islamic sectarianism, French colonialism and British imperialism—it all came, they all came, and saw, conquered and then vanished, hung on or hung out. And it's all still here, they're all still here, somewhere: a living multicultural museum.

To be Syrian—as it is to be American or Canadian—is to define a national identity, but not an ethnic one. If human history, or at least its post-Egyptian Western chapter, began in Syria, as Syrians like to believe it did, then this is the original melting pot, the crucible in which tribalism was first blended into an alloy used in forming a prototype of modern society. Admittedly, this prototype had and has problems that are still being worked on—all over the world. But Syria, contrary to most Western preconceptions, is in better shape than most countries I've ever visited.

Habib Boulares, a Muslim writer, says:

> As a Believer, one cannot deny the evident fact that this land has been chosen by God both to test men and to bring out their true qualities— for better and for worse. If one has no faith, one reverses the problem and concludes that such a land could do no other than engender exaltation, mysticism, fanaticism, proselytism and messianism . . .

It does both, of course.

One can hardly imagine a more fitting area of the planet in which Jesus could be born; for the mélange of faiths and philosophies that poured through him to emerge as Christianity still exists here in all its original and undiluted forms.

NURI AND NANI

Less than thirty miles up the Euphrates from Abu Kamal is the site of Dura Europos, a town founded by Nicanor, one of Alexander's generals, but taken over by the Romans, who clearly used it for their own multicultural experiment. A vast walled town covering nearly twenty acres, it was destroyed by the Persian Sassanids in A.D. 256, and lay forgotten, covered by the desert sands until 1921. Excavations, still incomplete, have so far located the temples of sixteen different religions, including a Jewish synagogue and a lavish early second-century Christian church. About as far from Rome as anything in the empire could be—and perhaps for a reason—Dura Europos was obviously far more than just a place of strategic and commercial importance. It formed a microcosm of the empire itself, and it seems likely that some pioneer Roman social scientist was based there to study the interactions between religious and ethnic groups with a view to possibly determining for military and political purposes which were weakest, which strongest, and, ultimately, which faith the empire might consider championing as its own and supreme Holy Roman Truth. The size and opulence of Dura Europos' Christian church perhaps has more to tell archaeologists than they've so far heard there.

Contemplating the curiosity of Dura Europos was all I had been doing for the hour it took Nuri to deal with some sort of business involving the form he'd been given by Blondie and Ginger. A government office noisier and more hectic than a stock exchange trading floor was where he had to deal with this business, advising me to wait with the camels: in case someone stole Mustafa's corpse? It wasn't clear, but the sunlight and bracing air were a much better deal than the government office.

Clutching yet another form, grinning and whooping, Nuri emerged, leading the camel and its baggage by hand a block, then telling me to wait again while he vanished inside the National Bank of Syria, whose facade could have easily been part of a temple to Baal or Marduk shipped down river from Dura Europos.

I squatted against one of its pillars, wondering if the Magi would have stopped at Dura Europos before heading on to Palmyra. The ancient trade route didn't go there—and thirty miles out of your way meant more to folk two thousand years ago—but I had little faith in the accuracy of maps showing routes taken through a wilderness by travelers thousands of years ago. Bedouin could find their way across five hundred miles of sand blindfolded, but they also—many of them—still firmly believed the earth was flat, too, and named areas after memorable people associated with them in the past. What was memorable about these people frequently, however, was some physical peculiarity. So half their deserts teemed with places called Big Nose, Goat Leg, Three Fingers or Cushion Bum; and these places consisted of one tree, a cave, or an oddly shaped rock. Some Bedouin thought there was a very big tent pole in Mecca that propped up the sky. Maybe there is. One old fellow once expressed amazement that I could believe God had created any people before the Prophet, who was obviously the First Man—which he is to many Muslims, of course.

The Magi must have used guides, though, I decided. Bedouin were the only guides they could have used, too, since the Persians might have been able to navigate by the stars, but they wouldn't have known where to find watering holes or edible flora.

I was examining a Bedouin map that resembled a circus tent covered in racing chariots, when Nuri woke me. He shoved a package wrapped in newspaper into my hands. Inside was a statuette carved from white limestone depicting a man wearing a skirt apparently made of feathers that reached his feet. His hands were clasped in prayer or supplication, or both. He had a beard hanging down to his waist, but no hair; and the pupils in his eyes, his eyebrows and eyelids were all highlighted with black paint. The effect made him resemble a crazed but harmless space alien.

"*Shokran,* Nuri. *Shokran gazeelan.*"

"*Aafwan.*"

"What is it?"

Where he had obtained it was what concerned me more. It looked convincingly ancient at first glance. But he wasn't apparently trying to sell the object to me: it was plainly a gift.

"Noon-yee," he announced.

Eventually, I gathered that this was Nani the Pious himself. He certainly looked pious—or looked as if he'd have to be pious to get away with looking the way he did.

Then Nuri thrust a ragged stack of Syrian pounds at me, which, I later found, amounted to some $230. What was all this about?

"Vor you gam-ell," he kept saying.

It took a good half hour for me to gather that the military—that is, the government—had compensated him for Mustafa's death by land mine. After all, no Bedouin would blow up his camel just to collect a fraction of its cost. Would they? I had the sneaking suspicion, however, that Nuri hadn't told them where the accident really occurred, but had probably claimed the mine was somewhere it shouldn't have been.

The Syrian government likes to keep all minority groups happy, and, since the country is made up entirely of minority groups, is very good at the task. Unhappy minority groups tend to expand into less inconsequential forces, united by grievances, and the government is very careful to avoid such potential problems. The Bedouin could cause more trouble than most minorities, too, so two hundred bucks was a small price to pay for social harmony in their case. I assumed, of course, that Nuri had received far more than $230 in compensation—but he needn't have given me a cent, so I felt like a kid at Christmas. Especially with Nani the Pious as a bonus.

Our next stop was a butcher's shop, open to the street, with raw carcasses hanging from hooks. Nuri proceeded to haggle with its proprietor, who resembled the emperor Nero in a blood-spattered apron. What did Nuri have in mind? I wondered, as he kept pointing to a flayed cow's leg, then to me. A roadside barbecue? Another gift? After twenty minutes, Nero shot across the sidewalk. For a moment I thought Nuri had sold him me, but the butcher carried on past and began hauling poor Mustafa down, then, helped by Nuri, dragged him into the store and through a rear door. He'd probably be dinner for several Abu Kamal families before I reached Damascus.

Nuri handed me another wad of Syrian currency—nearly $100 this time. A dead camel in Syria was apparently worth far more than a totalled automobile where I come from. Later, I saw a camel skin rug in Damascus priced at $200. Everyone had probably come out of the Mustafa deal a winner—except Mustafa.

I just wanted to leave town now on the next bus to Palmyra, but Nuri insisted on buying me lunch. In a sepulchral, smoky dive, I hunched wearily over yet more kebabs—dearly hoping I hadn't recently been riding them. Lunch was clearly the final item in Nuri's program, since when it was over he seemed relieved of a burden, happy to see me disappear into the six-seater minibus that was taking nine people and one goat to Palmyra.

"*Maa'az salaama*," he said, turning and walking back to his camel with light-hearted steps.

It must be nice not to have any ongoing cares in the world.

SOLOMON'S TEMPLE?

I awoke some three hours later. All the other passengers, except the goat, were asleep—and I had my doubts about the driver. Outside, a cerulean sky stretched far across reddish-ocher desert, as if testing the tenacity of horizons to resist giving in to infinity. I could certainly see how very appropriate the word "deserted" was here.

God only knows what the Bedouin's ancestors made of Palmyra in its heyday. I must have dozed off again, because my next memory is of dreaming someone had teleported half the ruins from ancient Greece and Rome to the middle of a desert for the sheer hell of it. Even stumbling from the minibus into a pleasantly cool late afternoon did not convince me I was awake.

All around were the most spectacular remains of an ancient city I've ever encountered: processional avenues lined with columns—Doric, Ionian, Corinthian—leading to an agora, a baths, tetrapylons, an amphitheater, courtyards, triumphal arches, palaces; then a gigantic temple that looked Indo-Egyptian, with some Greco-Roman additions, surrounded on three sides by lush gardens teeming with date palms. Northwest, high on a distant hill, perched an Arab castle. To the south there rose up tomb towers, almost identical to the Zoroastrian ones built by Darius for his showpiece capital at Persepolis—though here used for interment, not excarnation.

What was this place? The entire ancient world condensed into one fictional city? It was overwhelming. If the Magi hadn't stopped here— and they would have had no choice but to stop—I would have moved on immediately. But I had the place to myself, which is always enticing.

The reddish limestone of its columns and walls and courtyards was now deepening in tone as the sun began to drag shadows out from under their stone lairs, and a haunting perfume floated up from the emerald oasis gardens.

Half an hour in the magnificent precincts of what is called the Temple of Baal—or Bel—was enough to fuel months of research. It looked familiar, I realized, not because whole sections could have been torn from Egypt's great Luxor Temple, which they could have been, but because I was standing in a three-dimensional description of Solomon's Temple. The feeling was not unlike that I'd experienced at what was called Solomon's Altar in Iran, and what I later found identically matched in its dimensions the Jerusalem Holy of Holies.

There was the huge ablutions pool—the "sea of bronze"—in front of the raised cella or holy of holies, the temple's focal point, the walls around it lined with porticoes whose columns are still standing. Next to the ritual pool was "the altar of the holocausts," just like the huge sacrificial altar where Solomon had slaughtered 144,000 sheep and oxen. The cella was once surrounded by a colonnade, with capitals fashioned from bronze. Only the stone cores now remain, but the limestone lintels joining this colonnade to the wall behind still show the profusion of motifs—pomegranates, winged figures and animals— that the Bible recounts Solomon decreeing for his temple. One scene that Solomon certainly didn't decree for his Temple—at least according to the Bible—virtually glowed out of the stones.

In it a camel bore the great image of Baal toward an altar, passing by a group of elegant women wearing the traditional Palmyrene dress, a simple draped cloth tied at the middle. Following these, though, was another group of women who were veiled, their heads bowed in humble reverence, their whole demeanor far from the proudly independent stance of their Palmyrene sisters. These were Semitic women, beyond doubt; but were they Hebrews or Arabs?

The altar itself was heaped with offerings of the kind we read about in the Solomonic accounts: pomegranates, pine cones, fat bunches of grapes, a goat. And worshipping at the altar itself were two figures, both men in typical Parthian dress. The Parthians were an Iranian tribe from an area southeast of the Caspian Sea; but many Diaspora Jews also occupied this area. In the New Testament (Acts 2:9) we hear of Parthian Diaspora Jews present at the first Christian Pentecost. The followers of Simon Magus were Diaspora Jews, Western Magi, linked closely to their Eastern counterparts. It is thus tempting to read more into this image: the two Parthians worship at an altar that Baal has not yet reached, their offerings perhaps for an invisible god, while Palmyrene and Semitic women either flaunt themselves or cower before the pagan idol.

There were only two Persian Magi here: just as there were evidently only two buried at Saveh, only two portrayed on the enigmatic tiles, only two in the Mandaean account, and only two depicted in one of the oldest catacombs under Rome. As always, it is tempting to speculate . . .

Inside the cella were still more surprises. This sanctum sanctorum consists of two open shrines facing each other, both reached by steps, both containing huge square ceilings of elaborately carved monolithic slabs. The one to the left of the entrance, however, has a zodiac circling its lotuslike design; and the one on the right contains exceptionally fine geometric designs within a virtually identical multipetaled floral form. The Palmyrene trinity of Baal, Yarhibol, and Aglibol is also represented in the cella. Yet the opposing shrines were what I found most astonishing. They are overtly Hindu-Buddhist, with the lotus forms and a reappearing entwined swastika motif prominent among the geometrical designs.

It was almost an inner temple where East and West faced and complemented each other, showing the harmony of their ideas rather than the opposition. It's assumed that these shrines once held idols—and they may have done—but there is no evidence to prove or disprove this.

To view the ceilings properly one had to lie vertically beneath them.

These were not mere decorative additions, either, each solid slab weighing many tons, and each carved by a master mason in extraordinary detail, especially the zodiac and the geometric patterns. Was this mathematical conceptual thought facing that of a natural visual symbolism? Both, of course, represent the structure and mysteries of the universe in their own way. Was Pythagoras balanced by Zoroaster—his alleged mentor—here?

This zodiac appeared to be Nabatean, too, with Minerva as Virgo and a Virgo-Aries-Cancer connection to fertility symbolism. Hadn't Zachariah the ganzibra said that Nabatean priests had helped hide Jesus in Palmyra?

Little of sense has been written about the Nabatean civilization which, based at Petra in Jordan, vanished during the second century A.D. There seems to be much that could be made of the Nabatean obsession with dolphins alone. Nabat is also a common name among Mandaeans, deriving from a prominent biblical figure in their scriptures: is there a link here, too? No one can explain the tribal source of this name convincingly.

Whatever and whoever they really were, the Nabateans have left almost more evidence of themselves in Syria than they have in Jordan. How on earth, I wondered, could this ancient temple now have as its very core and purpose a cella so clearly Nabatean in design? The bizarre fusion of Indo-Romano-Egyptian motifs and architecture is unmistakable, although no one yet seems to have attempted to discover how or why or where the Nabateans arrived at such a style. Their civilization also—supposedly—spans merely the four centuries from 200 B.C. to the second century A.D.: the period of the most intense upheavals in Judaeo-Christianity. What are their trademarks doing in the cella of another, older henotheistic faith?

The Palmyra temple was allegedly constructed by Queen Xenobia in the late second century A.D., but it looks in places at least a thousand years older, and clearly has close connections with early Middle Kingdom Egyptian style. Ancient Egyptian temples were, however, living structures in a sense, supposed to be added to, rearranged, enlarged, or even demolished by successive generations, to reflect the eternal flux of life and also to embody astrological changes in the heavens. Why would Xenobia have reproduced Solomon's Temple?—if she had any connection to the original structure at Palmyra, that is—and was it really Solomon's Temple that was being reproduced here anyway?

Both temples, however, by description and visual evidence respectively, are undeniably Egyptian in style and concept. There are lintels at Palmyra weighing a minimum of ten or fifteen tons placed side by side thirty feet up, and at least one monolithic block in the Baal cella weighs thirty or forty tons. No one outside classical Egypt was lifting such weights three millennia ago; and two millennia ago no one anywhere was building like this. The Greeks never learned how it was done—and no one is entirely sure even to this day. It's worth remembering that Japanese archaeologists recently attempted to build a 1:100 scale model of the Great Pyramid—using methods they believed to be available five thousand years ago—and were unable to complete the project, conceding that aspects of the original structure are "beyond comprehension."

Yet Phoenicians, the "sea peoples," were sent to help both David and Solomon with their building projects by Hiram, king of Tyre—and at one time Solomon's business partner. Phoenicia—now much of Lebanon—traded constantly with Egypt. At one time, King David extended his Israeli empire far north into what is now Syria, including Damascus and almost reaching the Leontes River, but apparently not far enough east to touch Tadmur (or Palmyra, as it became).

In an almost ruby light now, the vast temple hummed with mystery. This was what Solomon wanted to build—and what the biblical scribes outline that he did build—yet, reading carefully, the Bible says that the Temple in Jerusalem was mostly made of wood—cedar from Lebanon. That's why nothing of it remains. There was no 10,000-gallon bronze ablutions pool there to disappear, either, I suggest. Nebuchadrezzar merely burned the place down and returned to Babylon with his captives. The real temple is one each person can construct within, where, according to Jesus, the kingdom of heaven eternally waits for its appearance.

Yet could this Syrian temple have been Solomon's after all? His final betrayal of the ancient and mystical truth which positively proscribed such material structures? Had his pursuit of "strange women" and "strange gods" led him here, to the desert oasis? Was this why he crops up so frequently in Arab mythology? Was this, too, why his name—though *Shelomoh*, "the peaceful," in Hebrew—is such a curious mixture of the names for solar deities in Egyptian, Greek, and Latin? Sol and Ammon are undeniably close. The Roman emperor Aurelian found his Sol Invictis, or Helios, at Palmyra—the god whose birthday was on the twenty-fifth of December. Ammon Ra was the sun, his solar disk becoming the Aten, the one true god proclaimed by Egypt's heretic pharaoh, Akhenaten—whom many associate with Moses, or at least with the henotheistic cult that became Judaism. Solomon's Temple sounds more like a structure for a solar cult than for an invisible and omnipresent God. And we know Solomon did in fact build for his Egyptian wife—on the Mount of Olives—at least one temple to a pagan cult. Why not more? He had seven hundred wives, after all.

In the Palmyra temple's courtyard I found a huge stone block bearing the image of a solar deity, with the sunburst nimbus behind his head that would eventually become the trademark halo of Jesus—and not long after Emperor Aurelian had dragged Queen Xenobia through Rome in chains, and made December twenty-fifth, birthday of his imported sun god, part of the most important holiday in the Roman calendar. Which it remains to this day, of course, for different reasons—but not *such* different reasons.

MISTRESS OF THE AFQA SPRINGS

Palmyra generally, in fact, contained too much for me to take in. There was even a medicinal spring called Afqa, which, according to undisputed evidence, was used for thermal hydrotherapy as far back as Neolithic times. Just like the Sialk civilization at Kashan—with "Solomon's Fountain" and his "altar" up in the nearby Zagros foothills.

Not far from the Neolithic votive altars in tunnels discovered near the Afqa spring is a relatively recent inscription. Dated October, A.D. 162—the year a five-thousand-seater Roman theater dedicated to Zeus was erected near the Acropolis in Athens, and the year the construction of the first Christian church in Britain began in Glastonbury—in Latin, it reads, "To Zeus, the Highest, the Master of the World, by Boldua, son of Zebida, at the time when he was surveyor of the Afqa Springs."

Water has always been important to the Master of the World: to destroy his fiefdom and inhabitants in order to save them, to have his heroes born from, or just to immerse mere mortals in symbolically before granting them immortality.

Three quarters of a century after Boldua's inscription, Xenobia, Queen of Palmyra, was mistress of the springs. More beautiful than any writer dares describe, she was also deemed more dangerous than Rome needed to tolerate. Some claim she announced herself a descendant of Cleopatra, others use the term "reincarnation." Either way, in the second century A.D. the last thing Rome needed was the Second Coming of Cleopatra, who was herself Isis reborn. The empire used as its excuse for taking offense that Xenobia had minted her own coin. She'd done this in Alexandria, at a time when it was probably the most civilized place on earth, and when Christianity still had promise, being blended with Jewish and Egyptian mysticism and Greek philosophy into what could have been a sane, exquisite neo-Platonist faith. But Xenobia's coin, like the fructifying ideas of Alexandria's Hellenized Jewish Christians, was a blatant affront to the divine rulers of Rome, the august Caesars who wanted what was theirs rendered unto them. A massive army was dispatched, and before long the brave and beautiful Xenobia found herself the centerpiece of "Aurelian's Triumph": she was led—in true Roman tradition—like a beast through the Eternal City, for all to see what became of those who challenged the Empire.

On the route to her Palmyrene palace, I noticed, were four pillars of Aswan granite, supposedly gifts from the Egyptian pharaoh to Xenobia. There was no real pharaoh in Egypt in the second century A.D., though, merely Ptolemaic quislings who had lost control of Upper Egypt or Nubia—where Aswan is situated. Yet this was unmistakably the finest pink Aswan granite—like that used for inner chambers in the Great Pyramid, and that later reserved for special obelisks and sarcophagi. How such mighty columns of solid granite were shipped here from Egypt at all is one question; who shipped them, when, and why is another. Such fine stones could easily have been adapted from an earlier structure to promote the living myth of Xenobia. We may never know, since an earthquake ravaged the site, confounding any attempt to chart the original positions of fallen stones. But yet again Egypt's presence here was powerfully evident.

By A.D. 270 Xenobia had taken control of Syria entirely, conquered Lower Egypt, and had armies proceeding across Asia Minor as far as the Bosphorus. The granite pillars could have been booty, but it's unlikely in the time frame available. By 274—a mere four years later—she was dead, a prisoner in a gilded Roman cage, and Palmyra had been crushed into submission. Its status was never regained.

It hasn't really been examined properly, either, particularly within the context of its relationship with the religions of the East and the religions that developed more locally. Anyone just comparing a ground plan of the Baal temple to that of Solomon's, extrapolated from the Bible, would have to admit that there's far more to Palmyra than historians have so far conceded. But Syria, like so many places, has been cut off from the West for much of this century—because of Cold War politics—and has just opened its doors again. Besides Egypt, nowhere in the Middle East is so rich in the remains of those civilizations upon which our own has been built. Palmyra will undoubtedly yield up its secrets over the next century, as the history books are once more revised, along with the preconceptions and prejudices that eternally fill them with errors.

Originally "Tadmor" or "Tadmur"—city of dates—it became "Palmyra"—city of palms—but is once more Tadmur. The fertility symbolism of palms and dates permeates not just Mandaean scriptures but, as we've seen, the Holy Koran and much Sufi literature. Like Babylon, Palmyra was a city that empowered its rulers—which is why the Romans destroyed it, as they'd destroyed Jerusalem a century earlier—but unlike Babylon, Palmyra was more feminine in nature, not quintessentially hostile and militaristic. Its rulers had something else to confer power on them, it would seem, and that "something" was a trade in ideas that complemented the trade in things but brought far greater profits. At Dura Europos, a few hours' drive away these days, the Romans were learning what the Palmyrenes already knew: that ideologies, not armies, were the real weapons of what would become the

Christian or Common Era—or Common Error, as I've heard the initials explained by anti-Christians.

WHILE SHEPHERDS WATCH . . .

In a magic twilight, I couldn't bring myself to enter the lavish hotel newly erected for tourists visiting Palmyra—when they start arriving. Instead I walked out along the Damascus Road. Syria's capital was still two hundred-odd miles away, though. Twenty minutes' walk from Tadmur—as its sign proclaimed it—I saw a shepherd watching his flock by dusk. With raised hands, a sign of friendship to the Bedouin, I approached him. Massive, clad in sheepskin abaya and layers of sweaters, with a kaffiyeh tied like a headscarf, he was touchingly shy, although his normal speaking voice was gravel and thunder. He spoke no English, and his Arabic dialect was baffling, but eventually he let me share his roomy tent for the night, with some dogs and sons. The women scampered off to an adjacent tent after he'd barked out something from fifty yards off.

It was a tranquil night, something I needed after the deluge of history that is Tadmur-Palmyra. More than ever now, though, I just wanted to go home. I sensed that something terrible was about to happen, that my luck had run out, and I suddenly realized what I valued, what I truly loved and did not wish reft from me. Within all philosophies, faiths, and even fantasies is a simple human reality: life, a family, a home, that is the battleground and the place where one's heart and duty belong.

SLOUCHING TOWARD BETHLEHEM

I

Next day I saw the Crac des Chevaliers, which T. E. Lawrence termed in his Ph.D. thesis "the most wholly admirable castle in the world." Built by the Hospitaller Order of Crusader knights, and finally conquered by the Mameluke warlord Baibars, it was indeed the most extraordinary castle I've ever seen—hardly a ruin, either, after nine hundred years. The more mystical Crusader orders were, in their minds at least, certainly here to stay. And, like the Castle of the Fire-worshippers at Saveh, the Crac was also as much monastery as fortress, with an early Gothic-style chapel at its core as magnificent as any in Europe's great medieval castles.

II

At Maalulla, near the coast northwest of Damascus, I found a church dedicated to two Roman centurions, Sergius and Bacchus, who were apparently among the earliest converts to Christianity. Not subterranean, like most very early churches, it was nonetheless all but invisible, concealed high among creviced hills reached by roads that twisted like sheep's guts. The stone altar still had channels for blood to run off when a sacrifice was performed—just like the altars in Solomon's and Herod's temples would have had. Whoever worshipped a Christian god here originally was doing it with very Jewish trappings. The altars had always been symbolic for Nazarean-Essenes and the original followers of Jesus, yet they were perfectly functional all the same: a reminder of the sacrifice really required, and that real death lay always just a heartbeat away. We all walk the knife edge to heaven across the gulf to hell that Zoroaster described—and daily, too.

An ancient icon showed the Last Supper, which was being eaten around a similar altar with, most unusually, Christ seated far to the left, not in the center. Another showed a crucifixion where the spear wound was on the right side—where it would not have been fatal—rather than on the left near the heart, where it is traditionally portrayed.

The people in this tranquil village were among those few hundred left anywhere who still spoke Aramaic, although they could no longer write it. Father Theo, the portly, red-faced priest who showed me around, and sold me a room for the night, recited—as if I'd demanded proof or called him a bare-faced liar—the Lord's Prayer: "As our Lord would have spoken it."

It was an alien, guttural tongue, Aramaic, yet with something oddly musical in it, like old Provençal, or dialects of Portuguese. I asked why it had survived so long here and almost nowhere else, and got no answer that made sense besides, "Because it did." Nobody showed much interest in anything I found interesting. Father Theo was more interested in selling me the wine he made. It was actually quite good—as home-made wine goes and compared to Mr. Yazdani's brew—until it induced a heartburn of such astonishing ferocity I felt like those pictures of Jesus performing a triple bypass on himself.

III

Not far from here was a sect called "Christians of Thomas." Unnaturally friendly and helpful, they did not believe Thomas was Jesus. Thomas had been Thomas. But he had also been Christ's twin brother. Certainly, he had. He spent time right here on his way to Mesopotamia and parts east, too. He wrote a beautiful hymn called "The Pearl" on this very spot—which was now a gas station. I wondered, though, if Jesus had had a twin brother, why a Nativity painting in their chapel nearby showed but one baby. It also showed shepherds, flocks, Magi and gifts, too, for that matter, as well as the entire Assyrian army.

It was all they could afford, I learned. Funds were short, and a Nativity painting was a Nativity painting. Besides, it had been a gift.

"From whom?"

The Syrian government was the answer. President Assad, himself a member of a minority sect, was, as I've noted, fond of other minority sects—even if uninformed about what made them so minor. But none of Thomas' Christians could tell me precisely what Assad's quasi-Shi'ite sect believed in, either. Maybe it was fifteen imams; or just three? No one was even sure in Damascus.

IV

The old city had not changed much since St. Paul allegedly fled it—lowered from a window in a bucket—but the new city beyond the old walls looked like Moscow on a budget. The ancient Christian section was hard to find in a maze of cobbled alleys, and not worth the trouble.

A cantankerous priest reluctantly answered some questions next to the tomb of a saint whose name he had forgotten, then brusquely kicked me out, saying I had been listening to Iranian propaganda and ought to read the Bible. I told him I had read it.

"Well, read it *again!*" he hollered.

Oddly, there's always been dispute over whether the word "religion" comes from the Latin *religare*, "to bind together," or from *relegere*, "to read again."

V

Basra is a Roman town more impressive than Pompeii; although people still live in it, and the 5,000-seat amphitheater is still used once a year for a Syrian "Cultural Festival." But many areas of the town show an extensive Nabatean presence, too, because Basra was once their second city, after Petra. Some of the only surviving Nabatean arches can be seen here: little miracles of architecture, spanning impossible gaps with a gentle curve, their elegant carving still intact and impressive in its quiet beauty after two millennia.

Basra is near the Jordanian border today. It was in this town some fifteen hundred years ago that a Christian priest had told the Prophet Muhammad's father his son was chosen of God. And Basra was also where the first Koran in Syria had arrived by camel. After hearing this and seeing the camel's miraculously preserved hoofprint—which was some eighteen inches wide—I talked to a man whose wife worshipped the "prophet Noah" at a tiny shrine in an abandoned temple once dedicated to Zeus.

What did this Noah worship involve?

Lighting candles and asking Noah for favors seemed to be all it involved. It struck me as refreshingly uncomplicated. The man also stated that the Prophet Muhammad's father had been a "Nazarean Christian."

What was that in Syria? I wondered.

It was nothing now, because such Christians had long ago recognized the truth of Islam and embraced it.

Had Muhammad converted his father?

My friend did not know, but, he suggested, what did it matter? All men of pure heart were brothers, weren't they? He and I were brothers, were we not? Of course we were. That was why I would give him a hundred dollars for "hospital expenses."

Medical care is free in Syria.

VI

OFF TO SEE THE WIZARD

Dazed with travel fatigue, I often wondered which century I was in—and sometimes if I had perhaps escaped from time altogether. It was a curiously peaceful feeling, one that made me feel close to those ghostly Magi I followed, and with whom I felt kinship now. I understood them, and they seemed to know that—wherever they were now. We were all eager to end this journey, it felt, because its real purpose had already been achieved. The only journey is an inner one, along the path from self to Self. Being alone so long gave me a heady sense of freedom, too, and I began to believe I would see my own world differently when I finally saw it again, that its petty conflicts would be easy to resolve with these new eyes I'd acquired.

If I saw my world again, that is: for the sense of something terrible was mingled with this feeling of release. I truly felt that a change had come, that we were all about to be freed from history's prison, awakened from its nightmare. But I wasn't at all sure that I, for one, would like the waking process. The Magi had probably felt like this, though, I reassured myself, knowing, as they must have done, how near they were now to the Perfect One promised by Zoroaster and the Hebrew prophets and the Vedic sages. Fear and God are never far from each other, in a man's world.

We were all near something profoundly extraordinary again, I felt, yet we would be better prepared this time. We needed to be. Those ancient feuds had gone now—hadn't they? The Peace Accords were about to be signed in the Middle East. Humankind was surely ready for a different future, a kinder, gentler world: a world of *partnership.*

VII

I must have floated through Jordan on this kind of heavy, heady fuel, because I scarcely recall the place. I was heading to the Promised Land: I didn't need scenery. I should have looked at what happened to others who believed such promises. But after Basra, it was just me, the Tin Man, the Scarecrow, and the Cowardly Lion skipping along the Yellow Brick Road to Oz—where all our problems would be solved . . .

EPILOGUES

*Now when Jesus was born in Bethlehem of
Judaea in the days of Herod the king, behold,
there came wise men from the east to Jerusalem,
saying, "Where is he that is born King of the
Jews? for we have seen his star in the east,
and are come to worship him."*

—The Gospel of Matthew 2: 1–2

Universally famed as astrologers, Magi tended to crop up at portentous events on a regular basis. A crowd of them are recorded standing
amid the smoke and ruins at dawn the day after the great temple of
Artemis at Ephesus burned to the ground. These Magi announced that
the great temple's destruction augured the (virgin) birth of Alexander
the Great.

Magi had cause to be interested in Alexander themselves, too. The
Egyptians may have deified him, but no one in Persia thought he was
so "Great" after 331 B.C., when he defeated Darius III and invaded the
country, ruling it for seven years. In the Zoroastrian tradition, he is
termed the "Accursed" (*guzastag*), an epithet which he alone shares

with Ahriman, "Spirit of the Lie": Satan. Another ancient text sets him among the worst sinners in history, his main sin being that he "killed Magi." Elsewhere it is said that he slaughtered "many teachers, lawyers, herbads [priests] and mobads [Magi or High Priests]"; he also "quenched many fires." Dousing the sacred fires was a sure way to lose Zoroastrian friends. Alexander carried off entire libraries of texts, too, among them many "lost" works of Zoroaster himself, which probably exist now in unattributed translations as the work of Greek authors— possibly even Pythagoras. The Persian religion suffered an enormous blow, and there are many decrees during later periods requesting that copies of missing texts be handed in, or pleading for people who have memorized religious works to step forward. Had the oral tradition not been still so strong, many Zoroastrian scriptures would have vanished for ever thanks to Alexander "the Accursed."

Whole processions of Magi also turn up as an ambiguous presence at celebrations hosted by dubious characters like the emperor Nero. They were both feared and respected—and also despised for charging too much for their arcane skills. Three wily lawyers will probably attend the next Nativity to offer their services: Gold, Frankensenz & Muir, Attorneys at Law.

Matthew knew what Magi were about as much as the next man; and he also knew the Old Testament by heart, since the function of his gospel is to prove that Jesus fulfilled all the Messianic prophecies in it. In fact, Jesus does almost nothing but fulfill prophecies in Matthew. The "fulfillment phrase" crops up so often that had Jesus purchased an apple on his way to raise the dead, Matthew would have concluded that this action was "that it might be fulfilled as was written by the prophets: Lo! He shall exchange silver of the fruit of a tree . . ." (it would be evidence for his forgiveness of the original sin, by now).

Oddly, however, there are no fulfillment phrases in the Magi section—which is only an amazingly brief twelve verses from their arrival to their departure. Matthew does not exploit Old Testament prophecies which he could easily have used to lend prophetic weight to the Magi's presence. Others, including Justin Martyr, have done that for him since, though, and mainly by turning the "wise men" into "kings" with certain kingdoms.

Several sections in Hebrew prophetic works predict that monarchs from places like "Sheba and Seba shall offer gifts" to the Messiah (Psalm 72), and even that these gifts will be "gold and incense" (Isaiah 60:6)—hold the myrrh—yet Matthew's Magi are not kings. Nor are they pagans acknowledging the superiority of Christianity. Nowhere does the gospel indicate that the Magi are anything but noble and re-spected figures, whose hearts are in the right place and whose esoteric talents are laudably employed in the service of Truth and God. Yet Matthew restricts his Magi's esoteric baggage to the bare minimum necessary for his story's purpose: a little astrological skill and one prophetic dream.

Everyone knew that the Magi were masters of the occult and spe-cialists in dream interpretation. Here, however, they don't even get to interpret their own dream, since in it they are "warned of God"—and God was obviously not warning in obscure symbols that night. It is al-most as if the presence of these major candidates for heresy makes Matthew nervous—which, in fact, lends his story more credence. Magi have to be there, but they're given the bum's rush as soon as it's feasible.

In the original Greek, however, Matthew's text contains far more ev-idence of the Magi's astrological talents than either Latin or English translations are able to carry. In the Authorized Version, for example, Matthew's Magi come "from the east" and see their star "in the east." The Greek has *magoi* coming from *anatolai*—"the east," usually writ-ten in the plural—yet seeing their star *en te anatole*, the singular form and thus not a reference to where they were when they saw the star. No writer of Greek in antiquity would employ two different usages to mean the same thing; but *anatole* also has a specific astronomical and astrological application. It refers to the achronychal rising of a star or planet—when the object is in direct opposition to the sun, rising in the east as the sun is setting in the west and visible throughout the night in an arc. We know from cuneiform tablets now in various museums that the Babylonian astrologers, for instance, regarded such a phenomenon as exceptionally significant, calculating positions for its occurrence with enormous accuracy for the potent outer planets of Mars, Jupiter, and Saturn, and able to predict astronomical events far into the fu-ture—as lucrative a business in those days as it's recently become in ours.

During Herod's absurdly brief audience with the Magi, all Matthew has the king ask these visitors is an inordinately precise inquiry about "what time the star appeared." Neither Latin nor English has a word for "appeared" that also carries a specific astronomical connotation the way the Greek *phainestai* does. In fact, the Vulgate Bible acknowledges this shortcoming by providing a Latin gloss on the Greek phrase, defining it more clearly *tempus quo coeperat lucere*, basically "the time when it was first visible." But even this does not quite convey the specific meaning of the Greek term, which refers to a star's heliacal rising—the earliest moment at dawn when it can be seen emerging over the horizon. Such an event takes place only once a year in the case of any star or planet in the ecliptic, and in Herod's day astrologers connected the heliacal rising with a person's exact date of birth. The king is thus bluntly asking the Magi exactly when this "king of the Jews" was born.

According to Matthew, the whole of Jerusalem appears to know why the Magi have arrived. It thus seems that Herod wishes to keep at least the details as secret as possible. He was king of the Jews—and governor of Jerusalem—and he had married, then murdered the mother of the sole Maccabean heir to the throne along with her son, just to make sure that he remained king of the Jews. Not being Jewish by blood was a bit of a stumbling block here, and Herod had ambitious plans for an empire and dynasty that would not be particularly assisted by the appearance of another claimant to the throne, especially one who was actually Jewish. In what is perhaps a deft literary flourish, Matthew establishes that the Magi are no more Jewish than Herod is, obliging the king to suffer the humiliation of summoning Jewish elders—the Sanhedrin probably—in order to ask where the Messiah is supposed to be born. As any Jew would have been able to reply, Bethlehem, according to Micah's prophecy, was this traditional birthplace. It was David's home town.

Bethlehem was only an hour's easy ride by horse or camel from Jerusalem, so one wonders why Herod, considering his vested interest in the Magi's quest, does not accompany them but simply requests trustingly that they report back on their return. There is, however, an ancient Jewish tradition relating to the star that "shall come out of Jacob," and the scepter that "shall rise out of Israel" in another Old

Testament prophecy (Numbers 24:17)—confirming the dual-messiah notion, as well as explaining why Simeon the Zealot called himself "son of a star"—and the tradition states that the Messiah would be born two years after this star's appearance. The Jewish elders would have known this. Possibly Herod did, too, for it explains both his lack of urgency in the matter and his order to slaughter male children under two years old—although there is no historical evidence to suggest that he ever issued such an order or that it was carried out. On the other hand, Bethlehem was not Tokyo, and such an order might have only doomed two or three children—or even none, if its few inhabitants had only produced girls for the last couple of years.

Another explanation for Herod's reluctance to accompany the Magi can be found in the encyclopedia of physical ailments which the historian Josephus lists—lists in rather gleeful and unnecessary detail—that he suffered from. And Josephus' patrons had reasons for wanting to hear the worst about Herod, so Josephus would have eagerly mentioned infanticide on hearing the vaguest rumor of it, but he doesn't. Besides violent mood swings, delusions of persecution and hypertensive cerebral attacks that created a reasonable facsimile of raving insanity, Herod had such horrors as ulcerated bowels, "gangrene of his private parts that produced worms," something that caused appallingly corrosive bad breath, something else that made his feet ooze whatever it is feet can ooze, and "convulsions in every limb." A cold will keep me indoors. It's certainly no surprise to find that the eclectic range of Herod's maladies drove him to suicide a couple of years later. One can imagine what a power of good it did the paranoid king's state to discover that the Magi had double-crossed him . . .

THE PROMISED LAND

A Sumerian text from the third millennium B.C. was discovered recently, its translation published on November 22, 1994. The gist of one sentence actually reads: "The Israelis have now made peace with their enemies the Palestinians . . ."

It is not a prophecy, simply an observation of relations between Semitic tribes settling in Palestine four thousand five hundred years ago and the indigenous population.

When I crossed over the Allenby Bridge from Jordan into Israel, I fell back deep within a conflict that had been raging long before the Magi passed this way. Israel's soldiers were hostile and edgy; the citizens of Jericho were hostile and edgy. Only up among the bare, ruined walls and desolate mounds of old hewn stone at Qumran was there any sense of peace. The view across the Dead Sea—the lowest spot on earth—has not changed, and in a way the ancient, noble dream once held here is still in place, too. Dreadful events occurred among these stones, though—you can feel it—but the heroic struggles and crushing defeats were to some purpose; thus there remains no rancor or bitterness. People did their duty, fought with absolute "zeal for the Law." What more could zealots have done? And there was no difference between Zealots, Essenes, Ebionites, Nazareans, or Nazarites, et al. These distinctions are mere obfuscation of a truth the Church has been reluctant to face: the purpose of Jesus' life was to prevent such a Church, such an institutionalization of spirituality, from ever existing.

ABRAHAM'S BOYS' BOYS

At Hebron things were very different. I recalled visiting the Tomb of the Patriarchs in 1974, when Jews and Muslims had still prayed side by side before their common father Abraham's great veiled sarcophagus. It was a moving and reassuring sight, a sign that nothing was as bad as it seemed to be, that differences could and would be resolved. Now, twenty years later, there were set times for each faith to use the sacred space alone: so Jews and Muslims would never again meet each other within the potent aura of memory radiated by the one person in whom they both truly do meet. But even Abraham's sons, Isaac and Ishmael, only met to bury their father. They never saw or spoke to each other again.

Ramadan was still being observed, so Muslims were allotted more time in the shrine than usual. This irritated the Jewish settlers, none of whom consented to discuss with me either their religion or their politics. They were all armed, some heavily, too. By the look of it, no one planned to obey the Sixth Commandment—if they hadn't already broken it. A young Israeli sergeant advised me to hit the road sooner rather than later.

"Jeez!" he cried. "You've got twice the odds of getting dropped than an Arab or a Jew!"

"Huh?"

"You could be either: *everyone*'ll shoot you!"

This was a war, the sergeant reminded me. I just wanted to discuss religion, but none of the settlers seemed remotely interested in religion. It was revenge that interested them, revenge for a catalogue of wrongs dating back to tribal feuds five millennia ago, and extending through the Holocaust to the latest Muslim terrorists' bomb. Vengeance had long since ceased to be the Lord's exclusive province. In fact, many of these settlers had no Lord to look out for them any longer. Like orthodox Christianity, rabbinical Judaism has become virtually secular in its concerns.

The Holy Scriptures to many Israelis are distilled into current events. There are new pharaohs, new kings in Babylon, and new Assyrian warlords to fight. The tribes all kept their feuds, but very few still have their God. Yet Hebron's Jews still wanted their fair share of time before Abraham all the same. On principle.

THE CITY OF GOD

On the morning of February 25, 1994, I skirted Jerusalem's walls, heading west from the Damascus Gate, then south, passing what remains of Herod's old palace. I pictured him quizzing the Magi in there, staring through the windows facing that point a few hundred yards from the southwestern corner of his new city walls where the road curves off toward Bethlehem.

I left the road at that point myself, walking east past the Essene Gate—where remains of walls that Zorobabel built for Darius the Great are still visible—along the curve of Hinnom Valley to Tekoa Gate at the southeast corner. Three thousand years ago the Wall of Zion surrounding the City of David would have faced me a little north of here. It was tiny, David's city: four hundred yards long and just two hundred wide, barely large enough to house a cohort comfortably. It was not a city at all, of course: it was just a fortified palace. And attached to its northern wall was Solomon's own palace—twice the size of his father's.

Solomon's walls curved along what was once called the Cheese-maker's Valley, or the Central Valley. Jesus would have known it as Ty-ropoeon Valley. It ends today where all that remains of Solomon's palace begins.

The Western or Wailing Wall is not a remnant of Solomon's Temple, merely a hundred-yard section of the walls protecting part of his palace and a larger part of Herod's palace. The Temple itself stood in the center of the palace on a hill just north of the point where the city wall extended off into what is now medieval Jerusalem. The Dome of the Rock mosque stands a little east of the same spot today, but not a trace of the Temple remains. Not a trace remained in Zorobabel's day, either. The famous Temple was no larger than a four-bedroom villa. Thirty such temples would have fitted easily inside David's little palace. Herod's Temple was nearly twenty times larger—because his had room for imported priests (local ones didn't like their employer). Solomon's only had room for the person it was built by and for: the king and his priest, alone with their mysteries—most mysterious of which was that the king really had no priest. And the Temple had no god.

As it was in Egypt, the masses were not permitted access to those great mysteries that dwelt deep within the temple courtyards and comprised the beating heart of an entire civilization. Mysteries must remain mysterious if priests and kings are to keep hold on the reins of power. Like Dorothy in Oz, the fear and trembling cease when someone parts the veil to show a little man with a big voice merely pulling levers.

When the Holy of Holies was shown to be empty, its occupant became emptiness itself: what wasn't there had to become what never could have been there in the first place. You cannot see an omnipresent and invisible God—there can be no idols—but it is possible to hear him. Thus, those who once acquired power through their lavish propitiation of God's image now retained that power by their miraculous ability to hear and speak to Him. And God spoke to the masses through them. The temples, however, remained at the heart of a darkness that was caused by denying anyone access to the light. The Brahmans, Magi, and Essenes taught only a religion of personal, subjective experience: thus they were called "sons of God," because all people contain the seed of God within them, the drop of water that is no different from the ocean it dissolves into. But children are only created by two parents; thus any religion that rejects the idea of God as both Mother and Father, both feminine and masculine, is both useless and dangerous. Partnership, not patriarchy, created us and all we know. And unity is our sole reality.

TWINS

Hundreds of people thronged around the Western Wall's massive blocks of limestone, some of which weigh many tons each and, after three thousand years or more, still fit together perfectly. Two Bar Mitzvahs were in progress: identical twins. They carried identical Torah Scrolls and wore identical powder-blue tuxedos with matching velvet yarmulkes. Could they be aware at thirteen of the real weight in those scrolls? I wondered. It also occurred to me that Jesus and Thomas might well have stood near this wall together when *they* were thirteen . . .

I pictured the Magi standing high above, looking where the sun itself was pointing a few hours after dawn. Herod seemed to them the epitome of everything they wished the world to avoid: a mortal tyrant whose goals were totally secular and selfish, yet whose methods were redolent of pagan superstition with its concomitant fear and trembling. Herod's own body was an image of this, at least according to Josephus' catalogue of the king's diseases.

The twins were now reciting, requiring a prompter for every word as they stared blankly at the writhing characters displayed between those two unrolled cylinders of The Law. It was this same eternal law that the Magi had come to protect, so that humankind did not lose its way. And so that men like Herod could not hold the planet's destiny in their fists.

TWO MAGI

Jerusalem seemed in ferment that day, as it had exactly two thousand years earlier. It was not an imminent messiah that made the locals restless now, though. It was an imminent peace treaty with the PLO and almost every other old enemy they had become accustomed to thinking of as old enemies.

I persuaded Father Cornelios, an affable young Greek Orthodox priest with great ingenuity and good connections, to help me rent a camel and even accompany me on the five-mile ride to Bethlehem. He cheerfully discussed all the theories I unloaded on him, and ultimately found them all most amusing. He seemed to find everything most amusing, including a feud his order was currently engaged in with the Syrian Jacobite Church and the Copts over some indescribably trifling incident connected with the rights to a shrine in the old city.

"The Copts are probably right," he conceded. "They do have an authority from the fourteenth century. But that's no reason we should let them have it, is it?" He exploded into a fit of mirth.

We had to settle for two horses. Camels were in short supply because the Bedouin were moving grazing grounds. Although, according to Cornelios, they were probably moving plundering grounds. It was still winter, after all.

The Bedouin walk tall in the world of biblical antiquities, apparently, and pitch their huge black tents over promising archaeological sites that no one has yet explored. Once established, they dig down within the tent to hide their finds from prying eyes. When a site is thoroughly exhausted they move on. Sometimes they buy up houses in the old city and elsewhere, digging down to the bedrock below cellars for the same purpose.

But did the Bedouin find much?

"God, yes!" Cornelios gasped. "They probably have more scrolls than the Rockefeller Museum and the Pontifical Biblical Commission combined."

As noted, The Pontifical Biblical Commission is the outfit still basically controlled by the Holy Inquisition, and the same one which had guarded the Dead Sea Scrolls so carefully until 1991. Cornelios announced that Bedouin had supposedly sold even more devastating scrolls than the ones currently being "liberated" by Dr. Eisenman, Professor Thiering, and others. They had sold them to private dealers for millions of dollars, too. One could only speculate what these texts contained.

Did this not worry him, as a priest?

"Why?" he exclaimed, as we approached a roadblock. "It won't affect anything. That's history, this is *faith*. Don't expect the Vatican to come tumbling down over some odd scrap of nonsense written two thousand years ago."

"That was what built it up, wasn't it—some two-thousand-year-old scraps of nonsense?"

"*Sanctioned* nonsense, old chap. Big difference." He laughed again.

The Church moved like a wary old chess master playing a prodigy. It only got around to pardoning Galileo a few years ago . . .

"Myth," Cornelios answered when I asked if he regarded Jesus more as history or mythology. "Some pope—Alexander, I think, though not which one . . . Anyway, he remarked—in an unguarded moment, no doubt—'How well we've done with this myth of Christ.' He *did* say that, you know . . ."

He did, too.

At a road block half a mile south of the Essene Gate, the soldiers seemed unusually fierce and nervous, checking papers and even asking me who the president of Canada was. I said we didn't have one, and got shouted at for being a smartass. A sergeant told us both we were insane to be going to Bethlehem without the protection of a car, then he wished us both a nice day.

A little farther on I noticed two Arabs driving a car festooned with little happy faces. They were the last ones I saw in Israel.

ONCE IN ROYAL DAVID'S CITY

In the claustrophobic crypt below the Church of the Nativity, Cornelios and I stood by the silver star that marks the spot where Jesus was born. It was the same one Sir John Mandeville saw in the fourteenth century, the one he believed marked the point of impact where the Magi's star fell to earth.

A Swedish priest was telling a small band of exhausted tourists, whom he had probably brought with him all the way from Sweden, about the Nativity—the Magi and the Shepherds and the no-room-at-the-inn manger—as a large candle slowly leaned from its six-foot holder, first dripping wax on his shoulders, then falling with a sudden thud on his pristine blond hair. There was a communal shocked gasp, then sudden nervous laughs of relief. The young priest laughed too, feeling clods of wax slowly hardening in his angelic hair. He looked up with a knowing smirk and said something cheeky to whoever he thought was listening high up there beyond the smoke-blackened vaulted stones, beyond the church and Israel, beyond the sky, and beyond that. It suddenly seemed such a very strange and unlikely thing we all believed in—or most of us believed in, sooner or later.

This holy place meant nothing to me, although my journey with the Magi was suddenly over. Soon we would depart to our "own country another way." In a sense, however, I felt that the Magi's journey would never end. Part of me would always be with them, too. "Symbols," the old Nazarean priest in Iran had said, *symbols . . .*

PEACE ON EARTH AND MERCY MILD

There's a heavy vibe in the Holy Land, all right, a great booming chord that could be thunder, or the quaking earth, or your heart attacking you. The Holy Vibe. It's no mystery why the place has produced thoughts higher than the heavens, lower than the lowest netherworlds, and crueler than a lover's hate. Everyone there seems to fly back and forth between its hellish and heavenly poles, or grasps a ledge while the current flashes to and fro between holy and unholy anodes, its path always through the heart and soul. Always.

I couldn't live there.

Cornelios had chattered on about another squabble his people were embarked on involving the Armenians. What with the odd drone of prayers, comments, grief, awe, and sheer silliness that filled this holiest of sites, neither of us heard the gunfire until we bent to creep through the Church of the Nativity's four-foot-high entrance and poked our heads outside.

A modest skirmish was underway between the usual masked Arabs hurling rocks and the usual Israeli soldiers firing tear gas canisters. Yet some of the Arab faces I could see were masked in something more than kaffiyehs: utter anguish, fear, a tear-stained and terminal anger that seemed to know it could never, never do enough damage to spend itself. The young soldiers seemed less cocky and less highly organized than usual, too. A group of Arab teenagers was screaming "Murderers, murderers!" at the Israelis, who were taking this quotidian abuse seriously for a change.

Bethlehem looked gray and grim and hopeless. What did humankind imagine it had achieved on the planet when this was still the way things were where a god of love was born? What a place! Yet, I presumed, it was just another day in the Occupied Territories, just the usual state of the State.

Only when Cornelios and I attempted to dart for a less hectic spot, then find our terror-stricken horses, did an Israeli major tell us that Baruch Goldstein had opened fire in the Tomb of the Patriarchs a few hours ago, killing twenty, fifty, a hundred Muslims—the major didn't have the count. But we could count on the fact that Bethlehem would be a bloodbath any minute, he thought, and we'd better get out while the situation was under control. The phrase sounded ridiculous.

TWO SPIRITS

I had hoped, foolishly and vainly, to find a peace treaty already signed when I arrived with the Magi at Bethlehem—hoped that there would be a little more hope for peace on earth and mercy mild. Which would, coincidentally, also make a very touching and appropriate ending for my book, of course. But this—the "Hebron Massacre"—this was bad. A very bad ending. This was worse then anything I had dreamed of happening. Nothing happening at all had once struck me as problematical enough. But now Arabs were talking of hideous reprisals, biblical revenges. Peace talks were broken off by those old enemies, who seemed to be new enemies once more, and the whole region threatened to go up in flames. Again. Its threats were rarely idle ones, though.

Even the weather was more like Good Friday than Christmas Day: low dark clouds swooped and swirled like the flapping cloaks of clashing warlords in the middle air. At any moment a giant hand would stab through the heaving charcoal vapors and wipe all of us poor little pawns from its board. *Check, mate!*

Yet it was, ultimately, all very much in the traditions I had steeped myself in over the past year. What seemed an awful evil produced a great good. Ahriman existed only so Ahura Mazda could overcome him in the end: for there was no doubt who would win. These faiths and philosophies all taught that evil existed so good could grow stronger, the way darkness existed so there could be light. But darkness is not really the opposite of light, it is just the absence of light, the deep well where you understand utterly the need for light, causing light to come in a flash—as if it has never been away.

Israel was not going to be Happy Valley overnight—that much was certain. But Baruch Goldstein's hideous blood sacrifice on the altar of Abraham's tomb seemed to jolt the cosmos and free something—a force long bottled up. It must have occurred around the same time that I stood near where Solomon's Temple had been, where he had sacrificed 144,000 sheep and oxen in the hope that God would move into his little box.

My journey was itself a Magian ritual, and like those cycles of hope and failure with which Magi were involved from Zorobabel to Simeon Bar Khochba, and like their sacred fires, the ritual is a cosmic drama of death and renewal. From light comes darkness, from life comes death, from hope springs despair—from which hope springs eternal. But the cycles are not endless. For Polo's Magi the fire becomes Truth, and the Philosopher's stone that Christ gave them was the wisdom that caused fire, that let light pour into the Sufis' "Well of Darkness" until not a shadow remained inside. Only the slave understands freedom. Only the Lie realizes that it is merely a lack of Truth. Darkness knows it is no opposite of light, too, and the terror of Baruch Goldstein's mass-slaughter recognized that it was not an alternative to learning the art of peaceful coexistence, taking a small step toward unity.

The Magi, as I now see them—thanks to Marco Polo—came to pay homage not to Christ but to the whole world; to celebrate the still, sad music of humanity, as well as its extraordinary ability to climb ceaselessly toward higher and higher goals, using the strength acquired through countless falls.

When, in a controversial *New Yorker* magazine essay forty years ago, the literary critic Edmund Wilson expressed his hope that, with the advent of the Dead Sea Scrolls, Christianity could be freed of superstition and viewed as just another episode in human history, he was hoping for a similarly fresh take on reality. As the recently translated Sumerian text shows, as ex-Yugoslavia shows, as Iranian theocracy shows, nothing stays still yet nothing really changes. Immortality and Utopia exist as ideals to force us into seeing their impossibility: no one will avoid death, no human society will be perfect. But in recognizing this as reality, we cease to be prisoners of limitations. This was what Zoroaster, Moses, and Jesus taught, and what Brahmans, Magi, and Essenes believed: the Truth literally sets you free, whereas institutionalized religion is just another prison. And individual consciousness is the first and last freedom.

I am the Way, I am the Truth, I am Life.

—The Gospel of John

Three Magi had become two Magi during my journey. A magical triangle had seemingly become a drab line between two points: the heavens and hells we fly in and out of daily, or the anodes between which life's fire lives and death's dull plumb line swings. But a few months ago, looking at a Bible illustration of Aaron with his rod, I suddenly saw the line as a simple stake of dry wood. All of us were hammering it into each other's hearts and feeling it hammered bursting into our own heart, while a voice, raining down from the skies yet also seeping out from the brain's soft, deep kernel, kept saying with each blow of the hammer on that stake: "*Wait until it flowers . . .*"

THAT'S HOW THE LIGHT GETS IN

Back in Jerusalem—shaken, and as edgy now as everyone else—I asked Father Cornelios some trifling question about Magi icons. He hooted with laughter, patting me on the back and saying:

"Enough with your three wise men, old chap. We're two hungry men, and if we were wise we'd go and have something to eat. And drink."

Without Zoroaster there would be no Christ. He was the bridge, and the Romans burnt it . . .

Toronto-Teheran-Damascus-Jerusalem, 1993–1995

A Christmas Carol

In the bleak midwinter
Frosty wind made moan,
Earth stood hard as iron,
Water like a stone;
Snow had fallen, snow on snow,
Snow on snow,
In the bleak midwinter,
Long ago.

God, heaven cannot hold him
Nor earth sustain;
Heaven and earth shall flee away
When he comes to reign:
In the bleak midwinter
Stable place sufficed
The Lord God Almighty,
Jesus Christ.

Angels and archangels
May have gathered there,
Cherubim and seraphim
Thronged the air;
But only his mother
In her maiden bliss
Worshipped the Beloved
With a kiss.

What can I give him,
Poor as I am?
If I were a shepherd
I would bring a lamb;
If I were a wise man
I would do my part
Yet what can I give him —
Give my heart.

—Christina Georgina Rossetti (1830–94)

Index